THE
MARRIOTT
CELL

Mohamed Fahmy

WITH **CAROL SHABEN**

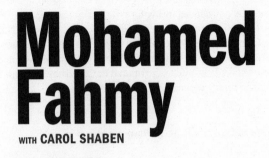

THE

FOREWORD BY AMAL CLOONEY

MARRIOTT

**An Epic Journey
from Cairo's
Scorpion Prison
to Freedom**

CELL

RANDOM HOUSE CANADA

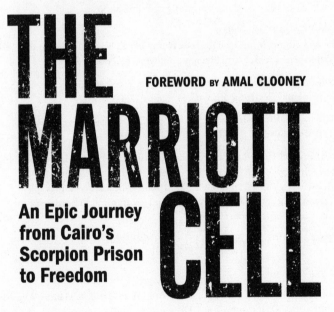

www.penguinrandomhouse.ca

Random House Canada and colophon are registered trademarks.

Library and Archives Canada Cataloguing in Publication

Fahmy, Mohamed Fadel, author
    The Marriott cell : an epic journey from Cairo's Scorpion Prison to freedom /
Mohamed Fahmy ; with Carol Shaben ; foreword by Amal Clooney.

Includes bibliographical references.
Issued in print and electronic formats.

ISBN 978-0-345-81635-1
eBook ISBN 978-0-345-81637-5

    1. Fahmy, Mohamed Fadel. 2. Fahmy, Mohamed Fadel—Imprisonment.
3. Egypt—History—1981–. 4. Egypt—Politics and government—1981–.
5. Journalists—Egypt—Biography. 6. Journalists—Canada—Biography.
7. False arrest—Egypt. 8. False imprisonment—Egypt. 9. Prisons—Egypt.
I. Shaben, Carol, co-author. II. Title.

DT107.88.F34 2016   962.05'6   C2016-904551-X

Book design by Lisa Jager

Cover images: (Mohamed Fahmy in court August 29, 2015) © Asmaa Waguih /
Reuters; (texture) © Benjaminlion | Dreamstime.com

Printed and bound in the United States of America

10 9 8 7 6 5 4 3 2 1

Penguin
Random House
RANDOM HOUSE CANADA

I dedicate this book to the thousands of people who were killed while raising the revolution banners of the Arab Spring, the hundreds of fellow journalists slain while doing their noble jobs, and to those still languishing behind bars.

I thank—from the bottom of my heart—my beloved family and friends who helped me win my freedom back and produce this book; especially the powerful women in my life: my most beloved wife, Marwa Omara; my mother, Wafaa Bassiouni; my lawyer Amal Clooney; my publisher, Louise Dennys; and, of course, my most admirable co-author, Carol Shaben, who in the course of writing this book has become like a sister to me.

I am most grateful to the millions of people who supported our #FreeAJStaff campaign worldwide and kept our plight alive for 438 days and defended our shared right to freedom of expression. You deserve to know the entirety of the story, and the truth about the men and the cause you fought for.

Finally, I believe the reader will understand that in order to protect the privacy of some individuals, I've occasionally replaced a name with an initial (which itself has no reference to the original name).

—Mohamed Fahmy

To my father-in-law, Dr. Baha Abu-Laban, and all other citizens of the Middle East whose lives have been forever changed by occupation, oppression and war.

Heartfelt thanks to Louise Dennys, publisher and editor extraordinaire at Penguin Random House Canada, and to the also brilliant minds and Herculean efforts of Angelika Glover and Rick Meier, as well as to my amazing agent and advocate, Jackie Kaiser. To Mohamed Fahmy, thanks for your passion, strength and perseverance. You are a true "Champ" and an inspiration. Finally, my love and gratitude go to my family, especially my mother, Alma, my son, Max, and my husband, Riyad, Sherpa, best friend, and love of my life.

—Carol Shaben

CONTENTS

FOREWORD

BY AMAL CLOONEY

When a government uses the law to silence its critics, freedom is under threat. And when judges become the government's willing accomplices, freedom cannot survive. This is why the Al Jazeera trial in Egypt was so important. The journalists were dubbed the "Marriott Cell" and faced a trial for terrorism through the "spreading of false news." They faced their judge from inside a cage in a packed courtroom, just a few years after the Arab Spring and in the Arab world's most populous country. Observers in the region rightly asked themselves if this heralded the end of free speech.

We are all worse off if journalists cannot do their work. We cannot fight corruption, discrimination, and oppression if we don't know about it.

But journalism has become one of the most dangerous professions in the world. Terrorist groups like ISIS have targeted and beheaded journalists, and in every continent journalists are killed or disappeared. It is a crime in many countries to insult rulers, religions or royals—and cartoonists, bloggers and mainstream media face lengthy prison terms as a result.

Stifling criticism has serious repercussions. It means there is only one version of every story, one view on every controversy. Yet history teaches us that the minority voice is the one that society must work hardest to protect. Because it is this voice that can challenge orthodoxy, confront complacency, and open the door to progress.

Galileo was prosecuted for "heresy" for his discovery that the earth moved around the sun. When Nelson Mandela first dared to argue that blacks were equal to whites, he was arrested for seditious activities. And Gandhi was sentenced to six years in prison because his views were "bringing or attempting to excite disaffection" towards the government.

It has always been the journalist's job to criticize the government and hold those in power to account—and this book is a powerful reminder that they should not be locked up for it. Our collective freedom is at stake.

Amal Clooney
Barrister
September 2016

CHAPTER 1

SCORPION

December 30, 2013

The night I am incarcerated, as I stand shivering and exposed, surrounded by half a dozen prison guards, I cannot fathom what losing my freedom might mean. Understanding will come later, stealthily, like the cold that creeps into my body from the concrete floor beneath my bare feet.

I am in a dingy foyer clad in only my undershorts and a thin, long-sleeved undershirt. Pain lances through my right shoulder, broken two weeks before my arrest and now cradled in a black canvas sling. I brace it against my chest as a prison guard approaches and tosses a set of white, pajama-like garments at me.

He gestures for me to put them on and I step awkwardly into the bottoms using only my good arm to pull them up to my waist.

"Take off the sling," he orders.

"It's broken," I say, but his face remains impassive.

I reach into the pocket of my jeans, which lie discarded on a nearby wooden bench and fish out a half-full pack of cigarettes. I hold it out to him, and he slides it into the pocket of his uniform.

I am struggling to pull on the top when I see my colleague Baher Mohamed escorted into the foyer. Our eyes make quick contact. Then I watch him suffer the same humiliation, stripping to his underwear as the guards look on.

A guard hands me two rough grey blankets and orders me to wait for the prison doctor. I drop onto the wooden bench, my shoulder throbbing. The doctor, when he shows up, is wearing a training suit and slippers, and strides aggressively towards me.

"Why are you wearing a sweater under the prison shirt?" His tone is sharp. "Take it off and give it to the guard."

The guard to whom I've given my cigarettes kicks me in the shin. "Get up when you're spoken to!"

"Sir," I speak directly to the doctor, "my shoulder is broken."

"Fine," he says, relenting unexpectedly, as if already bored with our conversation, "keep the extra shirt."

"May I keep these?" I ask, opening my left hand to show him the container of painkillers I have been clutching since my arrest twenty-four hours ago. He takes them from me, checks them over briefly, then hands them back without a word.

He looks at Baher with an indifferent eye, and then turns to the guards. "Send them in."

This is how I enter Scorpion, Egypt's notorious maximum-security prison. Reserved for terrorists, criminals and high-level political prisoners, Scorpion is one of seven blocks that make up the vast Tora Prison complex, a sprawling, foreboding and heavily fortified conglomeration of drab, desert-coloured buildings surrounded by seven-metre-high, barbed-wire-topped walls and watch towers, and located twenty kilometres south of Cairo. Little is known about

Scorpion, but it is nicknamed "the Cemetery," and some of the
region's most dangerous figures are incarcerated here. The bearded
face of Mohamed al-Zawahiri, the younger brother of the United
States' "most wanted man," Ayman al-Zawahiri, the al-Qaeda
leader who succeeded Osama bin Laden, floats into my mind. I had
interviewed Mohamed al-Zawahiri eighteen months ago for CNN,
following his release after ten years in this same prison where he had
been tortured and confined in solitary.[1] Mohamed, who was a
member of the violent Egyptian Islamic Jihad (EIJ) organization in
the '90s, a group that formally merged with al-Qaeda in 2001, had
insisted he was targeted mainly because of his brother Ayman. He
had been accused of participating in the assassination of President
Sadat and acquitted, but eighteen years later the CIA apprehended
him in the United Arab Emirates and extradited him under the
United States' extraordinary rendition program. Returned to Egypt,
he was sentenced to death this time on charges of plotting to overthrow the state.[2]

It had taken me weeks to land the interview with al-Zawahiri—
the first one he granted to foreign media after his brief release following President Hosni Mubarak's resignation. He would soon after
be rearrested by the interim government and thrown back behind
bars on new charges of "forming a terrorist cell" linked to al-Qaeda
and plotting attacks against targets in Egypt.

"Is al-Zawahiri inside?" I ask my guard.

"Yes," he answers sarcastically, "he and his friends are all waiting
for you in this seven-star hotel."

An entourage of guards march Baher and me through a maze of
decrepit concrete hallways and metal gates. There is a stale, fetid smell
that intensifies as the guards lead us deeper into the prison. Two
mangy, underfed cats appear in one corridor and follow us. After five
minutes we arrive in what the guards announce is the terrorist wing.
Its dim passageway, littered with broken chairs and other discarded

furniture, is lined with solid, gunmetal-green doors. The guards stop in front of a door marked with the number "7" in heavy black paint. One swings it open and I walk into a solitary confinement cell.

The door slams shut behind me and I hear the sound of the key turning the lock. I am imprisoned.

This is all a big mistake, I tell myself. *I will be out in the morning when my family and the network create an uproar.*

I take in my new home with a sense of denial. It is about ten by twenty feet, with a twenty-foot-high ceiling. I gawk for a moment at the toilet, a filthy, battered cement bowl that protrudes from one of the rough-hewn, grey concrete walls. I console myself that at least it is not a squat toilet—a hole in the ground flanked by two foot pads—which would have been difficult to manage with my injury. This small comfort disappears seconds later when I notice a line of cockroaches scuttling along the toilet seat. A concrete sink with a rusted dripping faucet in the far corner and a broken ceiling fan are the cell's only other adornments. Cut into the top corner of one wall is a narrow rectangular window, whether to the outside or to another prison block, I can't tell. This window, I will soon discover, is lit around the clock by a bright fluorescent light that casts a glare into my cell, robbing one of any possibility of a night's sleep. The only other opening is a brick-sized cutout in the cell door. I peer through it into the neglected hallway. No sunlight, not a breath of fresh air.

Fear, anger, disbelief. It's the first time I have had a chance to think, the first moment of solitude I have experienced since I was arrested. In the days and weeks before my arrest, I lived and worked in two small adjoining rooms in Cairo's Marriott Hotel: one served as the bustling temporary office of the Al Jazeera English news channel; the other was my bedroom and our storage room. I had recently accepted the job as bureau chief in charge of fifteen journalists, producers and cameramen providing live news coverage on Egypt for Al Jazeera's international English-language television channel.

It's late. My watch reads 8:00 p.m. An army of mosquitoes has descended on me and I swat them away. I cast about the cell for a spot in which to sleep and decide on the corner farthest from the toilet. I fan out one of the grey blankets on the hard surface and lower myself onto it. As I do, I notice the dense forest of scribbles scratched and inked onto the concrete wall. I run my fingers across them like a historian deciphering ancient messages: *Death to the oppressor! Death to Sisi! The revolution will never die! Islam is the solution.*

A slogan written in red ink stands out: *The thousands of Rabaa martyrs will live forever in heaven.*

The reference is to the recent Rabaa massacre. In August, a month before I accepted the position of bureau chief, government security forces had moved to end a sit-in by tens of thousands of demonstrators in Cairo's Rabaa al-Adawiya Square, which resulted in what Human Rights Watch described as "one of the world's largest killings of demonstrators in a single day in recent history."[3] The police and army had methodically opened fire on the crowds who had gathered over the previous six weeks to oppose the ouster of Egypt's first democratically elected head of state, President Mohamed Morsi.

Following Morsi's overthrow, the new interim government led by the acting president, Adly Mansour, fearful of the pro-Islamist tide that had risen under Morsi's rule, had spearheaded an unprecedented campaign to eradicate the Muslim Brotherhood, Egypt's oldest and largest Islamist organization, which had supported Morsi's Freedom and Justice Party. It disbanded the party, arrested Brotherhood members, shut down media platforms, banned books and harassed anyone who joined the Brotherhood's protests, promoted their cause or even wrote in their favour, finally designating the Brotherhood a "terrorist organization" days before my arrest. It reminded me of the McCarthyism that had swept the United States in the 1950s in an effort to uncover communists and communist sympathizers.

I'd visited the Rabaa sit-in with Ian Lee, a former CNN colleague, to help him report the story. The square had an eerie feeling about it that day. Dozens of Muslim Brotherhood protestors marched soldier-like in rows chanting verses of the Quran. They had built brick barricades at the entrances to Rabaa Square and the side streets leading to it, and many wore helmets and carried sticks and shields, in anticipation of a battle against the government's security forces. Was the sit-in a peaceful protest? It may have begun that way, but when the crackdown came after forty days, several protestors defended their positions with firearms and engaged the police from a nearby building—images caught on tape.

Some claimed that at one point there had been enough weapons at the sit-in to take on an army.[4] But that said, the vast majority of the nearly one thousand citizens killed were members of the Muslim Brotherhood, Salafis, and other supporters of Morsi's rise to power. By contrast, just eight police officers were killed, along with four journalists, including Sky News veteran cameraman Michael Deane, who was literally working alongside my good friend, the producer Omar Barazi, when he was struck by sniper fire.

I visited the Al-Eman Mosque near Rabaa Square in the days following the massacre to interview families trying to identify their loved ones, horrified by the sight of rows of corpses wrapped in bloodied white sheets—some bodies burned beyond recognition.

I wonder if the prisoner who occupied this cell before me was at Rabaa Square and if he lost friends in the massacre. I wonder what has become of him.

I had been angry at what seemed like an unjustified show of force by the new government. I wanted the powerful Brotherhood as far as possible from the ruling sphere, but I was appalled by the brutal way the military and police had dispersed the demonstrators, unlike anything the country had previously experienced. For the sake of its future, I hoped for another way out—one that did not perpetuate the terrible cycle of violence that had gripped Egypt since the start of the Arab Spring.

In my first days on the job at Al Jazeera English, I interviewed several Muslim Brotherhood members about the massacre. I also tried interviewing the mother of one of the police officers who had been killed, but when I mentioned I was with Al Jazeera she refused vigorously, assuming I was with the Al Jazeera Mubasher Misr channel. I explained that no, I worked for the network's *English* bureau—a separate, independent news-gathering entity not to be confused with the network's two Arabic-language sister channels: Al Jazeera *Arabic*; and (most especially) its local news affiliate, Al Jazeera *Mubasher Misr*. In the minds of many people not in the media, the names themselves (Al Jazeera English as opposed to Al Jazeera Arabic and Al Jazeera Mubasher Misr) sometimes created confusion. But everyone knew one thing: Mubasher Misr's mandate was to deliver propaganda: local news with a clear pro-Brotherhood bias that was upsetting to many people, including myself—and clearly to the interim government, which was cracking down on Brotherhood supporters wherever it could find them. I gently tried reminding the distraught mother that Al Jazeera English, broadcasting only in English, was renowned around the world for its objectivity and I promised we would tell her story with integrity. But tensions were now so high against the Brotherhood that her answer was an angry *No*.

Another slogan catches my eye. This one is scribbled in blue ink: *Port Said Forever! I didn't kill the 72 Ahly fans—I am innocent.* Port Said: the city of my father's birth, marred forever in my mind by an event I had reported on for CNN the previous year. As a child, I had run along its white sand beaches, swum in the transparent blue waters of the Mediterranean, teased the jellyfish until they stung me, and gorged on seafood fresh from the boats of returning fishermen. But the grim number "72" scratched on the wall brings back the day I stood outside the Port Said soccer stadium, too numbed to move.

During a match between Cairo's Al Ahly and Port Said's Al Masry soccer clubs, a band of men dressed as Al Masry fans and armed with knives, clubs, rocks and glass bottles, violently attacked Al Ahly fans while the police, instead of intervening, shut down the stadium lights and locked some of the gates. The massacre lasted twenty minutes. Unable to escape, dozens of Al Ahly fans were killed while others died in the stampede to get out, most of them between the ages of thirteen and twenty. One Al Masry fan and a police officer also died, bringing the total dead to seventy-four. Many of the men who participated in the attack were sentenced to death. Was the man in this cell one of them?

Stop! I tell myself.

I turn away from the wall and lie on the blanket. The cement is cold beneath my back and legs, and my shoulder throbs. I open my fist and peer at the bottle of painkillers. Maybe I should ration them? I pop a pill into my mouth. Without water, it catches in my throat. I swallow again and pull the second blanket roughly around me, both for warmth and to ward off the swarming mosquitoes likely coming in through the window high in the corner of the cell. I have no more power to stop them entering than I do the glaring light, so I cover my head with the blanket and pray for sleep.

I have barely closed my eyes when a voice calls out from beyond my cell.

"Newcomers. Brothers, look out your hatch."

I pull myself up and move to the door. Through the hatch, I can see the dark eyes of the prisoner in the cell across from me, and if I crane my neck and press my face against the opening, a lone guard slumped in a chair at the end of the corridor, sleeping.

"We have a ritual to welcome newcomers to our wing," the voice continues in a loud, conspiratorial whisper.

"Okay," I answer, matching his pitch. "Thank you."

I sweep my gaze one way and then the other down the row of cells, but can see nothing but the green metal doors.

"We will start with Essam," the voice announces.

From a cell somewhere to my left I hear another man speak.

"Essam al-Haddad," he says. "Executive aide to President Mohamed Morsi, responsible for foreign relations and international cooperation. I am married, have four children. One of them, Gehad, is in a different wing of Tora Prison. Another, Abdullah, a Muslim Brotherhood spokesman, is in London."

The high-level stature of my prison mate, who once met with President Obama, takes me aback and leaves me wondering why I am jailed among top-ranking political detainees now branded as terrorists, but I have no time to process this as the first speaker calls out: "Next!"

"Khaled al-Qazzaz, President Morsi's foreign affairs advisor, married, four children."

The voice comes from the man in the cell directly across from me and I am again surprised. My fellow prisoner is a well-known human rights activist in his thirties, married to a Canadian.

"I don't know why I'm here," he continues wistfully. "I was detained for three months at the presidential guard headquarters with no charges, where my family visited me regularly. They let me go. When I reached the street outside the building, a number of plainclothes policemen grabbed me and threw me into the back of a minivan, and brought me here. That was weeks ago. I haven't seen my family since."

My heart drops. I had assumed I would see my family the next day and that when I did they would extract me from this hellhole. Then another voice.

"I am Sheikh Murgan Salem al-Gohary. I am a Salafi jihadist who fought alongside brother Sheikh Osama bin Laden against the

Soviet and the American devils in Afghanistan. I have been married three times and have many children. I don't allow any of them to visit me to avoid humiliating them. I was released during the revolution and sent back here again for no clear charges. Arbitrary! This is all a play, a political performance by these pigs. History is repeating itself so don't let it get to your mind. Stick to the Quran."

This third introduction is alarming. Sheikh Murgan is well known for being an angry and murderous radical: he was a member of the Egyptian Islamic Jihad, had strong ties to the Taliban and was sentenced to death twice under President Hosni Mubarak. Not too long before my arrest I saw him on a talk show calling for the destruction of the Pyramids of Giza and the Great Sphinx. I remember thinking, *What a nut!* Now I am living with him and he is giving me advice, too.

"Amin Al-Serafi, Morsi's presidential secretary. Spent three months in detention with no charges. Now I am accused of spying for Qatar alongside President Morsi, and of selling classified documents containing military secrets to Qatar and to Al Jazeera."

Then I hear a familiar voice.

"Baher Mohamed. Al Jazeera English producer."

I press my face into the opening, turning in the direction of Baher's voice. I'm rewarded with a glimpse of his brown, almond-shaped eyes through the hatch of the cell door across the corridor—just to the right of Khaled al-Qazzaz. This small fragment of familiarity makes me inexplicably happy.

"I am married with two children," Baher continues. "The charges are being a member of the Muslim Brotherhood, funding the Brotherhood, giving them cameras, and . . ." He pauses a second before finishing with a laugh, "a bunch of other accusations."

"*Helwa*, good one," someone yells, and then another voice: "*Ya*, Baher, I know your father."

"Welcome to Tora," a third inmate cheers from afar, soon joined by a chorus of comments and knowing chuckles. The introductions continue, cell by cell, voices from beyond the metal doors floating through the corridor, sometimes fainter, sometimes louder, until it is my turn.

"Mohamed Fahmy. Al Jazeera bureau chief for the English channel. I am engaged. My charges are the same as Baher's." I recite them as if remembering by rote a childhood lesson. I still cannot believe the charges the prosecutor read out to me yesterday in an unemotional voice. I see myself as from a distance, on the edge of a chair, facing his mahogany desk; to one side of me sit two lawyers from Al Jazeera who have just scurried into his office, men I've never seen before and who do not speak to me, summoned in haste no doubt after our arrest: "You are accused of joining the Muslim Brotherhood Group, whose goal is to change the regime by force, including by terrorism, and to violate the freedom of individuals, target public institutions to undermine public order, and jeopardize the safety and security of society; of providing the Brotherhood with monies, supplies, equipment, machinery and information; of being in possession of communication and broadcast equipment without obtaining a proper permit from the relevant administrative authority; of intentionally broadcasting video clips, images, and false news to give the outside world an impression that the country is undergoing a state of internal strife and civil war . . . , which would have disturbed public security, harmed public interest, spread terror among the general public and stirred strife."

Dumbfounded, all I could say at that moment was, "Are you serious?"

I recall with a sense of irony two of the last stories I covered before my arrest. In the dawn hours of December 25, I announced breaking news on air that the interim government, under acting-president Adly Mansour, had designated the Muslim Brotherhood a terrorist organization following a deadly bomb blast at a police station north of Cairo. A swift government crackdown on anything Brotherhood had followed, and just three days ago, I'd sent a crew to cover a massive protest against the crackdown attended by large numbers of Brotherhood members and their supporters.

"Two days ago, Baher and I were arrested," I continue, "along with our colleague Peter Greste. Authorities raided our office and filmed the arrest. The state prosecutor has accused us of being terrorists."

"Welcome!" someone shouts. "We heard you guys were arrested in the Marriott Hotel!"

A number of other prisoners chime in, some praising Al Jazeera. A voice to my far left chants: *Allahu Akbar! God is great!*

"You journalists have been sent here to see the truth," the voice says. "There is a reason why God led you here!"

Several inmates call to the guard, already roused by the ritual, beckoning him to their cells. I catch a glimpse of a hand pushing something to him through the hatch of the cell to my left but don't fully understand what is happening until he opens my cell door moments later. His hands are full of gifts: an apple, a banana, a box of soap, a towel, a T-shirt, a bottle of water, a small roll of toilet paper, a small loaf of bread and mosquito repellent. I am both staggered and humbled by this unexpected generosity. It's oddly reassuring to have friends in this dungeon, even if that is because they wrongly believe me to be a supporter of the Muslim Brotherhood—one of them.

The ritual ends and moments later I hear the rhythmic voices of the prisoners reciting verses of the Quran.

I have just lowered myself to my blanket with my bounty when a voice calls out.

"Fahmy, open the box of soap I sent you."

I'm not sure who the speaker is, but I find the small box, remove the soap and discover a neatly folded piece of paper tucked underneath. I unfold it and begin reading:

Please rip up this note and flush it down the toilet after you read it. My wife is Canadian-Egyptian and I have heard you are too. I hold a permanent resident's visa. You must exert pressure for your case through the media in Canada and others like CNN and the BBC. Have your family start a very loud campaign and make sure they appear in the press. People die and disappear in this prison. Appeal to the Canadian government. The truth is that you won't make it out of here without international pressure. Try to get Amnesty, Human Rights Watch and the UN to support you before the case is referred to court.

Clearly the note is from Khaled al-Qazzaz. I'm of course distressed by the warning—and worried that I now possess information that could get me into trouble mere hours after I've arrived in Scorpion. I lift myself from the ground and walk to the toilet, ripping up the note as I do. I quickly drop the scraps of paper into the toilet, as if they are poisonous to the touch, and watch them float in the dark water, white fragments of an incriminating puzzle, and search frantically for the toilet's flush mechanism.

I can hear the heavy footsteps of the guard pacing up and down the corridor. *How the hell do I flush?* There is no lever attached to the primitive toilet bowl, no pull cord above. The footsteps approach and I cast about desperately for a solution, praying the guard is not returning with more offerings. Seeing the bottle of water, I grab it, open the plastic top, chug down half then pour the rest into the toilet. A few pieces of paper disappear, but the majority continue to float on the surface. Panicked, I search the room again. The dripping tap over the small sink on the other side of the cell catches my attention and I lurch for it. I fill the bottle with water, dipping my injured shoulder towards the faucet to hold the bottle steady and using my good hand to turn the tap to produce a weak stream of water. It takes some doing, but I eventually fill the bottle then empty it into the toilet. More of the paper disappears. I do this a second and then a third time, until the last fragments of the note finally descend out of sight. Though my cell is freezing, I am sweating. The thought enters my mind that I'll have to go through the same process every time I need to relieve myself.

For what may be minutes but seems like hours, I listen to the footsteps of the guard as he paces up and down. Finally, there is silence. I peer out of my cell into the quiet corridor and can see the guard once again slouched asleep in his chair.

"Mr. Qazzaz," I whisper, "I got your soap. Thank you. When do they let us out for some air? I want to talk with you."

There is no answer from the cell across from mine. Instead, I hear a voice from down the corridor.

"They won't let us out. We have not seen the sun for weeks."

Demoralized, I lie down on the blanket and again am swarmed by mosquitoes. I cover my face and head with the blanket, though it makes it hard to breathe. I can hear the buzzing mosquitoes beyond the rough fabric. Remembering the repellent, I throw off the blanket and find the small bottle, slathering the smelly liquid over my face and neck, and lie back, but it seems to make no difference. In the far corner of my cell I can see a row of cockroaches scuttling along the wall and more filing in from under the crack of the door. Miserably, I pull the blanket over my head again, and reach out for my bottle of pills, unsure whether to swallow another.

I think of Marwa, my beautiful fiancée, who delivered the pain-killers to me at the Marriott just before I was arrested. Tomorrow will be New Year's Eve, the second anniversary of our first date. I so clearly remember that final night of 2011 together and how, despite a year of revolution, 2012 seemed to hold promise and possibility both for Egypt and for us. President Hosni Mubarak had been forced to resign after three decades of repressive rule, and the country had held its first free ballot. Though the Muslim Brotherhood's Freedom and Justice Party had won a majority of the votes, I had remained hopeful in the run-up to Egypt's first presidential election. Now, almost three years after the start of the revolution, Egypt is mired in unprecedented violence. Still, this year, as 2013 drew to a close, I had vowed to do what I had always done, no matter where I was or what the circumstances: celebrate the coming year in a big way. I had purchased two airline tickets to Beirut where Marwa and I were due to be tomorrow night to bring in 2014 with a group of Lebanese friends I had met while working with the International Red Cross in Lebanon. Until this moment, I believed we would make that flight. Now, the words of my fellow inmate ring in my ears: *They won't let us out. They won't let us out. They won't let us out.*

In the early hours of the morning, there is a new sound. It is not the heavy, methodical step of the guard pacing the corridor or the unceasing electric hum of the fluorescent light somewhere outside my cell window, or the incessant buzzing of mosquitoes beyond the barrier of my woollen blanket or the steady drip, drip, drip of the faucet. This sound is an uneven, intermittent squeak. It starts, then stops. Starts then stops, slowly advancing. Then a man's voice calls from right outside my cell telling me to come and get my breakfast. My shoulder is in worse pain than the night before, and I cannot bear the thought of rising. I hear the sound of a key in the lock and the door swings open. A guard I have not seen before steps inside. Beyond him in the corridor is a stooped man dressed in blue prison garb, his hands resting on a wheeled food cart. I realize the mysterious sound was just the cart's squeaky wheels. The guard asks in an aggressive tone: "You are the Al Jazeera chief, right?"

I nod.

"When the man calls you to pick up your breakfast, you get up and pick it up!"

He reaches for the food cart and grabs a piece of flat bread, a chunk of white cheese and an orange, and throws them on the filthy floor of my cell. I catch the orange as it's about to roll past. As the door slams shut, I notice a cockroach advancing on my breakfast, and, cursing, I race him to it.

Though I win that battle, I am soon losing the cockroach war. At first I watch them skirting the length of the dirty grey blanket or marching in procession down the wall beside me, but soon I feel the tickle of their tiny legs across my feet or at the back of my neck.

Moments later, the door opens again. A guard tells me I am to get a haircut. "You can get up," he says, "or we will get you up."

Clumsily, using the wall for support, I pull myself upright. My legs feel leaden, as if not my own, and my head buzzes with hunger and fatigue. I follow the guard down a series of corridors. I feel relieved to be out of my depressing cell and able to walk more than a few steps. We arrive at another cell, one brighter and more spacious, occupied by a lone inmate with an electric shaver clutched in one hand. He instructs me to lean over and then presses the clippers to my skull. I will later learn that my barber has been imprisoned for murder.

With the first pass of the clippers I realize he is not giving me a haircut, he is shaving my head. I feel the nick of the razor against my dry scalp and protest, but he continues roughly and without pause, telling me I will thank him when the lice start looking for a home. I watch my hair drop in dark clumps onto the floor. Moments later I am bald.

I am being led back to my cell when I see a familiar figure approaching down the corridor. Though it has been more than eighteen months since we met for our interview, I immediately recognize the bearded face of Mohamed al-Zawahiri. A group of officers and guards encircle him and as the gap closes between us I search for words to address him. But before I can open my mouth, he stops before me. "Mohamed Fahmy," he says. "Now, you see it with your own eyes, the oppression, from the front seat. Pray. Pray that you make it out alive."

I am taken aback that he recognizes me, even though before he agreed to the CNN interview he had subjected me to a series of tests to verify my identity and intentions. When I met with him in his modest Cairo home in July 2012, he was not accustomed to using a mobile phone, on which I was recording our interview, and told me he had not been photographed for over a decade. He was calm, his eyes intense and darkly ringed, his face encircled by a woolly wrap of long grey-white beard. When he spoke, his words were carefully measured—it was clear he did not trust me or the international media, especially the US media, which he despised for labelling him a terrorist. He spoke about his efforts to free the supporters he had left behind in prison, and talked about a peace treaty he had written in prison proposing a truce between al-Qaeda and the United States. We were all skeptical of his influence in al-Qaeda's hierarchy considering the ten years he had been locked up.[5] Although I wondered then, as I do now, if he was in contact with his fugitive brother Ayman al-Zawahiri, leader of al-Qaeda. "Could you get in touch with your brother Ayman to implement this peace treaty if the Americans agreed to your conditions?" I had asked.

He answered cagily. "I could get in touch with my brother if the American government allowed me to."

It had taken me a long time to gain his trust, and it was only after CNN agreed to publish sections of his proposed peace treaty, in a link embedded in my story online, that he allowed the renowned correspondent Nic Robertson to conduct CNN's first on-camera interview with him.

The police confiscated my mobile phone during the Marriott raid, and the recording of that hard-won interview will become so-called evidence of my collusion with the Muslim Brotherhood.

Back in 2012, this shadowy international figure and I had seemed to exist on opposite sides of a vast political and philosophical landscape. Today, under the same roof, it occurs to me, incredibly, that Mohamed al-Zawahiri and I are both accused terrorists.

How in hell did I get here?

CHAPTER 2

BREAD, FREEDOM, SOCIAL JUSTICE

January 22-27, 2011

I flew into Cairo on January 22, 2011, three days before the beginning of Egypt's Arab Spring. It had been almost two decades since I lived here, having moved to Canada at sixteen, and then eventually becoming a correspondent in the Middle East at twenty-seven. I longed for the people of Egypt to one day have the same democratic freedoms I enjoyed as a Canadian citizen, and the growing rumble of anti-Mubarak sentiment I had heard coming out of Egypt fuelled my hope. When I awoke that first morning in the Om Kolthoom Hotel overlooking the Nile River in the upper-class neighbourhood of Zamalek in central Cairo, I felt that I was exactly where I wanted to be. The sun shone brightly through the sheer white curtains as I revelled in the unfamiliar freedom of not having a pressing deadline or a staff of thirty-four to manage. It was a blessedly quiet moment but in just a few days the peace would be upended, with reverberations that would spill across the region and the world.

The previous night I had said goodbye to Dubai and the luxurious apartment I'd rented while employed as senior producer and manager at the Middle East Broadcasting Network's Alhurra Television. The past two years had left me weary of the highly sanitized culture of television news coverage in the United Arab Emirates. Any story involving sex, religion and politics had been off-limits and every time a subject arose that touched on these, a network battle was not far behind. Though the job had been prestigious and the pay generous, working in the opulent, apolitical bubble of the UAE had made me feel hollow and disconnected from the gritty, real-world journalism I'd grown to love. Instead of covering stories that mattered, my team reported on trivialities: the construction of Dubai's Burj Khalifa, the tallest building in the world, or the Dubai Mall—this, too, the biggest on the planet, complete with an indoor ski hill smack in the middle of the desert. I had filled airtime with reports of excess—the largest man-made island or the richest horserace—or inanity: the cloning of a camel. The tiny sheikhdom with its sandy beaches and income-tax exemptions might have felt like utopia for many residents, but for me it was a journalistic wasteland.

As I looked out over the bustling streets of Cairo below, any uncertainty I had about abandoning my job evaporated. I felt a surge of excitement. A month earlier Tunisians had successfully initiated the "Jasmine Revolution," a widespread civil resistance movement that erupted the day after a twenty-six-year-old fruit-and-vegetable street vendor, Mohamed Bouazizi, doused his clothes with gasoline and lit himself on fire. An act of desperation to protest police and government corruption and abysmal living conditions, his tragic self-immolation sparked widespread pro-democracy demonstrations. Those demonstrations had ended when Tunisia's strongman president of twenty-three years, Zine El-Abidine Ben Ali, fled the country.

I had closely followed the events unfolding in Tunisia via Facebook and Twitter. Social media had emerged as a vital news source and powerful communication medium for the protestors, accelerating the Tunisian revolution. I remember sitting in my Dubai apartment electrified by the tweets that soon began emerging from Egypt, too. It seemed Bouazizi's death had not only been a catalyst for revolution in Tunisia, it had ignited a movement in Egypt and across the Middle East that the world would soon come to know as the Arab Spring.

One tweet in particular had moved me to action. Posted by a friend blogging under the alias "Sand Monkey," the tweet announced that a protest was being planned in Egypt for January 25—also known as Police Day—to oppose police brutality and demand justice from President Mubarak's government after years of repressive dictatorship. I immediately made a couple of calls to Egyptian journalists and colleagues who confirmed that a protest movement was indeed brewing in Egypt. Days later I quit my job and scrambled to book a flight from Dubai to Cairo.

Being back in Egypt, a country ripe for change, felt enticingly familiar to me. My career as a journalist had begun on the first day of the 2003 Iraq War when I slipped into the country as an interpreter and assistant reporter for the *Los Angeles Times*. Over the next year I had helped cover the dangerous and bloody events unfolding in Iraq from a moving van, which often doubled as our sleeping quarters. By 2006 I was an assistant reporter and stringer in the UAE for the *New York Times*, discovering a passion for my profession and a conviction that a good journalist's job is to hold governments accountable and to give voice to the voiceless. However, arriving in Egypt for the anti-government protest reminded me that it was not solely my profession that had prompted me to place myself in the midst of the action. It was also my father.

I grew up in Egypt and Kuwait listening to my dad's complaints about Hosni Mubarak, and his decades-long despotic rule. My father was constantly writing freelance articles that alluded to the epic corruption and mismanagement of wealth that had left our seven-thousand-year-old nation underdeveloped and in debt. He was a highly educated engineer who, like millions of Egyptians seeking a higher standard of living, had emigrated to the Arabian Gulf, looking for lucrative work in the oil business. Most judges, doctors, teachers, engineers and labourers who lived in and built Kuwait had come from Egypt. The Kuwait National Petroleum Company, where my dad worked, provided our family with housing and paid for my education at the Universal American School-Kuwait. Though I had spent the majority of my youth there, I never stopped counting down the days to my three-month summer vacation when I could go back to Egypt to be with my grandfather, a former police general.

My father's words did not resonate with me as a youngster, though I clearly remember him ranting about the country's pitiful press and personal freedoms and lack of social justice. I also remember the day Egyptian president Anwar Sadat was assassinated during a military parade in 1981. Though I was just seven years old, I still recall the shock and sadness that gripped my parents as we sat in our Kuwaiti home watching the news emerging from Egypt. The country's shattered dreams for political and economic reform were not something I could grasp, but my father's tears and anger were.

As a middle-school student, mastering Microsoft's newly launched Word software in the late eighties came with a price: my father pressed me into typing his handwritten articles before he sent them to be published. I became his personal typist and no matter how onerous my school assignments or how late the typing kept me up on a school night, there was no escaping it.

Later, when I was in high school, he wrote a petition calling on Mubarak to step down. In it, he called for national civil disobedience and asked the Egyptian people to stop using public transport services, shutter their shops, and stay home on a specific date to protest Mubarak's government. By then I understood the magnitude of what I was typing and the ramifications for my dad and our family if he carried through on his promise to mail copies to the State Department in Washington, the Egyptian Parliament and various newspapers. I remember the fear I felt for my dad's safety as I typed the words over my mother's protests, and watched her try to rip the addressed envelopes from his hands. Our opposition could not dissuade him. He had pushed my weeping mother out of his way and stormed out the door like a man possessed. I had a sense of terrible foreboding, with good reason. Shortly after he mailed those envelopes, Kuwaiti authorities, on the request of the Egyptian government, had arrested him. I visited him in prison, listening to him proudly explain that he slept on the concrete floor of the cell "for democracy." The Egyptians had asked that he be deported to stand trial in Cairo and our family fought fiercely for his release until at last an influential Kuwaiti sheikh from the royal family obstructed his deportation.

I had once been angry with him for what he'd put our family through, but that January morning as I stood looking out at Cairo from the Om Kolthoom Hotel I felt proud of his courage, and happy to be back among my many friends and extended family. Egypt, the land of my ancestors, has an ancient and unparalleled cultural history, and in recent times I had also come to love and admire its sophisticated movies, its writers and musicians, and its vibrant social scene.

Even my stately three-star hotel was named after one of the most influential Arab singer-songwriters of the twentieth century, beloved from the twenties to the seventies throughout the Middle East, and indeed the world. Known as Kawkab al-Sharq, "The Star of the East," Om Kolthoom's voice and lyrics fuelled the country's patriotism. She sang of love and nationalism, drawing on stories sung and listened to for generations. It is said that President Anwar Sadat refused to hold his weekly news conferences when her live concerts were being broadcast on the radio because he knew no one would listen to him. Admired by fellow artists from Bob Dylan to Beyoncé, her enchanting songs were engraved on the hearts of kings, presidents and soldiers and were a siren call for ordinary people seeking to escape the reality of the region's bloody wars, and the increasing difficulty of simply feeding one's family.

Each guestroom door in the Om Kolthoom Hotel bears the title of one of her songs, and I felt buoyant as I walked along the hall to the elevator, testing my knowledge of her music as I went.

At the café next door, a crowd of people sat smoking their *shisha*—tobacco pipes—the air rich with the smell of fruit-flavoured smoke. I took a seat at a small round table, ordered a tea with mint leaves and settled in to wait for Wael Omar, an Egyptian-American friend and filmmaker I'd arranged to meet. All around me patrons were talking about recent events in Tunisia and what they might mean for Egypt. At one table, a young, boisterous group, who I pegged as college students, discussed how it was impossible to compare ninety million Egyptians who wanted change to the ten million Tunisians who had achieved it. At another table, I recognized an activist known for her anti-government views typing away on her laptop. Beyond her, a group of low-ranking police officers hovered near the hotel parking lot. I watched as one of them approached a car as it entered the lot, and witnessed the all-too-familiar scene of the driver slipping a bill to the officer before proceeding.

"Welcome to the land of the pharaohs, *Habibi!*" I turned to see Wael striding towards my table, his baseball cap on backwards as always on his wild curly hair, and stood to embrace him. "How's the hotel?" he asked. "Better than home?"

By "home" he was referring to the house my parents still owned in Maadi across the city, where I could have stayed. "I want to be close to the action," I said, calling the waiter over. "What's going on with the protest on January 25?"

"*Everyone* is going!" Wael declared. "It's going to be huge. The government is so stupid—it's just announced the twenty-fifth as a national holiday." He handed me a flyer. "This is being distributed across university campuses."

I studied the photo on the front. It was a post-mortem snapshot of the bloodied, disfigured face of Khaled Said, a twenty-eight-year-old amateur blogger who had allegedly posted a video online showing Egyptian police involved in a drug deal. Seven months ago, police had dragged him from a café in Alexandria and fatally beaten him. When his family had visited the morgue to identify his body, Said's brother had snapped the photo, which he'd later posted on the Internet. The photo had gone viral. One of the people to see it, Wael Ghonim, a Google marketing executive in Dubai, had started a Facebook page called "We Are All Khaled Said." The page had not only grown into Egypt's largest dissident Internet site, attracting hundreds of thousands of followers across the country and internationally, it had become the go-to source for up-to-the-minute information on plans for the protests.

I scanned the slogans on the flyer: *Join us on January 25! Come to Tahrir Square! Egyptians Rising Up Against Torture, Corruption, Poverty & Unemployment. Tell the Police We Are All Khaled Said.*

"You really think this will be different from other protests?" I asked.

"People have had enough," Wael replied with conviction. And I wondered if Khaled Said might become Egypt's moral equivalent of Tunisia's Mohamed Bouazizi.

The streets of Cairo were quiet two days later as I walked towards Tahrir Square where Wael and I had arranged to meet at ten o'clock. Searching the faces of the people heading in the same direction, I detected a firm resolve. A light breeze freshened by a mist that shrouded the city made the day feel full of possibility. Though I'd covered dozens of political events, I had never before participated in a protest and had no idea what to expect. *Just be an observer,* I told myself. My journalism career had kept me at a properly objective distance from the stories I'd reported on, but today I was entering unknown territory.

Half an hour later I crossed the bridge over the Nile. Here, the crowd thickened. I checked Twitter and confirmed what my eyes already told me: protestors were streaming towards Tahrir Square from different sections of the city. Most tweets I read made no mention of any violence and reported that the Central Security Forces, though out in numbers, were standing idle. I marvelled at how quickly and widely the demonstration news was being disseminated on Twitter. As I approached the square, I saw at least a dozen officers marching in formation. I discreetly snapped a photo of the men dressed from head to toe in black uniforms and shiny helmets, their Plexiglas shields and large batons held at the ready. I attached the image to my Twitter handle and pressed the tweet button.

There were thousands of protestors in the centre of Tahrir Square when I arrived. I was struck by the diversity of the people around me. These were not organized thugs or members of fanatical religious groups but ordinary citizens: men, women, teenagers and the elderly alike—an unprecedented fusion of students, illiterates, aristocrats, housewives, holders of doctorates, businessmen, vendors and street kids, musicians, actors and the average unemployed man—all standing together, many carrying signs that captured the essence of Egypt's populist discontent: BREAD, FREEDOM, SOCIAL JUSTICE.

I spotted my friend Wael filming freely and smiled—he'd been unsure whether it would be safe to bring his video camera. He noticed me and nodded, not pausing in his interview with a young woman who was speaking passionately into the camera. He wrapped up and turned to me with a grin. "I said this was for real!" He told me of the simultaneous protests in many of Egypt's twenty-seven governorates, or administrative jurisdictions. "Suez is big."

I looked around, unable to fully comprehend the enormity of the demonstration and what I was seeing. Across the square several young men held a massive Egyptian flag. I spotted Omar Barazi, a dual Egyptian-Syrian citizen and friend I had not seen in years. He rushed towards me and hugged me.

"When did you leave Dubai?" he asked, adjusting the baseball cap on his head. "Is your father back in Egypt?"

"I wish," I said, thinking how much he would have enjoyed this moment. "He's been on a no-fly list since 2004—Mubarak's government would arrest him if he returned."

Omar knew that my parents divided their time between Kuwait and Montreal. "I wish I could live in Canada," he said, and I was reminded of how lucky I was to hold Egyptian and Canadian passports.

I was revelling in the atmosphere of brotherhood around me when I heard a loud noise—half bang, half pop—in the distance. A ripple passed through the crowd. Was it a gunshot? It took a moment for us to realize that the police assembled in front of the American University had fired a tear-gas canister. It landed yards from me. I heard another pop. I looked up to see a white plume of smoke ripping through the air before a second canister landed nearby. Each released a thick cloud of tear gas, which rapidly engulfed us. I ran from the smoke, burying my nose and mouth in the crook of my arm and squinting to protect my eyes from the burn of gas. Chaos had erupted and I lost sight of Omar and Wael among the hundreds of people fleeing from the tear gas. I could sense a shift in the atmosphere. I saw a young protestor, his face covered by a bandana, grab one of the tear-gas canisters from the ground and throw it back towards the row of policemen. Dozens of younger kids began hurling rocks.

"Don't throw rocks!" some of the protestors yelled. *Selemya, selemya. Peaceful, peaceful.*

I felt a ripple of fear about what the boys' actions might provoke, shocked at how quickly the situation was escalating. I was now standing in a group of strangers gathered on the green patches of grass in the centre of Tahrir Square. I looked in vain for my friends. I could see journalists running into the square to film the commotion. Young protestors began dragging metal barricades toward the leading edge of the crowd, creating a wall of defense in the event the police decided to storm the crowd.

The police fired another tear-gas canister. I was squinting into the chaos when I felt the sharp crack of a rock hitting my forehead. I doubled over in pain and heard the pop of more tear gas. Smoke billowed around me and my eyes burned. Through my tears I saw a rock on the ground and grabbed it.

I tried to retreat, but was paralyzed by spasms of coughing. The air was so thick with gas that I could not breathe. Suddenly, I felt someone grab my arm and half lift, half drag me away from the centre of the square and the hundreds of panicked protestors. I remember seeing puddles of water on the ground as we pushed through the crowd, trying to keep our balance. When my eyes cleared, I was startled to see that my rescuer was the actor Khaled Abol Naga.

It took me a few minutes to recover, but when I did, I felt myself charged with anger. Together, Khaled and I began walking back towards the frontlines. The rock was still in my fist. The situation had changed dramatically: protestors were badly injured and greater numbers were banding together to confront police. The chants no longer revolved around bread or social justice. People were yelling, *Down Mubarak! Down police thugs!* The mood of the crowd was becoming increasingly angry, its chants louder. I stood in the middle of it, chanting as loudly as I could and pumping my fist in the air. Then I cocked my right arm and hurled the rock at the police. For the first time in my career as a journalist, I had become part of the story. It would not be the last.

The Arab Spring that had begun in Tunisia had arrived in Egypt.

I remained in Tahrir for hours that day. News reached us that three protestors had been killed in Suez. I watched once peaceful citizens hurl rocks and gas canisters back at the police. Social media was at the forefront of the news, tweets and Facebook postings racing far ahead of traditional news reporting. Even when the government managed to block Twitter later that day, tech-savvy protestors found ways of publishing tweets using Twitter third-party clients. Web proxies were now the only way to tweet. One called "Hide My Ass" was a favourite among young protestors, and the Facebook page "We Are All Khaled Said" was releasing minute-by-minute photos from the ongoing clashes in Tahrir and Suez. I lost all track of time and it was not until I put a hand to my throbbing and swollen forehead hours later that I realized it needed attention. I was done.

I walked out of the square and caught the first cab I could.

"The government has unleashed its civil servants," the driver said angrily, referring to the reporters who provided state-sanctioned news. "Their journalists are insulting our intelligence, saying many of the protestors are Iranians and Hezbollah agents."

I told him I was worried that such fabrications would worsen the violence. I'd seen very few Western journalists in the square that day who might counter such false information.

"How many people were there?" he asked.

"Thousands." I paused. "No, tens of thousands."

"I'm going to join them tomorrow," he announced as I got out of the cab.

In my hotel room I examined my injury in the mirror. My forehead was red, bruised and sore, but otherwise okay. I lay exhausted on the bed, pressing a makeshift icepack to it as I watched the coverage on the government-owned state TV. An interesting narrative was emerging about who had been behind that day's protests. One news banner read, "Muslim Brotherhood cells have rioted in Tahrir Square." I wished I could help the true story get out.

The next day, while part of me yearned to be back in the throng of protestors standing up for what I believed in, for the ideals my father had fought so long and hard to achieve, I was very distressed by my unbridled impulse towards violence the day before. As a journalist my aim had always been to champion the voiceless, challenge government oppression and corruption and to encourage positive change. To do that requires an objective distance. Yet I had lost sight of all that and surrendered to the revolutionary fervour in Tahrir Square. It was hard to make sense of the feelings I had experienced: the powerful sense of purpose I had felt as I helped a woman clear the tear gas from her eyes, or an elderly man avoid being trampled by the surging crowd; the hatred that filled me as I hurled that rock at the police. I thought about how quickly peaceful intention could morph into violent action. If I go to the square today, will I be moved to throw Molotov cocktails at the police? No, I told myself, but without conviction. I realized that I, like my Middle Eastern compatriots, carried suppressed anger over the state of the country. What frightened me was how little it took for me, for all of us in the square, to unleash that anger.

So I avoided Tahrir Square over the next couple of days but I could not stop thinking about it. As I sat at an Internet café a block from my hotel, a young woman handed me a pamphlet calling for a massive protest on January 28. She introduced herself as Mona and told me she was a member of April 6, an activist group formed to support thousands of workers who had banded together in El Mahalla El-Kubra, an industrial town north of Cairo on April 6, 2008, to protest the legitimacy of that year's re-election of President Mubarak. After she left, I read the pamphlet. The movement had the same logo of a raised fist used by the Otpor movement in Serbia, which

was credited with toppling the regime of Slobodan Milosevic. Like
Optor, April 6's mandate was to use nonviolence to encourage the
government to create a democratic state. It instructed protestors to
wear goggles to shield their eyes from tear gas, long sleeved sweaters
with hoods, sneakers, and gloves for protection. One image portrayed
a protestor spray-painting the windshield of a police car to immobi-
lize it. Another image showed a protestor presenting a rose to a row
of police officers. Surfing the Internet, I spied a more detailed version
of the same protest guide on several sites and grasped how truly large
and widespread the grassroots opposition movement had become.
I decided to rejoin the demonstration the next day, although in spite
of all the non-violent directives I had seen and heard, the organizers
had dubbed January 28 the "Friday of Rage."

The nervousness that gripped me that evening reminded me
how I had felt on March 20, 2003, the day before I entered Iraq.
My uncertainty now was so acute that I called my parents in Canada
to seek their opinions. My father, naturally, wanted me to join the
protests, while my mother was fiercely opposed. The conversation
left me jittery and unsettled and I decided to call Sharif, an easy-
going, apolitical American-Egyptian friend who had been a source
of light-hearted, party-loving company in the past. He suggested we
meet later that night at the Omar Khayyam Casino.

The casino is housed in Cairo's majestic Marriott Hotel, a luxurious, sprawling property that commands acres of prime real estate in
Zamalek. The district, known for its quiet leafy streets and nineteenth-
century villas, is not only one of the most attractive areas in the city, it
is the neighbourhood where Cairo's sizable non-Egyptian population
lives. With its large pool, manicured grounds and more than a dozen
restaurants, the Marriott had always been a sanctuary in a city of more
than twenty million people that constantly pulses with activity.

The lobby was full of well-heeled guests, many from Arabian
Gulf countries such as Kuwait and Saudi Arabia, as well as journalists

who had flown in specifically to cover the mounting protest movement. I made my way past a BBC television crew checking in at reception and headed to the casino, flashing my Canadian passport to the woman at the door. Only foreign passport holders were allowed into the lavish casino hall. I scanned the crowd for Sharif. Gamblers stood in clumps around felted tables. A number of elegant call girls hovered around them, balancing their drinks and making small talk. I spotted my friend near a blackjack table. He was a regular gambler who enjoyed the free food, booze and cigarettes offered to casino patrons.

"Hey, Mr. Tahrir," he said with a grin when he saw me. "Welcome back. You ready to play?"

"I need a drink," I said.

"So, are you going tomorrow?" Sharif asked, when I explained that the political situation had put me on edge. Though he lived across the street from Tahrir Square, he couldn't understand why people were protesting. I had sought him out precisely for his lack of political engagement, but his response annoyed me. A waiter stopped by our roulette table with a tray of drinks and offered me a beer. I needed something stronger and ordered us each a whisky.

I placed a bet and watched the roulette wheel turn, my mind spinning too, full of unease about what the next day would bring and how such a dichotomy of perspective and privilege could co-exist in one country. "Twenty-seven red," the dealer called. It was my number but I felt little satisfaction in my win.

"That's the Mo I know," Sharif said, clapping me heartily on the back. "Forget politics, man. Let's party."

My heart was not in it. I scanned Twitter for updates under the hashtag #FridayofRage. The Twittersphere was on fire and I noticed that a number of prominent Western journalists I followed had posted that they were in or on their way to Egypt. I decided to text Wael. He had suggested we meet outside Mostafa Mahmoud Mosque at noon and I wanted to confirm I would be there. I texted him, but the message did not go through. I checked Twitter again. Strangely, there were no new tweets on my feed. Sharif was standing next to me. I dialled his number. Nothing happened.

"That's weird," I said to no one in particular, though a nearby waiter overheard.

"The phones are disconnected?" he asked, looking over the shoulder of another patron who was trying to get his mobile to work.

"I'll try rebooting," Sharif said.

I knew it would make no difference. Something more sinister was going on. A Western journalist whose face I recognized but could not place overheard us and came over.

"The phone lines are out. Does this happen often?"

I shook my head. "Never."

A quiet commotion had begun throughout the casino. What was happening to the phones was no accident. I was witnessing a moment both astonishing and portentous. The government had convinced or coerced the three major phone companies, who supply land and cellular coverage across the whole country, to suspend their services for the first time in Egypt's history.

CHAPTER 3

FRIDAY OF RAGE

January 28-February 11, 2011

I awoke late on the morning of Friday, January 28, my body tense with anticipation. After noon prayers, Egyptians would begin the march to Tahrir Square to demand a more just and equitable society. Today the sky was a dull winter whitewash outside my window, an unwritten slate for what lay ahead. I quickly showered and dressed, then zipped up my favourite jacket. I had worn the dark blue leather bomber while reporting on events in various conflict zones and superstitiously hoped the immunity from harm it had given me in the past would hold true today. I recalled the protest pamphlet's advice as I adjusted my hoodie. I did not own thick goggles, but tucked my sunglasses into my jacket pocket, feeling like I was preparing for battle. I picked up my cellphone and glanced at the screen. Though there was still no reception, I slipped it into the thigh pocket of my cargo pants.

The street in front of the Om Kolthoom Hotel was eerily empty. Though it was not unusual for Cairo's streets to be quiet around

Friday prayers, today the city felt ghostly. I hailed a taxi and directed the driver to the Mostafa Mahmoud Mosque a few blocks away. Although the walk would have taken me less than ten minutes, I felt a sense of urgency to get there.

"Any cellphone reception?" I asked the driver.

He shook his head. "No. The radio is spreading fear and warning people against participating in the protest. But," he added, "I'm parking my cab soon and joining it."

As the taxi closed the distance to the mosque, we fell silent at the sight of dozens of black-clad Central Security police standing in formation in front of government buildings and at intersections along the route. A large contingent of police conscripts along with generals in full uniform were clustered nearby as we pulled up outside the mosque. The crowd there was massive, overflowing from the modest domed white structure onto the wide street in front of it. Again, I was struck by the diversity of people I saw gathered shoulder to shoulder: ordinary men, women and youth from all walks of life as well as recognizable faces—famous actors, musicians and sports stars.

Though I do not consider myself an adherent of Islam, and had not prayed in years, as I listened to the voice of the Imam booming from the minaret, I felt compelled to join the hundreds standing on carpets placed on the pavement outside the mosque to accommodate the worshippers who could not fit within it. I walked to the area reserved for ablution and approached one of the many sinks, removing my boots and placing them to one side away from the wet ground. Pushing up my sleeves, I began *wudu*, a ritual washing of different parts of the body required of Muslims before prayer. Feeling somewhat uneasy about my ignorance, I furtively copied the man standing next to me; I washed my hands three times, splashed water on my face three times and cleansed my ears inside and out three times. As I finished I looked up and saw two longtime family friends in the crowd. I had last seen them in Montreal almost a decade earlier,

before I headed to Iraq for my first journalism job. We shook hands
warmly. We did not need to exchange words: as Egyptians who had
lived and studied in the West and experienced its democratic freedoms, we understood what was at stake in today's protest.

The call to prayer echoed once more and I positioned myself
beside my friends, copying their movements to make sure I got
things right as we first lifted our hands to our ears, then placed them
at our navels and finally performed a series of prostrations. My voice
was a barely audible mumble as I mimicked the words of prayer
while my eyes remained open, observing everything around me.
The policemen were not praying and stood immobile on the sidelines. For ten minutes the huge crowd moved as one, standing then
kneeling, foreheads bowing to touch prayer mats then lifting and
bowing again. I felt an indescribable sense of solidarity with those
who had gathered for this collective moment of worship. Then, as if
the crowd was possessed of one mind, one single sentiment, the
second the prayers ended a unified chant erupted from within and
outside the mosque:

The people want to topple the regime!

It was like nothing I had experienced. I raised my own voice in
chorus with the others. Chanting loudly, I put on my shoes and fell
into step behind my two friends. I nodded to their sixty-year-old
father as he joined us and we slowly began moving down El-Shaikh
Saleh Mousa Street. Our voices reverberated off the surrounding
residential towers and our fists pumped skyward. The police formations moved to block the crowd but retreated just as quickly, overwhelmed by our numbers. The protestors turned east towards the
Nile River, which separated us from our final destination: Tahrir
Square. As we marched on that cool winter day, our numbers swelled.
Many watched from their homes and hung flags from the ledges of
their balconies and open windows. *Come Down! Come Down!* the
protestors called up to the onlookers, and citizens joined us by the

thousands, bringing their banners with them, streaming in from side streets, chanting, waving Egyptian flags, and calling on others to do the same. I felt invigorated as I watched shop owners, cab drivers, and elderly women abandon their daily routines and rush into the throng. The crowd remained peaceful and civilized as it overtook police formations along the route to Tahrir Square, not by force but sheer volume.

The chanting alone, the act of speaking out freely on the streets of Cairo in unison with total strangers, evoked entirely new emotions in me: pride, belonging and fearless resolve. I noticed several media vans following the protest, filming it as it snaked through the city past the Cairo Opera House and towards the bridge that would deliver us into Tahrir Square. I could picture the headlines and news tickers, and imagine TV anchors around the world reporting the breaking news of this grassroots protest movement.

It was early afternoon when we reached the Opera Square roundabout and streamed around it to the entrance of the Kasr el-Nile Bridge. That's when everything changed. Police suddenly fired a barrage of tear-gas canisters directly into the crowd. The offensive came from behind three large Central Security trucks parked at the bridge entrance and flanked by dozens of soldiers, many of whom wore gas masks. I watched in disbelief as they aimed their rifles at us, firing one tear-gas canister after another. The crowd split in two, each group running for cover towards the residential buildings on either side of the street. On our march to the bridge a fellow protestor had handed me an onion and I pressed my nose into it, hoping it would protect me from the stench of tear gas. It seemed to help. Several young protestors began hurling rocks and I dropped to my knees and picked up two.

"Drop the rocks! No!" I heard someone yell.

Selemya, selemya. Peaceful, peaceful. Others echoed the familiar chant, and I felt embarrassed that for a second time I had let my baser instincts get the better of me. I immediately dropped the rocks, silently vowing I would not resort to violence again. I straightened and watched the crowd reassert itself. Several feet in front of me on its front line I spotted the familiar face of Amr Waked, one of Egypt's most famous actors. He was boldly leading the chants, his green eyes flashing with intensity above the blue surgical mask hanging loosely below his chin. His fist pumped the air and his presence seemed to fuel the masses, giving them the courage to reassemble and press forward. A young woman pushed through the crowd, her arm aloft and waving the same blue masks, which she distributed among the protestors. Armed with these as well as scarves, swimming goggles and hoods pulled low, and carrying lemons, onions and homemade spray bottles of vinegar and Coca-Cola as protection against tear gas, the crowd continued its advance on the bridge.

Police responded with a second volley of tear-gas canisters. A young man nearby hurled one of the canisters back at the police. The crowd cheered, but the scene was turning ugly. Someone set one of the police trucks on fire. Dark smoke and flames engulfed it, spreading panic among the officers who began to break rank. The crowd reacted with a unified roar and surged forward. From the corner of my eye I saw another protestor pick up a gas canister that had just landed in the crowd. It was my friend Wael. I watched him throw it back and tried to reach him, but there was no way to move forward through the crush of people or to attract his attention amid the clamour. Fire trucks had been dispatched to the burning building and the wail of sirens added to the din.

The gas hung rank and heavy in the air and my eyes, nose and mouth burned. Tears streamed down my cheeks as I watched protestors spray vinegar and Coca-Cola on each other's faces. The police continued their onslaught of tear gas and fired water cannons mounted on trucks to keep the crowd from advancing. I retreated from the centre of the action to sit on the curb. Nearby, young men dismantled the sidewalk, smashing the concrete blocks into small chunks for ammunition. Like me, the crowd seemed tired, an army in need of direction. But this uprising had no Che Guevara, no Gandhi, to unify them around a single strategy. Instead a new wave of protestors streamed into the square, men and women yelling that they had come from Giza through the pyramids to join the protest. They surged towards the bridge equipped with fresh lungs and fresh legs and fuelled by sheer collective determination.

Their advance turned the tide and the police forces that had held the bridge suddenly retreated. It felt like an important victory. We now occupied most of the bridge leading to Tahrir Square. The police had stopped firing tear gas which enabled the demonstrators to congregate and regroup.

It was close to four o'clock, more than three hours since we'd reached the bridge. Rejoining the crowd, I paused in the middle of it, admiring the Nile, watching boats speeding towards it to get a closer look, and taking in the sense of camaraderie among the haggard crowd. I could see none of my friends. I didn't care. Everyone around me was a friend now, I thought, as I drank in the revolutionary fever. A number of men dropped to the asphalt and began praying, metres from the police line. I was just a row or two back and allowed myself to relax and enjoy what seemed like a welcome moment of truce.

A moment later tear-gas canisters again sailed through the air, this time accompanied by the sound of gunshots. A muscular police-man wearing a gas mask moved quickly towards us, his rifle seem-ingly aimed straight at us. The men who had been praying stopped, frightened and caught off guard. No one was sure whether the police were firing blanks or bullets, but there was no time to figure it out. I turned to run and found myself locked in a crush of retreating bodies, all of us hemmed in by the bridge and desperate to move away from the gunshots, and I found myself trapped in a slow motion stampede, a sea of humanity so dense I could not even raise my hands to cover my face. I placed my hand against the back of the man ahead of me to keep him from becoming plastered to my body. A girl stumbled and fell in front of me and I yanked her up off the ground as her dad pulled her into the safety of his arms. I began to lose my own balance and felt someone behind me lift me up. Crazily, I spotted Wael an arm's length from me as he was going down beneath the crush. I watched in horror, unable to reach him, exhaling in relief as the man beside me pulled him up. I saw his baseball cap fly off and managed to snag it and return it to his head, which was now tucked into the back of the man in front of him. He glanced back at me and his eyes held a mixture of surprise and fear.

"They're firing birdshot," he yelled. I didn't have a chance to respond as the crowd behind us pushed forward. I could see fear drawn on the faces of the people around me. Women screamed and gunshots rang out in staccato succession. There was nowhere to go, so we surged in a tight knot together, each of us praying not to lose our footing, to stay upright as we retreated to the entrance of the bridge and mercifully spilled out into Opera Square.

Relief poured through me. We'd made it. I stood in shock over what had just happened, unable to fully digest it. But police boats on the Nile now turned their water cannons on us, drenching the crowd with powerful spumes of water. As we ran for cover I heard more gunshots. Less than a moment later, a group of men came running back from the frontline carrying a boy in his early twenties. He was bleeding profusely from his neck, his white T-shirt and jeans drenched in blood.

"Help us!" one yelled. "Find us a taxi!"

The men stopped right in front of me, laying the body on the pavement. A man pressed a hand to the boy's neck trying to staunch the flow of blood, but it was no use. He was dead.

At that moment it seemed to me that the hopes of the revolution also died.

A taxi arrived, driving right through the crowd, and I helped several men lift the body and carry it to the car. I sat on the curb, feeling utterly sad and defeated.

Then something unexpected happened. It began with the distant sound of a powerful chorus of chants, a sound that grew ever louder. I saw a seemingly endless parade of thousands of people marching like an army towards the bridge. Unlike the rest of us assembled in the square, this civilian army was not comprised of men, women and youth of diverse educations, religious persuasions and backgrounds. The group was all male, most of them bearded, with banners emblazoned with the insignia of the Muslim Brotherhood, two crossed swords with a Quran and a single word in Arabic: PREPARE! One banner demanded the release of prisoners. Those at the leading edge of the group carried police uniforms on long wooden sticks like barbarian war booty—and most, if not all, of this tide of men were members of the Muslim Brotherhood.

The Muslim Brotherhood was founded in Egypt in 1928 by a schoolteacher named Hassan al-Banna as both a political and social-service organization, promoting the implementation of Sharia (or Islamic) law and pan-Islamic political unity, including an Islamic state. The Brotherhood's primary political efforts were focused on opposing British imperialist occupation in Egypt and the corruption within Egypt's long-ruling royal family, but it also gained rapid, widespread grassroots support by providing much-needed services such as health care and education to the poor. I recall filming a story for CNN in a poverty-stricken neighbourhood in Cairo where the Muslim Brotherhood had set up a distribution point and was handing out medicine, food and school supplies to a long line of people. Recipients were required to register their names and contact details before receiving assistance. Later I learned the Brotherhood used these registration lists to call up thousands of welfare beneficiaries when they needed them to swell anti-government protests.

In 1948, amid rumours that the Brotherhood was plotting a coup, Egypt's prime minister Mahmoud an-Nukrashi disbanded the organization, seizing its assets and imprisoning many of its members. At the end of that year, a Muslim Brotherhood student assassinated the prime minister, an act that the Brotherhood's founder Hassan al-Banna condemned, saying terror was not the way of Islam. He was shot and killed on the streets of Cairo six weeks later.

Over the years the Brotherhood has had an uneasy relationship with successive Egyptian governments, many of which have incarcerated and tortured hundreds of its members. Others fled to nearby Arab countries, including Saudi Arabia, Syria, Iran, Iraq and Jordan, where they continued to operate, whether with open support or in secrecy. Over the last sixty or so years, the Brotherhood has become a worldwide organization, and to this day remains the largest and best organized political opposition force in Egypt.

In the days following the January 25 protests in Tahrir Square, the Muslim Brotherhood, comprised of close to 500,000 members across Egypt, had announced that they were officially joining the youth on the streets to protest the police brutality. Now the Brotherhood had arrived in force, and all of us, regardless of our feelings about them, charged with emotion over the death of our fellow protestor, eagerly joined their ranks. Not even the impressive police force amassed on the Kasr el-Nile Bridge could hold back the sea of tens of thousands of protestors marching towards them. As the front line of the crowd approached the police barricade, I watched two officers jump off the bridge into the Nile. The chants were deafeningly loud, so loud I could not hear my own shouts. "The people want to topple the regime," I yelled in unison, as we crossed the bridge and streamed into Tahrir Square. *Tahrir* means "liberation" in Arabic. Around me, citizens from every socioeconomic stratum and walk of life cheered and chanted, all of them unwilling to accept anything less than President Mubarak's immediate resignation.

We had won the battle of the bridge, but the standoff in the square was just beginning. The Egyptian military had dispatched tanks and thousands of soldiers, positioned at various locations around the square. It was early evening and an uneasy tension hung over the crowd. Though the government had ordered the police to stand down, many around me believed they had simply sent the military to take their place. Others insisted the military was on the side of the protestors. Buildings and cars burned in the distance and I could hear the occasional pop of gunfire.

In the midst of this chaos, I saw a tall, familiar-looking man with blond hair striding towards me. It was Ivan Watson, the National Public Radio reporter I'd worked with in Dubai in 2006. Though we had not seen each other since then, I had sporadically kept in touch and only days earlier had sent him a message via Twitter to say hello and ask how he was.

"Hey, Moody," he said, blue eyes alight, as if it had been five days rather than five years since we'd last seen one another. "I got your message. What the hell is going on in your country? Why don't you come work with me? I'm with CNN now. We need help. I need some eyes on this massive story."

I did not hesitate. Tahrir Square was *the* story on the planet, and I had been yearning to report the story. What I did not realize was how completely CNN would dominate my life for the next two and a half years.

Ivan led me across the road to the modest City View Hotel, which overlooked the square. CNN's main Cairo office was located in the Hilton Hotel a couple of blocks away, but the network had rented a room to be closer to the action. I soon learned that many other news agencies had done the same. The room Ivan took me to was cramped and cluttered with cameras, lights and other equipment all set up and ready to broadcast at a moment's notice. He quickly introduced me to Joe Duran, their cameraman, and Hossam Ahmed, CNN's

Egyptian office administrator, and to a youthful, blue-eyed reporter with a shock of short grey hair, perched on one of the two double beds—Anderson Cooper. I said hello, but my attention was on the large window and fifth-floor balcony beyond: the view of the square that it offered was mesmerizing. I had been in the midst of the protests the entire day, but the scale of what was happening had not hit me until I looked out over the sea of bodies below. The numbers were almost incomprehensible, as was the sense of order and community that seemed to have organically emerged. Citizens on the periphery blocked the entrances to the square while those in the centre banded peaceably together, chanting and singing. The square pulsed with life like a massive, new beating heart of the city, perhaps of the entire country, the beautiful blue artery of the Nile stretching out to the horizon beyond it.

I stood there oblivious to the high-voltage energy of the journalists behind me until Ivan called me back inside. He told Hossam Ahmed that I would need a press pass issued as soon as possible.

I was buoyant and filled with purpose when I returned to Tahrir Square the next day to start my new job. The mood was cautiously festive. Overnight a tent village had emerged in its centre, revolutionary artwork had begun to appear on banners and brick walls, yellow, happy-faced helium balloons bobbed above a small section of the crowd, and music from several bands filled the air. Egypt's famous artists, poets and performers all seemed to have joined the fray and many entertained the crowd. I listened for a moment to a passionate young man named Ramy Essam sing a song he'd written for the revolution. A large crowd gathered around him and again I was struck by both the solidarity and diversity of the protestors. The rich rubbed shoulders with the poor and disenfranchised, and the passion and vigour of youth was everywhere.

Egypt's young intellectuals had long been a leading force for change. Many had begun advocating for an end to corruption and a fair political system a decade earlier. One particular pressure group called Kefaya ("Enough") had risen to prominence during the 2005 presidential referendum and the revolution had returned this grassroots coalition to the forefront of the uprising.

Hossam secured my press pass that afternoon and my days immediately became relentlessly long. I juggled duties that varied from gathering news, securing guests for interviews and acting as an interpreter, to writing web stories and ferreting out key background information on the various political parties, youth groups and members of the Muslim Brotherhood involved in the ongoing uprising. It was as far removed as I could imagine from my previous job as a manager in Dubai with a huge, modern desk and a plump leather sofa, daily editorial meetings and a generous budget. None of that was important now. I was working with some of the most redoubtable reporters on the planet, but above all, this was not just another story in another country. It was my story. And covering the news on streets where I had lived carried a heavy emotional burden. Each time I looked at the hundreds of thousands of protestors occupying Tahrir Square, I remembered how it had felt to be among them, hopeful and afraid, caught in the stampede on the Kasr el-Nile Bridge, carrying the lifeless body of the boy, fighting for democratic freedoms and rights that had been denied my father and grandfathers for generations.

In my first few days it seemed we were mostly watching teenagers throwing rocks and charging at the military. Some wore flip-flops, others were barefoot. There were adults among them, but increasingly, as I witnessed youngsters being continually tear-gassed only to return with defiance, it occurred to me that there was an entire generation of Egyptians who felt they had nothing to lose. Some, like me, were foreign educated and had experienced democratic freedoms first hand, and scores more, facile with social media, could no longer be duped into accepting the status quo.

I was committed to being meticulous about listening to and objectively representing all sides of the story, though I knew that the Mubarak military regime would brand me a traitor for reporting news of the revolution to America, the same country that, ironically, had invested billions of dollars propping him up. His government was intensifying its smear campaign against the protestors, branding them anti-Egyptian: conspirators. On the ground, however, it was obvious that the Muslim Brotherhood and the secular movement were now a powerful and united front which the army was struggling to control.

At the same time, something suspicious began happening. Thousands of pro-Mubarak protestors suddenly appeared on the streets to defend the status quo. In contrast to the protestors who occupied Tahrir, these were almost entirely young males. Most were aggressive, even violent, and acted like trained thugs. They were openly hostile to journalists, too, and speculation was rampant that they were police conscripts dressed in civilian clothes, hired by Mubarak's security apparatus.

Then, on February 2, the situation turned precarious for foreign journalists. That morning Mubarak supporters attacked Anderson Cooper and his CNN team as they crossed an expanse of open pavement in front of the Egyptian Museum—a kind of no-man's-land separating pro- and anti-Mubarak supporters. The incident happened close to where Ivan and I were reporting. It began when several men began shouting and blocking Anderson and his camera crew. Without warning or provocation, the commotion escalated into physical violence. Anderson's cameraman kept the camera running and in the video footage Anderson can be heard shouting, "I've been hit now, like, ten times . . ."[6] Egyptian soldiers did nothing to protect the journalists as men punched Anderson and his camera operator in the head and pulled at a female producer's clothes. The sense of lawlessness, of an ominous, unbridled potential for things to go unstoppably wrong, was acute. Only when we reached the relative safety of the square, did I exhale.

Then an extraordinary scene unfolded. Like a tableau from a medieval battlefield, men mounted on horses and camels charged into the square brandishing bladed weapons and whips and lashing out at the protestors. A brutal battle erupted. We were caught in the middle. Men from both sides pelted rocks, bricks and glass bottles at one another. Military officers in nearby tanks fired bursts of automatic gunfire in the air, while the battle raging around the mounted men grew more and more bloody in what would become known in the media as "The Battle of the Camel." The centre of the violence was only yards away from the Egyptian Museum, frighteningly near our hotel, but with no other option Ivan and I ran to it and from our room watched the violence escalate. We later learned that pro-Mubarak thugs had harassed the CNN anchor Hala Gorani, who had been a short distance from us in Tahrir, and that Mubarak supporters had stormed the Hilton Hotel searching for journalists. That night some CNN reporters took refuge in a secret location farther from Tahrir to report on the events unfolding. That location was the Marriott Hotel.

The next day we reported the escalating situation in Cairo from the safety of the hotel, the streets becoming increasingly dangerous for foreign journalists. The situation was exacerbated by the former head of intelligence Omar Suleiman, in an address to the nation on state television (Mubarak had appointed him to the long-vacant position of vice president just five days earlier): "I actually blame certain friendly nations who have television channels—they are not friendly at all—who have intensified the youth against the nation and the state [. . .]. They have filled the minds of the youth with wrongdoings, with allegations, and this is unacceptable."[7]

That day, scores of foreign journalists were beaten with sticks and fists and dozens detained by government forces. The Committee to Protect Journalists (CPJ) reported that thirty journalists had been detained and twenty-six assaulted. "This is a dark day for Egypt and a dark day for journalism," Joel Simon, the executive director said. "The systematic and sustained attacks documented by CPJ leave no doubt that a government-orchestrated effort to target the media and suppress the news is well underway."[8]

Tahrir Square had become the epicentre of the revolution. The death toll in the square rose to thirteen with many more killed across Egypt and hundreds more injured. Yet Mubarak remained defiant, insisting that the country would fall into chaos if he resigned.

It had taken Tunisians twenty-eight days to topple their long-time president. The question everyone was asking during the violent days that followed was: How long would it take Egyptians to topple Mubarak?

What I did know from my experience during the Iraq War is that no matter how ardently people may profess that victory is close at hand, democracy is not acquired overnight. I had entered Iraq on the first day of that war hopeful, like many, that removing Saddam Hussein from power would usher in a true era of freedom. When President Bush gave his "mission accomplished" speech on May 1, 2003, proclaiming the war over, I was in Baghdad feeling like we were just starting. As I tried to make sense of what the US had in store for post-Saddam Iraq, I was quickly realizing that while Bush had planned for war, he had not planned for what would come after. Few of us foresaw the disastrous results of the decision by the US presidential envoy to Iraq, Paul Bremer, to disband Saddam's 400,000-strong army—releasing a tsunami of trained and armed servicemen from Iraq's Sunni Islamic sect across the region. Thousands of these suddenly out-of-work Sunni servicemen joined militias and Islamist groups that later swelled the ranks of al-Qaeda and morphed into present-day ISIS. Many wonder today if it was worth exchanging one unacceptably brutal dictator for the inhumane killers that followed, who have terrorized local citizens with suicide bombings, beheadings and the wholesale slaughter of thousands of innocent people. Millions more Iraqis remain internally and externally displaced as warring coalitions battle extremist Islamic groups. Thirteen years after Saddam's execution, Iraq is more politically divided, the sectarianism is worse than ever (ISIS didn't exist back then), and it's a ruined country that may hardly be able to stand on its feet again or even taste the promise of democracy.

While Egypt hadn't suffered Iraq's violent sectarianism, democracy had remained elusive. Egypt is considered the birthplace of political Islam and groups that originated on its soil have exported radical Islam across its borders to implement Islamic governance in all sectors of life by way of Sharia law.

Though I understood this unfortunate reality, I felt personally offended when Vice President Suleiman, during an exclusive interview with Christiane Amanpour on *ABC News*, suggested that Egypt was not ready for democracy.

"When you see what's happening on the streets of Egypt, of Tunisia, and now of Jordan and Yemen and Syria, what do you think?" Amanpour asked Suleiman earnestly. "These are young people who want a different world."

"It's the Islamic current who push these people," Suleiman replied.

"You think that?" Amanpour's voice held a hint of disbelief. "You don't think it's young people who want their rights? Their freedom?"

"It's not their idea," Suleiman insisted. "It comes from abroad."

"Do you believe in democracy?" asked Amanpour finally.

"For sure. Everybody believes in democracy. But when will you do that?" Suleiman asked rhetorically. "When the people here have the culture of democracy."[9]

While the former head of the General Intelligence Directorate, the country's national and transnational intelligence and security

apparatus (also known as Mukhabarat), may have been correct in
saying that a "culture of democracy" was not prevalent in Egypt, he
failed to grasp that the actions of its citizens, particularly of its youth,
were not the result of shadowy Islamic figures inciting violence from
beyond Egypt's borders, or the news media of "friendly nations"
causing unrest, but of the government's own repressive policies.
Suleiman, whom the *Daily Telegraph* had labelled "one of the world's
most powerful spy chiefs,"[10] had not only spearheaded Mubarak's
vendetta against the Muslim Brotherhood and the country's other
Islamic groups for the past quarter century; he had, since 1995, col-
luded with the US government in its infamous extraordinary rendition program. In Egypt (as in many of the fifty plus countries that
have been party to the agreement), they were then incarcerated in
secret "torture camps."[11] [12] Or they "disappeared." What had arisen in
Egypt, therefore, was a culture of fear rooted in a deeply entrenched
police state that served the small, powerful elite who ran the country
but did nothing to further the democratic freedoms and institutions
of its citizens, 40 percent of whom were functionally illiterate and
one quarter of whom lived below the poverty line.

As the protests raged against Mubarak's dictatorship, Suleiman
blamed everyone but his own government for what was unfolding.
He accused the Muslim Brotherhood, Hamas, Palestinian militant
factions, the Hezbollah and Shiite militants based in Southern
Lebanon with conspiring against Egypt, a view not surprisingly
echoed in the Egyptian media which was largely controlled by the
country's state security apparatus. But while the government's stran-
glehold on national press freedom tightened during the protests,
news from foreign media could not be suppressed.

The eyes of the world were on Mubarak, including those of
his longtime ally, the US government. The Obama administration
quietly began urging reform as the standoff between protestors
and the government threatened to boil over across the Middle East.

Mubarak responded by removing senior members of his party from office, including his younger son, Gamal, long touted to take his father's place, who was wildly unpopular with the country's youth. The protestors, however, refused to be placated, and on February 10, Mubarak finally prepared to address the nation.

Expectations of his resignation were high in Tahrir Square that night. After days of tense clashes the mood had again turned festive, even celebratory. All around the square people sang, danced and hugged one another, waving banners and Egyptian flags. Bands played on several stages across the square, and on one a wedding was under-way. A massive white sheet had been strung up at one end of the square and soon an image of the eighty-two-year-old leader, dressed in a dark suit and tie and standing behind a podium, appeared on the makeshift screen. A semi-hush fell over the crowd as he began to speak, dedicating his words to the youth of Egypt and promising to honour their demands. Mubarak announced that he would not seek re-election, but immediately added he would stay in office another six months to ensure an orderly transition to an elected government.

Joy gave way to anger, the shouts and insults drowning out his speech. As the mood turned sour, people removed their shoes and waved them in the air as a sign of contempt. *He must leave*, they chanted loudly. *We're off to the presidential palace! We will give our lives for our freedom!*

Early the next afternoon Ivan, CNN's cameraman Thomas Evans and I took a twenty-minute taxi ride northeast of Tahrir Square to Al-Ittihadiya Palace, Mubarak's private residence and administra-tive headquarters. In the brooding centre of Cairo (and other cities across Egypt) protests had continued to rage since Mubarak's speech the previous night, but we arrived to a modest crowd of several hun-dred. Dozens of presidential guards and several tanks stood behind a barrier of barbed wire that had been erected at the entrance to the palace. A lone protestor argued with a guard, waving his shoe in the air. More media began to arrive on the scene. At one point the crowd broke into a frenzy as two helicopters lifted off from the palace and the rumour spread swiftly that Mubarak was leaving the country, but otherwise the protest in front of the palace remained relatively civilized. Then, moments after the helicopters disappeared from view, a sea of several thousand protestors appeared, marching up the street toward the palace. Their chants echoed off the surrounding apartment buildings as they yelled, *Erhal! Erhal! Leave! Leave!* I translated the chants for Ivan who was preparing to do a "stand up" to use in the package for the day. He interviewed some of the newly arrived protestors who told us they had walked three hours from Tahrir Square to reach the palace. I could see the presidential guards preparing for the possibility of a confrontation, readying their weapons and repositioning themselves closer to the barbed wire that separated them from the crowds.

Hours had passed since we had arrived. Chilled and hungry, our team decided to head down a side street in search of a bite to eat and a place to recharge our camera battery. We found a burger restaurant not far away, ordered dinner and plugged in our battery pack. While we ate and waited for it to charge we eavesdropped on the conversations among the patrons. Several of the younger ones were hatching plans to engage the presidential guard in a violent clash; others urged a peaceful approach and suggested staging a sit-in outside the palace similar to the one taking place in Tahrir Square.

I was tired, but not only from the eighteen days of consecutive protest. It had been almost two weeks since I'd joined CNN. It was a gruelling job that on a personal level left me torn between the unquestionable need for journalistic impartiality and my private feelings towards a president I despised: I dreamed of an Egypt free of Mubarak's repressive rule.

A sudden commotion arose in the crowd outside the palace. Chants echoed through the street. Ivan asked me to grab the battery pack while he paid the bill. The restaurant owner had no TV, but quickly turned on the radio the minute he understood what the protestors were chanting. The vice president, Omar Suleiman, was preparing to make an announcement on state television.

Not a soul in the café spoke or moved. The streets had gone silent as the spy chief's measured voice echoed through the neighbourhood, emanating from TVs and radios in every apartment and business in the city. Suleiman's announcement was brief, little more than half a minute: "President Hosni Mubarak has decided to step down from the office of president of the republic and has charged the Supreme Council of the Armed Forces to administer the affairs of the country." He added sombrely. "May God help everybody."[13]

Jubilation erupted among hundreds of thousands of Egyptians in Cairo, among millions throughout the country. People around me jumped up, hugging and crying. It was over! After thirty years of dictatorship, Egypt had been liberated.

I shot off a quick text to my father who had dreamt of this moment for so long, whose calls for liberation I had typed as a boy, then I ran with Ivan and Thomas towards the palace to film the ecstatic crowd, many waving Egyptian flags above their heads. I felt tears streaming down my cheeks and hastily donned my sunglasses though the sun had set long before. My cellphone vibrated in my hand and from the corner of my eye, I saw its screen light up with an incoming call. I recognized the number immediately—my father's—but had no time to answer it as I watched Ivan's back. He was balanced precariously in the euphoric crowd as he spoke into the camera capturing the power of the historic event. Some of the demonstrators tried to lift him up on their shoulders as they screamed their joy into the camera. My phone rang and rang and finally, as Ivan's recording ended, I answered. It was impossible to hear or be heard amid the thousands of people around me crying, laughing and shouting. I knew my father would be crying, too, and that even if we had been able to speak to one another amid the deafening sounds of celebration, there would have been no words to capture the depth of our emotion. So I simply held my phone in the air and let him listen.

CHAPTER 4

BROTHER'S KEEPER

January 3, 2013

I lie awake on the cold floor. My shoulder is swollen and tender, throbbing. I wrap the rough wool blanket around me in an attempt to stay warm but I shiver convulsively. Four days in and I have barely slept. With every movement pain radiates through my arm, ribs, jaw and neck.

At night I hear the mournful howls of feral cats beyond the walls of my cell. The sharp crack of gunshots in the distance creates a harsh counterpoint. Mosquitoes buzz in my ears, sting every exposed bit of flesh. Thoughts turn endlessly in my head. *How will I get out? Does anyone know I'm here?* The words the unknown prisoner muttered to me when I arrived reverberate in my mind: *They won't let us out. We haven't seen the sun for weeks.*

I try to quiet my thoughts, focusing on the things I took for granted: coffee, fresh juice, the sugar rush of a Coca-Cola. Pillows. The embrace of my beloved Marwa, the warm comfort of her smile, her soft skin. Everything I cherish seems distant and unreal. My family. My friends. Freedom.

On New Year's Day, I was taken out of my cell for a second round of questioning at the state security headquarters. It was a momentary joy to find my colleague Peter Greste there, too—he had been brought in from Luman Prison, somewhere distant in the Tora complex—but we were then separated for the interrogation. I was nervous as I entered the spacious, air-conditioned office for the second time. The same state security prosecutor who had interrogated me the day after my arrest—an overweight, bespectacled young man with a closely cropped head of tight curls and expressionless green eyes—motioned me to sit in the chair in front of his massive mahogany desk. He wore a dark suit, perfectly knotted tie and a tight smile. Beside the nameplate on his desk, which read *Rami el-Sayed*, an ashtray overflowed with cigarette butts. As before, a stenographer sat beside me, ready to record my every word.

I nearly jumped from my chair when Ragia Omran burst into the prosecutor's office, trailed by two junior lawyers from Farag Fathi's law firm—Al Jazeera's legal counsel in Cairo. Ragia, a whip-smart human rights lawyer who I had come to know well during my time at CNN, had learned of my arrest and come of her own volition. We had crossed paths many times amid clouds of tear gas and the chaos of the protests. I admired her fearless representation of activists and protestors during the January 25 revolution and had frequently cited her work in my CNN reports. We had last seen each other at a Halloween party two months earlier under more jovial circumstances, me dressed as a Rastafarian in a wig with long dreadlocks, and she bewigged in blond curls.

"You have come here as a pack, I see," el-Sayed remarked, asking the lawyers to place their union identification cards on the desk in front of him.

As Ragia leaned over to submit her card, she whispered that my parents were on their way from Canada. The interim government had removed the names of many citizens, including my father's, from the no-fly list—a positive outcome of Mubarak's ouster.

El-Sayed silenced her sharply—talking to the suspect was not allowed and he would have them all removed if he heard another word. This seemed ironic, given my so-called lawyers said not a word. Whatever counsel they may have had, they did not share it with me.

I answered a barrage of questions about my work with Al Jazeera, feeling frustrated, wanting desperately to speak with Ragia, to get word to Marwa and my family.

A small opportunity presented itself after the interrogation. Ragia caught up to me in the hallway as a guard, who had placed one handcuff on my wrist and the other on his own, was leading me down the corridor to the elevator.

"Don't worry, Moody," she said, "the whole world is behind you."

"Don't talk to the suspect," the guard shouted, yanking me by the handcuff.

"Don't yell at me," Ragia replied fiercely. "I'm a lawyer and I have the right to speak to him. I know the general who runs this building and I will call him if you don't let me speak to my client."

"Ragia," I whispered, "my Twitter password is 'MarwaCanada.' Delete any tweets that could be incriminating or could be perceived as pro–Muslim Brotherhood."

The media is all over the story, she reassured me, as another guard stepped between us. "They'll make sure the truth gets out. And," she warned as the elevator doors closed, "get rid of the Al Jazeera lawyers. They have a bad reputation."

Several days later I saw the guards take Baher for interrogation. When he returned that evening, he stopped at my hatch. "Fahmy, we will be out soon. Fifteen days. I took care of it. The prosecutor gave me assurances." His smile was like sunshine, but before I could ask him what he meant, the guard hustled him to his cell.

I hold fast to Baher's words as I lie in my cell. I nourish myself on hopes of freedom, of seeing Marwa and my parents, of the possibility that the whole world is indeed behind me. Yet I worry, too. Worry about my colleague's penchant for wishful thinking. I worry about Al Jazeera's lawyers, who I barely acknowledged in the interrogation and who scurried off as soon as they could. I worry about how I will get proper representation or medical attention for my broken shoulder if I am shut away in solitary confinement.

I decide to distract myself by memorizing every detail of my cell. It has a foul, rancid odor, a smell of piss, sweat and, probably, my own fear. The close concrete walls, the rough-hewn ceiling, enclose me like a burial vault. The cables of the broken fan snake across the walls of the cell to a useless electrical box. An army of cockroaches swarms out of the electrical box and marches across the wall, carefully avoiding the spider webs. They, at least, know how to survive in here.

When I hear the call to prayer, I know it must be dawn and check my watch, which, to my surprise, the guards did not confiscate when I entered Scorpion. The recitations rise from neighbouring cells and drift through the air. The sound of the Quranic verses at least gives me a sense of anchored existence, of peace. I try to join in, although I do not know the words. I have not prayed since I was a child, other than on the Friday of Rage when I marched with thousands to Tahrir Square and everything seemed achievable. My prison mates pray five times a day—dawn, midday, late afternoon, just after sunset and late evening—and there is comfort in marking the passage of time in this dungeon where the twenty-four-hour glow of fluorescent light prevents us from distinguishing day from night.

As I mumble half-remembered verses, my rational, Western-educated mind rises up in protest—it is, after all, a group of incarcerated Islamists with whom I pray. I feel self-conscious. Silly, almost. *I need to get out of here. I need to do something. I can't leave it to God.* But a few of the prayers I learned as a young boy return and wash over me, drawing me along in their tide.

The next morning I hear the squeaky wheels of the food cart. The guard opens the hatch in the door, yelling at me to come and get it.

"I can't, I need medical help," I shout.

The guard ignores me and instructs the old prisoner to leave the flat round of *balady* bread and salty white cheese in the hatch where I fear the cockroaches will get to it before I can. For four days now, food has been a welcome relief from the boredom and discomfort of solitary. Some mornings there is a lentil soup that feels nourishing and substantial. There are beans, sometimes an egg, and for dinner the occasional piece of meat, or perhaps vegetables. But I have become afraid to eat because everything I put in myself must also come out.

The toilet, as I found out the first night, doesn't flush. There is a bucket I am supposed to fill up and pour into the toilet to flush down my excrement, but with my right arm immobilized it is impossible to lift and tip the heavy water-filled bucket one-handed. The solution I devise is to use my plastic water bottle to push the excrement down the toilet. I plunge furiously with one arm, trying to break up my own shit and force it into the drain. The smell is so revolting that I gag and vomit. I am literally, as well as figuratively, in deep shit.

My cell smells as pungent as those of Beirut's Roumieh Prison where, in 2007, I served as a prison delegate and interpreter for the International Committee of the Red Cross (ICRC). Roumieh was the most infamous prison in Lebanon. As part of a delegation in charge of protecting the rights of political prisoners, most of my work had been inside the terrorism wing. Our ICRC team visited

cells three times a week to register and interview prisoners, document torture and ill treatment and communicate messages between
prisoners and their families. After each visit, we relayed the findings
and requests of specific detainees to the prison's warden. I think
about my team partner at the ICRC, Claire Higgins. Claire was a
British national, self-tutored in Arabic, whose diplomatic skills,
black belt in karate and intellect could break the habitual stubborn-
ness of whatever prison warden we dealt with. We had worked well
together, a kind of good-cop, bad-cop team, hounding Lebanese
prosecutors with our findings which clearly revealed a systematic
use of torture. We also carefully monitored the medical issues of the
detainees and lobbied for those in need to be transferred to hospitals. The prisoners included Saddam Hussein's nephew, and suicide
bombers who had been apprehended before they could blow up
themselves or others—radical Islamists who criticized me for working with an organization whose symbol was a cross.

Now, nearly a decade later, I am the one who needs medical intervention and legal help. I need Claire, or someone like her, someone
on the outside. As a journalist and foreign correspondent I am accustomed to the dangers of war zones. I have seen respected colleagues
injured and detained. But it never crossed my mind that, simply for
doing my job in Cairo, I would end up here, shovelling my own shit
in the terrorist wing of a maximum-security prison.

I know that the government is not taking kindly to the US
critique of its human rights abuses—including the recent Rabaa
massacre—given that the US is holding more than seven hundred
prisoners indefinitely in its military prison on Guantanamo Bay
Naval Base. I can imagine Egyptian diplomats using that argument
behind closed doors should the Americans ever try to intervene.

Speaking the truth has always been hardwired for me—the
foundation of all my actions. With the ICRC, I had to keep my
mouth shut. I was not allowed to report to the media about our

findings in the prison system. That frustration led me to leave the organization after just one year. Being a journalist was the antidote. For me it meant the opportunity to report truthfully, honestly, accurately. The freedom to do so meant everything to me. Naively, I never thought I would be jailed for it.

Throughout the day I huddle on the floor and drift in and out of a groggy half-sleep. At one point I wet an undershirt a prisoner has given me and wrap my face to repel the insects. Blindfolded with the wet cloth, and skewered by the discomfort of my shoulder, I try to stay perfectly still.

I am startled out of my stasis by loud voices, and the hard metal jangle of keys and a bolt sliding. I tear the wet shirt from my face and lift my head. Two men in trench coats stand at the door to my cell holding a young man in the same white uniform as me. One of them gives a hard shove and the young man trips and stumbles into the cell.

He is in his early twenties at most, frail and brown-skinned. He carries two blankets, but is barely able to stand straight. Scrawled across his back is the same word emblazoned on my own uniform: TAHQEEQ, under investigation. He is shaking and his eyes dart around the cell, confused, obviously nervous. Finally he places his blankets on the ground and sinks to the floor.

"Did they torture you, too?" he whispers, pointing to my arm. I shake my head No.

I notice dried blood around his nose. His ears, bright red with pressure wounds, are crusted with blood. Gingerly he begins to clean his face.

"The blood must be from the blindfold," he says. "It was tight and they kept it on my face all the time." He tells me his name is Shadi Ibrahim, and he is the former head of the student union at Ain Shams University in Cairo. He and his two friends have been tortured for three days in a row at Lazoghly State Security. He speaks in a low, fearful tone.

"Don't worry," I assure him. "I haven't heard anyone in our wing being tortured." I feel a protective surge. He is barely out of childhood. "What are you accused of?"

He shrugs. "I don't know, but it's somewhere between the usual accusations of belonging to the Brotherhood or assaulting cops. We haven't seen a prosecutor yet." He says they were arrested in a cab at a checkpoint in the Cairo suburb of Mokattam.[14]

I recover my manners and introduce myself.

Shadi stares at me. "You are *Mohamed Fahmy*?" He shakes his head in disbelief. "Your story is huge, it's all over the news. They asked me over and over during the torture if I knew you or your colleagues."

I am puzzling over why on earth the authorities would question him about me and my colleagues when we hear a voice shout out. "Newcomers, introduce yourselves!"

Shadi's eyes grow wide with alarm. "It's okay," I say, extending a hand. "Help me up. There are introductions to make. Everyone will want to know who you are."

He uses his slight body weight to pull me up. I walk to the door and peer through the hatch. Across the corridor in the hatch to the right, I glimpse Baher. When our eyes meet, I see the skin around his eyes crinkle, as if he is smiling. This small expression of resilience tells me he is staying strong. I smile back.

The roll call begins as one by one the prisoners call out their names. Shadi calls out his own name, and calls to his friends to do the same.

"Khaled Abdel Raouf." A voice booms down the corridor. "Media student at Cairo University. I am a cameraman, and I'm not sure why I'm here. I was picked up with Shadi Ibrahim and Sohaib Saad in a taxi in Mokattam."

"Sohaib Saad, political science student and cameraman. Detained with Khaled and Shadi. We were punched and abused. They put cigarettes out on our bodies. I don't know why we are here."

I get the sense from Sohaib's voice that he is the feistiest in the group. Their attitude is a combination of innocence and bravado. I motion to Shadi to step aside and press my face to the hatch. Sohaib's cell is adjacent to Baher's. If I squint I can just make out the young man's bulging eyes and a fringe of curly hair. I introduce myself and Baher follows suit.

"Fahmy!" Sohaib shouts, his words laden with sarcasm. "Emir of the Marriott Cell. Baher, Marriott Cell deputy!"

The words echo down the corridor. The Marriott Cell. It takes a moment for me to absorb their meaning. "Cell? What is the Marriott Cell?"

Sohaib laughs as if it's funny. He tells us we are famous, saying that student protestors are carrying posters of us in rallies. "You guys are heroes!"

As a journalist, I am familiar with the convention of naming terror cells for the locations at which the terrorists gather. It strikes me suddenly that the Marriott hotel room from which we temporarily ran Al Jazeera's English bureau is being framed as a terror cell. I look to Baher. His eyes bore into me from his hatch. I know from my interrogation at the prosecution office that we are being accused of being members of the Muslim Brotherhood, now deemed a terrorist organization, but the ring of this label—the Marriott Cell— sends a small electric shock through me.

"We aren't heroes," Baher calls out. "We are just journalists who were doing our job. We will be out in fifteen days, *Inshallah.*"

I can hear the other prisoners stepping away from their hatches and the beginning of muttered evening prayers and Quranic verses.

Afterwards, perplexed by Sohaib's enthusiasm for our supposed heroics, I call to him, as quietly as possible, to ask what kind of camera work he did, and what he had been filming prior to his detention.

"I operated one of the main cameras on the stage at Rabaa al-Adawiya [sit-in]. Do you remember the twenty-one Brotherhood girls sentenced to eleven years in Alexandria for carrying balloons to protest peacefully against the coup?" he says.

Of course I remember the story—we covered it out of the Marriott. The girls, seven of whom were under eighteen, had been sentenced for carrying balloons with the Rabaa insignia, the four-fingered salute that is used by supporters of the Muslim Brotherhood. Although their sentences were suspended after an international outcry, the message to the world was loud and clear. In Egypt now, the expression of any opinion in support of the Brotherhood, or critical of the government, was interpreted as terrorism and could be criminalized.

"I provided footage of the girls' protest to Al Jazeera Mubasher Misr," continues Sohaib proudly. "They paid me to do that. Not much, but not bad for a beginner."

His admission rocks me. Now I understand why our names were raised during the students' interrogation, and why we are detained in Scorpion together. With a sick feeling I think of the stories we produced at Al Jazeera English. I know of two that were translated into Arabic by the network without my permission, and rebroadcast on Al Jazeera Mubasher Misr, the network's local news channel that was banned from broadcasting in Egypt. It concerned us at the time, infuriated us. But Sohaib's comment suggests a more systematic connection, one I had no knowledge of as Al Jazeera English bureau chief.

I turn back from the door and see Shadi sprawled on his blanket.

"My brother was arrested, too," he confides, "along with his friend, Anas Beltagy. I've no idea where they are."

I recognize the name Beltagy; his father is a prominent Brotherhood member rumoured to be incarcerated somewhere in Scorpion. Could it be that Al Jazeera used these young Brotherhood supporters behind my back to provide footage to the banned channel broadcasting illegally from Doha? Were Peter, Baher and I really Brotherhood heroes? Despite the prosecutor's assurance to Baher that we'd be out soon, it is dawning on me that I need to find a way to get expert legal representation or we could be here for a very, very long time.

The next morning, the guards come and order Shadi as well as Khaled and Sohaib out—they are going to see the prosecutor. After they leave, Khaled al-Qazzaz calls me to the hatch. Since he quietly passed me that forbidden note on my first day here, I have considered him an ally. The former senior aide to Morsi, married to a Canadian, Sarah Attia, speaks excellent English. He talks dreamily of Canada, where he met her. Now he tells me that he will be going to see his lawyer later that afternoon. He offers to smuggle out a note to my family.

"I wish, Khaled, but I have no pen or paper."

Al-Qazzaz calls out to the inmate in the cell next to me, Dr. Ayman Ali, a presidential advisor and Brotherhood member, to pass me a pen. Waiting until the guard is out of sight, Ali reaches his arm through the hatch and extends it to me, holding a pen. I push my left arm through the hatch and grab the pen like a lifeline. There is no paper. The meagre roll of toilet paper that was given to me four days ago is gone. Then I remember that yesterday Baher passed me his last two cigarettes. I still have the package. Working quickly in case the guard comes around unexpectedly, I split open the empty pack and rip off a thin piece of cardboard.

I write out Marwa's mobile number and scribble the following note:

Please come visit me. Bring twenty servings of chicken. Push the embassy to come see me too and get a powerful lawyer. Not the Al Jazeera lawyer. I love you. Stay strong.

The chicken is for my companions on the cellblock. I have already learned that trading favours is part of the game in here. There is no doubt that I will be expected to return the kindness of the pen.

Half an hour later, I hear the guard unlock al-Qazzaz's cell door. I press my forehead against the hatch to see him being led out of his cell. His gait is stiff and awkward. He is a large man, at least six feet tall, and stooped. He has told me about the excruciating pain in his neck and back and that his health has deteriorated during his months of detention from sleeping on the cement floor, and from the cramped conditions and lack of movement. He needs medical attention, and to be moved to a prison hospital.

As the guard moves ahead, al-Qazzaz steps towards my door and thrusts three bananas through the hatch. I reach for the fruit and as I do I press the small note into his palm. Success! My heart races but I am deliriously happy with this small victory. For the first time since seeing Ragia, I have hope. I also have a pen. I scan the dingy cell for a hiding place, a crack in the wall, a hole where the concrete has eroded. There is no safe place. I cannot risk losing the pen in a surprise search. The pen must stay with me. I tuck it carefully into the waistband of my pants.

The irony that the pen, now my lifeline, is a gift from one of Morsi's presidential team, and that his former advisor is now smuggling a note out on my behalf is not lost on me. These men, who I reported on as a journalist, the same men I wanted ousted from the palace, are now my first line of defense. We are in a strange alliance as neighbours in this cellblock.

I down the last painkiller, which doesn't help much but I drift off. A fitful sleep comes over me. I do not know how long I am out for, but I am awoken by a cacophony of yelling, and the clang of metal, the sound of cell doors opening and closing. I push myself off the floor and drag myself over to the hatch. I catch a glimpse of Shadi and Sohaib being led into two cells down the wing.

"Baher, Fahmy," shouts Sohaib. "We are with you in the case! We are being charged together for our work with Al Jazeera." He laughs, as if this is some kind of triumph.

"What do you mean?" I ask.

Once the guard is gone, Shadi excitedly tells me that we have been accused as one group of working for the Brotherhood. My colleagues and I are bundled together with these young Brotherhood activists, all of us accused of broadcasting false news and conspiring to undermine the state. Our captors are attempting to build a case around us as airtight and suffocating as it is false. It is something I would never have imagined possible as I marched to Tahrir Square with my friends to call for democratic elections.

CHAPTER 5

WHO GETS THE CAKE?

February-October 2011

On February 11, 2011, the night of President Hosni Mubarak's resignation, and well into the next day, the country held massive celebrations from Cairo to Alexandria to Suez, marking the greatest grassroots uprising in the country's history against a dictator who, for many younger Egyptians, had been the only ruler they had ever known.

In Tahrir Square, hundreds of people worked shoulder to shoulder to remove the mountains of rubble and garbage that had accumulated over the past two-and-a-half weeks of occupation, fuelled by their belief that they had ushered in a new era of democracy. Until the coming election the government would be in the hands of the Supreme Council of the Armed Forces, led by Egypt's seventy-five-year-old defense minister, Field Marshal Mohamed Tantawi. Although Tantawi had been commander-in-chief of Egypt's military for two decades under the ousted Mubarak, he had not unleashed his armed forces, and had shown good will in standing with the people against Mubarak. Anyway, most citizens believed that even if the military did not fully support the goals of the revolution, the sheer size and determination of Egypt's uprising would ensure that the interim government remained accountable. A smaller number of demonstrators, however, stayed in the square, vowing to continue their sit-in until Mubarak's regime had been completely dismantled and a democratic transition achieved. Tantawi seemed off to a positive start, appointing an eight-member constitutional committee to help manage the transition and to develop guidelines for presidential and parliamentary elections.

Four days later, the Arab Spring uprising swept into Libya; just weeks later it would erupt in Syria. In Libya, there were protests in Benghazi against Colonel Muammar Gaddafi, the iron-fisted dictator who had controlled his country for forty-two years. The CNN correspondents, cameramen and producers, including Ivan Watson, immediately left Cairo to cover the next big story.

I recall watching CNN's Cairo bureau chief Ben Wedeman— who had led the coverage of the Egyptian revolution—now breaking the Libya story. I sat glued to the big-screen TV in our CNN Cairo office marvelling at Ben who, after decades of living and reporting in the Middle East and fluent in Arabic, had used his impressive network of friends and contacts to help him and camerawoman Mary Rogers slip across the border from Egypt. Their sensational coverage aired from a rooftop overlooking Benghazi. Below them, tens of thousands of Libyans chanted in the streets; beyond the chaos, the waters of the Mediterranean shimmered blue. Ben's excitement was palpable as he spoke into the camera.

"We arrived in this city, and [. . .] everywhere we went, I felt like I was an American soldier going into Paris during World War Two," he said. "Everybody [was] clapping and cheering. We are the first television crew to get to this city. And we were just overwhelmed by

the welcome here. People were throwing candy inside the car [. . .].
An incredible experience."[15]

I yearned to be on the frontlines alongside him and Ivan.
Although I'd cut my teeth with the *LA Times* in the Iraq War and
had ten years of journalism experience under my belt, I was on a
lower rung of the CNN ladder, and stories like Libya were still out
of my reach. I longed to lead the coverage of a breaking international event, but staying behind in Egypt provided some unexpected positives. The first was developing close friendships with
two members of CNN's Cairo bureau, the Iraqi photojournalist
Sarmad Qaseera and the rookie American-Egyptian journalist Dina
Amer. Sarmad, a longtime member of CNN's Baghdad bureau,
had grown up under Saddam Hussein's dictatorship. The son of an
Iraqi scientist assassinated by Hussein, Sarmad had covered the war
in Iraq for CNN, eventually fleeing after receiving death threats
from religious extremists. Bald, round-faced and filled with good
humour, Sarmad was deeply compassionate. I called him "the gorilla
cameraman" for his short, stocky build and ability to muscle his
way into any situation, but it was his constant laughter that kept us
buoyant and grounded throughout the intense months of reporting
that would follow.

Dina, like me, had arrived in Cairo days before the revolution,
she too drawn by a connection to her Egyptian heritage. Born in
Cleveland to Egyptian parents, she and I shared chameleon-like
identities, moving fluidly between our Arab and North American
nationalities. As dual citizens, we felt inured against serious harm
and carried our respective Canadian and American passports tucked
away in our back pockets like get-out-of-jail-free cards.

The second positive—though the events themselves were far
from positive—about staying behind in Cairo was unexpectedly
finding ourselves on the frontlines of the dramatic events unfolding
around us. The first event occurred on March 9 when the military

tried to forcibly remove the protestors who had remained in Tahrir Square. I stood close by as military officers accompanied by plain-clothes thugs charged into the square, ripping up the tent camps and beating protestors. I saw dozens being dragged into the nearby Egyptian Museum until, fearing for my safety, I fled the square.

Later, the protestors detained in the museum told stories of being tortured, beaten and electrocuted. One of those unlucky individuals was Ramy Essam, the twenty-three-year-old musician who I had heard captivating the masses during the protests, and who had returned to Tahrir Square by chance that day. Essam had inspired hundreds of thousands of Egyptians with his impassioned songs. One of them, entitled *"Irhal"* ("Leave"), uploaded to YouTube during the height of the revolution, had gone viral. Essam had instantly become an international hero and *"Irhal"* the anthem of the revolution.

Days after his arrest, I tracked the university student down in his hometown of Mansoura, 120 kilometres northeast of Cairo. Our CNN crew—Iranian-American correspondent Reza Sayah, Sarmad and I—were the first foreign journalists to interview him. When we arrived at his home, he was lying sprawled, stomach down, on a narrow single bed, a thin sheet covering his body from the waist down, his back a terrible tapestry of bloody purple welts and bruises, the most prominent a boot-shaped mark from which an angry red bulge of clotted blood protruded. As his family looked on I knelt down next to him and gently took his hand, introduced the team and asked if we could film him.

"Please, put it all out there," he said in a half whisper. The mili-tary were supposedly now protecting us, and Essam was a shining symbol of the cause we had all fought for together, but he told us that soldiers stood by as plainclothes thugs beat him. "They took off my clothes. They beat me with sticks, metal rods, wires, whips, and electrocuted me. One soldier jumped on my face with his feet."[16]

When, appalled, we discussed it later, Sarmad, an Iraqi, saw it differently. "Revolution?" He laughed. "What revolution? The military is just beginning, *Habibi*! Egyptians are so naïve."

But my faith in the uneven process towards democratic reform was restored a short time later while covering the March 19 referendum. Tantawi had promised to hold a vote to allow citizens to approve or reject constitutional amendments, prior to the coming election in September. CNN had dispatched several teams to the polls before they opened at 9:00 a.m. That morning I breathed in the fresh air and silently rejoiced at what appeared to be the dawn of Egyptian democracy. Citizens from all walks of life flocked to polling stations at hundreds of schools across the country to exercise their right to vote—an act that had meant nothing under Mubarak's regime. Military officers efficiently and patiently helped the elderly and the infirm. Although the lineups were long and slow moving, snaking hundreds of metres around building perimeters and down rubble-strewn streets, the day unfolded in a civilized manner that encouraged my sense of optimism. I gently ribbed Sarmad and Dina who had been skeptical about the military honouring the spirit of the revolution.

At the Cairo polling station to which I had been assigned, I hugged many of my friends as they stood in line waiting to cast their votes. More than forty-five million eligible voters turned out that day and when the ballots were counted, 77 percent of them had voted in favour of the proposed constitutional amendments. These included limiting the president's term in office to two four-year terms, restricting the duration of emergency law to six months, requiring judicial oversight of elections, and forming a commission to draft a new constitution after the September parliamentary elections.[17] I was prepared to be patient: there was no magic wand to instantly erase three decades of despotic rule but the constitutional amendments provided a way forward.

So I was confounded when just days later the military announced a ban on all protests and imposed severe punishments for anyone publicly expressing opposition to the regime. On April 1, tens of thousands of Egyptians responded by returning to Tahrir Square for a protest dubbed "The Friday of Saving the Revolution." Chants once more rang out, this time calling for a civilian council to replace the military administration and for Tantawi's resignation.

I entered Tahrir Square without a crew; with Libya and Syria in turmoil, and Syria heading towards civil war, CNN was still focused on live coverage of events there. A young protestor, dressed in a T-shirt emblazoned with the ever popular face of Che Guevara, handed me a flyer that read: *We want to ensure our revolution is not stolen from us.* It seemed the youth, labour and leftist movements that had spearheaded the revolution felt they were being sidelined. But it wasn't the military that concerned me as much as the Muslim Brotherhood. As I stood amid the chanting crowd, the question on my mind was: What were the ambitions of the most organized and politically savvy opposition in Egypt, amply funded by a network of wealthy businesses and the oil-rich emirate of Qatar? And what would the Brotherhood, with its ultimate aim of imposing Sharia law, do to take advantage of this political vacuum? Having operated successfully as a clandestine political movement for decades, the Brotherhood was well situated to step into the post-Mubarak power void.

The Arab Spring had left the political sphere ripe for extremist groups: ISIS, Jabhat al-Nusra, Boko Haram, al-Qaeda, and many more, dotted across the deserts of Africa, Iraq, Libya and Syria.

All of these groups fall under the umbrella of Salafi jihadism. Salafi jihadists—like Osama bin Laden's successor, Ayman al-Zawahiri—promote a religious-political ideology rooted in "physical" jihadism, promoting violence against individuals, political leaders and entire regimes they consider heretical. The Salafi jihadists most barbaric attack to date is the destruction of the Twin Towers of the World Trade Center by al-Qaeda on September 11, 2001. And it was as the manhunt intensified for Osama bin Laden in its aftermath that the links between the Salafi jihadist groups came more closely under the microscope.

Salafism is a way of thinking, not itself an organization, such as ISIS or al-Qaeda, or even the Muslim Brotherhood, power-seeking organizations that interpret Sharia (Islamic principles or ways of living) to justify political aims. Both Salafis and Salafi jihadists believe in implementing a literalist interpretation of Sharia to revive Islamic practice from the time of the Prophet Muhammad. But whereas ordinary Salafis work through preaching, social services, and sometimes politics to achieve this goal, Salafi jihadists embrace violence and warfare as a primary tactic. Article 2 of the Egyptian Constitution states that "the *principles* [italics mine] of Islamic Sharia are the main source of legislation." [18] But the violent tactics of Salifi jihadists like Ayman al-Zawahiri and his followers aim to enshrine Sharia law in its strictest forms as the *source* of all legislation. A critical difference: as a result, the constitution itself would be at risk and any tool of democracy subverted—whether free elections or referenda. Any hope of peace with Israel would vanish along with modern Egypt—the overnight banning of alcohol and dancing would be the least of it.

Although the Brotherhood announced in April that it would not seek the presidency, it formed a new political party—invoking the goals of the revolution by calling it the Freedom and Justice Party (FJP)—but indicated it would run candidates in only 45 to 50 percent of seats for the September parliamentary elections—not enough for a majority. The FJP also stated it would not field a candidate for president, but chose Dr. Mohamed Morsi, a prominent member of the Muslim Brotherhood, as the party's chairman. [19]

A former independent member of Parliament, the American-educated Morsi had served on the Brotherhood's Guidance Bureau, or ruling body, and many believed him to be an Islamist at heart. Still, I reported their announcement in an April 30 wire story for CNN with a sense of cautious optimism. It suggested that the Brotherhood was not out to rule Egypt and turn it into an Islamic state as many feared; if the announcement that day was any indication, Egypt's future government would have room for leftists, liberals and moderates.

Two days later, on May 2, Osama bin Laden met his end at the hands of the Navy Seals, and Egypt's Ayman al-Zawahiri stepped into his shoes as head of al-Qaeda.

It was soon after bin Laden's death that I landed my first exclusive story: an interview with a former Egyptian intelligence officer turned filmmaker named Essam Daraz. Daraz was the first to chronicle Osama bin Laden's fight against the Soviets in the mountains of Afghanistan in the 1980s.[20] He believes his film, *Arab Supporters in Afghanistan*, which featured bin Laden and his original group of 120 fighters, helped promote the guerilla leader's notoriety and inspire thousands of disaffected Arab youth to join his al-Qaeda movement. He spoke to me about how he had spent time with bin Laden in the caves of Afghanistan and how he had met Ayman al-Zawahiri, his personal advisor and physician.

"Bin Laden was a member of the [Saudi] Muslim Brotherhood," the old filmmaker told me as we sat in his Cairo home. "Starting in the late 1970s, he galvanized its Saudi cells with the help of Egyptian and Syrian exiles from the Brotherhood." He explained that though the relationship was not clearly formalized, the Saudi Brotherhood maintained links to the Muslim Brotherhood in Egypt, as well as throughout the region. He talked about how bin Laden had been influenced by the books and teachings of Sayyid Qutb, the Egyptian author and educator considered the intellectual godfather of the

Muslim Brotherhood, who wrote prolifically on Islamic ideology in the fifties and sixties. Qutb had spent two years at Colorado College and Stanford University in the 1940s, during which time he faced overt racism. As a result, the young man developed a strong dislike for the US and began to view Western society as hopelessly materialistic, corrupt and morally bankrupt.

Qutb was not only offended by the treatment shown to Arabs in the United States, but also by its strong support for Israel. On his return to Egypt he encouraged Muslims to take a violent stand against Western democracy and secularism as practiced in the United States and wrote his seminal book, *Milestones (Ma'alim fi al-Tariq)*. He described his reaction when, as a student, he stopped in to see a church dance in 1949, describing the scene as "the animal-like mixing of the sexes . . . the halls swarmed with legs . . . lips met lips . . . chests met chests." "The worst sight of all," Qutb wrote, was "the outline of women's breasts in tight sweaters."[21]

Milestones became a manifesto for political Islam that continues to inspire thousands of followers, known as "Qutbists," to violent, anti-Western action. Among its disciples: al-Qaeda's current leader, Ayman al-Zawahiri, who joined the Muslim Brotherhood as a teenager before breaking away to join the jihad in Afghanistan against the Russians.

Before Daraz and I parted, he spoke wistfully about a conversation he had had with bin Laden. "I warned him against attacking civilians, but he wouldn't listen."

During the intense early months of the Arab Spring, CNN correspondents moved in and out of Egypt's Cairo bureau. During one posting, I arranged an exclusive interview between Ivan Watson and the radical Salafi jihadist Aboud el-Zomor, one of the men convicted of masterminding the assassination of President Anwar Sadat in 1981. Sadat's efforts, which led to the Egypt–Israeli Peace Treaty, jointly earned him and Prime Minister Menachem Begin the 1978

Nobel Peace Prize as well as the hatred of many Arabs who accused him of befriending the enemy. El-Zomor had been released from Scorpion after Mubarak's downfall, and Ivan and I travelled to his hometown near Cairo for the interview. A massive banner stretched across the main street congratulating him on his release and hailing him as "General el-Zomor."

"I only wanted change," Zomor told Ivan as I translated. "In 1981 there wasn't a peaceful mechanism to pressure a ruler, like there was during this January 25 revolution. Back then, if there were protests, the regime was able to crush them because there was no watchdog media presence like Al Jazeera or CNN."[22] The assassin admitted he had been envious watching the events of the Arab Spring unfold, insisting that he and his followers in the Gamaa al-Islamiya—a militant Egyptian movement dedicated to overthrowing the country's government—had renounced violence in favour of democracy after the ouster of Morsi (they had formally renounced it earlier, too, in the nineties).

The old leader ended our conversation with an unexpected announcement: "I plan to form a political party and run in Egypt's next parliamentary elections. The January 25 revolution has opened up new possibilities for change."

The revolution had also opened up new dangers. I felt increasingly uneasy about the growing instability in Egypt. At times the country felt adrift and lawless. Nowhere was the lawlessness more evident than in the Sinai region along Egypt's uneasy eastern border with Israel. One of Mubarak's achievements through his lengthy tenure had been to keep the peace with Israel. Now, with Mubarak gone and the administration consumed with the task of steering the country towards a new future, the government's tight hold on border security had dissolved. The lack of state authority in the Sinai was becoming a source of anxiety for Israel and a potential powder keg that could reignite an Arab–Israeli war.

During the revolution, Bedouin tribesmen had revolted against Sinai's police force in revenge for decades of oppression under Mubarak's rule and taken control of large areas of the region. More recently saboteurs had been bombing the cross-border pipeline that supplies Israel with much of its natural gas. I'd remotely reported on several of these incidents, but over that summer got the opportunity to travel to northern Sinai on several occasions, see the charred pipeline for myself and speak to the Bedouin families living around it.

The first time was in June 2011 when the CNN reporter Diana Magnay, a cameraman and I drove to El Arish, a small picturesque resort city on the Mediterranean. Its fine beaches are dotted with palm trees and a string of luxury resorts extends along the coast, promising tourists a quiet paradise. But in the aftermath of the revolution, El Arish had become anything but that. A well-armed Salafi jihadist organization and Muslim Brotherhood splinter group called Takfir wal-Hijra had swept into town, burning police stations and intimidating the local population. A pamphlet the group disseminated criticized the Camp David Agreement, and called for an Islamic state. The pamphlet bore a chilling attribution: *A statement from al-Qaeda in the Sinai Peninsula.* Egypt's waning control over the Islamic forces and the political power vacuum created by Mubarak's ouster seemed to be giving rise to a dangerous new reality.

A trusted Bedouin I knew escorted us to meet two brothers leading this radical group. They welcomed us in the desert at night, offered us camel milk and agreed to an interview for the CNN website.[23] They insisted that they had not killed innocent women or children and that they were bearing arms to defend themselves against the Egyptian military who have "tortured us and killed members of our tribes in cold blood for years." They praised al-Qaeda's role in Afghanistan and its new leader, Ayman al-Zawahiri, stating firmly: "To fight in Afghanistan is totally acceptable jihad for the sovereignty of a Muslim country attacked by the infidels."[24]

In the midst of this volatile situation, our crew discovered a thriving and illicit cross-border trade between Bedouin tribes in the Sinai and another Muslim Brotherhood affiliate inside the Israeli-occupied Gaza strip: Hamas. Hamas was working in coordination with the Bedouins to smuggle goods ranging from Coca-Cola to stolen cars through a series of close to a thousand underground tunnels between Egypt and Gaza. These tunnels were not only a lifeline for Palestinians suffering under the Israeli blockade of Gaza, but a huge source of profit to their owners. Hamas siphoned off taxes—thousands and thousands of dollars—on any goods passing through the tunnels and, with the help of some Bedouins on the other side, used the tunnels to transfer cash, weapons and militants into Sinai to fight the Egyptian military.

"Olives cost about a hundred dollars per carton," one Bedouin tribesman named Salem, a fugitive convicted of weapons smuggling and targeting police officers, told us as we filmed inside the tunnels. "Marijuana sells for double the price in Gaza than it does in Egypt. And animals, such as a tiger or small elephant for the Gaza Zoo, cost as much as twenty thousand dollars."

As unbridled and mercenary as Salem was, there were lines he would not cross.

"I refuse to allow suicide bombers through the tunnels to bomb Israeli targets from the Egyptian side. And my tribe won't smuggle weapons or hostages either. I was once offered $500,000 to smuggle an Israeli hostage to Islamist groups in Gaza," he said. "I refused."

Why? I asked.

"It's just not worth it for me," Salem said. "The Israeli fighter jets would demolish my tunnels in a second."

The tacit approval of these tunnels by Egyptian and Israeli security forces underscored the precarious balance that existed along their shared border. Keeping a lid on instability in north Sinai depended increasingly on the continued control by and goodwill of the sovereign Bedouin people—tribesmen with a reputation as professional outlaws.

The simmering tensions that existed along the Israeli–Egyptian border erupted in August when terrorists crossed the border from the Sinai into the southern Israel tourist town of Eilat and killed eight Israelis. Israeli counter-terrorist operations immediately responded with an attack that killed five Egyptian soldiers.[25] Watching the news, I couldn't help but think of the tunnels I had visited and Salem's prophetic answer to my question of what would happen if he allowed insurgents access to Israel.

On the morning of September 9 I was back in Cairo on my way to the office in a taxi when I noticed hundreds of protestors gathered on the Cairo University Bridge overlooking the twenty-one-storey residential tower that houses the Israeli embassy on its top two floors. The day after the Israelis killed the soldiers in Sinai, a wave of anti-Israeli sentiment had swept Egypt and appeared to be spiking outside the embassy.

Following Mubarak's departure, the military, as a precautionary measure, had erected a sixteen-foot-high wall made of cement slabs running two hundred feet along the north side of the bridge to shield the building entrance from onlookers. Now that wall had attracted a large crowd. I asked the driver to stop and watched as dozens hoisted a giant Egyptian flag while others waved placards that read: END CAMP DAVID and THE MUSLIM BROTHER-HOOD IS THE FUTURE OF EGYPT. Hastily I made notes on my BlackBerry and headed to the office. Throughout the day, I scanned social media for updates. Then a Reuters wire caught my attention: hundreds had congregated outside the embassy and begun destroying the wall.[26]

CNN had no reporters or camera operators in Cairo so I jumped into a taxi and raced to the scene anticipating CNN would be calling for a live beeper, or on-site interview. I arrived to witness protestors using a battering ram to bring down the blocks of the wall, their chants resonating more loudly with each crashing blow. Many were shouting for Egypt to stop exporting its natural gas to Israel, a demand I'd also heard at the height of the Arab Spring demonstrations. By six o'clock most of the wall had been destroyed, and as night fell, the sky was alight with celebratory fireworks.

When the call came from CNN, I retreated to a quiet nearby street and crouched between two parked cars to relay events to Hala Gorani, anchoring CNN's *The World Right Now*. Minutes later, I received information that several Israeli diplomats were trapped inside the embassy unable to escape. I spotted the uniformed military commander of the district standing in the crowd discreetly filming the scene with a small camera and ran back to ask him for confirmation of the news. He explicitly denied it, just as a CNN email appeared on my cellphone stating that the embassy had been breached and diplomatic documents were being thrown from its windows. I got to the embassy in time to grab one of the thousands of confidential papers raining down. The mob pushed and shoved one another, grasping for the printed sheets as if they were high-denomination currency. Twenty-one floors above us, the Israeli flag had been ripped from the building and replaced with an Egyptian flag. The crowd roared its approval, and as I stood among it reading the Hebrew script of the page in my hand, another request came from CNN, this one for a live report for Wolf Blitzer's *Situation Room*.

"Are any Israeli diplomats there [inside the embassy]?" Wolf asked, and I passed on the denial of the military officer.[27] It would prove to be false. Six Israeli security personnel were in fact bolted behind a fortified door inside the embassy. Tempers on the street continued to escalate until around nine o'clock they erupted in violence. By the time I returned to my hotel, thirteen hours later, exhausted but unable to sleep, three people had been killed and hundreds more injured. I took a quick shower and changed my clothes. Ivan Watson and Joe Duran were on their way from Turkey and would be in Cairo that morning to cover the fallout, and news outlets everywhere hummed with the ominous threat of potential war. Half an hour later I was in a cab on my way back to the Israeli embassy.

Hundreds of protestors still loitered there, along with military and security personnel, and other curious citizens who had woken up to news of the dramatic events. I had arranged to meet Ivan and Joe in the vicinity, and despite gridlocked traffic and a huge crowd, they managed to get to our agreed-upon location on time. Ivan is a consummate journalist and my relief at having him and the CNN crew there was high.

The three of us were discussing our coverage when I spotted Dina Amer and an unfamiliar Western cameraman walking towards the crush of people gathered on the bridge overlooking the embassy. Dina had recently left CNN and we'd not been in touch over the past weeks. Surprised to see my friend and a little concerned for her safety, I waved her over, and she explained that she was freelancing for American PBS. Her cameraman was apparently quite new to her. I felt uneasy about her working the streets with a cameraman she didn't really know but I didn't have time to dwell on the situation. Ivan, Joe and I had to discuss strategy for coverage.

Less than five minutes later, I saw the PBS cameraman running from the bridge with several men in pursuit. Frantically my eyes swept the crowd for Dina, but I couldn't see her, only a commotion in the direction from which the cameraman had fled. I bolted towards the disturbance. There had been several incidents of female reporters being mobbed and sexually assaulted during the uprisings. Lara Logan, a CBS correspondent who had been brutally gang-raped and almost torn to pieces by a large group of men in Tahrir Square on the night of Mubarak's resignation, was the most publicized of these. I'd reported on another incident involving a British reporter who had a similarly terrible experience in Tahrir Square. I feared the worst for Dina as I lunged into the melee. Sure enough, she was in the middle of it. Dozens of men surrounded her, two of whom were pulling her towards them. Another attacker had a hold of her shirt and was beginning to pull it up.

"She's an Israeli! A Jew!" I heard someone in the crowd yell as I bulldozed my way through the crowd. I didn't think as I crashed towards her, pulling the men around her away.

"She is with me!" I yelled. "I am her brother!"

"*Gassosa Israelia! Yahoodia!*" a veiled woman screamed in Arabic. "Israeli spy! Jew!"[28]

I wrapped my arms around Dina's waist from behind, tightly clenching my forearms as if my life, as well as hers, depended on me not letting go. "She is Egyptian! I am Egyptian!" I yelled as the men pushed and pulled at us propelling us along the bridge. I stumbled several times over my and Dina's feet, desperate to stay upright, but eventually lost my balance. The two of us fell hard to the pavement, my forearms protecting her body even as mine landed on top of hers. I tightened my grip around her as several men kicked my back and tried to drag me off. Next to mine, Dina's face was drawn with fear, her brown eyes wide. For a second, as the men yanked on my legs, I thought I'd lose my hold. Then a young man, a complete stranger, was beside me, talking in my ear.

"Your van is right here," he said urgently. "Let me help you stand up. Now."

I lifted my head and saw a white minivan a merciful few yards away. With the man's help, I exerted every ounce of energy I possessed to hoist myself to my feet, pulling Dina up after me. Then, as the good Samaritan shoved back the crowd in front of us, Dina and I stumbled forward, lunging towards the van and diving head first through its open side door. I glanced up to see Margaret Warner, the distinguished chief foreign affairs correspondent for PBS's *NewsHour*, sitting in the passenger seat, her driver having fled. Dozens of men had chased us and were grabbing at me through the open door as I tried to shield Dina with my body. Scores of others surrounded the van and began pelting it with rocks. I turned my body to face my attackers, holding myself up on the doorframe and viciously kicked out at the men trying to climb inside.

"Drive!" I shouted at Margaret. "Get in the other seat and *drive!*"

She clambered swiftly across into the driver's seat and started the car. "There's a crowd in front of me," she yelled.

"Drive through them!"

Without hesitating, she stomped on the gas and drove through the sea of young men, who fell away in front of us.

"I don't know where I'm going," she called back to me as I pulled myself inside the van and yanked the door closed behind me.

"Left—straight ahead!"

For the next five minutes, Margaret weaved adroitly through the streets of Cairo as I navigated, leaving behind our attackers, the crowd surrounding the embassy, Ivan and Joe, and the scene of my first international CNN story.[29]

A week later, unexpectedly, I got the reporting break I'd been hoping for: Bruce Conover, CNN's senior international editor in Atlanta, assigned me to Libya. I had less than twelve hours to throw clothes into a bag and mentally prepare myself to head into a war zone. Most welcome was the news that Sarmad Qaseera would accompany me as my cameraman, and our two-hour flight from Cairo to Tunis was filled with non-stop laughter, our unspoken way of lightening the weight of uncertainty about what lay ahead. Both of us had experienced the terror of the 2003 Iraq War and had few illusions. The excitement we felt over our new assignment was muted by memories of bloodied Iraqi civilians, orphaned children, frightened families begging for deliverance from the destruction that had suddenly stolen their loved ones and turned their once-ordered lives to chaos.

Less than a month before, the country's despotic ruler and his family had fled, and Gaddafi and one of his sons were reportedly holed up somewhere inside Libya. Another son was rumoured to be leading rebel forces somewhere near the city of Sirte. Speculation was rampant on Muammar Gaddafi's whereabouts and the hunt for him continued to capture the headlines. Libya had slipped into the anarchy of civil war. Rival groups, and varying tribes and armies, held running gun battles throughout many Libyan towns and cities, and what we had seen so far of the daily clashes between rebels and what remained of Gaddafi's armed brigades seemed surreal, like something from a gratuitously violent movie set.

In Tunis, a longtime CNN fixer—a local guide for CNN—met us at the airport and we began the long drive south to Tripoli, crossing several hundred kilometres of dusty and largely deserted landscape before we reached the border and crossed into Libya. Signs of battle dotted the road, bullet-riddled buildings and charred remains of automobiles appearing along the route like ominous sentinels.

When we arrived at Tripoli's Meridian Hotel many hours later, there were few signs of Gaddafi loyalists in a city that had served as his military command post for forty-two brutal years. Armed rebels, however, roamed the streets, and the close and constant sound of gunfire surrounded us. The most intense and dangerous fighting was now raging south and east around the pro-Gaddafi strongholds of Bani Walid, and the city of Sirte, Gaddafi's birthplace, located some six hours southeast along Libya's Mediterranean coast. As Sarmad and I hauled our bags, flak jackets and helmets into the CNN newsroom, the anchor in Atlanta was relaying very upsetting news. Our CNN colleague, Ian Lee, had been hit in the leg with shrapnel and a paramedic killed when the anti-Gaddafi convoy they were travelling with near Sirte had faced incoming fire from small arms and rocket-propelled grenades.[30] I watched in horror as news of the attack involving the blond-haired, blue-eyed Wyoming native I'd nicknamed "Intrepid Ian" flashed on the screen. Ian and I had developed a strong friendship and healthy rivalry during the uprising in Egypt, and though I'd admired his willingness to dive into any situation no matter how treacherous, I also knew he was no cowboy.

Ian's injury was a painful reminder of the ugly, unpredictable reality of war. Eight years had passed since I'd been in Iraq, but the images flashing across the screen were intimately familiar: armed rebels in military fatigues, a desert dotted with pickup trucks mounted with heavy artillery; charred vehicles and smoke billowing from buildings. I paced the large suite that would serve as my new workplace for the next month, taking in the charts pinned to the walls and the cameras and equipment set-up. I stepped onto the wide balcony and looked out over the harbour. Huge ships lay calmly at anchor or tied up alongside massive cement piers. All looked placid, but I knew that the days ahead would reveal a different reality.

And in the ensuing weeks, I found myself once more bearing witness to anarchy. On the streets of Tripoli, I was often stunned at the sight of boys, some of them barely teenagers, outfitted in stolen army fatigues and brandishing semi-automatic weapons. As in Iraq, the most heart-wrenching stories were of the civilians killed in the crossfire, of the children murdered or made orphans, the families ripped apart. These were the stories I tried to tell alongside the heavy schedule of CNN assignments—hoping that what I was reporting in distant places might help move politicians and ordinary people find ways to stop the carnage.

CNN asked me, as an Arabic speaker, to keep close tabs on local opposition groups and revolutionaries in hopes we might unearth untold stories and unheard perspectives. Part of my daily routine was calling these groups to fish for news. One of those calls led reporter Phil Black and me to two of Libya's senior air-force pilots, Colonel Abdullah al-Sahi and Colonel Ali al-Rabti. During the early days of the Libyan revolution, Gaddafi ordered the two men to bomb civil-ians in Benghazi and other cities. Instead, they flew to the nearby island of Malta and requested asylum.

"It was a difficult decision—to place our country before our families," said al-Rabti who, in the six months he was away, lived in constant fear that there would be terrible repercussions for his wife and children. Mercifully, there had not been, and recently, with Gaddafi in hiding and his loyalist forces losing ground, the two pilots had returned to Libya. As we talked, both men expressed their gratitude to NATO and the multi-state coalition that had intervened to support the uprising: American and British naval forces had fired hundreds of missiles and enforced a naval blockade; French, British and Canadian jets had also participated in destroy-ing hundreds of Gaddafi's tanks, airplanes, rocket launchers and air-defense capabilities.

A controversial partner in the coalition was Qatar, the tiny Arab state of only 1.6 million people. It armed and funded the rebel fight-ers against Gaddafi with hundreds of millions of dollars of aid, dispatched its jets, set up an opposition Libyan television channel in Qatar and sent hundreds of troops to support and train the rebels—including radical extremist Islamists. I remember seeing Qatar's Al Jazeera crews on the frontline receiving prime positioning alongside the rebels amid the fog of war so they might cover it all in depth. At the time I did not know what to think of the relationship—or understand the *why* behind Qatar's interventionist approach.

Although a highly divisive figure internationally, many Libyans had lauded Gaddafi's anti-imperialist stance and his efforts to foster pan-African and pan-Arab coalitions. Within his country, he had provided free health care and education, and the country had main-tained one of the highest standards of living in Africa and a literacy rate of more than 80 percent among the seven million people he ruled. On the other hand, he had governed the oil-rich state with brutal authority and killed thousands who opposed him. So while most Libyans supported the NATO-backed offensive that had helped oust their leader, others worried about what a post-Gaddafi Libya would look like—and, indeed, Salafi jihadist groups and al-Qaeda-inspired extremists were now flocking to the country.[31] I had a strange sense of déjà vu as I interviewed its citizens, their hopes and dreams so reminiscent of the hundreds of thousands of Iraqis who had supported Saddam's overthrow in 2003. Where was Iraq now? Would Libya face the same fate, I wondered? Would Egypt?

Despite these dark concerns and the devastating stories we covered, Sarmad and I helped one another stay buoyant. We laughed when we could, holding onto humour like a high handlebar, hoping to leave the weight of all we'd seen and experienced below us. One story we covered gave us a rare opportunity for lighthearted antics. A group of revolutionary fighters had called me, hoping for news coverage of a "treasure" they had stashed in a remote desert location. We travelled with a security guard—hired by the network to accompany journalists on such outings—to a villa where half a dozen armed rebels, including the man who had called me, were waiting. There was Gaddafi's brand-new beige Hummer outfitted with bulletproof glass parked in front—a sight so unexpected that Sarmad raced towards it with his camera like a child towards a new toy.

The rebels explained how they had taken it and other personal belongings from his palace and moved them to their newly acquired abode, where they'd also amassed old communications equipment and clothing from the palace. Among the looted goods were a number of Gaddafi's extravagant robes. Sarmad grinned as he filmed me in one of the robes talking about the former dictator's penchant for flamboyant clothing—we knew the story would be perfect for CNN's *Back Story*.

"*Yallah!* Hurry!" a voice called from an adjacent room. "Come see the guns."

We moved to the next room, and stopped short, aghast at the stockpile of handguns, rifles, and boxes of hand grenades lined up against the wall. I held up a pistol in one hand and a rifle in the other as Sarmad snapped a photo on my cellphone. (That, too, would become evidence against me when I was arrested.) Then Sarmad examined the guns, brandishing them like so many rebels we'd seen in our travels, while our security guard took photos as a record of our bizarre afternoon.

But such moments of levity were rare, and by the time Sarmad and I made our way back to Cairo in mid-October, we were more than ready to leave Libya and her lawless war behind. Gaddafi's assassination days after our departure left me feeling unsettled. Certainly I was happy that the Arab world had rid itself of another repressive dictator, but I couldn't but wonder what that meant for the boys with guns I'd seen on the streets, or the Libyan people whose country had been plunged into civil war and overrun by Islamists armed to the teeth. Again those images of lawlessness reminded me of the people of Iraq when they cheered the removal of Saddam, unaware that it heralded the beginning of the hell they are living today.

If I'd hoped for respite in Egypt, it was nowhere to be found. Less than twenty-four hours later I was on the street covering deadly clashes between protestors and security forces who fired live ammunition, rubber bullets, tear gas and birdshot at the demonstrators from behind a fortified wall they'd erected on Mohamed Mahmoud Street off Tahrir Square. These battles, far more violent than anything I'd witnessed during the eighteen days of the revolution, raged for six days, killing dozens of civilians and injuring hundreds. CNN had again rented a room in the nearby City View Hotel and for the duration of these brutal and bloody confrontations this is where I lived, sleeping only sporadically, the acrid smell of tear gas ever present. My dreams were a horror show, mashed up images of all I'd seen. Most recently, I had reported on the disturbing incident of a young protestor being shot in the eye—he was one of many deliberately targeted by the suspected Central Security Forces marksman Mahmoud Sobhi El Shinawi, who the people and the media were calling "the Eye Hunter."[32] One man, who had lost an eye during the Friday of Rage months earlier, had the other eye taken out by the sniper during the Mohamed Mahmoud uprising.

The violence erupted just as Egypt was preparing for its first democratic parliamentary elections in history. Rather than taking to the polls, many protestors called for the elections to be cancelled, deeming them premature as the military continued to cling to power and protestors to be killed. Almost a year had passed since the revolution had toppled Mubarak's regime. The youth and liberal coalitions that had led the charge and the millions of citizens who had supported them seemed farther from the dream of a civil society than they had been when I'd left for Libya. The fate of the country hung in limbo, suspended between the entrenched interests of Egypt's long-ruling military regime and the increasingly seditious campaigns of the Muslim Brotherhood. As I tried to make sense of this descent into chaos, I was reminded that the one person who had predicted it was none other than the deposed president, Hosni Mubarak. For he knew that he was leaving behind weak political institutions, non-existent democratic parties and an Islamist organization he had allowed cosmetic political participation because its threat lent legitimacy to his heavy-handed rule. That organization was the Muslim Brotherhood and, watching the growing dissolution, I feared where its increasing power would lead.

CHAPTER 6

MARWA AND THE
MUSLIM BROTHERHOOD

December 2011–July 2013

A Christmas party at the home of Dr. Z came as a welcome reprieve at the end of the long, politically charged year of 2011. Z and I had spent our teenaged years and twenties together and I looked forward to reconnecting with my old friend, now a doctor living in the upscale neighbourhood of Maadi.

Growing up, Z and I had not given much attention to Mubarak's political machinations. Our relationship had been all about impressing the ladies and living on the edge. He had recently resurfaced in my life as a married man. I showed up at their home in good spirits, carrying complimentary copies of my newly published photo documentary book, *Egyptian Freedom Story*, chronicling the days of the Arab Spring in photographs and art.

I had been working intensely in any downtime I could find, and was proud of how it had turned out, a fruitful collaboration with my friend Sami Al Tobgy, who managed his own printing company and advertising agency. One guest who flipped through the pages was enthralled with the chapter entitled "The Art of the Revolution," which I'd added after sifting through dozens of photos of powerful graffiti and street art that had been painted on the walls, streets, buildings, bridges, barricades and doors all across the country during the revolution. I had been especially moved by the art honouring the martyrs of the revolution. No one had yet been held account- able for the deaths of the hundreds of protestors shot in cold blood, so including photos of their portraits, their names and explanations of their murals was one thing I could do to make sure they were remembered after the streets had been scrubbed clean and the walls painted over. The artists who had immortalized the faces and names of courageous protestors killed during the revolution had themselves risked arrest.[33]

At one point as we were speaking I looked up to see a woman sitting quietly on a bar stool near the dining table, listening in from a distance. I stopped short. She was stunning. She had captivating doe-like eyes framed by dark lashes and long, silky-straight hair.

I launched into a story of my favourite Egyptian graffiti artist, raising my voice to ensure the beautiful woman sitting across the room would hear. The artist, I began, painted under the alias of Ganzeer to protect his identity. Despite his popularity and prolific work, no one, including the police, had any idea who he was. Thus he evaded arrest until one day the police spotted him hang- ing one of his murals. It featured a head, blindfolded and gagged, and the message: *New . . . The Freedom Mask . . . from the Supreme Council of the Armed Forces to the beloved people. Now available for an unlimited time.*

Soon after his arrest, I explained, when his identity was finally revealed to the Egyptian public, I received a barrage of frantic phone calls and text messages from family, friends, and CNN colleagues. I looked up to make sure the woman was still listening and felt my pulse quicken when I saw that she was. "Ganzeer's real name," I said, pausing for effect, "is the same as mine: Mohamed Fahmy."

From across the room I saw her eyes light up, a lovely half-smile on her lips.

Z led me towards the table where she was seated, and his wife joined us, handing me a drink and introducing me to her friend, Marwa Omara. Still smiling, Marwa shook my hand but did not say a word. I took the opportunity to lean in towards her and offer her a drink.

"I don't drink," she declined politely, crossing her long, slim legs.

"Are you good friends with Z's wife?" I tried again.

"She's my best friend," Marwa said.

Hoping to impress her, I told her I was a journalist with CNN.

"I work a lot with local journalists," she replied. "It's part of my PR job at Vodafone." Vodafone was one of two major telecommunications companies in Egypt. The journalist in me got the better of the teenager. What happened to the phones on January 28? I asked her.

"My boss had no choice. Government officials forced him to shut us down. It was out of our hands."

"Fortunately even four days without internet didn't stop the revolution," I quipped. "It just sent everyone out onto the streets for news."

"I don't care for politics at all," Marwa said. "I actually think this so-called revolution has destroyed the country. Egypt was a much better place under Mubarak."

Taken aback, I steered the conversation to other topics: the Christmas season, my home in Canada. I learned that she was twenty-eight, liberal and independent, and that she drove four hours a day to and from her demanding job. On several occasions she had taken a wrong turn and ended up in the midst of violent protests. Muslim Brotherhood protestors had harassed her for not wearing a hijab, but she had managed to speed away before they could block her car.

I would have been happy to monopolize her company, but my friend B interrupted our conversation.

"Hello, Marwa," he said, laying a hand on my shoulder. "I see you've met Moody. I've known this guy since high school. Where there's trouble, there's Moody. Iraq, Libya, probably Syria tomorrow," he rambled loudly, his tone good-humoured and slightly tipsy. B was the son of a wealthy businessman close to the Mubarak government. I had seen him in Tahrir Square once. "I wanted to see what all the fuss was about," was how he'd explained it. I liked the fact that he had strong opinions against Mubarak despite his own father's close affiliation with the regime.

"So, what are you doing for New Year's, Marwa?" he asked, inserting himself between us. "I'm having a party at my house and I'd love you to come." He turned to me with a grin. "I won't ask you to come, Moody, because you'll be off as usual covering some news story."

Marwa excused herself and walked away.

I spent the rest of the party chatting with other guests but constantly watching her across the room. To my surprise she approached me as I was about to catch a ride home with B.

"Here's my business card," she said, handing it to me. "I would like to invite CNN to some of our events." I stared at the card happily. "If you want to give me your business card, I will add it to the database," she said.

I was quick to seize the opportunity. "Why don't I give you my cell number and you can feel free to send me any invitation."

Driving home with B, I felt lighter than I had in months. Cairo at night is magical, something I'd all but forgotten, and never more so than that night.

"Do you see her around much?" I asked.

"I wish. She's quiet, never drinks, and loves to smoke *shisha*. I've never seen her with a man though, only with Z and his wife."

The screen of my cellphone suddenly lit up indicating I'd

received a text message. I read it with amazement, then excitement: *Hi. I enjoyed your stories. You are a funny guy. Let me know what you are doing for New Year's. Marwa.*

I grinned happily, pumping my arms in the air. "She just texted me!"

"Who?"

"Marwa! She literally just texted me and we have a date!"

For New Year's Eve, I hired the driver I'd used during my coverage of the protests to drive the two of us to the Tamarai, an upscale nightclub with an outdoor lounge overlooking the Nile. Marwa looked sensational in a black dress and high heels, and we spent most of the night talking, our conversation flowing easily across a range of topics—politics being the exception. Marwa, I now knew, was not shy, but she was not keen to get embroiled in politics.

While I was careful not to push my own politics and passion for journalism on Marwa, less than a month later, on a cold January day, she chose to join me as I observed a protest staged by hundreds of Syrians outside their Cairo embassy. The protest was against President Bashar al-Assad's bloody crackdown on the recent uprising, which had erupted in Syria two months after Egypt's. That night Marwa wore cargo pants, sneakers and no makeup. I teased her about her new rebel look, but was impressed by how tough and adaptable she was, and watched her take in the energy and passion of the hundreds of people calling on Assad to step down. The violent turn the Syrian uprising had recently taken was becoming increasingly evident in Egypt and in neighbouring countries as tens of thousands of refugees flowed across the borders. Little did we realize that this was merely the beginning, that it would become an unstoppable tide of desperate men, women and children.

The Egyptian government had agreed to provide Syrian refugees with education and access to medical treatment, and to ease their integration. I felt proud watching Marwa as she engaged the Syrian women, asking about their tribulations with a warmth and strength that drew them out. Later that night, she surprised me by sending me a text message containing the phone numbers of the female spokesperson and members of several families of injured Syrians being treated in Egyptian hospitals.

Marwa quickly became the most important person in my life. She was generously understanding of my demanding, often unpredictable CNN schedule and supportive when CNN pulled me away, whether from a social occasion or a quiet evening together. On February 1, Marwa and I were at a friend's house having dinner when the phone rang. The urgent and familiar voice on the other end belonged to the editor on CNN's assignment desk in Atlanta.

Had I heard about the soccer clashes? he asked. I signalled Marwa to turn on the TV as I checked my Twitter feed. "We are seeing tweets and a Reuters wire that just surfaced about clashes at two soccer games. Something about Port Said. We need you on air in eight minutes."

Egyptian channels were already playing footage of hundreds of soccer fans clashing in the Port Said soccer stadium. Wires claimed that dozens had been killed, but I needed confirmation. I called two sources at the interior ministry without success. An Arabic tweet posted minutes earlier cited the death toll at thirty. From the corner of my eye I could see Marwa dialling her cell and heard her asking for a number. I watched her jot it down on a piece of paper as I continued trying to reach my contacts to confirm the death toll.

I had three minutes to go before I was live on air and was sweating when she pushed the paper in front of me, quickly explaining that the number was for Mohamed Sultan, head of the ambulance authority in Port Said. She had organized an event there months earlier and when the CNN request came in she immediately called the Vodafone branch manager in Port Said to get the number.

MARWA AND THE MUSLIM BROTHERHOOD

Sultan answered, confirming the number of deaths at seventy-four. I flipped to an Egyptian channel and it was also reporting seventy-four dead.[34] I ended my call to Port Said just as CNN's Atlanta number flashed on my phone. When I finished my live beeper to the anchor, Jim Clancy, I turned and wrapped my arms around my talented new private producer.

As 2012 unfolded, I was constantly amazed at the courage and dedication of journalists covering the events of the Arab Spring, both on the frontlines in conflict zones—Libya and Syria—and in Egypt. One of those journalists was Steven Sotloff, a young, idealistic Jewish-American freelancer from Miami who had lived in the Middle East for many years and who I had crossed paths with during various protests in Cairo. Marwa and I invited Steven to dinner at my apartment one evening and listened to him talk about his desire to cover the plight of Syrians from within Syria. His cherubic face was animated, his eyes alight behind his glasses as we shared war stories before shifting our conversation to sports and his favourite team—the NBA's Miami Heat.

Although a lot of foreign journalists were reporting on the Syrian crisis by interviewing refugees stranded abroad or living in Turkey or Egypt, only the most fearless were attempting to report from inside—journalists such as James Foley and Steven. Steve wanted to go to the frontline; he said he knew the risks, but was full of confidence in the contacts he had made, some of them through Vulture Club, a Facebook group that helped freelance journalists and aid workers find fixers and translators, and aimed to build a non-competitive community of war reporters, photographers and human rights activists. He saw the two bulletproof vests and helmets that hung on my bedroom wall and before leaving that night asked to borrow one of my flak jackets. I explained that they belonged to CNN so I wasn't at liberty to lend them, though I wished I could.

His charged talk of crossing the border into Syria worried me, but he was experienced and had produced great reports from Libya, Yemen, and Egypt, so I brushed my anxiety aside.

Egypt was grappling with its post-Mubarak predicament. Though the protestors had been very clear about not wanting the repressive leadership of the old state, they lacked the organization, resources or ideas to achieve a new one. In the early months, the field of candidates vying for the presidency was robust; by the time the votes were counted following the first round of elections on May 24, it was clear that only two were seriously in the running for the title of Egypt's first democratically elected president. One candidate was Mohamed Morsi, leader of the Muslim Brotherhood's newly formed Freedom and Justice Party—whose announcement that they would not seek the presidency I had covered earlier. His rival was Ahmed Mohamed Shafik, former air force pilot and senior commander in the Egyptian military whom Mubarak had appointed prime minister during the Arab Spring. For liberal and secular voters, neither candidate offered high hopes for a more democratic Egypt. The highly educated Morsi—he had obtained his PhD in engineering from the University of Southern California in 1982—had been a member of the Muslim Brotherhood since 1977. Shafik had close ties to the military and was a member of the former Mubarak regime that the revolution had opposed.

When Election Day arrived I headed under a scorching sun to Tahrir Square with a recovered Ian Lee and camerawoman Dana Smillie. The excitement in the square was intense, the crowd largely Morsi supporters. Ben Wedeman and camerawoman Mary Rogers were positioned on the other side of Cairo where pro-Shafik supporters had gathered to await results.

People waved Egyptian and Muslim Brotherhood flags, many prayed, some passed out dates and cold water, others smiled at us and flashed victory signs as we walked towards a large tent in the centre of the square. Inside, dozens of men, Morsi supporters, huddled around a small TV perched on a wooden chair. They fell silent when we entered. Several eyed the camera and us suspiciously. I greeted our host, a bearded, middle-aged man named Mohamed, as another heavily bearded man served us tea. Dana began filming while Ian, who had learned enough Arabic to carry on a reasonable conversation, conducted a brief interview.

Suddenly there was a commotion: the head of the electoral committee appeared live on television to announce the winner of the election. The crowd outside fell silent. Some men in the tent began reciting verses of the Quran. Others dropped to their knees, praying aloud to Allah to deliver their candidate, Dr. Mohamed Morsi, to victory. I said a prayer of my own: I wanted his opponent, Ahmed Shafik, to win.

Then, loud and clear across the square, the name of the victor: *Mohamed Morsi Al Ayat*. The Muslim Brotherhood had won.[35]

There seemed to be no air in the tent. Outside, the crowd erupted, jubilant. Dana and I emerged to see everyone crying, shouting and dancing. A man, tears streaming down his face, ran through the crowd distributing candy. Dana was catching it all on camera. My mouth felt chalky, my throat tight. My cellphone vibrated.

"Can you hear me?" Marwa asked. "Are you still in Tahrir?"

"Yes," I shouted, barely able to hear her over the din of celebration.

"I am watching with my friends. We are all depressed here. The Brotherhood will destroy Egypt."

When the votes were counted, Morsi had won by the narrowest of margins: 51.7 percent to Shafik's 48.3 percent. Worse, only 52 percent of the population had voted, despite voting being compulsory and the failure to vote punishable by fines or imprisonment. Many liberal, progressive Egyptians had refused to cast a ballot, unable to stomach either the Muslim Brotherhood and their mandate to establish an Islamic state, or a candidate linked to the regime they had fought so hard to overturn.

While the journalist in me continued to report the news as it unfolded in Egypt, the private citizen in me increasingly detested everything about the Brotherhood. I cringed when a businessman I knew told me he had begun growing his beard to appeal to Morsi's new minister of investment and members of his recently appointed cabinet. But objectivity was critical, so I forced myself to attend Islamist events: it was my job to maintain a good contact list and keep close tabs on key players in the new political arena.

One of those players was my future prison mate Mohamed al-Zawahiri, who was considered a leading Salafi jihadist with significant potential to capitalize on the stature of his brother Ayman al-Zawahiri, a man with a price now of US$25 million on his head.[36] In my interview with Mohamed five weeks after the election he showed himself determined to extend his influence, and as usual had nothing good to say about the West.

"We only try to regain some of our rights that have been hijacked by Western powers throughout history," he told me, describing the Brotherhood's rise to power in Egypt as "merciful times." With Mubarak gone, he dreamt of an Egypt governed strictly by Sharia law and had little time for democracy.

"I don't believe in constitutions, or this secular system created by America to distort the true Islam. Democracy is not against dictatorship, as some try to portray it. It is against Allah's supreme authority. Against Islam."

I continued to nurture my relationship with al-Zawahiri in the months that followed, calling him on occasion for his opinion or a comment, mostly around stories related to the daily terrorist attacks and slayings of Egyptian security forces in Sinai. One such occasion

came on September 11, 2012, the anniversary of the attack on the
World Trade Center, during a protest by a group of Islamists outside
Cairo's heavily fortified American embassy.[37] That evening I reported
for CNN as protestors scaled the embassy wall, tore down the
American flag, burnt it, and replaced it with the black Islamist flag
used by many extremist groups, bearing the words: THERE IS NO
GOD BUT ALLAH AND MUHAMMED IS HIS MESSENGER.

The protest had begun in response to an anti-Islamic short film
entitled "Innocence of Muslims," recently released by an Egyptian-
American Coptic Christian on YouTube. The low-budget drama,
produced in California, portrayed the Prophet Muhammed as a
womanizer, alcoholic, child molester and merciless killer, and while
the response was not surprising, the brazen attack by Islamic funda-
mentalists on one of the country's most guarded compounds was. In
Mubarak's time, it would have been unthinkable for these radicals
to attend a public event let alone carry out such unbridled anti-
American actions.

As I prepared to go live on CNN, protestors chanted angrily in
the background: *"Down, Down America! Obama, Obama, We Are All
Osama!"* I couldn't believe what I was witnessing: radical Islamists
not only breaching the grounds of the US embassy, but publically
gloating about it. A barrage of gunshots caught me off guard as I
dialled in my report. As soon as I had finished it, I retreated to a side
street, crouching again between two parked cars—fast becoming my
go-to safe zone—and called al-Zawahiri to get his insight. I had
heard that he had been seen in the vicinity of the embassy earlier that
day, and I told him that I had not only seen Muslim Brotherhood
faces in the crowd of protestors, but supporters of Sheikh Omar, also
known as the "Blind Sheikh," who was currently serving a life sentence in a US prison after being convicted of conspiracy in the 1993
World Trade Center attack that killed six people and injured close
to a thousand.

"The protest came out of nowhere," I said. "Did you know about it?"

"Yes," al-Zawahiri replied. "We called for a peaceful protest, joined by different Islamic factions including the [Egyptian] Islamic Jihad and the Hazem Salah Abu Ismail movement." Both were ultra-conservative reform groups of Islamists broadly categorized as Salafi or Salafi jihadists. "We were surprised to see the big numbers show up [. . .]. How would Americans feel if films insulting leading Christian figures like the pope, or historical figures like Abraham Lincoln, were produced? The film portrays the prophet in a very ugly manner [. . .] which is not acceptable. . ."[38]

"Did you see them remove the US flag off the pole and replace it with our flag in the name of Allah, raising the pride of our peaceful Islam?" he asked. "Should we not defend our religion and prophet when attacked?"

"Can I quote you on that?" I asked.

"Yes, feel free."

I wondered how involved al-Zawahiri had been. Two months later, Egypt-based Al Farooq Media, an online platform that while not officially sanctioned by al-Qaeda, openly promotes its ideology, praised Mohamed al-Zawahiri and Rifai Ahmed Taha Musa among other Salafi jihadists for their role in orchestrating the US embassy attack. Musa, also in the vicinity the night of the attack, was a signatory to the February 1998 fatwa "Jihad against Jews and Crusaders." (He would be killed in a US airstrike in Syria in April 2016.)[39]

Within hours of the embassy attack, international media attention abruptly shifted. Across the border in Libya, another Salafi jihadist group called Ansar al-Sharia, which means "Supporters of Islamic Law," attacked the US consulate in Benghazi, killing the US Ambassador Christopher Stevens and Foreign Service officer Sean Smith, and subsequently two CIA contractors.[40]

As I tried to unravel the unholy mess that the region was becoming, I couldn't help but ask: Who was to blame for the mistakes that had given birth to the Islamist insurgency crippling our lives today?

I was already nervous after the violence I'd seen a month earlier in Sinai when on August 5 armed militants ambushed an Egyptian military base in El Arish in Sinai, killing sixteen soldiers as they broke their fast during the holy month of Ramadan; they then stole two armoured cars and drove them into Israel where they engaged in a deadly gun battle with Israeli soldiers.[41] The day after the attack, our CNN crew followed convoys of Egyptian tanks to cover the beginning of "Operation Sinai," aimed at crushing the unexpected insurgency. There news reached us that Morsi had forced the resignation of Egypt's twenty-year army chief, General Mohamed Tantawi, naming as his successor Abdel Fattah el-Sisi, a relative unknown who had held various command positions in the Egyptian Army, including former head of military intelligence during the revolution.

When President Morsi announced he would hold a military parade to commemorate his first one hundred days in office, the date he chose was October 6, 2012. It was the thirty-seventh anniversary of Egypt's 1973 war with Israel and the date of President Anwar Sadat's assassination eight years later. The event was another show of force by the Brotherhood, and many of its prominent members were in attendance that day. As Marwa and I watched the spectacle on television at my apartment, I was appalled to see Tarek el-Zomor, brother of Aboud el-Zomor, the man Ivan and I had interviewed, and who had also been sentenced to life imprisonment for his role in Sadat's assassination, sitting in a prominent spot. (Almost a year later, Tarek el-Zomor was caught on film at the Rabaa Square sit-in, urging Brotherhood protestors to "crush" the new interim government following Morsi's ouster; and he would later appear on Al Jazeera's Arabic channel from Qatar inciting violence.) "What arrogance!" I yelled to Marwa. "To seat Sadat's killer in the front row!"

I turned off the TV angrily while she tried to calm me.

Since his election, Morsi had adopted an exclusionary policy in rebuilding the country, and his plans to reshape Egyptian society according to the Brotherhood was alienating huge segments of the population: many citizens were furious at the rushed constitutional process and Morsi's controversial appointments of Muslim Brotherhood members as state governors, an approach the media had labelled "Brotherhoodization."

A plethora of religious TV channels had also emerged, anchored by bearded men intent on ensuring the population's Islamic indoctrination. As I flipped through these channels after a long day at work, they seemed a stark harbinger of the new Egypt. And the two Al Jazeera Arabic-language channels broadcasting into Egypt (Al Jazeera Arabic and Al Jazeera Mubasher Misr) had abandoned any effort at neutrality, blatantly endorsing the Brotherhood's agenda in their reporting. It was disgraceful to watch. Al Jazeera English, on the other hand, upheld its objectivity, maintaining a balanced view, just as we did at CNN.

The modernity of our country seemed to be rapidly slipping away. Marwa, my mother and my female cousins all told me they had started to feel threatened on the street.

Just when I thought life in Egypt could not get worse, on November 22, Morsi issued a radical decree stripping the judiciary of the right to challenge his decisions—and outraged protestors immediately took to the streets in the thousands.

International reaction was swift and unequivocally negative, and locally, political leaders united in a rare show of solidarity, holding a news conference during which they issued a scathing rebuke. I decided to visit Tahrir Square on my way home from the office that night to check out the anti-Brotherhood protest taking place there. A huge banner positioned at the entrance to Mohamed Mahmoud

Street read: NO IKHWAN, NO BROTHERS, ALLOWED INSIDE. Morsi was driving the country to the brink of civil strife.

Like others, I wondered if he had been emboldened by his recent success in brokering a truce between his friends in Palestine's Hamas movement and Israel. That success had landed him on the cover of *Time* magazine with the headline "The Most Important Man in the Middle East."[42] That day, however, as I gathered reports of assailants setting fire to the offices of the Muslim Brotherhood's Freedom and Justice Party, and of anti-Morsi protestors clashing with his supporters across Egypt, it was evident that Morsi had unleashed widespread, violent opposition.

In spite of all our critical reporting, nothing seemed to make a difference. The killers of the protestors got away, or were never identified. The new government seemed to have no accountability and little transparency. The same police officers in black uniforms, helmets and shields who had opposed our efforts to oust Mubarak in January 2011, now served the Brotherhood. Their enemy of yesterday had become their master of today. Most of the police conscripts beating civilians and journalists with their batons were illiterate, besieged young men from Egypt's poor and remote suburbs who could not comprehend that they were demolishing their own futures.

Another blow—a literal one—came weeks later, when, on my way to cover a protest outside the presidential palace, I was struck in the chest by a tear-gas canister. I remember falling to the ground and awaking in the hospital with an oxygen mask strapped over my nose and mouth. That day left me questioning my future as a journalist. As much as I believed in what I did, I was burned out and depressed. The new year loomed and Egypt, it seemed, was no further ahead that it had been two years earlier when I had arrived on its doorstep full of optimism and enthusiasm.

———

In a welcome reprieve and to ring in 2013, Marwa and I flew to
Beirut for a couple of days over New Year's. Not only did our trip
mark the one-year anniversary of our first date, it was a celebration
of our engagement. As is custom in Egypt, we'd quietly gotten
engaged at Marwa's parents' home in late December in the presence
of my mother and Marwa's parents.

There was no better place in the Middle East to be on New Year's
Eve than Beirut, a city whose citizens had truly learned how to celebrate amid times of war. Marwa looked dazzling that night as we
took in the live entertainment at Beirut's Music Hall and talked
about our future. We decided I needed to throttle back and make
more time for our personal life together. We spoke of stability, shared
dreams of perhaps starting a new life in my "other home"—Canada.
We weren't sure exactly what that future looked like, but we were
sure we'd be spending it together.

I was back at work in early January when CNN's Wolf Blitzer
arrived for an interview with President Morsi. CNN had assigned
me as a producer on the story and I felt re-energized as our team
drove through the gates of the presidential palace in two cars. Dana,
Ian and I, with the help of our driver, unloaded the half-dozen bags
of equipment we'd brought and carried them into a hallway inside
the palace designated for the interview. Wolf was animated as we
chatted briefly while the crew set up the cameras. He had secured
the exclusive one-hour interview through a man I would come to
know intimately in prison: Essam al-Haddad, one of the president's
chief aides.

Wolf had connected with al-Haddad on his recent trip to the
US, during which al-Haddad had also met with President Obama.
In his interview, Wolf was warm and earnest, drawing Morsi out even
as he asked tough questions about the government's uneven six-
month record. Morsi urged patience, saying it would take months,
and perhaps years to achieve the democratic country Egyptians so

badly wanted, and claimed that he intended to honour basic freedoms, including allowing political opponents to speak their minds. He backed the international calls for President Bashar al-Assad to be tried for war crimes in Syria and, on the subject of Israel, promised to "respect the will of the world" as long as it did not conflict with his support for the Palestinians and their rights to self-determination. On a more radical note, he called for the United States to release the Blind Sheikh.[43] After the interview Wolf and I stood with the president and had our photo taken. Then I deliberately presented Morsi with a copy of my book, *Egyptian Freedom Story*.

That interview, with the exception of Morsi's controversial request to free the Blind Sheikh, played well in the US and across the Western world; but Morsi's stature as a moderate soon came under attack when a 2010 Arabic video recording surfaced in which he referred to Jews as "apes" and "pigs."[44]

Morsi's promises made no difference to the lives of those living within Egypt's borders. Violence continued on the streets of Cairo and in cities and towns across the country, the patience that Morsi had urged nowhere to be found.

As I had promised Marwa, I began pulling back from covering news on the street. I spent more time with her, listening, observing and dancing my worries away in the bars of Egypt. I enjoyed meeting and socializing with reporters I had not had time to get to know, given the hectic pace at CNN. One of those journalists was Baher Mohamed, a thirty-year-old, fresh-faced Egyptian with expressive eyes and a close-cropped cap of curly dark hair who worked as an assistant reporter for *Asahi*, an English-language newspaper based in Japan. I was very taken by his love for his craft, and his idealism reminded me of my own passion at his age. Indeed, I loved sharing some of my Iraq stories with him and he shared entertaining ones of his own.

But talk on every street corner, in every café and bar, was of the Brotherhood, and I could not avoid being drawn in. The Morsi government continued to alienate a growing segment of society including many of those who once voted for it. As the violence escalated leading up to the one-year anniversary of Morsi's election, I started thinking seriously about leaving CNN. Yet quitting felt like a betrayal—an abandonment of my duty to inform the public and the wider world of the abuses of power and the turmoil gripping the region. I saw where the likes of Mohamed al-Zawahiri were taking Egypt: he and many Salafi jihadists were telling me of their aspirations to create a morality police to enforce Islam, and to devise a model of mandatory prayers and religious indoctrination similar to Saudi Arabia's. Islamists surrounded Media Production City, the country's largest production and broadcast complex, calling for the slaying of certain liberal TV anchors.[45]

To understand the mind of the Brotherhood and the Salafi jihadists, and to grasp the infighting and their plan for the country's future beyond the diplomatic rhetoric, was to know that unprecedented violence was about to overtake Egypt. I didn't want to witness it. I wanted out.

As I was wrestling with my decision a comment from the late *Los Angeles Times* reporter Mark Fineman came back to me. I was a cub reporter and the two of us were in Iraq together when the talented veteran had warned me: "Don't let journalism rule your life—it will take away everything precious you have—wife and all." Then twenty-seven and full of bravado, I had barely registered his words. Fineman died of a heart attack in Iraq at the age of fifty-one, and though his journalism remains legendary, the meagre possessions he left behind in Baghdad, including a box of cigars, a case of booze, and the jewellery we bought together in Baghdad's gold district for his daughter's wedding—one he never got to attend—tell a sadder story.

I quit CNN in June 2013. I continued to write op-eds for various publications including *Foreign Policy* and *Al Monitor* as a way of keeping sane, paying the rent and staying engaged. By now fuel shortages were common, the Egyptian economy was in peril, and its beleaguered citizens were once again chanting in the streets: *Bread, Freedom, Social Justice!* I had become convinced that the cancer of political Islam needed to be extracted before it crippled what was left of Egypt, but what or who would take its place was the big question.

A quasi-grassroots campaign called Tamarod ("rebellion" in Arabic) had arisen on the streets of Cairo in opposition to President Morsi, and created a petition demanding he call early elections. Legions of young men and women canvassed the streets, schools and coffee shops across Egypt urging citizens to sign. Some TV anchors signed live on TV. I signed it while stuck in traffic, as I sat in a taxi. The movement, led by Egyptian activist Mahmoud Badr, announced that as of June 29, a day before a massive street rally was planned, Tamarod had collected more than twenty-two million signatures. There was no way to verify the number of signatories or the Brotherhood's claims that the military was behind the movement, though some military officers I spoke to confirmed they had person-ally donated money to the initiative. Still, Morsi and the Brother-hood insisted it was a conspiracy. Then a leaked audio conversation between the top brass of the military confirmed that the UAE had indeed funnelled money to champion the Tamarod movement.[46] The oil-rich Arabian Gulf nations had begun to realize the political threat a Muslim Brotherhood regime in the region might become. The longstanding ruling families of UAE, Saudi Arabia and Bahrain particularly worried that the empowerment of the Brotherhood now ruling Egypt would ripple across the Middle East and end their monarchies, including UAE's Al Nahyan family and the powerful House of Saud. The Saudis, hoping to stave off the Brotherhood in their own country, injected billions of dollars of social welfare spending to placate its citizens following Mubarak's ouster, as well as generously funding both Egypt's military and the non-violent Salafis against anything Brotherhood.

But what these governments failed to recognize was that the Arab Spring had been a grassroots movement driven by young progressives desperate for democratic reform—a movement hijacked by Islamists. If anyone doubted the magnitude of Tamarod, those doubts were dispelled the next day. On June 30, 2013, the one-year anniversary of the inauguration of President Morsi, millions of Egyptians took to the streets in what could well have been the largest protest in Egypt's history. I joined Marwa and a couple of her colleagues, once deemed members of the "couch party" for their lack of participation in the political process, in two peaceful rallies against the Brotherhood. I proudly watched my fiancée, her entire being radiating passion and conviction as she chanted alongside other protestors. The shy yet incredibly strong woman I'd met eighteen months earlier had come out of her apolitical shell.

I held Marwa's hand almost too tightly as we followed hundreds of thousands of protestors carrying Egyptian flags across the Kasr el-Nile Bridge and into Tahrir Square. I looked around me at all the people, young and elderly, moving steadily forward. I'd been part of another crowd that had crossed this bridge two years ago, united by the same fierce desire for freedom. We had called it *Revolution!* It seemed like a lifetime ago. Today there were no bullets, tear gas, or water cannons. Instead, military choppers flew overhead in formation, dropping tiny Egyptian flags to the protestors.

The next day, General Sisi issued an ultimatum: President Morsi and his government had forty-eight hours to meet the "people's demands" to step down or the army would impose a road map for the nation's future. Thousands of people had continued to stream into Tahrir Square, joining the multitudes that were now camped out there demanding Morsi's resignation. Military choppers again flew overhead, this time dragging national flags across Cairo's summer skies. Marwa and I watched the situation unfold from the living room of my apartment, as we held one another and yelled fervently. "He's going to do it! He's going to do it!"

Sisi's actions were branded as a "coup d'état" by many world leaders and most of the Western media, whereas millions of Egyptians insisted that the military was upholding the will of the people. The military itself was quick to deflect the "coup" allegations, insisting it was saving Egypt from entering a "dark tunnel of conflict." And when Sisi finally announced the ouster of Morsi and the Brotherhood on July 3, Marwa and I kissed and danced like delirious children before taking to the streets to celebrate with millions of Egyptians. For the first time in a year, I felt as if life had possibility. Tragically for Egypt and, as it would turn out, for Marwa and for me, the honeymoon would not last long.

CHAPTER 7

AL JAZEERA

September 1-December 24, 2013

On the morning of September 1, 2013, my cellphone rang, jarring me awake. Although it had been several months since I left CNN, I still slept with my phone under my pillow and jumped to answer it. That morning, however, a Qatari number flashed across my screen and the caller introduced herself as Afaf Saoudi of the Al Jazeera English channel. The call was brief and after I hung up, I stared dumbly at the phone, both surprised and intrigued. She had just offered me a plane ticket to Al Jazeera headquarters in Doha for a job interview.

I shook the sleep from my head and tried to recall the unexpected conversation. The woman had told me that a senior position was available and that Salah Negm, director of news for the network's English channel—a man I had met briefly in a Cairo hotel lobby a year earlier—had referred me for the job.

A couple of days later, Marwa helped me pick out the shirt and tie I would wear with my suit, and fired interview questions at me as I packed a small carry-on for the trip. We laughed as we role-played and chatted about the possibility of starting a new life outside of Egypt. Just ten days earlier the network had launched Al Jazeera America, headquartered in New York. Although it was a long shot, we were giddy at the prospect of relocating, if not to the US then perhaps to one of the several dozen Al Jazeera English news bureaus located on every continent across the globe. Al Jazeera English was very appealing to journalists with liberal values—like CNN, it had received a Peabody Award for its globally acclaimed coverage of the Arab Spring uprising. But I didn't want to be associated with the marred Al Jazeera Arabic-language channels—nor work in the Doha headquarters under the same roof. I told Marwa I would have to decline an offer if that was any part of it; and, if it wasn't, I would still need assurances that I would be able to report independently and objectively. I was becoming increasingly antagonistic to the editorial stance of the Arabic-language channels—they were becoming daily more explicit in their support for the Muslim Brotherhood, and as a mouthpiece for the Qatari government which owns Al Jazeera 100 percent. Egypt's closure of both Arabic-language bureaus in Cairo a few months earlier made independence essential.

The English and Arabic platforms had since their inception been positioned as entirely different animals. Qatar's Emir had launched Al Jazeera, which means "The Island," on November 1, 1996, and its English-language channel—known simply as Al Jazeera English—a decade later. The Emir and his network bosses had allowed Al Jazeera English's independent stance, which was central to its international success and reputation. In more recent years, that had been upheld thanks to the man who was its managing director from 2008 to 2010, the highly regarded one-time Canadian Broadcasting Corporation (CBC) producer and news editor-in-chief Tony Burman, who vig-orously maintained the English channel's commitment to objectivity and ethics, and to reporting the news of the Middle East accurately and regardless of political interests.[47]

I arrived in Doha on September 4. My position as a producer for Dubai television had me crisscrossing the Gulf, covering stories in Kuwait, Saudi Arabia, Oman and Bahrain. While I hadn't worked in Qatar specifically, I had freelanced for Al Jazeera English's website during my year as a stringer in Iraq—a time when Al Jazeera English, with its intimate access to the Iraqi people, had been a professional player in the coverage of the war. After it was over, I'd even flown to Doha to meet Al Jazeera Network executives and explore employment options. At that time the job offer, a junior position with Doha's Arabic-language network, hadn't appealed to me, but this time around, the possibility of a senior journalist position with Al Jazeera English did. I thought the Peabody Award certificate I'd received earlier that year, for my part in covering the Arab Spring uprisings for CNN, might be a helpful calling card.

In Doha, the network put me up in the same hotel they had for my first interview, but that was the only similarity. Qatar had changed dramatically in the decade since I'd visited—its skyline glass fronted and futuristic, and its waterfront polished and pristine. The tiny but very wealthy oil-producing nation boasted the highest GDP in the world and had positioned itself as a key player in the Middle East. With its soaring towers, sprawling malls, expensive sports cars and cosmopolitan citizens, Doha gave every outward appearance of a modern Western-style city, glittering and rich and sophisticated. The Gulf state had even won a questionable bid to host the 2022 FIFA World Cup. Yet the Qatari government's political views were anything but progressive, and since the Arab Spring it was daily becoming more blatantly and ambitiously pro-Islamist.

The next morning, I met with Afaf Saoudi, news editor at Al Jazeera English, and Ramsey Zarifeh, head of planning. Afaf was poised and professional as she asked me questions about my previous experience. Then she surprised me by saying: "We have an opening for English bureau chief in Egypt."

Was *that* the job they were interviewing me for? Before I could query it, Ramsey presented me with a hypothetical scenario involving a security issue at a news bureau, asking how I would deal with it. After a few more scenarios and questions, Afaf nodded, and as she moved towards the door said she would like me to meet with Salah Negm, Al Jazeera English's director of news.

Before I left the office, I turned to Ramsey to ask a question of my own: "Do you have an administrative team to provide press passes and permits and deal with any accreditation or security issues for Al Jazeera English in Egypt?" It was a fair question, given the government's recent closure of the two Arabic bureaus in Cairo.

Ramsey reassured me that they did as he shook my hand, and I turned to follow Afaf down the hall to meet the news director.

Salah Negm is a short, slight man in his late fifties with a gaunt face, thinning cuff of grey hair and a thick grey moustache that stands out like the rim of a thatched roof over his upper lip. We found him on a balcony in the humid afternoon air smoking a cigarette. Salah had been news editor for BBC's Arabic television before being appointed head of news at Al Jazeera English. Afaf introduced us, and then left us alone.

"I've heard good things about you," he said, as he offered me a cigarette. "I've also seen some of your live reports on CNN and our reporter, Mike Hanna, asked Ben Wedeman about you."

I hadn't expected the position of bureau chief. It would be a huge step up. I told him I knew a couple of the reporters in the Cairo bureau and admired their work. Salah, exhaling a cloud of smoke, now explained that the former bureau chief had left suddenly so the position was available, but assured me everything at Al Jazeera English was fine. I repeated that for me to take on the job, Cairo's

Al Jazeera English bureau would have to be able to operate totally independently from the network's Arabic-language bureaus—essential, I said "to ensure we get good interviews and steer away from any backlash against Al Jazeera Arabic [and Mubasher Misr] in the present climate."

Salah again reassured me and extended his hand to indicate our very brief discussion had come to an end. "Thank you, Mohamed. Afaf will be in touch with further details."

I walked to the lobby in a state of confusion. *Had they actually offered me the job?* I believed I would be able to bring a unique perspective and insight about Egypt to the world, given my experience and my dual Egyptian–Canadian background; I was enthusiastic about the opportunity to bridge the gulf in mutual understanding between the Middle East and the West. I also knew it would give me the freedom to choose how much time I wanted to spend on the streets. Back in my room, I jumped on the bed in a buoyant mood and texted Marwa and my mother with news that I had just finished one of the strangest interviews of my career but was, it seemed, being considered for the position of English bureau chief in Cairo.

That evening I sat glued to the television watching coverage of an assassination attempt on Egypt's Interior Minister, Mohamed Ibrahim, that had taken place in Cairo minutes before. I scanned the news tickers running under the screen then, out of curiosity, switched to Al Jazeera English's channel. Oddly, no Al Jazeera English reporter appeared on-air from Cairo. Instead, Al Jazeera English ran a video package containing footage acquired from agencies such as Reuters or AP. Every other channel had reporters on-air talking about the horrific car bomb that had injured twenty people. I assumed the sudden departure of the bureau chief was the cause for Al Jazeera English's absence from the air.

I was in a cab on the way to the airport the next morning when I received an email from Afaf saying I'd been hired for the English bureau chief position. The email noted that more details would follow in an introductory message to the Cairo staff. Three hours later, when I landed in Cairo and opened my phone, the promised email popped up on my screen. They were moving fast: Afaf was asking me to show up the next morning at the Marriott Hotel at ten o'clock to meet the staff. I scanned the names of the fifteen journalists she'd copied on the email and smiled. The name of Baher Mohamed was among them.

The next morning, I rose early. I had arranged to meet with senior correspondents Sue Turton, Nadim Baba and Nicole Johnston in the lower restaurant area ahead of meeting the entire staff. I introduced myself and we ordered coffee. I liked them all and knew them as competent and seasoned journalists. Sue, a British anchor and war correspondent, had a quarter century of experience reporting all over the world. She was impressively tough and effective, as was Nicole, an Australian reporter who had spent seven years with ABC before joining Al Jazeera English. Nadim, an Iraqi-British national, spoke fluent Arabic and had reported from Gaza prior to Egypt. He came across as faintly reserved, and was, I knew, a fearless reporter.

The news they had for me was disturbing. While I was preparing to leave for Doha, their Al Jazeera English office had been raided by the government, and the network had asked staff to temporarily relocate to the Marriott Hotel and set up shop in a room, registered in Sue's name. While the raid was not totally surprising considering the recent wave of arrests of journalists and closures of media offices, the news that the former bureau chief Abdullah Mousa had secretly fled to Doha after the raid without telling the staff, was. I wondered why Salah had not shared this remarkable detail about the former chief's sudden departure.

The four of us left the restaurant and rode the elevator to the nineteenth floor. The other staffers were packed inside the room and it was obvious they were on edge.

Mostafa Hawa, the office administrator, said, "When they raided the office, the police confiscated some equipment and arrested me for a couple of days."

"The security of the team," I began, "comes before any story, and I will do whatever I can to ensure that." I took a deep breath. "No one mentioned any of these issues to me in Doha."

One of Al Jazeera English's two producers, Fawzy Abdel Maksoud, interjected with a heartfelt plea that he and his colleague, producer Heba Fahmy, be allowed to work from home. "I don't want to sound like a whiner," Fawzy said, "but I don't feel safe operating out of the Marriott. For my family's sake, I can't afford to let anything happen to me."

"Wait a minute," Sue Turton jumped in. "I need a producer feeding me news lines and securing guests. I don't see how Fawzy and Heba can do that from home."

Then Baher Mohamed, who had joined the bureau three months earlier, revealed that several weeks ago, he and three Al Jazeera English foreign reporters had been arrested for operating without proper press passes. The team was now talking all at once, clamouring for answers.

"Let's calm down," I said, trying to exude a confidence I did not feel. "There's lots of new information here. I will speak to Salah about all this right away. I don't have all the answers right now, but if we stick to good journalism, we should be okay."

I retreated to the balcony overlooking the Nile to collect my jangled thoughts. When I flew to Doha I had not expected to be offered a position as senior as bureau chief. It looked to me now as if my arrival at Al Jazeera's headquarters had been a convenient solution to a crisis. It seemed I had been made captain of a sinking ship.

I heard someone approach and turned to see my young friend Baher, with his ready smile.

"Consider me your black box," he said. "I can tell you whatever you need to know and I'm happy to do anything you want."

I asked him to just tell me about his arrest. It appeared that after they were picked up, Al Jazeera had hired a lawyer to represent them—Farag Fathi—but he never even showed up to their interrogation and he sent another young lawyer to represent him at their court appearance.

"I'm very surprised," I said angrily. "I was told none of this in Doha."

Baher replied, "They've been too busy launching Al Jazeera America."

I tried without success to reach Farag Fathi, Al Jazeera's lawyer. I called his office several times, but he was either not there or would not take my calls. His legal assistant came across as unprofessional and sheepish, just as Baher had described him. I wrote to Salah Negm.

From: Mohamed Fadel Fahmy
Sent: Saturday, September 07, 2013
To: Salah Negm; Afaf Saoudi
Subject: AJE Legal/Security Situation in Cairo

Dear Mr. Salah,
I have met with the whole team yesterday on my first day and I am impressed with their attitude and energy considering the pressure they have been dealing with lately on the ground.
[. . .] However, the staff is very concerned where Al Jazeera stands legally and I would like to be able to comfort them at some point regarding their security and well-being. As you know, the producers yesterday expressed their concern with the security situation and preferred to work from home.

I would just like to suggest that I am willing to meet the lawyers myself to try and get a better picture of where we stand legally and what to expect in the near future. I can get a copy of the prosecutor's report.

The network's brief response came a day later:

From: Afaf Saoudi
To: Mohamed Fadel Fahmy
Subject: RE: AJE Legal/Security Situation in Cairo
Date: Sunday, 8 Sep 2013

Dear Mr. Fahmy, I appreciate your concern about the legal issue but Doha management will deal with it from here.

I continued to bombard the Doha office with emails and phone calls, Al Jazeera continued to provide assurances that they would send a letter containing our names and job titles to our office administrator and accountant, Gamal el Sherif, so he could apply for our press accreditation, and that they were in communication with their lawyers who had given them assurances that we would be able to return to our office soon.

My focus turned to raising the morale of my team. In the days that followed, I negotiated a raise for the two veteran cameramen, secured phones for local staff, and negotiated a US$50 per day raise for Baher, who was working on a freelance contract, to bring his day rate to US$150, closer to what CNN and BBC were paying. My priority was to ensure our coverage was both balanced and accurate to separate our team from the stigma attached to Al Jazeera Mubasher Misr. On September 3—the same day that the English office was raided—the interim government had officially declared Al Jazeera Mubasher Misr closed by a court order that stated the channel was biased towards the Muslim Brotherhood and a threat to national security.[48] Digging into it now, I learned that two months earlier, on July 9, four days after the ouster of President Morsi, twenty-two of its employees had resigned over "biased coverage."[49] The pattern was troubling.

I intended to be vigilant about every story emerging from our bureau. I submitted clear conditions to management: given we are a separate entity, keep our work and our team as far removed as possible from Al Jazeera Mubasher Misr, which was now being covertly—and illegally—broadcast into Egypt from the Doha headquarters via a different satellite frequency; I would not duplicate any reports emerging from the Arabic channels: my staff would conduct only first-hand newsgathering, sourcing and booking.

And in terms of news, there was no shortage. The ouster of Morsi had sparked the bloodiest event in memory—the Rabaa massacre, which was still fresh in everyone's mind. The army had declared a month-long state of emergency, imposing a strict 7:00 p.m. curfew to maintain order. While Cairo remained relatively peaceful—with the exception of Fridays when protests often ended with tear gas, clashes and deaths—violent protests by defiant Brotherhood supporters and Salafis continued across the country. Dozens of churches were burnt, police stations torched, and businesses shut down.

As a bureau chief with limited resources, I tried to pick and choose the protests that resonated politically. However, a new wrinkle: I was told by the management in Doha that the decision was not to be mine alone. They wanted us to report on every Friday protest against the government as if each was a major news event. I determined to balance their importance in our weekly coverage but it still meant that when Friday rolled around each week, there was our Al Jazeera English team, on the streets after noon prayer, filming the pro-Brotherhood protestors.

"Why are we covering a protest every time a gas canister is fired?" Sue exclaimed in frustration, as we sat in our Marriott Hotel room discussing possible stories. She made a good point. To make matters worse, the network bosses had recently made an inexplicable decision to ban PTC ("piece-to-camera") story segments, during which reporters address the viewing audience by speaking directly to the camera. They also decided they would not display reporters' faces, locations, or names on the screen when their stories aired. Management countered my inquiries by saying that they were protecting their journalists' identities from an aggravated public—the very public whose views we were trying to openly represent. So not only did it not make sense, it was something I had never seen a TV network do.

"I'm not working in radio! If I remain dark, then I'm leaving," Sue announced one day as I tried to reassure her, promising yet again to talk to Salah.

Dominic Kane, another British reporter who had been deployed to Cairo from Doha on assignment for a short period, voiced his growing frustration. "Fahmy, I'm working on a story about the new protest law," he said. "We've filmed the founder of the April 6 protest movement, but can't get an expert to comment. No one wants to talk to Al Jazeera."

"Fine," I said, scrambling for an alternative. I suggested we get Dr. Omar Ashour, an Exeter University scholar to comment and compare it to the protest law in the UK.

"Okay," he said, mollified for the moment. "What about the piece-to-camera? Are we still hiding our faces?"

Again, I improvised, asking them to continue to film PTCs in the hope of pressuring management to run them. We sent the full package, including the PTCs, to Doha for airing, but they ignored them—in the days and weeks that followed, our reports continued to air without identifying journalists.

The demands of my new job quickly took over my life. I worked ten- to twelve-hour days juggling three to five deadlines in addition to scheduling staff shifts, paying salaries, managing office finances, planning weekly news coverage, calling on my contacts to comment on stories, and reviewing editorial packages. Even after I'd arrived home, typically around ten at night, I was often still on duty, emailing the next day's lineup to the night staff. The apartment that had been a sanctuary for my fiancée and me had ceased to exist as such. Marwa, too, had experienced a change in her work life. She was unhappy with her new boss, a Muslim Brotherhood sympathizer who she felt was prejudiced against women. On one particular night Marwa was tearfully flipping through the TV news channels as I comforted her over her boss's misogynistic treatment. When the Al Jazeera Mubasher Misr channel flashed on the screen, I literally jumped off the couch, snatching the remote control to increase the volume.

To my horror, a video package I had recently produced on 140 teenagers detained in adult prisons was showing on the pro-Brotherhood Al Jazeera Mubasher Misr channel. Our package had been dubbed into Arabic and rebroadcast from Doha. It was a good story—one I would have been proud to run on any channel, but not on a banned one broadcasting into the country illegally.

Before the report had ended, my phone rang. It was Omar Fouad, the cameraman who had filmed it.

"Fahmy, you won't believe what the network has done," he said in a panicked voice when I answered. "I can't work like this! I will not go to jail!"

"I just saw it," I said, furious. "I can't fucking believe those idiots! I'm emailing headquarters now and will call you back later."

Marwa had stopped crying and was staring at me in alarm.

Though livid, I tried to be diplomatic in my email to Salah, Afaf and Heather Allan, head of global newsgathering for Al Jazeera English. After all, I had not yet been on the job three weeks.

From: Mohamed Fadel Fahmy
Sent: Friday, September 27, 2013
To: Salah Negm; Afaf Saoudi; Heather Allan
Subject: Inquiry about AJE package running on AJ Mubasher

Dear Mr. Salah,
We produced a package on hundreds of children wrongfully
detained with adults after their arrest in Raba and Nahda
sit-down dispersals. I personally reached out to the lawyers
and families profiled in the story and made the distinction
between Al Jazeera English and Al Jazeera Egypt Mubasher
due to the increased tension on ground here toward the
Arabic channel.

Our AJE package ran at least 5 times but last night I
noticed that the package was voiced into Arabic and broadcast on Al Jazeera Mubasher Misr. [. . .] I would imagine that
due to the security situation this action may come back to
bite us.

From: Salah Negm
Date: Friday, 27 Sep 2013
To: Mohamed Fahmy, Afaf Saoudi, Heather Allan
Subject: RE: Inquiry about AJE package running on AJ
Mubasher

I will handle this. Thank you for alerting me.
Best
Salah

A leaked video circulating on social media a week later raised the
political stakes. It showed army chief General Abdel Fattah el-Sisi
discussing in a roundtable with his senior officers how to deal with

the country's media.[50] The recording starts with an officer urging Sisi to find a way to prevent journalists from criticizing the army: "We must re-establish red lines for the media. We need to find a new way of neutralizing them; the media in Egypt is controlled by twenty or twenty-five people. [. . .] We should engage with these people directly, and individually either terrorize them or win them over."

Sisi interrupts the officer: "I know how to win them over, but tell me, how do you suggest I terrorize them?" Then he can be heard saying: "I want to tell you that we've been concerned with controlling the media from the very first day the army took over power in 2011, and we suffered a lot. Because in order to achieve what you're talking about you need to have influence, it's not as simple as just setting up a committee or task force."

The officer replies: "It takes a long time before you're able to affect and control the media. We are working on this and we are achieving more positive results but we are yet to achieve what we want."

The leaked video reinforced that the top brass was trying to bring back the old days and quash the democratic press freedoms we had briefly tasted. The military had enjoyed a level of immunity during Mubarak's era—no journalist could question or challenge the generals freely. The January 25 revolution changed all that and left the military caught off guard in the avalanche of media freedom. (In fact, it seems Sisi had had a change of heart about his approach to power and the media, because in 2006 he had written a paper at the US Army College he attended called "Democracy in the Middle East." He wrote: "The media will be an obstacle to a democratic form of government until it can be trusted more than the government's perspective. This will be an immense challenge because those in power must be willing to let go of media control.)[51]

Al Jazeera's told us the Arabic channels would run the leaked footage immediately along with a critical commentary. I asked them to slow down while I located a reputable English-speaking analyst to contextualize it objectively for our English audience. The request was ignored. Instead, the management asked an Al Jazeera English reporter, Jamal Elshayyal, to produce the story from Doha right away.

As September rolled into October, I was still receiving the network's assurances that they would have us back in the office "soon," telling me to continue to book the hotel room on a week-to-week basis only, and—when Sue Turton reassigned to Doha—to transfer the reservation to my name—it was cheaper, they said, for me to book with my Egyptian identification card and take advantage of the 50 percent discount provided to Egyptian nationals. The hotel moved us from the nineteenth to the twentieth floor in order to make repairs to the room we'd been occupying. The new room, Suite 2056, was at least more spacious with separate sleeping and lounge areas, which would ease the congestion we'd often experienced when interviewing subjects. The suite also had a door to an adjoining small room. I was willing to put up with our temporary quarters, but I was uneasy about the lack of press accreditation for many staff, including me, despite the repeated reassurances from Doha that they were handling it.

I took them at their word and got to work making our team the best it could be. Ours was now the only Al Jazeera channel operating legally in Egypt and I wanted to keep it that way. An encouraging sign that my requests were being heard came in mid-October when the network resumed showing the faces and names of our reporters on air, though with no clear answer as to why or what had changed.

I decided to let a couple of people on the Al Jazeera English staff go to create more efficiency, including one of our producers, Sherif Elhelwa. Baher, by contrast, was every reporter's first choice and someone I'd quickly come to rely on. He was fast, dependable and with a talent for relating to anyone on the street, be they a Muslim Brotherhood hardliner or a secular moderate, and for convincing subjects to speak on camera. I'd always said that if a person was in journalism for the money, he or she was in the wrong business. Baher, it seemed to me, loved his job for all the right reasons: the pursuit of truth, justice and freedom of expression. I groomed him to do live phone reports from the field and recommended him for a permanent staff position, a request Doha rejected, to my astonishment: Baher had been arrested and held for four days, risked his life on the street and been beaten and threatened more times than I could count on two hands. He was also a father of two, a family man, and could use the stability and income that came with a full-time contract.

But stability was precisely what we had to worry about. I was alone one night in the hotel office when I received an unnerving call from an editor in Doha asking where I was and if I was okay.

"Don't tell me there is a huge bombing in Sinai?" I'd said half joking.

"No," he said, his voice serious. "Reuters just reported that Al Jazeera's Cairo office has been raided."

"What!" I practically yelled. "There's nothing wrong here. Send me the wire."

Indeed, Reuters was reporting that security forces had raided the office of Al Jazeera's television channel in Cairo and arrested eleven Qatari citizens, including four Qatari police officers. In the wire, Reuters referenced *Al-Ahram*, Egypt's state-owned newspaper, which quoted security officials saying they had searched the office after receiving reports of firearms inside.[52] The story concluded by saying Qatar "was a strong financial backer of Muslim Brotherhood rule and vehemently opposes the army's overthrow of Mursi [*sic*] and the ensuing bloody crackdown on his movement."

Given we were the only Al Jazeera bureau now operating in Cairo, I moved into damage control, emailing the managers in Doha and demanding Al Jazeera release an official statement contesting the story. I called Reuters to ask them to take down the story, but it was too late: although they printed Al Jazeera's denial of a raid the next day, the damage was done—the article had been syndicated and widely circulated. I was pissed and on edge. Something wasn't right.

We hunkered down into a routine. Protests against Morsi's overthrow carried on, demanding accountability from Sisi and the generals for the deaths of dozens of students killed in the recent massacre and for others still dying in ongoing protests. The treatment of female protestors, some of whom had been assaulted by police and had their hijabs pulled off, also sparked outrage. The epicentre of this movement, dubbed "the campus revolution," was Cairo's Al-Azhar University. In October the dean had called in security forces to end the protest after a group of students broke into the university's administrative headquarters and ransacked the building. We reported on the verdict: twelve students convicted of attacking university personnel and sabotaging public and private property were sentenced to seventeen years in prison. That day, I hosted a live shot for *Inside Story*, a popular Al Jazeera English program, from our hotel room balcony with a pro-Morsi, Muslim Brotherhood college student, her head covered in a hijab, who had just returned from a student protest incited by the verdict. The placid backdrop of the Nile seemed incongruous with the reek of tear gas on her clothes and her impassioned description of the violent campus uprising during which a student had been killed when security forces fired tear gas, rubber bullets and birdshot into the crowd.

The director of *Inside Story* wanted a guest from the opposing camp and I quickly found a vocal representative from a pro-government group called the Sons of Mubarak and linked her in via Skype.

"No one can deny the rights of students for protesting," the young, anti–Muslim Brotherhood spokesperson said, "but when you go violent, you have to be stopped. Other people going to university

are going for an education [. . .] so if students want to protest, why
don't they do it after hours?"⁵³ The director immediately switched
to a split screen showing the two women as they fiercely debated
one another. It turned out to be a very successful show—just one
example of the balanced reporting Al Jazeera English was renowned
for and we were upholding. We also covered the fallout when the
interim government introduced a draconian and highly controversial
anti-protest law, which decreed that anyone protesting without a
permit would face three to five years in prison. One ludicrous example was the incident of a fifteen-year-old boy jailed for possessing a
plastic ruler. The minute I saw the tiny news blurb about his arrest,
I asked Baher to locate the boy's lawyer, while I tried to do the same
through my own sources. "Race you," I said to Baher, and we placed
a friendly bet on who could track down the boy's attorney first.
Baher won.

I called the lawyer, taking notes as he relayed the details, assigned
Nadim Baba to the story and dispatched a camera crew, producer,
and driver to the city of Kafr el-Sheikh, three hours north, where the
story was still unfolding. The lawyer provided me with the official
document from the prosecutor's office, and we asked our designers in
the Doha head office to quickly recreate the government statement
in a bold, typewritten graphic to appear on screen as part of Nadim's
report. It accused the boy of distributing exam schedules imprinted
with the four-finger insignia associated with the Rabaa protest, and
for possessing a ruler with the same mark. "He was defaming the
military and spreading inaccurate information to the students," the
statement concluded.

Two days after the story ran I was alone in the office at night
sifting through various news feeds, and thinking about getting away
with Marwa over New Year's for a desperately needed break, when
I spotted a tweet in Arabic promoting a feature about "The Ruler
Student" being aired from Doha on the banned Al Jazeera Mubasher

Misr channel. I clicked on the link and when it opened, I felt the air leave my body.

The channel was running an entire show about the imprisoned teen complete with our graphics, a panel of studio guests, and an anchor using the report we'd produced—which had now been dubbed into Arabic and was being rebroadcast in the background. This time there was no question of a programming glitch. The management in Doha had knowingly put us in an incredibly dangerous position: not only had they ignored my stipulation about not running the content we'd produced for the English channel on the illegal Arabic channel, but their anchor and guests had added pro-Brotherhood rhetoric when discussing the video report we had worked hard to keep balanced. Such deliberate negligence could easily put us on the radar of the authorities or worse.

I immediately called Doha, but at that late hour no manager was there to answer my call. Seething, I emailed the managers of the English and Arabic Al Jazeera channels, and the director general of the network. "We will be targeted if this continues. Please stop the program. The authorities will not accept this approach."

I called Doha again the same night, desperate to stop a repeat broadcast of the show, and complained angrily to a producer working at the Arabic channel.

The next day, Afaf Saoudi apologized: she would make sure "it would not happen again."

Working in Egypt as a journalist seemed to get harder by the day. Our roving reporters, Dominic Kane, Nicole Johnston, Nadim Baba and Sue Turton, took turns flying in and out of Egypt on assignment, many of them hesitant to return due to the security situation around Al Jazeera. I felt powerless to change the toxic political climate so I focused on what I could control: I pressured the network to find me a veteran reporter, one based in Egypt permanently, so I could plan coverage for the next big story—the upcoming referendum in

January. Salah, however, was having a hard time convincing reporters even to travel to Egypt, at one point advising me to prepare myself to go on camera and cover the upcoming referendum myself. Afaf finally responded telling me she had located a reporter willing to cover over Christmas. His name was Peter Greste, an award-winning journalist based in Kenya and a former BBC correspondent who had covered Egypt very briefly during the uprising. He had a reputation for attention to detail and accuracy and was precisely the kind of experienced journalist I needed. For once the network had come through for me.

Peter entered Egypt on a tourist visa a week into December and the two of us clicked immediately. I appreciated the calm, unruffled and confident demeanour of the blue-eyed, balding Australian. I briefed him over breakfast about the tenuous political footing at the bureau, dismayed again—as he was—to discover that management had failed to fully inform him of the security issues we faced on the ground. Still, he remained stoic and inquisitive, and asked about the Cairo Opera, expressing interest in seeing a performance during his time in Egypt.

Peter, Baher and our cameraman, Mohamed Fawzy, instantly became my A-team, though for the first time since I'd taken over the bureau three and a half months earlier, there was a blessed lull in breaking news. We produced features on the start of the soccer season and on Tawseela, a new fleet of colourfully painted, comfortable, air-conditioned commuter buses with high-speed wireless Internet. Baher and Peter chatted about taking an Arabian horseback tour of the pyramids and developing the experience into a tourism story.

I had begun using the gym in the hotel after hours to stay in shape and to clear my mind at the end of a long day. I was working out on the night of December 11 shortly after Peter's arrival when the editor on the Al Jazeera English desk in Doha called to alert me about a breaking story. An audio recording of the minister of defense,

General Abdel Fattah el-Sisi, had been "leaked" on YouTube, and Al Jazeera had immediately run it on the banned Arabic channel. I listened with curiosity; it was purported to be from an off-the-record interview with a renowned local paper during which Egypt's powerful defense minister described a series of long ago dreams and premonitions he had that revealed he was going to be the next president of Egypt. He recalled how in one dream he was wielding a sword on which the Islamic creed "There is no God but God" was emblazoned and wearing "an Omega watch with a big green star." When asked by people in the dream, "Why do you have this watch?" Sisi explained, "It is because of my name—it is Omega and I'm Abdel Fattah, so there is something universal between us."[54] I could not believe these nocturnal visions would be seen as anything but ludicrous—Sisi's words made absolutely no sense to me.

"I'm not going live on TV to report *that*," I said.

"It's an order from Salah," the editor replied in his lilting British accent. "He called the desk from his home."

"Tell Salah the cameraman has gone home," I said, my voice sharp. "And tell Salah, Fahmy says 'it's not a TV-breaking-news live shot.'"

I hung up, but it wasn't the end of it. The editor called back moments later.

"Okay," he acquiesced, "we will run it on the ticker. Can you send us an English translation?"

"This is absurd," I said. "Why is this news?"

At that point Sisi had not clearly indicated that he would run for the presidency in the upcoming election to end the interim government and I suspected someone close to him might have deliberately leaked the recording to gauge the public's reaction.

It was after eight o'clock and I stood in the gym staring at the TV positioned above the rack of weights. CNN was running a report on the Syrian uprising. Within minutes, however, news of Sisi's dream was running on the ticker on Al Jazeera's English channel, mocking the general and giving the recording plenty of airtime.

The next day, Baher and I were in the office following up on university protests spiralling out of control, with Peter sitting nearby on the couch tapping away at his laptop, when Sherif Elhelwa, the producer I had let go, barged into the office and confronted Baher. A heated discussion ensued and the two men stepped outside onto the balcony. I was monitoring the protests on TV and tried to ignore the argument, what sounded to me like a personal feud between the two men, yelling at them finally to knock it off. Then security forces began firing tear gas and the clashes escalated on TV, and I slid the balcony door open to ask Baher to come back in. Sherif followed him in and continued to hound him, standing in front of the screen and accusing Baher of lying to him. I asked Sherif to save his argument for later, but he wouldn't stop. Finally, I lost my temper. Grabbing him by his shirt, I pulled him towards the hotel room door, swiftly opening it with my free hand. As we stepped over the threshold, he began to resist and our feet tangled. I felt myself losing my balance and the two of us fell hard to the ground, the weight of Sherif's body landing full force on my right shoulder. I heard a crack and an excruciating pain shot through my right side. Sherif quickly got up, but I couldn't move.

A trip to the hospital a short time later revealed I had fractured my right humerus and torn my rotator cuff. The doctor advised that I avoid any unnecessary movement and immobilized my right arm in a sling, telling me it was the best chance to avoid surgery. The pain was acute and I felt like an invalid. I was unable to use my laptop—I sent all crucial emails on my BlackBerry—dress or undress myself, or use a knife and fork. The painkillers the doctor prescribed robbed me of appetite but did little to mute the pain, which was still debilitating after ten days. As Christmas approached, and with movement still very limited, I decided to move from my apartment into the room adjoining our office space, where I sometimes slept and we stored equipment, to avoid the daily commute.

Marwa was one of the few bright spots in my life. On Christmas Eve she visited me in my hotel room despite the risk to her reputation or worse. While she'd been relatively safe dropping by my apartment, morality police could arrest and imprison an unmarried Egyptian woman caught in a hotel room with a man to whom she was not related.

"I hate this," Marwa said, as she closed and bolted the door behind her and handed me a plastic bag with a refill of the painkillers I'd requested. "I hope hotel security didn't see me."

She sat down in the armchair beside the bed and begged me to consider taking more time off than the few days I'd negotiated over New Year's.

"I can't, Marwa," I said. "I just started. Besides, I'd hardly be able to enjoy myself in this state."

Before she left that evening, she shut the curtains, turned off the lights and silenced the ringer on my mobile phone. Then she handed me two painkillers and placed a glass of water on my bedside table. For several hours I lay motionless in the pitch-black room, my eyes wide open and my mind racing. At some point the reflection of an intermittent light on the ceiling above me caught my attention. It took me several seconds to realize it was coming from my mobile phone. I shifted slightly to pick up the phone and stared at the screen. On it flashed a text message from Ahmed, our local Al Jazeera English security guard.

"Turn on Tahrir TV!" it read. "Big bomb in Dakahleya!" Dakahleya is a region northeast of Cairo with a picturesque capital city, Mansoura, situated on the Damietta River.

I manoeuvred carefully out of bed and turned on the TV. The scene it showed was horrific. The central police station in Mansoura had been all but destroyed and burning police cars littered the smoke-filled street. The bomb also appeared to have badly damaged neighbouring buildings. I immediately texted an email to the desk in Doha, which requested a live breaking news report. I called Peter's cell, but received no answer. I stared at the time on my screen. It was 1:25 Christmas morning. I gathered what updates I could from my sources and called the editor in Doha, telling him I'd be doing the live report. Then I stared at the carnage on the muted TV as I waited for the anchor's cue. Soon I heard the familiar voice of the anchor from the network headquarters, say: "A car bomb has exploded outside a police station in Mansoura, Dakahleya. We have our Egypt bureau chief, Mohamed Fahmy, following the story from Cairo."

I filled in the details that I knew: ten policemen had been killed and no group had claimed responsibility for the bombing. I'd also learned that the same station had been attacked several times, but the damage had been nothing compared to the devastation viewers were now seeing on screen.[55] "We will follow the story as it develops," I said, as I hung up.

Peter called a short time later to report that the desk wanted him in vision on Skype—could I email him any developments?

"Of course," I replied, filling him in on what I'd learned from our ministry stringers and officials. "The death toll is up to thirteen—" I stopped in mid-sentence as a news banner flashed across the TV screen in front of me. "That's weird. The prime minister's spokesman just announced that the Muslim Brotherhood is responsible for the bombing."

"That was fast," Peter said. *Too fast*, I thought, as I continued relaying what I was seeing: "The banner now says that 'The Muslim Brotherhood has been declared a terrorist organization.'"

Peter and I were puzzled: Why the sudden declaration now?

I didn't know the answer, but whatever it was, I feared it was going to make our jobs as journalists a hell of a lot harder than they already were. That morning I called my lawyer friend Khaled Abou

Bakr, who I'd often turned to for comment on the legal repercussions of government decrees and announcements during my time with CNN. He had also made a name for himself as the host of a popular TV talk show. Khaled confirmed what I already knew: life was about to get very difficult for the Muslim Brotherhood and for anyone who supported them. But nothing he told me could have prepared me for what would happen next.

CHAPTER 8

HARD KNOCK

December 25–30, 2013

Christmas was a festive time at the Marriott Hotel. Two towering evergreens with tiny white lights framed the marble plaza in front of the entrance. Inside the lobby, green garlands, hundreds of red poinsettias and a steady stream of tourists added to the holiday spirit.

My own spirits, however, were far from bright. The deadly terrorist attack affected us all and the government immediately followed up its decree designating the Muslim Brotherhood a terrorist organization with an aggressive crackdown, within days arresting dozens of citizens across Egypt, seizing land and assets belonging to Brotherhood members, and shutting down hundreds of social and charitable organizations associated with the group. They did so even though many of these charities, deeply rooted in the country's social and civic life, provided vital medical and food relief to thousands already suffering from violence and economic instability. Defense Minister General el-Sisi and the interim government had set the tone for how they intended to deal with the Brotherhood—vowing that "those who harm [Egyptians] will vanish from the face of the earth."[56]

The Al Jazeera English management had asked me to cover the Friday protests on December 27, and to interview Muslim Brotherhood members in the hotel to get their reactions to these events. I'd refused to host Brotherhood members in the hotel but dispatched Peter, Baher, a cameraman and a security guard to briefly cover a protest staged outside a mosque.

"You interviewed a Brotherhood student in the hotel just last week," one of the managers in Doha had argued, but I stood my ground.

"Last week they weren't terrorists," I told Marwa, when she dropped by the hotel after work on December 29, bringing more medication for my shoulder. The pain coupled with Egypt's bleak political climate had put me in a dark mood.

Peter had invited Marwa and me to join him for an evening out, but I'd declined on the doctor's advice to move as little as possible. I lay on the bed brooding about how far the government was willing to go with its anti-Brotherhood campaign. I thought about what it would take for the pro-Brotherhood managers in Doha to realize what a precarious position its journalists in Egypt were in—even though we were independent—and how much more essential our proper accreditation was than it had been even weeks ago.

A loud knock on the door interrupted our conversation.

"Did you order room service?" Marwa asked, sitting up in the chair.

I shook my head. Struggling up from the bed, I walked to the door and peered through the peephole to see a waiter standing on the other side, a fruit tray held aloft.

"I didn't order anything," I called through the door.

"Complimentary, sir!"

Marwa had already risen from the chair and looked alarmed. I cursed living in a country where I could not associate freely with my fiancée without impugning her reputation and I wished that we were in Canada instead.

"Okay. Give me a minute," I yelled to the waiter as Marwa crossed the room to the balcony and slid open the door.

"It's freezing out there. Why don't you just wait in the bathroom?" But she had already stepped outside and closed the door behind her. I drew the curtains and walked back to the door, wondering who would have sent a complimentary fruit tray. An uneasy feeling tripped down my spine as I turned the lock.

Several men rushed into my field of view. Too late, I jammed my foot against the door to block their entry. A tall man in a black trench coat forced it open, pushing past me into the room, followed by a distinguished-looking man in a black, brass-buttoned uniform, and close to a dozen others in civilian clothes and uniforms. The distinguished officer said nothing, but seemed to be directing the others. A man with a video camera filmed the entire scene, and behind him another held a still camera, its flash unnerving. I knew, even as my mind shuttered in denial, that the moment my staff and I feared had arrived. The Cairo office of Al Jazeera English was being raided.

I thought of Marwa. I glanced towards the balcony, a motion the uniformed officer was quick to pick up on—he nodded to the man in the trench coat who parted the curtains and opened the door. I wanted to cry out to her, but held my tongue. Her back was to the room and I could see her hands tightly gripping the rail. Beyond her, the backdrop of the city skyline and the tranquil waters of the Nile seemed surreal. I stepped towards the balcony, but the man in the trench coat stopped me before I could reach her, ordering me to sit in a nearby armchair.

"Please, come in," he asked her.

Marwa took her hands from the railing and covered her face, but didn't move. "Turn off the camera first," she said.

The man in the trench coat turned to me. "Tell her to come in. We have to photograph her face."

"Who are you people?" Marwa demanded.

"We are with national security," he replied. "We have a warrant to search this room."

"Marwa, just come in. It will be okay," I said, though I had little confidence that it would be.

"Tell them to turn the video camera off," she repeated, her voice muffled behind her hands.

The officer who seemed in charge silently signalled the cameraman and photographer to move to the adjoining room and, when they'd left, Marwa finally stepped inside, though she didn't remove her hands from her face.

"Why are you doing this?" she asked, her voice high with alarm.

"Marwa, please," I said, willing her to calm down.

"I can't be photographed! It will be in the newspaper. I can't be seen here in the hotel with you. My reputation will be ruined."

I pleaded with the officer to let her go as the man in the trench coat led her over to a desk on the other side of the room and started questioning her. He turned back to me briefly, ordering me to open the room safe where I kept my Canadian passport and several hundred dollars cash.

"Count it." He gestured towards the cash.

One by one I thumbed the bills and set them on the top of the bureau. When I finished, I looked up to see the video camera trained on me and the man in the trench coat at my side.

"Again," he said. "Slowly."

Through the haze of stress, I grasped that I had become part of a production, a sinister story in which I was the villain. Around me, officers rifled roughly through the contents of the room, throwing everything they considered evidence on the bed: gas masks, flak jackets, laptops, cameras, lights, tripods, printers, TV screens, monitors, hard-drives, cables and live broadcast units. The camera-man and photographer filmed the growing pile as another officer documented each item on paper. All the while, the uniformed officer watched silently.

Now the man in the trench coat motioned for me to take a seat. "It seems you have a whole TV channel here, Mohamed," he said. That he knew my name and addressed me with such familiarity unnerved me, but his next question shocked me.

"So you are the Al Jazeera Mubasher kingpin, operating secretly from the Marriott?"

It was so preposterous, I wondered if this was all a mistake. "I don't work for Mubasher Misr," I said.

"Are you the bureau chief here?"

The mention of the banned channel worried me, and I tried side-stepping the question. "I run my own production services and give content to many channels."

His face flushed with annoyance.

"Google me," I said, hoping my bluff would work.

He grabbed an open laptop from the bed and pushed it towards me. "Enter the password."

I told him I didn't have the passwords, that the laptops belonged to the video editors. At that moment, another officer rushed into the room with a piece of paper. "We found a copy of this ID at the front desk," he said as the man in the trench coat skimmed the page.

"Who is Baher Mohamed?" he asked.

"He's a friend. I put his name on the room so he can get free access to the pool, gym and breakfast hall."

"Do you know any foreigners in the hotel?"

"None at all."

He pressed on with his interrogation. From time to time, my eyes met Marwa's with a look that I hoped was reassuring. She had given up hiding her face and now sat near the desk looking forlorn. He questioned me for the better part of an hour, then abruptly announced we were leaving.

"Please let her go," I said quietly as I saw the terrified look on Marwa's face. "She has no part in this."

He said nothing, only ushered us towards the door. On the way out I grabbed the plastic bag containing the refill of painkillers and my favourite jacket, the dark blue bomber that had kept me safe during the January 25 revolution. Almost a dozen men escorted us down the hallway to a service elevator. As we waited for the car to arrive, the man in the trench coat leaned his head towards mine.

"Don't worry, Fahmy," he whispered. "We will let her go."

Relief flooded through me. "You do that," I said, "and I will speak more openly."

When the elevator opened on the ground, I was relieved to see an empty service corridor. While I cared little for my own reputation, I did not want Marwa paraded through the Marriott Hotel lobby by Egypt's security police. The officers led us through a maze of hallways to the hotel's security surveillance room where a uniformed security guard sat monitoring a bank of TV screens. I looked around the room and my heart skipped a beat. Sitting on a gold-coloured couch in the corner, surrounded by a cluster of officers, was Peter Greste, his beloved Akubra hat resting on his lap. I said "hi," with what I hoped sounded like cheerfulness. But at that moment, I knew our situation was very serious.

I told Peter I would try to handle it, then warned him I had said I wasn't the bureau chief, a strategy I hoped would redirect their suspicions away from us and towards the management in Doha.

Then the silent officer spoke for the first time, gesturing me towards the couch. "You can sit there beside Detective Columbo."

I dropped onto the couch beside Peter. Marwa, her face pale, remained standing amid a group of officers.

"Come, sit here." I patted the empty cushion beside me, but

she shook her head vigorously, retreating to the far side of the room.

The officer now moved away to stand silently again in the corner, while his trench-coated colleague sat on the edge of the desk in front of us and smiled, nodded towards Peter. "Your Al Jazeera buddy," he said. "Are you going to talk now, Fahmy?"

"All right," I offered. "All the equipment upstairs belongs to Al Jazeera English. Not a piece of it is mine."

Our interrogator signalled the cameraman over. He positioned himself to Peter's left and began filming. Marwa had been wise to refuse to sit beside me on the couch. The man in the trench coat asked me to repeat what I'd just said so it could be captured on tape and I complied. Then he began a new round of questions.

"Who are your cameramen? How many are there?"

The last thing I wanted to do was expose my unaccredited staff to danger. "There's more than one," I said, stalling for time.

"Tell me their names."

"They are all registered as press. They have press passes." This was true. My cameramen Omar Fouad and Mahdy el-Anani had been in the business for decades.

"What are their names," he asked again, "so we can check what you are saying is true."

The camera was unnerving, the flash making me see stars.

"Do you not know their names?"

"Of course I know their names."

"Okay, then, who are they? Who is working here with you?"

I thought of Omar's two little daughters and how horrific it would be for them if their dad was arrested at home. And what about Mahdy Al-Anani? He was in the middle of planning his wedding. "I don't want to say," I answered after a long silence. "They have press passes from the ministry."

"Right," the man in the trench coat said, before changing tack. "When you conduct interviews, shouldn't the cameramen be there?"

I regarded him warily, wondering where he was headed with this question. An image of the pro–Muslim Brotherhood protestor we had recently interviewed in our hotel room popped into my mind. Could it be that he was trying to connect us to the Muslim Brotherhood?

"We don't conduct interviews inside," I said.

"So why are there cameras and lights in the room?"

My shoulder throbbed and I held it briefly with my left hand. "There are no interviews in that room," I repeated emphatically. "We go outside to conduct interviews. On the street."

He looked at me shrewdly. "The cameras in that room were ready to film. They were obviously set up in that room to be used."

"The cameras are ready so the correspondent can speak on air."

"Who is this correspondent? What is his name?"

"Me," I said, "and sometimes the man sitting next to me." I looked at Peter, wishing he could speak Arabic and help us manoeuvre out of this nightmare of a situation.

"Who is he? What is the name of the man sitting next to you?"

"Peter," I said, and Peter turned to look at me.

"Mr. Peter," the man in the trench coat addressed him directly, "what was the last interview you conducted?"

Peter shook his head and raised his hand to indicate that he didn't speak Arabic.

The trench-coat man turned back to me, and the questions continued, round and round. "Who purchased the equipment?"

"It's owned by the channel." I felt as if I was walking through a minefield where any wrong answer would come back to hurt me.

"Who is paying the rent for the room?"

"Not me. The channel."

"How long have you been here?"

"Three months."

"In three months you couldn't find another place to be?"

His question sent a jolt of anger through me. He was asking me the same question I'd been asking Doha since I started. At that moment, I wished to hell that Salah Negm, my boss in Doha, was sitting in this hot seat, not me.

"It's a place to work. Nothing more," I said with a nonchalance I didn't feel.

"Who handles your business at the Al Jazeera channel? Who directly corresponds with you, one-on-one?"

"The management."

"Who are they?"

"The management team in Qatar." The moment the word "Qatar" was out of my mouth, I knew I'd made a terrible mistake since the government of Qatar was so staunchly pro-Brotherhood. I could sense the ears of my interrogator perk up.

"In *Qatar*?" He drew out the word. "Who are these people in Qatar?"

"The managers there." I was kicking myself for my carelessness. *Why had I gone there?*

"What are their names?"

One of the other officers leaned into the conversation, demanding, "Do you have a permit to film?"

"I have an expired press pass from CNN." Even to my ears, my answer sounded weak.

"The last time you were in Qatar was when?"

"September, for the job interview."

"Did you go from Qatar to Turkey?"

"No, I came right back to Egypt and started working." I knew what he was insinuating. Turkey's President Erdogan was also a staunch Muslim Brotherhood supporter.

"Where do you film?" My interrogator pressed on. My shoulder throbbed and I worried about Marwa, wishing I'd never asked her to deliver the painkillers to the hotel. For what seemed like an eternity, the questions kept coming: What do you film? Was there a time you went out and filmed protests? Who handles the money? How do you give the footage you film to Qatar? Do you work for other channels?

At one point he circled back to the issue of press passes. "Does anyone have credentials on the team you work with?" he asked.

"Yes, of course."

"Who? Tell me their names so we can check the information."

"The two cameramen."

"What are their names?"

"Omar and Mahdy."

"Omar what? What is his full name?"

"Omar Mohamed," I said, stopping short of revealing my cameraman's last name.

"Omar Mohamed *what*?"

I looked at Marwa, her huge eyes dark pools of anxiety. "I don't know."

"Okay, Mahdy?"

"Mahdy el-Anani," I said, feeling defeated. "They have credentials; they have been working in this industry for thirty years. These are very respectable workers."

I was angry with myself for having given the name of one of my staff and angry with the officer in front of me.

"I have been with Al Jazeera for *three* months," I said bluntly, "and I asked more than once: 'Is our legal situation all sorted in Egypt?' and they said 'Yes, legally, everything is in order at Al Jazeera English.' Otherwise, I would *never* have accepted the job."

"We are not accusing you of anything," the interrogator said, catching me off guard. "We are simply asking you to verify information before you are brought in front of the general prosecutor."

I slumped back on the couch, cradling my broken shoulder, unsure how to interpret his unexpected words.

"We will take this information to the proper authorities and they will confirm it," he said. "It is up to them. If there's been an error they will say, 'Thank you, we were mistaken.'"

I felt a glimmer of optimism. *Of course* they were mistaken. The state prosecutor reviewing the case file would realize it immediately.

He stood up from the desk. "Let's go," he said.

It felt bizarre to have the camera follow Peter and me as we walked down a service hallway and emerged from the hotel into a dark alley where a black sedan and white minivan waited. We were accustomed to producing stories, not being subjects in them.

As I climbed into the minivan I looked around for Marwa. I called out to her—"Phone Al Jazeera!"—feeling utterly helpless as I watched the man in the trench coat usher her into the back seat of the sedan.

"Tell me the truth," an officer riding next to me asked in a conspiratorial tone as we started moving. "Is this girl, Marwa, a prostitute?"

"No," I said, shocked. "She is my fiancée, and she is a good girl."

I glanced over my shoulder to Peter sitting in the back seat of the van—we said nothing. I could tell we were heading to the Kasr el-Nile police station near Tahrir Square—I knew the station well. For my last story with CNN, I'd arranged for Ian Lee and me to tour the city with a unit from the station to report on how police were enforcing a recently imposed curfew. I had interviewed the station warden, smoking and drinking tea in his office. After we had finished, he ordered his officers to drive me home so I would not encounter trouble at the military checkpoints. I hoped the warden would be at the station, but when we arrived, the man I had met was nowhere to be seen. Another sat behind the warden's desk, and I was back inside the station as a prisoner rather than the confident journalist I had been only months before.

The officers who had brought us in seated Peter and me on a wooden bench, taking Marwa inside the warden's office. I was agonizing over how I could get her out of the situation, sick at the thought of anything happening to her, when I saw her brother enter the station. He walked into the office and moments later Marwa emerged with him and bolted towards the exit. I got up and rushed to her.

I turned to her brother. "I am sorry for all of this," I said.

I returned to the bench to try to give Peter a sense of what was happening. He was silent, and I thought of how hard this must be on him, not speaking a word of Arabic. Moments later the police escorted the two of us to a windowless cell crammed with a dozen men ranging in appearance from downtrodden to downright frightening. It smelled of stale food and unwashed bodies. The entrance was a massive black metal door, and once closed, the room's only opening to the outside was a small cutout hatch affixed with a sliding metal plate. A clutter of clothing, prayer mats, plastic containers and personal items lined the walls and the grimy floor, and rows of plastic bags hung like albino bats from nails pounded into the concrete walls. One of the inmates, a strapping, lightly bearded man dressed in black, approached us immediately.

"This is my cell," he said.

My heart raced as several others moved in behind him. I recalled the story of Eric Lang, a forty-nine-year-old Frenchman and longtime Cairo resident who had been picked up by police several months earlier for breaking curfew and held in this very station. He'd never left because fellow inmates had beaten him to death. Many of the men looked as if they had been living in the cell for weeks—we later learned that some had been there for months. Others seemed almost delirious, with eyes like dark houses where no one lived. Thankfully, the leader turned out to be more curious than hostile and began asking questions about who we were and why we were there. Several inmates volunteered their own stories, their words coming to me as if through water, muffled and distorted by my unease. I translated for Peter, relaying the gist of what I heard. Our fellow cellmates came from all walks of life, had been arrested for myriad reasons.

One of the most frightening was a wiry, middle-aged Syrian with fair skin and brackish-green eyes. The cell leader, who I came to think of as "the bodybuilder" for his heavily muscled physique, told us that the Syrian had been accused of killing several boys during a protest, a claim he seemed proud of. The bodybuilder, by contrast, said he had been arrested simply for attending the Rabaa sit-in. "It took half a dozen officers to pin me down and handcuff me."

An emaciated man with a long bedraggled beard complained he'd spent half his life in prisons because of his religious beliefs. Another, a cloying textile merchant, complained that his wife had framed him to get his money; he was obsessed with Peter's grey felt Akubra hat and asked to feel its texture. After the introductions, our cellmates laid out several trays of cooked food their families had delivered and invited Peter and me to eat with them. The two of us huddled close together in a corner of the room, legs crossed, backs against the wall facing the other inmates and plucked stuffed grape leaves and kebabs from trays passed around.

Peter leaned over and whispered to me. "I have eight thousand dollars cash in my pocket."

I looked at him, my eyebrows rocketing up my forehead.

"It's to pay my hotel and per diem expenses."

I looked around the room nervously. I couldn't have felt more like a target had someone painted one on my back. "We'll hide it in our shoes when they go to sleep," I whispered.

Around us, prisoners continued telling stories of their arrests. I half listened, my eyes following the murderous Syrian's every move, scrutinizing his body language, the direction of his slack gaze, his incoherent mumblings. After dinner the bodybuilder ordered the men to clear their dishes and tidy the cell. They complied without question or complaint, tucking leftovers into containers shoved against walls and into dim corners or stuffing them into suspended plastic bags. Then they spread prayer mats and knelt in cramped rows.

As they began to pray, their backs to us, bodies prostrate, I seized the opportunity. "Where's the money?" I whispered to Peter.

He surreptitiously pulled a thick fold of bills from his pocket and we quickly divided it and then placed equal-sized stacks into the bottoms of our shoes. We'd exchanged few words since our arrest, but I was grateful for his familiar presence. I was also filled with gratitude when, a short time later, the guard slid open the hatch in the door and I saw the face of Mohamed Suleiman, one of our Al Jazeera English security guards, peering in. I waved to him as Peter helped me stand.

"I came as soon as I saw it on the news," Mohamed said. "It's all over the Egyptian and Western TV. Are you guys okay?"

"Fine," I lied. "What are they saying?"

"The government's accusing you of being members of the Muslim Brotherhood and calling you terrorists. They arrested both Baher and Mohamed Fawzy from their homes. We don't even know where they are."

Shaken, I translated this news for Peter and watched Mohamed hand the guard money and cigarettes—a bribe.

"How can they accuse us of being Muslim Brotherhood if the state prosecutor hasn't even questioned us yet?" I asked. "Who leaked this to the press?"

The prison guard closed the hatch before I had time to say more and Peter and I numbly returned to our corner of the cell. The bodybuilder, who had overheard the conversation, literally crawled over to give us advice.

"They will torture you at state security," he whispered. "Keep your answers short."

"I have a Canadian passport. They can't touch me," I said quickly, before my bravado left me. "What kind of torture are you talking about?"

"If they take you to Lazoghly [one of the main Homeland Security locations in downtown Cairo] you will be electrocuted, beaten and hung by your hands until you talk, even if you have nothing to confess."

I shut my eyes and leaned back against the rough wall, feeling sick. He was right. I'd covered stories where suspects were brutally tortured during interrogation. I opened my bottle of painkillers and popped two into my mouth. The pills lodged in my throat and I swallowed in hard, dry gulps, choking them down. I looked at Peter. Should I translate what I'd just heard, I wondered, and thought the better of it.

In the cell men bedded down, lying haphazardly head to toe or curled back to back like brooding spouses. A prisoner banged on the door, yelling for someone to let him out to use the toilet. With so little space it was impossible to recline without the unwelcome intrusion of a stranger's touch, the moist, heavy brush of breath. I struggled in vain to find a position that didn't send shards of pain lancing through my shoulder and enviously eyed Peter who, hanging his hat on a nail, had curled into a fetal position beside me and fallen asleep. I lay on my left side, my back propped against the wall, willing sleep that would not come. The stacks of money in my shoes felt like bricks, visible to anyone who looked my way, and my eyes darted nervously towards the Syrian. Neither he nor the bodybuilder slept, the latter constantly cursing the accused murderer. After the guards had turned off the lights and the prisoners had fallen into fitful sleep, his harassment escalated to slapping and verbal abuse.

"How long has it been since you've been fucked in the ass?" the bodybuilder whispered, and then: "If you don't watch yourself, I will have you sent downstairs to the cell where the Frenchman was killed."

I lay wide awake through the night recoiling with every rustle of movement, every inadvertent touch. At one point the bodybuilder and the Syrian scuffled, falling on sleeping prisoners, awaking several who cursed and yelled at them.

"What's going on?" Peter mumbled.

"It's nothing," I said, "Go back to sleep."

Morning arrived when a guard opened the hatch to tell us we were being transferred to the State Security Prosecution headquarters for questioning. I peered through the opening and saw armed police escorting a handful of hard-edged men, handcuffed in twos, out the door. Moments later the guard yanked open our cell door and ordered us out. He snapped one ring of a pair of handcuffs on my left wrist, the other on Peter's right, and led us outside. I gulped the fresh morning air as guards prodded us towards a police-transfer truck. I'd reported stories of men who had been seriously beaten or died of heat exhaustion while in the coffin-like vehicles. Cramped and airless, these metal sweatboxes often carried dozens of men crammed inside. When guards opened the back door, I was relieved to see it was empty. Peter climbed inside and I followed, balancing with difficulty as I navigated the three narrow steps into the truck. I glanced up and saw to my relief our Al Jazeera English security guard standing at a distance beside our car and driver, waving to us—I'd been worried that the truck might drive to some unknown location and that Peter and I would simply "disappear."

The cage was strewn with garbage and smelled of urine. Peter and I sat silently on a long metal bench as the truck began moving. I gripped the bench with my handcuffed hand, trying to protect my shoulder from the unsteady ride, and stared through a tiny mesh-covered window at Cairo's early-morning streets. Perhaps thirty minutes later we passed through the gates of the State Security Prosecution headquarters, a four-storey building located in Cairo's Fifth Settlement neighbourhood. We were escorted up to an empty second-floor office. A short time later, a delegation arrived from the Australian embassy to speak with Peter. When they left he told me they merely wanted him to sign consent forms for access to information and representation.

We waited with a guard for what seemed like hours in the empty room. The handcuffs chafed and Peter and I nodded in and out of sleep, alternatively slumping in our chairs and shaking ourselves awake. My shoulder throbbed and the pressure in my bladder eventually became unbearable.

"I need to use the bathroom," I said, finally.

The guard called another in to keep an eye on Peter before handcuffing himself to me. As we walked down the hallway towards the bathroom, I saw Baher, handcuffed to a guard, sitting slumped on a chair puffing nervously on a cigarette. I quickly lurched in his direction, pulling the guard with me.

"I just want to ask him for a cigarette," I said without stopping.

Baher looked up, his brown eyes heavy with worry. "Fahmy, they raided my home, took my laptops and passport and shot my dog," he said in a rush. "They took me to a Central Security Forces camp in the desert. What's happening?"

I asked him for a cigarette, leaning in as he reached for his pack. "It seems we're in deep shit. I don't know, something to do with the Brotherhood," I said.

Baher handed me a cigarette and held up a lighter. "They raided Mohamed Fawzy's home, too. I just saw him handcuffed to an officer, but he didn't even look at me."

I inhaled smoke, my eyes searching the hall for our cameraman before my guard yanked me away toward the bathroom.

After another period of waiting, the guards escorted Peter and me to separate prosecution rooms. I was nervous as I entered a spacious, air-conditioned office where the state prosecutor assigned to our case sat at a large mahogany desk. The brass nameplate on the desk read *Rami el-Sayed*. He motioned me to sit in a chair positioned sideways to his desk. A court clerk sat in a second chair that faced me across a low wooden table. Behind him was a comfortable seating area with a couch and two armchairs; beyond, a large window through which I glimpsed a parking lot. The prosecutor sat smoking, sifting through papers, a nearby ashtray mounded with butts. There was a knock on the door and an office boy entered. "The lawyers are here, sir," he said.

Two men walked in and introduced themselves, saying they were with the Farag Fathi law firm representing Al Jazeera—the lawyers Baher had spoken disparagingly of and who had not returned my phone calls. El-Sayed asked them to take a seat on the couch where they could observe the interrogation but not ask questions. Reassured by the presence of legal counsel and sure of my innocence, I decided to break the ice with a lighthearted comment. "Sir, I have no idea why I am here, but I can recommend the breakfast at the Marriott." I smiled at the prosecutor and, to my relief, he smiled back, offering me a cigarette and ordering the office boy to serve me a Turkish coffee.

"How's your coffee?" he asked after a minute.

"Wonderful, thanks," I said, feeling more reassured—until his next words snapped me upright.

"You know you are going to pay the price for Al Jazeera and Qatar's war against Egypt. And yes," he said with a smirk, "I will visit the hotel with an investigative team tomorrow to try the breakfast."

The coffee was bitter on my tongue. "I work for the English channel, not the Arabic. And I have worked there less than four months," I said. "Before that I was with CNN. What am I even accused of?"

El-Sayed picked up the phone, requesting the evidence against me be brought in. A clerk appeared, setting a stack of paper on the desk.

"Mohamed Fadel Fahmy," the prosecutor began in a formal tone, "you are accused of joining the Muslim Brotherhood Group, whose goal is to change the regime by force, including by terrorism, and to violate the freedom of individuals, target public institutions to undermine public order, and jeopardize the safety and security of society; of providing the Brotherhood with monies, supplies, equipment, machinery and information; of being in possession of communication and broadcast equipment without obtaining a proper permit from the relevant administrative authority; of intentionally broadcasting video clips, images, and false news to give the outside world an impression that the country is undergoing a state of internal strife and civil war . . . , which would have disturbed public security, harmed public interest, spread terror among the general public and stirred strife. What do you say to these accusations?"

I looked incredulously at the lawyers and then back at el-Sayed. "Are you *serious?*"

"Answer," he said sharply.

"I deny all these accusations."

"The suspect denied," el-Sayed said and I watched the clerk record his response. When he'd finished, el-Sayed asked, "Don't you know Al Jazeera is banned in Egypt?"

"I know Al Jazeera *Mubasher Misr* is banned." I said, emphasizing the words. "I work with Al Jazeera *English* and I have assurances from my bosses that we are operating legally."

El-Sayed repeated my response to the clerk who wrote it down. This procedure, awkward, stilted and repetitive, would continue throughout the interrogation.

"Your English reports were broadcast on Al Jazeera Mubasher [Misr] on many occasions. Do you think you can fool us?"

"It only happened twice and I have emails voicing my objection and responses from my bosses in Doha promising it won't happen again." I later learned that our reports were aired at least half-a-dozen times.

"Is Al Jazeera not all one network funded and managed by the same CEO, the Emir's cousin?"

"I would not have taken the job if there was no separation between the editorial line of the Arabic and English arms of the network. I placed conditions on management that I conduct independent newsgathering, booking, and reporting. I don't like what Al Jazeera Mubasher [Misr] does."

"Why didn't you have a press pass?"

I mentioned my expired CNN pass again, and that Al Jazeera had promised me many times that they were in the process of getting us accreditation and passes.

"Who in the world leaves CNN for this cheap Al Jazeera channel?" He held up a hand to the clerk to indicate his comment was off the record.

Before I could answer, he asked for a detailed account of my career. I described every job I had taken, conflict zones I had reported from, books I had written, even mentioning my grandfather's high-ranking position as police general. El-Sayed appeared unmoved, parroting my words to the clerk and stopping only when interrupted by a knock on the door. Two men entered with a cart carrying equipment seized from the hotel room and piled it on the floor in front of the prosecutor's desk.

"Suite 2056 was booked under your name," el-Sayed said. "All these gas masks, flak jackets, hard drives, cameras and their content—everything confiscated from the hotel—is registered to you personally. The investigation states you distributed sixteen keys to foreign agents and you hosted Brotherhood terrorists in the room."

"They are not 'agents,'" I retorted emphatically. "They are journalists. As for the room—I arrived to a makeshift office and a room registered in a British reporter's name. Al Jazeera asked me to transfer it to my own to avoid paying double the rate foreigners pay."

I answered each question with a sickening sensation that the interrogation was going downhill fast. How did I know Peter and Baher? What did I think of the Muslim Brotherhood? Who was Dominic Kane? Sue Turton?

"What about this Dutch woman, Johanna Ideniette?"

"I've never heard of her," I said. I had met for coffee, once, with a Dutch reporter at the hotel, but her name was Rena Netjas.

El-Sayed lit a cigarette and rocked back in his chair. "Strange," he drew out the word, exhaling slowly before dropping his bombshell. "Do you know we have been watching your every move in the hotel since October, monitoring your phones, and even observing your private dinners with Marwa Omara?"

He indicated to the clerk that his last comment was off the record as I tried to keep my composure.

"If you've been watching me," I said, "then you know I am no Brotherhood member. I'm a liberal. I drink. I hate the Brotherhood."

The prosecutor smirked.

"Mr. el-Sayed," I said earnestly, "I am *innocent.*"

"Mohamed," his voice was condescending, "I have detailed evidence in front of me. Egypt is going through very tough times and we have many who would destroy us. Qatar, your employer, is our number-one enemy. We have to cleanse the country," he said. "So, we collect all the apples, and pick out the bad ones."

His words underscored what I most feared: that my staff and I had, overnight, become ensnared in the escalating tensions between the Egyptian government and the Muslim Brotherhood.

At that moment, I became very worried. "Sir, I have a broken shoulder. Can you please transfer me to a hospital?" I said, grasping for an out.

"Don't worry, I will take care of you," el-Sayed promised.

He ordered the clerk to put the pages of his transcription on the table in front of me and asked me to sign every page, attesting to their accuracy. Then he announced that the questioning was over and called in the guards to take me away.

In shock, my panicked brain clutched onto his last words: *Don't worry, I will take care of you.* Did he understand, I wondered? In the tumult of distress, I became convinced that the hospital was indeed where I was headed, not prison.

Downstairs, the guards escorted me back to a blue transport truck. I clambered awkwardly inside to find Peter already there.

"Can you believe this shit?" I said in disbelief as a guard handcuffed us together. "They're accusing us of being terrorists."

Peter was dumbfounded—his interrogation had been cut short because there had been no interpreter available.

"I think they're taking me to the hospital, Peter," I said, my mind fixated on that hopeful possibility as we merged into traffic. I peered through the window as the prison truck sped through the dark streets of Cairo. Lights and buildings blurred, the truck accelerated and slowed, wove one way, then another towards our unknown destination. Twenty minutes later I saw high walls, light poles, felt the truck slow, then stop. A voice ordered us out and Peter and I emerged into a dimly lit yard where a few men in civilian clothes waited. Beyond them loomed a squat, nondescript building, weak light filtering from small high windows. A man in our welcoming party fumbled through pockets, jacket, pants, produced a small key, unlocked our cuffs.

We were ushered towards the building. Then, a hurried conversation in Arabic. Words drifted in the air, indecipherable to Peter, but clear to me. Only I was to enter the building. A military hospital? There was no time for goodbyes, as the men hustled us in opposite directions, Peter back into the blue truck, me inside the building. I left the cool night air behind and entered a large deserted foyer. It was only then, as I stood on the stark cold concrete, took in the pale green walls and high inner metal gate, that I fully grasped where the blue truck had delivered me. I was in prison.

CHAPTER 9

DUNGEON OF RADICALS

January 6–30, 2014

Scorpion prison is a concrete tomb. Days into my incarceration, time warps, my thoughts scatter. I hunch under my blanket in a dank corner of my cell like a skittish animal, deadened by the whine of mosquitos, the low timbre of voices raised in prayer, occasionally startled from my stupor by the shout of a guard, the clank of a distant cell door, the moans of other prisoners.

Then, on January 6, I hear a guard moving down the corridor, shouting the names of prisoners, and hoist myself to a sitting position, until—"Fahmy, get ready! You're going for interrogation."

The thought of leaving these close walls, moving my body, breathing fresh air, glimpsing the sun, buoys me. After the guard unbolts my door, I cross the corridor to Khaled al-Qazzaz's cell, extending my hand through his hatch. President Morsi's one-time foreign affairs secretary shakes it, moves to one side, points to a photo of his wife and four children on his wall. The guard down the corridor is opening other cells, when Essam al-Haddad, one of Morsi's top four presidential aides with responsibility for foreign affairs and promoted by the former president to the Brotherhood's Guidance Bureau, calls me over. I peer through his hatch, two cell doors to the right of my own, surprised to see that he is much smaller than I imagined, just over five feet. He wears thick glasses and sports a heavy black mustache. "Fahmy," he says, as he reaches out to me through the hatch, "take this small Quran with you."

I stare at the tiny holy book, accept it graciously. I do not tell him I am not a devout, or even practicing, Muslim.

"If you see my son, Gehad, please let him know I am in good health and holding up well." I'd met Gehad al-Haddad on occasion through my work. He had been arrested in September after the interim government's crackdown on officials loyal to the ousted Morsi—he had been the spokesman for the Brotherhood and with his flawless English, the charismatic go-to guy for Western reporters.

The guard calls my name and I fall in with the others. I scan the prisoners: sixteen men in white, pyjama-like garb, we shuffle along to Scorpion's main hall. With the exception of the three students, the men are unfamiliar, many from other wings of the prison. Some appear frail and haggard, others strong and fearsome. Almost all carry Qurans and a few clutch prayer mats and plastic bags. A guard approaches me and, without warning, hooks the metal curve of a handcuff around my left wrist, then snaps the other side closed around the right wrist of a tall, bearded man. He nods, acknowledging my Quran. Minutes later, the guards march us into a garage and a blue truck backs towards us. Awkwardly, we ascend the three steps into its dark, cramped cage.

The prisoners take their seats, eight a side and crammed, knee-to-knee, shoulder-to-shoulder on the narrow metal benches lining opposite walls of the truck. I lean forward to avoid the painful crush of contact. The smell of urine is overpowering and the heat and stench of unwashed bodies makes me want to gag. As the truck emerges from the garage, I crane my neck towards the natural light streaming through the mesh-covered window. The familiar cacophony of Cairo street traffic is a balm. The driver has turned on a small portable radio, and one prisoner lets out a whoop at the news of three policemen recently killed at a checkpoint by terrorists. Joyfully he begins singing the lyrics of a jihadi song. Soon others join in, drowning out everything outside:

> Brandishing our guns along with our explosive belts,
> We will cut off the head of the snake,
> Blow up . . . blow up . . . blow up the courthouse,
> And the Ministry of Defense.
> Jihad, Jihad, Jihad is our path.

I have often cringed hearing Osama bin Laden's and Ayman al-Zawahiri's audio recordings calling on the "soldiers of Allah" to indulge in jihad. The violent struggle against enemies of Islam is associated with "jihad," even though it is an Islamic term referring to the religious duty of Muslims—the act of struggling, persevering, striving in the way of God to spread and protect Islam. It is now often misunderstood as only a "holy war." I interviewed jihadists in Lebanon's Roumieh Prison during my job with the Red Cross in 2007—radicals from Fatah al-Islam, a group inspired by al-Qaeda, who had been arrested on the field after a three-month-long battle with the Lebanese Army. Some of those young, bearded fighters had never pulled a trigger or carried a weapon. Their job was to cook and clean for the fighters and by performing these chores, they committed self-prescribed jihad. One of those five poorly educated cooks, a twenty-five-year-old Saudi man, had been caught with a suicide belt, wrapped around his waist by his masters on a whim, and instructed to push the trigger if apprehended. He did. Only destiny saved the officers—and him—when the trigger jammed.

"Violent jihad" has to be declared by someone who disciples consider an Islamic authority (which leaves it open to many comers), who sanctions it as a "just war" on the grounds that Islam and its people are facing a threat so great that they can only overcome it by bearing arms. This matter of a "just war" remains controversial, leaves many defenders of the religion confused about which scholar to listen to, and finds fighters on the ground turning their guns on various "enemies."

Being imprisoned among these self-proclaimed jihadists, and listening to their murderous song, convinces me more than ever that "just wars" sanctioned by extremists like Ayman al-Zawahiri, whether he is hiding in a cave or a palace, easily attract lost souls longing for a cause to give their world meaning—young, disenfranchised and economically disempowered Muslims and mercenaries alike living in the Middle East, Paris, London, New York, or anywhere on the globe—who sign on to jihad.

Author Lawrence Wright states in his book *The Looming Tower* that Ayman al-Zawahiri hopes to restore the caliphate, which has not exercised real power since the thirteenth century and ended in 1924 with the fall of the Ottoman Empire. Wright outlines his ambitions: that when the caliphate is re-established, "Egypt would become a rallying point for the rest of the Islamic world, leading the jihad against the West." The last caliphate, the Ottoman Empire, had numerous barbaric practices, including selling non-Muslim girls as sex slaves—much the same as what ISIS is now doing in its self-prescribed capital of Al-Raqqa in Syria. "Then history would make a new turn, God willing," al-Zawahiri writes, "in the opposite direction against the empire of the United States and the world's Jewish government."[57]

The Muslim Brotherhood is viewed as moderate because unlike ISIS and al-Qaeda, who only know the language of blood, it's willing to seek theocracy through the ballot box or other political tools at its disposal. But the patient and often more politically savvy Brotherhood, whose philosophy derives from the same Qutbist handbook as al-Qaeda follows—is not opposed to using violence if and when necessary. Whatever the means, the Brotherhood, al-Qaeda, ISIS, al-Nusra and others share the same ideological end: ultimately establishing a global Islamic state.

I feel shaken as the prisoners continue to chant their jihadi songs. In due course they will become words I cannot forget from hearing them so often.

The prisoner leading the chant sits directly across from me, head shaven, green eyes flashing with intensity. He is short, menacing, with the body of a prizefighter. I do not chant and, feeling his eyes on me, drop my gaze. Sohaib, one of the students I am being charged with, filled with his usual reckless energy, booms out the words, and the driver, in response to the outpouring of anti-military fervour, increases his speed, deliberately brakes abruptly. Bodies slide and slam against one another and I press my right arm against my chest, trying to stay upright. The men curse and take up the song again. I brace myself. Close my eyes.

"Brother, why aren't you singing?" The harsh question comes from my neighbour—the huge man I am handcuffed to. I manage to reply calmly, "I make jihad with my pen."

The green-eyed prisoner across from me stops singing. "He is the Al Jazeera journalist!" he calls out.

I hold my breath, expecting the worst, but my Al-Jazeera-Muslim-Brotherhood-terrorist reputation turns out to be an asset. The man smiles, tells me his name is Ammar and that he's a boxer and a bomb-maker. The man I'm handcuffed to introduces himself as Abu Omar, tells me he has just returned from Syria to join what he calls the "jihad in Egypt against Sisi and the illegitimate regime that overthrew President Morsi and the Brotherhood." Another prisoner confesses: "They caught me on my way to Turkey," and others follow, share their stories. They become quite a cheerful bunch as the truck driver continues to speed and weave maniacally through the streets of Cairo for the forty-five minutes it takes to get to the state prosecution building.

As we pull into the parking lot, Sohaib yells, *"Allahu Akbar! God is Great! Allahu Akbar!"* They all chime in. The chanting intensifies as we file out of the truck. We walk past a line of riot police, descending a staircase into a cavernous dark space like an underground garage. Abu Omar whispers to me that it is a huge holding cell. They call it "the dungeon."

Suddenly Ammar, the boxer and bomb-maker, who is ahead near the front of the line, begins bellowing out verses from his jihadi song. I see anger on the faces of the policemen, their emotions surely raw over the recent murders of fellow officers. Two of the guards begin pushing him, and he turns on them, landing several powerful punches with his free arm. I watch as the guards raise their batons and begin beating him and other prisoners rush into the bloody fray.

Abu Omar, who is still cuffed to me, lunges forward, too, pulling me with him down the stairs into the melee. My shoulder wrenches and I cry out in pain, resisting with every ounce of strength I possess as I'm dragged into the hot chaotic centre of the brawl. More riot police charge in, separating us all from the officers and we are shoved into the holding cell.

Ammar's hand is bloody and there are red spatters on his prison whites. Abu Omar shuffles beside me as I take in our surroundings, a massive, windowless, dimly lit bunker crowded with several hundred prisoners. The sight is staggering. They huddle in groups, circle the graffiti-filled walls of the perimeter in twos and threes, eat, pray and proselytize. Many are bearded or built like Ammar, tough, hardcore Islamists who have been trucked in from prisons across Cairo for questioning.

A guard removes our handcuffs, and Abu Omar hurries off. "Come with me," the guard shouts, and I follow to a small adjacent room with a dozen men dressed in prison whites. Minutes later a different door opens and a prison official yells my name, beckoning me into a barren room where a uniformed guard sits at a desk. I am taken aback to see Nancy Youssef, a reporter from McClatchy News who I know well, and another female reporter I do not, and behind them—thank heaven—Marwa.

"Relatives," I hear Nancy say, and the guard's curt reply: "Two minutes. We are doing you a favour."

I am disoriented by their sudden appearance and inexplicably embarrassed by my own. I haven't bathed, brushed my teeth, shaved in more than a week. I find myself almost unable to look at them.

"*Habibi*, how are you?" The term of endearment, the catch in Marwa's voice, her presence here, beyond my reach, is almost too much for me. I am afraid if I look at her I will come undone.

"I am fine," I say, avoiding her eyes.

"Did you get the pillow and sleeping bag I sent?"

"They wouldn't allow it. I'm in solitary. There are so many insects. Can you bring food?"

Marwa holds out a duffle bag and four other bags, tells me they are full of food, toiletries, clothing, water, towels, notebooks, a pen. There are cigarettes "to bribe the guards." I glance at the bags, but make no move to take them. When they leave, the guard will confiscate them.

"It's the insects that are the worst. Why have they put me in the most highly secured prison?" Even to my own ears my words sound confused. Garbled. "I am trying to get to the hospital but it is slow."

Marwa's face crumples. She whispers that she has hired a lawyer, my friend and media legal source Khaled Abou Bakr. Nancy, who would normally be full of questions for her article, is very still, staring at me with distress on her face. Then the guard yells that the visit is over and mutely, I turn and let him lead me away.

Back in the underground dungeon I stand for a long time, scan the crowd, feeling bereft and disoriented. As my eyes slide across the crowd of slow-moving men, I am startled to see Peter Greste leaning against a far wall. I stumble towards him, call his name. He sees me, his eyes light up and he shifts from his sitting position as if to stand. I motion him to remain seated and lower myself painfully to the ground beside him. He looks haggard and one eye is red and appears infected.

"Are you all right?" I ask

"I could be better." He smiles ironically. "I'm in Luman Prison, in solitary." He tells me the prison confiscated the money he had—they will hold it in safekeeping till his release.

"Mine, too," I say.

He watches me cradle my right side. "How's the shoulder?"

I tell him I've asked numerous times to see a doctor. He asks about Baher and I say he's okay, that I can just see his eyes through the hatch of his cell across the corridor from mine. I describe the hellish conditions in Scorpion. Peter tells me about the prisoners he has met and the more humane situation at Luman—the prisoners there receive four-hour daily outings, he says. He speaks positively about the detainee who occupies the cell next to his—Alaa Abdel Fattah. I know Abdel Fattah by reputation, a secular blogger who became one of Egypt's beloved voices of the revolution. Peter says he speaks good English and they talk a lot, and play soccer in the yard. Alaa has lent him an MP3 player containing a variety of songs and books to read.

"Fahmy," a voice interrupts us. "What happened to your arm?" I look up to see Gehad al-Haddad, Essam al-Haddad's son, standing before me and I struggle to my feet to greet him.

"Gehad, your dad sends his greetings. He's in the cell adjacent to mine at Scorpion."

He looks pleased, shares news of his brother to take back to their father. I introduce Peter as my Al Jazeera colleague and manage a light-hearted quip. "He only arrived in Egypt a few weeks ago and he's already a Brotherhood supporter, a terrorist!"

Gehad suggests we walk, and the three of us begin circling the perimeter, joining a stream of men making laps around the huge holding room, taking advantage of the rare opportunity to exercise.

Gehad was one of the first leaders of the Brotherhood arrested after the Rabaa protest, in a highly publicized raid by Sisi's new government—a good "get" for the regime given that he was the inspirational Western-educated spokesman for the foreign press and had worked for several years as head of the Clinton Climate Initiative in Cairo.

Despite the military's significant advantages in arms and capacity, Gehad and the Brotherhood genuinely expected to win the post-Morsi power struggle. They believed that only a small number of generals had supported Morsi's toppling, and that the protests would foment a split within the military, and thus restore Morsi to power. As Eric Trager of the Washington Institute wrote:

> The Brotherhood further believed that it could withstand any attempt to disperse the protests, given that its members were willing to die for the cause. "If they want to disperse the sit-in, they'll have to kill a hundred thousand protestors," [Gehad] told journalist Maged Atef [days before the massacre]. "And they can't do it [because] we're willing to offer 100,000 martyrs." At the same time, the Brotherhood called for pro-Morsi protests across the country. Demonstrators blocked roads and clashed with security forces. All these activities were intended to send a very clear message to the new regime: Egypt would not know stability until the coup was reversed.[58]

As we walk, Gehad describes his arrest after the Rabaa massacre, along with several other high-ranking Brotherhood members, from an apartment near the square, and I wonder why he wasn't in the thick of it with his foot soldiers and the Brotherhood's youth on the ground. I can see Peter soaking in this strangely exclusive interview. I leave the two men and wander the dungeon alone, mesmerized by the volumes of graffiti plastering every inch of wall. The pro-Brotherhood and anti-military slogans are emblematic of the intense ideological battle that has ensnared millions of people—and landed us in prison.

My thoughts are interrupted by a booming call to prayer. I watch scores of inmates obediently line up behind a prisoner who appears to take the role of Imam, a scraggly-bearded man with an upraised arm who shouts at the dark ceiling as if speaking directly to God.

"Allah," he intones in a loud voice. "We ask you to kill the infidels, Abdel Fattah el-Sisi, and prosecutor general Hisham Barakat, and his minions. We ask you to champion our cause and defeat the oppressors!"

The prisoners around him roar like an army heading to battle, shouting, *Allahu Akbar!* They kneel and ready themselves for prayer as I stand gaping in awe at the spectacle. Several stare suspiciously at me and I seek an exit, holding my Quran in plain sight, moving towards Peter and Gehad, who stand away from the circle of worshippers. It seems Gehad has delayed his prayers to capitalize on the opportunity to converse with a Western journalist. "How far have you gotten in your history lesson?" I ask. "January 25?"

"I am talking to him about God now," Gehad says seriously.

I wonder briefly how Peter, a non-believer, feels surrounded by extremists with no sympathy for those who do not embrace Islam. Several men later approach me, asking if I will help them communicate with Peter, hoping they can convert him to Islam, but I deflect them with political small talk.

I spot the three students sitting in a far corner of the room in a cluster of detainees who listen intently to an older bearded man. I walk towards their circle to eavesdrop. The speaker is a hardened Islamist glorifying the extremist path. With a feeling of disgust, I hear him boast of his long career on the battlefield, watch as he fuels the young disciples with tales of glory, inciting them to cross the border and join the fight for global jihad. I realize that this massive holding room for the accused—innocent, guilty or merely disenfranchised—is fertile ground for radicalization.

If idealistic but misdirected young men like the accused students Shadi, Sohaib and Khalid aren't currently radical Islamists, they could possibly be by the time the system is done with them. The Egyptians are repeating the same terrible mistake the Americans made in Iraq, bundling young men into the prison systems with veteran extremists who know exactly what recruitment chords to strike to achieve radicalization of as many Muslims as possible.

It is no secret that ISIS leader Abu Bakr al-Baghdadi spent time in US prisons in Iraq in 2004, including Camp Bucca—through which at least a hundred thousand detainees are said to have funnelled—and the infamous Abu Ghraib. This provided ample opportunity for him to collude with the leadership of al-Qaeda and other incarcerated extremists, further his terrorist ideologies, recruit, and give birth to the world's most dangerous insurgency—thanks to the naivety of his Americans captors at the time. According to the Soufan Group, an organization specializing in terrorism analysis, nine members of ISIS's top command, including former senior officers in Saddam's army, were detained in Bucca, most notably the group's former official spokesperson (he was killed in a US targeted attack in Syria in August 2016) and second-in-command, Taha Subhi Falaha—widely known as Abu Muhammad al-Adnani. In a September 22, 2014, speech considered the first official public order to kill nonbelievers in Western countries, al-Adnani said:

> If you can kill a disbelieving American or European—espe-
> cially the spiteful and filthy French—or an Australian, or a
> Canadian, or any other disbeliever from the disbelievers
> waging war, including the citizens of the countries that entered
> into a coalition against the Islamic State, then rely upon Allah,
> and kill him in any manner or way however it may be. Smash
> his head with a rock, or slaughter him with a knife, or run him
> over with your car, or throw him down from a high place, or
> choke him, or poison him.[59]

The radical leaders in Camp Bucca were easily able to target the youth imprisoned alongside them, many disaffected by their impoverished lives.[60] In the dungeon, I am watching it happen before my eyes. I am witnessing the birth of "bin Ladens and Baghdadis."

Disheartened, I walk away, stopping near another gathering on the far side of the dungeon where Abu Omar, the fighter to whom I'd been handcuffed, is holding court. The hardened jihadist recalls how, after weeks at the Rabaa sit-in, he had fled Egypt to join the war against Bashar al-Assad's forces in Syria. He tells us how he fought alongside ISIS while his brother was killed in Syria fighting for ISIS's nemesis, Jabhat al-Nusra. It was the stuff of ancient myth: two brothers fighting Bashar al-Assad's forces under opposing terrorist flags to reach the same goal—an Islamic state governed by Sharia law.

ISIS was conceived in the womb of al-Qaeda in Iraq in 2006 as the Islamic State of Iraq (ISI), primarily comprised of Sunni insurgents fighting the US coalition and the Iraqi armies. Abu Bakr al-Baghdadi became its leader in May 2010 and, after claiming territory in Syria's Sunni-majority provinces of Al-Raqqah, Idlib, Deir al-Zour and Aleppo, announced the formation of ISIS (Islamic State in Iraq and Syria) on April 8, 2013. ISIS violently opposes any form of Islam that does not adhere to the rigid, often medieval rules of Sharia law, and immediately turned its fury on Syria's leader, Bashar al-Assad.

In December 2011, a jihadist named Abu Mohammad al-Julani established Jabhat al-Nusra, largely comprised of Syrian fighters with a focus on the "enemy at home" versus global expansion promoted by ISIS. Al-Julani later reaffirmed his oath of allegiance to al-Qaeda and its leader, Ayman al-Zawahiri.

In June 2014, ISIS proclaimed itself a global caliphate under the religious, political and military leadership of Abu Bakr al-Baghdadi, its caliph. By December 2015, ISIS had gained control over territory in Iraq and Syria with an estimated population of between 2.8 and 8 million people.[61]

Al-Qaeda rejected this caliphate, and the ongoing feud between the warring groups in Syria has resulted in numerous casualties. ISIS even published "Wanted Dead" posters on the Internet for senior Al Qaeda figures, including Ayman Al Zawahiri. The feud has also distracted these extremist groups from battling their common enemy—President Assad and his military who have been responsible for the slaughter of hundreds of thousands of Syrians and created the worst refugee crisis since WWII. Al-Julani announced in a recent interview with Al Jazeera Arabic reporter Ahmed Mansour that ISIS had killed seven hundred of his fighters. Ironically, 90 percent of ISIS victims are Muslims—an outcome that amounts to a war of Islam on Islam.[62]

While the varying factions in Syria share the objective of establishing an Islamic state based on Sharia law, al-Nusra and al-Qaeda advocate its gradual implementation, and they openly criticize ISIS for enacting an ultra-conservative and barbaric form of Islamic governance: forcing women to wear full-length black burqas, strictly prescribing the length of men's beards, banning music, TV sets and smoking, endorsing slavery and, worse, sanctioning the murder of apostates. This *hudud*, or extreme punishment, for serious crimes is meted out by an Islamic arbitration tribunal in accordance with Sharia law, and prescribes penalties such as amputations, flagellation,

chopping off hands and beheadings—images we've all seen broadcast on international news networks worldwide.[63] The Brotherhood does not sanction *hudud*; but when Supreme Guide Mohamed
Badie was asked about it in 2006, he stated that in narrow circumstances "we would execute the *hudud*"—another example of the
Brotherhood's duplicitous approach. Meanwhile, al-Qaeda's leader
has openly criticized the brutality and mass broadcast of ISIS murders, and has rejected killing others who do not subscribe to the
same Islamic ideology.

I had recently reported on Egyptians fighting in Syria and Abu
Omar's story piques my interest. "Did you get into Syria through a
network in Egypt or did you cross on your own?"

"Mainly through Turkey." He scowls at me. "There were several
groups helping us take our jihad to Syria to rid the country of Assad."

Abu Omar tells me that al-Nusra is strengthened by funding
from nations like Qatar and Turkey who use its members as frontline
soldiers in their own proxy war against Assad. Abu Omar adds that
these governments recruit from rival militias by promising better
pay and support. "But stay away from al-Qaeda," Abu Omar warns,
his voice thick with disdain. "Its leader, Ayman al-Zawahiri, is senile.
ISIS has done what brother Osama bin Laden could not have dreamt
of in our generation by cleansing and conquering so much territory
in such a short period of time."

"Sheikh Abu Omar," I interrupt, "I did a story months back and
the Egyptian jihadist I interviewed who fought in Syria told me he
had to buy a weapon from the militia out of his own pocket."

"He must have been affiliated with a very poor group," says Abu
Omar, and the men around him laugh. "Any of you who travel to
join ISIS would get excellent training before pulling the trigger,"
he enthuses. "Like I did. I met Muslims from the US and Europe,
doctors, students, taxi drivers who had never used a gun. Today, they
are raising Allah's word on the battlefield."

Unable to stomach his rhetoric, I turn to walk away. "Brother Fahmy," he calls, "in your newspaper, make sure to champion Allah's word, and remind the tyrants in the West that their war on Islam is a losing battle."

After several hours in this dungeon of radicals, a guard calls me upstairs for questioning. As I enter the prosecutor's office for the third time, trepidation turns to relief when I see the three people with him. The woman introduces herself as Iman Sabry, the Canadian consular representative. And there, as Marwa promised, is Khaled Abou Bakr, the celebrated lawyer I know from my work, and behind him a lawyer from Farag Fathi's law firm, appointed by Al Jazeera to represent me. The mood is tense. Rami el-Sayed is stone faced as he motions me to take a seat in front of his desk, but he orders me a coffee and offers a cigarette.

"How is your arm, Fahmy?" he asks, and before I can reply tells me he has signed papers authorizing me to visit the prison doctor. "Of course he will need to submit a report before I can transfer you to a hospital."

"May I add"—Iman Sabry turns to me, her face full of concern— "that the Canadian embassy has submitted a request to the Foreign and Interior ministries requesting a hospital transfer. Your family and the embassy have received permission to visit you in prison."

I want to tell her that I'm afraid her fax or email request is probably sitting on the dusty desk of a junior official without authority to make that decision. I know from experience, unfortunately, that what Canada considers an "intervention on the ground" often goes unrecognized. I would like to say that nothing less than a personal phone call or visit from a high-level Canadian official will get action in Egypt, but I can't tell her that in front of the prosecutor.

Instead I ask, if we must wait for the hospital transfer, if I can be transferred to the medium-security Luman Prison where Peter is being held. I tell them that there was a bloody brawl today between police and extremists as we entered the state security building and that I fear for my safety. I say to el-Sayed: "I am a journalist. Why do you bundle me with these mad extremists?"

Abou Bakr jumps on it and interjects strenuously, dark eyes flashing from behind rimless glasses. "As the lawyer representing the defendant Mohamed Fadel Fahmy, I want to document that his life was endangered today during the fight that took place in the vicinity of the building."

"I heard what happened," el-Sayed replies dispassionately, "but I am not responsible for prisoner housing, the Interior Ministry is." He turns to Iman. "Madame Sabry, we will start the official interrogation now."

She rises reluctantly, protocol not permitting embassy representatives to be present during interrogation.

As she heads for the door I entreat, "Please, would you ask my family to bring me a pair of white running shoes and extra white clothes?" As a detainee, white is the only colour I am permitted to wear inside Tora Prison. "And please have them put everything in paper bags," I add, desperate for writing paper and hoping this time the guards will not confiscate everything.

The coffee arrives and I set down the Quran I've been clutching. El-Sayed tips back in his chair, eyes me shrewdly. "Fahmy, what is this Quran you carry? Have you become a jihadi?"

I realize my error too late. "A prisoner gave it to me on my way out of Scorpion," I say, flustered. "I don't even pray."

"Mr. el-Sayed," Abou Bakr adds, "my client is no Brotherhood member. I've known him since he worked for CNN and he's interviewed me many times. I also know he has protested against the Brotherhood."

I can see from the look on el-Sayed's face that he is unconvinced. He questions me about my relationship to the students incarcerated with me in Scorpion and I insist that I do not know them, have had no dealings with them. Still, it seems that their connection with Al Jazeera Mubasher Misr has become my problem. El-Sayed tells me that some of the students have confessed to opposing the military, participating in the Pro-Brotherhood Rabaa sit-in, and accepting money from the Al Jazeera Arabic channels for providing film footage of protests. In his mind, these students, agents of Al Jazeera's banned local channel, and I, as bureau chief of Al Jazeera English, are inextricably linked—we are all Brotherhood sympathizers operating illegally, without even proper accreditation, to support the Brotherhood.

He asks for my computer password to access my email. I hesitate and refuse. Abou Bakr notes for the record that I have personal photos in my email and wish to keep them private. The interrogation is brief and again I must sign each page of the transcript attesting to its accuracy. Then guards hustle me out of the room, leaving me no time to speak further to the lawyers or Iman Sabry.

In the prison foyer, each prisoner is informed of his next interrogation date—in my case, a week. The administrative officer also informs me that my detention has been extended for at least fifteen days. At least I am relieved at what comes next: I am to report right away to the prison clinic.

I slow my pace crossing the prison yard, breathing the fresh air, cherishing the orange-red sunset that slashes the horizon beyond the high stone perimeter and imposing watchtowers.

We arrive at an air-conditioned waiting room with white walls and a spotless tiled floor. I can hardly believe I'm in the same prison. Another surprise greets me when the guard directs me to a wooden bench where several prisoners wait for the doctor. Sitting among them, wearing a white skull cap and matching prison garb, calmly reading a Quran while stroking his long grey beard, is Mohamed al-Zawahiri. I watch his expression as he takes in my own cropped hair and unshaven face, dirty clothing and trussed arm. The old man smiles benevolently, without a trace of the suspicion that marked our interactions when I interviewed him after his release from this very prison complex where he had allegedly been tortured for years.

At least he is a familiar face. "*Assalamu alaykum*, peace be upon you, Sheikh al-Zawahiri," I greet him. I recall his statements the year before on Egypt's CBC TV in which he denied belonging to any specific Islamic organization—including his older brother's al-Qaeda—but stated firmly that he was "ideologically speaking . . . in agreement with all of them. Our common bond is Islamic Sharia." His statements on Israel at that time were inflammatory: "Fighting Israel, fighting the Jews, is a religious duty incumbent upon us all." And he criticized the Morsi government for not "fighting the Jewish enemy . . . as a religious duty incumbent on all Muslims."[64] When he was rearrested in August after the overthrow of Morsi's government, he was arraigned with sixty-seven others and charged with forming a terrorist group and seeking to undermine the security of the country. So as we sit side by side I ask him about the new charges that brought him back to Scorpion: forming an al-Qaeda terrorist cell.

"We are not bloodthirsty merciless killers. We merely defend ourselves, organize protests, demand our rights of establishing a governance based on Islamic Sharia," he says, adding that he hasn't seen his al-Qaeda brother since 1996.

He has not answered the question, so I ask if it is his connections in Sinai—certain Jihadi militants who have been committing bloody acts along the volatile Egyptian-Israeli border—who might be the reason for the charges against him.

"What Sinai!" a prisoner sitting next to al-Zawahiri erupts angrily. "Those are legitimate resistance fighters. Whose side are you on?"

Al-Zawahiri raises his hand, silencing him, and signalling me to join him, gets up and moves to a quiet corner of the room.

"Brother Fahmy, don't mind his tone. He's angry because we are paying the price for the Brotherhood's inexperience. The naivety of

their leaders has failed us. We criticized Morsi for not implementing true Islamic Sharia when he won. He should have done so." He
stares hard at me. "Mohamed: the military was choreographing
President Morsi's overthrow from the day he won the election."

"Sheikh, it could be," I say, unconvinced. "But . . ."

"There is no 'could be.'" Al-Zawahiri is emphatic. "Morsi and
his Guidance Bureau sensed the coup was coming before it happened: some of the Brotherhood leaders in the government came to
me months before the June 30 civil protests even began. The Salafi
jihadists and I may have disagreements with the Brotherhood, but I
agreed to support them secretly by any means necessary to raise
Allah's word and to help secure their legitimacy against the plotting
of Sisi and the military under his control."

I know that the al-Zawahiri brothers have criticized the Muslim
Brotherhood for accepting "man-made" constitutions and laws, and
for not immediately enshrining strict Islamic Sharia as the sole legislative force; and that this man and his ultra-conservative Salafi
jihadist clerics had opposed and criticized the mild stance of the
Morsi government, echoing a statement released by his al-Qaeda
older brother. But his comments about his secret pact with some of
the Brotherhood leadership against a common enemy stun me.
Despite their disagreement it seems Morsi realized that maintaining
ties with the brother of the influential al-Qaeda leader was preferable
to losing control of the government. It would, of course, have also
facilitated communication and influence over thousands of militant
Salafi jihadists who were regularly launching attacks against the
Egyptian military in Sinai. From my own experience, I know there
have been other such moments when they used each other's influence. I recall my conversation with al-Zawahiri at the time that
Morsi's chief of staff, his first cousin, had asked him to negotiate the
release of seven Egyptian security officers kidnapped by militants in
northern Sinai.

I wish to hell I was on the outside breaking this story to the world, but the doctor calls me in before I can ask al-Zawahiri more about his connections with the Morsi government. Unlike the doctor I saw when police first brought me to Tora, this one shows genuine concern. He helps me remove my sling and shirt, appraises me. The skin is purple-black on my shoulder, down my arm and beneath my armpit, and on as much of my back as I can see. The doctor lightly grasps my arm, manoeuvres it upward, and I stifle a scream. He shakes his head, his expression grave. "You need an X-ray immediately. I'm referring you to the Kasr El Aini Hospital." He helps me to put on my shirt and the sling. "You need to keep this on at all times," he says. "Move your arm as little as possible."

A week later there is a bang on my door, the jangle of keys—*Fahmy, visitors!* I feel self-conscious as I pass by the doors of my fellow inmates, and the guard roughly shoves me along. Brotherhood prisoners have been boycotting family visits to protest the new visitation facility, which has added glass partitions to separate inmates from loved ones. Any communication now must take place through phone receivers on either side. The guard escorts me through the derelict maze of hallways to the visitor's room, and I shuffle behind him, buoyed with joy at the thought of seeing Marwa, and my parents who have come from Montreal.

I see my father first, sitting in a chair behind the glass. He wears a blue suit and is drawn with age and illness. It hurts to see his hands shake uncontrollably as he struggles to maintain his composure. His Parkinson's has gotten much worse since I last saw him nearly a year ago. He has also been diagnosed with colon cancer. I know he needs surgery, but instead he has come all the way from Canada to see me.

Marwa and my mother are crying. My mother looks frightened by my appearance, my rough beard and shaved head. My own emotions are a chaotic mix of shame, embarrassment, joy, despair. I want to reassure them, and at the same time I want to fall into their arms. I grab the phone handle as Marwa picks up on the other side. We both start speaking at the same time.

"*Habibi*, I love you," Marwa says, even less composed than when I had seen her briefly outside the dungeon. Like my parents, she looks exhausted. "The whole world is fighting for you." She wipes tears away, but more come. "Are you all right?"

I find it hard to get the words out, repeat myself. "I'm okay, I'm okay. Thank you, thank you, thank you for coming. How are you doing? I know this is hard on you, too."

My father says, "Be strong. This will soon be over." And we hold our hands to the glass partition so that our fingers almost touch.

"I need to get to the hospital," I say. I told them I had seen a doctor who had recommended an X-ray, but nothing had happened since, and the pain was worsening. And it was my best way to get myself out of the prison quickly.

"We're trying, *Habibi*." My mother tells me they're lobbying the Ministry of Interior, which oversees Egypt's prisons, but have received no answer.

I ask if they know what Al Jazeera is doing. My father raises his trembling hands, motions for me to be careful what I say. But I am so anxious that I go on, insisting that I don't want their lawyers representing me and I'd like the network to pay for Abou Bakr, whatever legal fee he needs.

Marwa quickly explains that Al Jazeera has put out a strong statement, condemning the arrests of Baher, Peter and me, and calling for our immediate release. Our photos are being flashed on news bulletins. In a torrent of words, she tells me she has reached out to the UN, Human Rights Watch and Amnesty International. Christiane Amanpour and my old friends at CNN have covered the story, and my brother Adel has already done two television interviews. "Even me," says Marwa. "I am talking to everyone I can."

I am overcome to hear this, moved by their efforts, by my colleagues' efforts, by her efforts. She is very shy, especially of media, and there is no doubt that her involvement is a direct risk to her own safety and the security of her position with Vodaphone.

We suddenly realize we don't need to use the telephone receivers, and we exchange information in a rapid-fire volley. My brothers, who both live in Kuwait, are flying in to help; my parents are working with Abou Bakr. Even in these difficult conditions, the sound of my mother's voice is as soothing to me as it was during my childhood.

Peter, I learn, has managed to smuggle out a powerful letter critiquing the government that has been circulating in the media. "He expressed worry for you and Baher in Scorpion," says my father. "How is it in here?"

I suspect one look at me tells them everything. Then a swell of frustration: "How can they call me a Brotherhood member? I protested against those guys. There must be photos of us protesting against the Muslim Brotherhood. Can you find them?"

Marwa nods, but when I ask her to contact Khaled al-Qazzaz's wife to let her know not to visit, that he is staging a protest against the degraded prison conditions, she flares up.

"No way. I am not contacting anyone associated with the Morsi government. They have destroyed the country. If my phone is tapped I could be in serious trouble."

She is of course right—and I realize for the first time that she, like me, must be a subject of hatred on the outside if people believe the government propaganda, that I am a journalist working for the Brotherhood, and I am mortified.

"How are the streets?" I ask. "We have no newspapers. Are people still protesting and dying?"

Alarmed, my father places a trembling finger to his lips, warning me again not to talk about politics. My mother looks terrified.

"Shh," she adds. "They are branding anyone who protests the government as members of the Brotherhood and locking them up."

Suddenly the guard announces that the visit is over. Marwa and I press our hands to the glass. "I gave the guard two buckets of Kentucky Fried Chicken and slipped him some money to let it in. There are also some new white clothes, toilet paper, juice and more painkillers," she says. Unable to touch each other, we are both overcome with emotion. "I love you, I love you," she says, but I am unable to speak.

Back in the cellblock, the guard asks me what to do with the chicken. I tell him to give two pieces to me, and the rest to Amin Al-Serafi who manages the wing. He organizes the wives and distributes the food they bring—usually packaged or home-cooked meat, macaroni, rice, vegetables, fruits, in addition to bags of chips, cookies, things that don't spoil. Now that the Brotherhood is abstaining from visits, this warm chicken will be a valuable contribution.

Slumped on the floor of my cold cell, I feel too depleted to eat. The sight of my family crying evokes feelings more overwhelming than anything I felt in Iraq, on any frontline, or in any battlefield I have covered. I replay every word we exchanged, memorize it. There was so much to say, but the visit was far too short. As I fall asleep I am filled with regret over the things I forgot to ask.

I awake to angry shouts from some of the prisoners who are yelling at the guards from their hatches. The prisoners requested permission to leave their cells to worship together in the hallways of the wing for congregational Friday prayers—apparently some prison wings have allowed it, but not Scorpion. I watch from my hatch as an officer relays the warden's decision: he refuses their request. The men hotly discuss their next move. One suggests starting a hunger strike, but others dismiss the idea. As a show of defiance, we decide to stage what we dub the "million man" protest, referencing the name commonly given to many Friday protests Baher and I have covered in Egypt since the revolution, even if they drew only thousands of protestors. We agree that when the time comes for noon prayer, we will all remove our shoes and bang them on our cell doors.

As midday arrives on Friday, January 17, I remove my shoe, and, joining my fellow inmates, bang it against the door as hard as I can. The din of hard soles on metal is thunderous, reverberating so loudly that prisoners in other wings hear it and begin banging and yelling, "*Allahu Akbar! Allahu Akbar!*" We stop for an instant, hear their chants of solidarity, and begin again, reinvigorated. The clangour escalates unabated and my arm tires, turns to jelly, but I do not stop. Instead, I let it hang limply for a moment and begin fiercely kicking the door. I take up my shoe again, striking it against the metal with every ounce of strength and passion I possess. Tears roll down my cheeks as I hit harder, yell louder, and I taste their salty wetness on my lips. My emotions are a tumult of frustration, anger and disillusionment. I am crying not just for myself, but for my country, for its failed revolution, for young students being radicalized in prisons and filthy prosecution holding rooms, for protestors killed in Tahrir Square, for the look of horror on my fiancée's face when she first saw me outside the dungeon, for the pain of watching my mother cry behind a glass partition, and the sight of my dad's hand shaking uncontrollably as he waved goodbye, watching a son now suffering as he suffered fighting for freedom and justice in Egypt.

In the ensuing days—as a result of our protest or pressure from the outside, I cannot be sure—conditions in Scorpion improve. The administration does not grant us the right to congregate for Friday prayers, but gives us beds, one hour per day outside in groups of three, and access to newspapers. I wish I could be let out with Baher, but regardless, I am in heaven during my first outing, a stroll in the empty, sunlit prison lot with Essam al-Haddad and Ayman Ali, two of President Morsi's most trusted presidential advisors. They discuss Morsi's final days in office, and the Egyptian armed forces' forty-eight-hour ultimatum or "offer" to Morsi and the Brotherhood government to conduct a referendum and hold early elections, and resolve their differences or they would impose "a road map" for the future. Al-Haddad tells us that Morsi *categorically* refused the military's offer. The day after the offer expired, the military "kidnapped" him and hustled him away in secret to an undisclosed naval base. Months later the former president, now accused of being a terrorist and a traitor, showed up at the Borg Al-Arab Prison in Alexandria.

As the three of us walk and converse, looking back on recent events, Ayman Ali insists that Morsi's favourable policies towards Iran were only strategic, despite the visit by President Mahmoud Ahmadinejad, that Morsi hoped to weaken Iran's determination to destabilize Syria. The visit was criticized by the US as naïve, given that so many ordinary Egyptians have little love for Iran (ever since the then-Iranian supreme leader Ayatollah Khomeini stirred Egyptians to rise up against Anwar Sadat). It seems Ahmadinejad did hope his trip would be a new starting point in relations between Egypt and Iran, and Morsi believed that this nascent relationship, if it materialized, could position the Brotherhood as a key powerbroker between Washington and its longtime enemy, Iran. So Morsi publicly kissed the president when he landed, and gave him a red-carpet reception. The visit only highlighted the rifts in the theological and geopolitical differences between the two countries, and—there was some laughter at this point—it all ended badly when a bystander tried to throw a shoe at Ahmadinejad because he was angry at Iran's support of Syria's murderous campaign against its own people.

A week after our shoe-banging protest we read in the paper that four bombs have rocked Cairo. The first and most powerful hits the Cairo police directorate. Two Islamist groups claim responsibility and, as Baher and I exchange looks of concern through the hatches of our cells, prisoners in our wing chortle in amusement when one reads the newspaper aloud, relaying news that bystanders at the scene had chanted, "The people demand the execution of the Muslim Brotherhood!"[65]

But no one laughs the next day when, on the third anniversary of the revolution, dozens of Central Security Forces flanked by investigators from the Ministry of Interior, raid Scorpion. The men strip the blankets and pillows from our beds, confiscate our food and personal belongings and subject us to body searches. Hearing the commotion in the cells down the wing, the officers knocking on walls, upturning beds, demanding inmates hand over their watches, I somehow manage to hoist myself onto the concrete sink and, balancing precariously, reach up and deposit my watch and pen—the two items I am not prepared to lose—on the dusty ceiling-side blade of the overhead fan.

When officers storm my cell and demand my watch, I tell them I don't have one.

"An Al Jazeera journalist like yourself doesn't carry a watch?" one confronts me angrily. "I don't understand how you're the only prisoner not carrying a watch!" He and the investigators return three times before giving up the search. After they leave I retrieve my treasures, and sit furiously penning a note I will smuggle out during my next family visit. In it I pour out my frustration over our arrest and inhumane treatment, decry the death of the democratic movement and criticize Egypt's backslide into Mubarak-era oppression.

The administration cancels our outings and revokes our newspaper privileges. By taking our watches, it seems the prison also hopes to thwart the Brotherhood members' prayers. My quiet confession that I have managed to hide my watch is met with jubilation. Keeping the watch, however, comes with a price. My fellow inmates, ironically, ask me to wake up the wing every dawn for prayers and to call them to worship five times each day. I take pleasure in my new role as religious steward, finding a sense of purpose that keeps me grounded. When my family visits a week later, I decide, in the wake of the security forces' search, not to chance smuggling out the note.

I can barely contain my anticipation. Marwa and my parents seem calmer, more composed than the previous visit, but something also feels wrong. I stare at Marwa's drawn expression beyond the glass partition, and tilt my head in a question: "What?"

"The prosecutor issued a press release listing the names of twenty people implicated in your case and calling you 'the Marriott Cell.' There is unconfirmed news that you're being referred to trial."

A trial means months in prison. I feel my entire body go slack. "When?"

Marwa shakes her head. "The date hasn't been announced yet." Her eyes fill with tears. "Don't worry, my love." She tells me a number of Western journalists have signed a petition and delivered it personally to Diaa Rashwan, the head of the journalism syndicate, that friends and colleagues—David Kirkpatrick from the *New York Times*, Sharif Kouddous of *Democracy Now!*, Nancy Youssef from McClatchy, Ian Lee from CNN, Heba Saleh from the *Financial Times*, Sarah El Deeb from Associated Press, and Sonia Dridi from France 24—are hounding the presidential spokesman and bringing up our story at every possible opportunity to embarrass the government.

A guard abruptly tells us our time is up and as I walk to my cell, I glimpse Baher in his, back from his own family visit, his face pale with disbelief. He calls out from his hatch, confirming after a visit with his brother, a cameraman for Sky News Arabia, what my family has just told me: the Marriott Cell has been referred to Cairo's criminal court.

CHAPTER 10

THE AL JAZEERA LIVE
SCORPION RADIO SHOW

January–February 2014

Later that night, Amin Al-Serafi, Morsi's former presidential secretary, calls all the inmates to their hatches for the ritual reading of the Quran. After the reading of the verses is over, al-Qazzaz calls out, "Let's add a new flavour to our night. Let's hear from our famous journalists: Baher and Fahmy."

The work of a journalist is bred in the bone, and the possibility of a good story is irresistible. Would they talk in this bizarre, insulated setting? I was trying to score interviews with many of these men for the longest time and was not able to get close. Now we are living together under one roof. "Even better," I call out. "Let us interview you."

Baher jumps on it. "Welcome to the Al Jazeera Live Scorpion Radio Show, broadcasting from Tora Prison," I hear his voice spark with enthusiasm, as if we are back in the office and a great story is breaking.

"Not more than a one-hour program, please," cracks someone down the hall. "We need to be finished for *Salat al-isha*." This is the fifth and final prayer of the day between sunset and midnight.

I can't wait to get at Essam al-Haddad. He served not only as a member of the Muslim Brotherhood's Guidance Bureau, handling foreign relations, he was a trustee for Islamic Relief Worldwide (IRW), a conglomeration of fifteen aid agencies mandated to alleviate the suffering of the world's poorest people. IRW has also been linked to militant groups like Hamas. His visit to the United States in 2012 had been controversial on both sides.[66]

"Sir, you had a forty-five-minute meeting with President Obama in December 2012. What can you tell us about that historic visit?"

Al-Haddad plays along, telling us that he lobbied Obama for a strategic partnership between the two countries and pushed the idea that Morsi was committed to democracy. He also tells us that he met with Pentagon officials and requested advice on democratic control of Egypt's armed forces (DCAF), namely how to mitigate the power struggle between the democratically elected civilian government and the military leadership.

"When I got back," al-Haddad says, "one of Egypt's top military brass, General Mohamed al-Assar, had found out about my meeting and told Defense Minister Sisi, who wasn't happy to hear I asked the US for such advice."

Al-Haddad thinks General al-Assar misunderstood his request, assuming Morsi's increasingly Brotherhood-directed government was looking for ways to control the military.

I interrupt to ask him, jokingly, if I can write this in my book. A number of inmates laugh.

"*Allahu Akbar*," someone cries and I recognize the deep voice of Sheikh Murgan, who fought with the Taliban in Afghanistan and alongside al-Qaeda and had blown up the ancient Buddha statues. On Egypt's Dream TV he had called for the destruction of the

Sphinx and the Great Pyramid of Giza because he considered them pagan idols.[67] He had also praised the assailants of the Boston Marathon attack that had happened the day before that interview and stressed the importance of fighting Americans and the West, France in particular. "Because [the French] are leading the war against us," Murgan had said.[68]

I subsequently learned that he had been instrumental in founding the Salafi jihadist movement in Egypt and had published numerous books on Islam. Ayman al-Zawahiri described him as a dear friend and brave jihadist in an audio recording, and praised Murgan for training fighters and schooling them on the fundamentals of Sharia law in Afghanistan and Yemen. In a meeting between various Salafi jihadist groups in Cairo in May 2013, Murgan openly announced that he was sending Egyptian men to wage jihad against Assad's government.

"You two journalists must have been sent here directly by God to write 'the word of truth,'" he yells through the bars in the prison.

Al-Haddad says go ahead, add anything you want to your book. I quickly pull the pen out from my waistband, and use my left hand to try to scrawl the points he is making on the wall. He tells us Obama said he had not opposed the rise of the Brotherhood, and considered the group moderate Islamists; and that he supported the idea of Egypt having a system similar to what he and President Erdogan had implemented in Turkey—cooperation on mutual regional and global interests in addition to military cooperation. Al-Haddad said he felt that the US, at that time, wanted an open dialogue with the Brotherhood in Egypt.

I was conscious I could not push too hard in this setting, nor reveal that I did not subscribe to the Brotherhood's ideology—after all, they considered me one of them. Erdogan was a dangerous man to get into bed with, but al-Haddad was not wrong about the fellowship between the Brotherhood and Erdogan who had decided to make Syria his "domestic affair" and was fast becoming one of the region's most repressive dictators. His record for imprisoning and killing journalists was topping the charts. I had covered Erdogan's November 2012 visit to Egypt with CNN when thousands of Brotherhood supporters welcomed him at the airport with signs that read: THE BROTHERHOOD AND ERDOGAN ARE ONE HAND.

I remember al-Haddad had also been involved in facilitating CNN's access to Morsi. "Wolf Blitzer told me you set up the interview between him and President Morsi," I say. Al-Haddad agrees he did.

Baher interrupts. "I want to ask a question about el-Sisi to anyone who cares to answer." Then, in his characteristically polite manner, he delicately frames an incisive question, one I had raised with Mohamed al-Zawahiri, but am intensely curious to hear from Morsi's inner circle on: Had Morsi's presidential team not noticed that Sisi was going to turn against Morsi and the Brotherhood?

"Once Sisi started wearing black sunglasses, I knew something was really wrong," I hear a prisoner say from a cell down the wing.

"*Allahu Akbar*," Sheikh Murgan shouts his familiar refrain from the far end of the corridor. His voice alone sends a shiver down my spine. "You Brotherhood should have chopped off the heads of all the generals. They didn't listen, that is why we are all here."

There is no love lost between the likes of Murgan, one of the most radical Salafi jihadists, and the Brotherhood members—behind bars together, however, they, at times, agree to disagree. Listening to Sheikh Murgan, a longtime comrade of the al-Zawahiri brothers, is a constant reminder of the inevitable clash of ideologies between the Salafi jihadists and the Brotherhood. For starters, the Salafi jihadists would resort to any means to derail a relationship with Israel, including assassinating President Sadat in 1981 shortly after he and Menachem Begin had brokered the Egypt-Israeli Peace Treaty. Morsi, on the other hand, was more of a pragmatist, giving assurances on taking power that he (and therefore the Muslim Brotherhood) would respect the treaties with Israel. I have often wondered if violent clashes would have erupted between the Salafi jihadists and the more moderate Brotherhood had Morsi remained in power. Sisi seized the credit for preventing such an outcome, arguing that the police and the military would now "take the blows" to avoid the "civil war" that could have erupted and led to civilian deaths. He anticipated the backlash from the radical Islamists who had turned their guns on Egypt. Today, it seems that indeed most of the casualties are from the ranks of soldiers rather than the protestors on the street.

I press my face into the hatch, hoping to catch a glimpse of Murgan's toffee-toned skin, his intense, dark-rimmed brown eyes, his long, scraggly grey-white beard. "Sheikh Murgan," I yell out.

"Listen to me," he adds before I can ask my next question, "Sisi's government will find you guilty even if you are innocent."

"What is your official charge?"

"Brother Fahmy, I am imprisoned for promoting true Islam. I fought alongside the Lion Sheikh Osama bin Laden to champion our religion. If we get the chance I'll show you the scar on top of my head from a US rocket that targeted our location," he boasts. "I met some of the nineteen men who brought down the World Trade Center towers in New York. I never knew what they were training for until the news emerged. I fired off almost all my ammunition during the celebrations we held on that joyous day."

Seeing Baher's eyes grow huge through his hatch, I say I am— metaphorically—handing the microphone to my "co-host" Baher.

Baher apologetically excuses himself before throwing out a bold question. "What mistakes have you committed as the Brotherhood? What could you have done better?"

The "guests" are silent. Finally, Abdel Meguid Al Meshary replies. Al Meshary, a former telecommunication executive with scant media experience, had been in charge of President Morsi's media relations department.

"We could have communicated better to influence perception and to establish a more transparent system to debunk the many rumours and false information against us in the media. At times we had a hard time controlling the nation's own State TV."

I interject. "This is for the floor. Do you think your governance was inclusive of all Egyptians?"

"I can say that wasn't a priority," Amin Al-Serafi, Morsi's secretary, responds.

"But it became a major issue, didn't it? It turned the masses against you."

"That is what every government does," a voice shouts. "They bring their own people; men they can trust."

"Our strategic decisions post-revolution"—I recognize the voice of Osama Yassin, a senior member of the Brotherhood and the former minister of youth—"did not encompass the big changes and unite the conflicting parties as happened in South Africa during the period of reconciliation. We made more enemies than friends. Now let us pray together."

So Osama Yassin ends our first show by reciting several verses from the Quran. For a moment, I stand listening to his humble voice. I am electrified by the frank intimacy of our exchanges. It has been entertaining for them, but I'm hyper-aware that I've also been conducting an interview. It is dead-serious work. These men are willing and waiting to open up, eager to share their stories and points of view. Baher and I have access to some of the highest-ranking leaders of the Brotherhood, but we can neither tape it, film it, nor broadcast it. Instead, I make cryptic notes on the cell wall and on pieces of scrap paper.

My days are marked by the five daily prayers that I signal for all with my precious watch, the creaking wheel of the food cart, and the

distraction of our evening radio show. The long night after the evening prayer becomes the prison for my thoughts. When others sleep
I lie awake, my mind crazed with ideas that go nowhere, only churn
incessantly round and round.

One night Sheikh Murgan leads the final *Salat*, or daily prayer.
I listen to him recite the *Fatihah*, the opening verse of the Quran.
This one I know: *Bismillah ir-Rahman ir-Rahim . . . In the name of
God, most Gracious, most Compassionate . . .* The men chant in unison
and I join them, my voice stretching out with each word. Although
my broken shoulder prevents me from prostrating, I sit on the floor
and lower my head in supplication. My mind floats on the rhythmic
sea of prayer. For a moment it seems that this act of devotion I have so
often mocked has become a kind of solace, and that these men whose
politics I have long despised are now welcome company. The prayer
unfolds and I lose the words, mix up my verses, but carry on, matching the pace and intonation until my voice blends with the others.

CHAPTER 11

THE BUDDHIST AND MR. BEAUTIFUL

February 3–19, 2014

The news that our case has been referred to court weighs heavily on me as we wait to hear the actual date. I've covered enough criminal trials in Egypt to know that my colleagues and I are in for a long and terrible ordeal. The hopes I've harboured for my release on medical grounds are dashed. To make matters worse, the prison authority announces it's banning family visits to prisoners in the terrorism wing. Still, fate isn't done with me. After a sleepless night, I hear the sound of the bolt sliding in the lock. "Pack your stuff," a guard yells—it seems they feel they always have to yell an order—as the door swings open. "You're moving!"

I labour awkwardly to shove my possessions into the bags my family had brought the clothes and food in, and hear guards ordering Baher and the three young students to do the same. "Take your mattresses, too."

They march us out of Scorpion, across an open area inside a fortress-like perimeter that encircles the sprawling Tora Prison complex. I try to keep my mattress off the ground, but with the use of only one arm, it drags in the dirt. I shuffle along, hunched and squinting in the sunlight like a cave-dwelling creature unaccustomed to the light of day. The walk tires me, sends hot pokers of pain through my shoulder. We approach a squat, rundown building. I'm afraid. As bad as Scorpion is, it is the devil I know and I have established personal connections and a routine there.

If Scorpion was unlivable, this place is far worse. Baher and I are thrown together into a filthy six-by-seven-foot cell. Mould and dampness darken its cement walls. There is a fetid toilet, and a rusted tap protruding from the wall. The air is rank with the smell of excrement and decay. Cockroaches scuttle across the walls, floors and low ceiling. There is no window. I look at Baher, his eyes reflecting my own despair, as we take in our new home. I pull my mattress into a damp corner, drape one of my grey blankets over it, and lower myself onto its rough surface. Baher stands in the centre of the cell and begins to pray. Sitting in these vile surroundings, I pray, too, hunching forward from my seat on the mattress to exert minimal movement on my broken shoulder.

Later, we lay out breakfast—leftover bread and hard cheese and a ration of dried provisions we've brought with us from Scorpion. Within minutes the cockroaches and ants are upon it and I can't stomach it after that. The prison's recent ban on family visits means we'll have to eat the repulsive prison food and fight the insects for it.

Our day passes in a fog of cold, discomfort and depression. As evening approaches, we lie on our mattresses facing one another, speculating about why we've been moved. Had the officers found out about our mock Al Jazeera talk show? As wretched as our conditions are, I feel grateful for Baher's company. Conversation erupts haltingly until the two of us somehow manage to gain enough equilibrium to joke weakly about our situation. We compare the repugnant, insect-infested toilet in the corner of our cell to the lavish bathroom we had at the Marriott weeks before. We recall the hotel's extravagant open-buffet breakfast, the choice of meats, cheeses, muffins and jams, and the smell of freshly brewed coffee. Through the night, as Baher sleeps, I hug these recollections to me.

The next morning, as I am finally drifting into the oblivion of sleep, a guard arrives and calls Baher out of the cell, telling him he's headed for interrogation. I hurry to retrieve a note I wrote on January 25 but haven't had a chance to pass to my family.

"Take this," I whisper, passing it to him as the door swings open. "Try to give it to the lawyer. Be careful." I lie back on the damp mattress, both praying the note won't get Baher into trouble and fretting that it will never see the light of day.

A couple of hours later a guard bursts in yelling the familiar and now terrifying refrain: "Pack your stuff! Pack Baher's stuff!" I look around helplessly. It was painful and awkward to manage my own mattress and possessions the day before. Fortunately, the officer has brought two prisoners to help carry Baher's things. I leave the cell with a mixture of relief at escaping the horrid conditions and trepidation over my next destination. As I follow the guards out of the wing one of the students—I can't make out which one—calls out from a nearby cell, "Fahmy, don't forget us." I turn and glimpse the forlorn face of one of them pressed against the hatch of their cell door.

I shuffle behind the guards back across the open expanse of Tora's internal lot, this time to the prison garage.

"You must know some people in high places," the guard says snidely as we enter the dim interior. Any hope that his words portend a positive outcome evaporate when he ushers me into a small metal cage and locks me inside. It reminds me of the shark cages that divers climb into before being lowered into the ocean. Mine smells of feces and urine and I imagine prisoners before me who have been

left inside for long stretches with no means to relieve themselves. I
vow I will not suffer the embarrassment of relieving myself where
others can see it. Thankfully, it takes less than fifteen minutes until
a blue truck pulls into the garage.

"Okay, Fahmy," the guard says, "you are being transferred to
Mulhaq Al Mazraa."

Mulhaq Al Mazraa is a lower-security prison located a ten-
minute ride away, still within Tora. When I arrive at the building,
my new jailers force me to strip while they search my belongings.
Once again I stand in my underwear, shaking with cold and humiliation. They confiscate my most prized possessions—the watch and
pen I've managed to keep hidden. I'm then escorted to a small,
sterile room where a doctor soon arrives to check me. Unlike the
last doctor, he makes no mention of medical treatment—which had
come to nothing anyway. Still, I feel weirdly optimistic about this
prison as guards lead me to my new cell. It is situated on the ground
floor of a two-storey wing that I later discover houses close to
twenty of Egypt's highest-profile political detainees.

The guards lock me inside what will be my home for the next six
months. I look around with an immense sense of relief. The cell is
small, about nine by twelve feet, but with clean, dry walls painted a
soothing pale green, and a thirty-foot-high ceiling. A barred window
is cut into the top of one wall and covered with a thick plastic sheet.
I feel almost euphoric at the thought that I will not have to fight
off the mosquitoes that plagued me day and night in Scorpion. The
only other opening to the outside is a barred rectangular slot in the
metal cell door about eight feet from the ground, too high to peer
through. The cell contains two metal bedframes, a single next to the
door and a bunk bed pushed against the adjacent wall. If I am happy
to have a bedframe for my mattress, I am ecstatic to see a bathroom
stall with a conventional toilet. I rush towards it, giddy as a child as
I push down the functional flusher and watch fresh water swirl

around the bowl and disappear down the drain. The sink is fitted with hot- and cold-water taps, as is the shower, and I play with them all. I drag my mattress onto the single bed, cover it with a blanket, and lie down, happily revelling in the comfort of the metal springs beneath the thin layer of batting and filthy fabric.

"Hello," a voice calls from the cell to my left, interrupting my solitude. "Who are you?"

"Mohamed Fahmy," I call back.

"Welcome. I am Abou Elela Mady." I recognize the name—it's well known in Egypt's political circles. As president and founder of the Wasat Party, Mady welcomes Christians and women, advocates for a more modern, tolerant version of Sharia law, and supports liberal democratic ideals and respect for civil and human rights, something he felt the political ideology of the Brotherhood did not aptly address. He had formed the Wasat Party after renouncing his membership in the Muslim Brotherhood in 1996. His attempts to register it as an official party failed several times, but he succeeded, finally, days after the ouster of Mubarak. He has since been vilified by both sides: by the Brotherhood for trying to split the movement and by the government who accused him of establishing his party as an Islamist front. With the ouster of the Brotherhood in July, Mady was imprisoned and charged with "inciting violence." He is probably the most progressive political prisoner and open-minded thinker I met during my incarceration—a leader I wish I could have interviewed under better circumstances.

Abou Elela Mady tells me that he may have been unjustly thrown into prison because of a comment of Morsi's that he repeated in the press. Morsi, he said, had informed him that, many years back, Egyptian intelligence had established a militia of 300,000 thugs and positioned 80,000 of them in Cairo alone. Some of those hired thugs were dispatched to various violent protests during the Brotherhood's tenure armed with guns and knives, and the president told him that this militia was recently transferred to the authority of the Homeland Security apparatus.[69]

Before I can respond he tells me he's read about the Marriott Cell in the paper. "Where are the other two—Peter Greste and Baher Mohamed?"

I am surprised that the three of us and our story are known here. I tell him that Peter is in Luman. And that Baher and I were in Scorpion, where they kept us in solitary and recently banned family visits. "This place is not so bad, it seems."

"We get an hour outside in the sun every day and family visits where we can sit together. You'll see, the warden here is fairly reasonable."

I am exultant at this news and think immediately of how good it will be to see Marwa without a glass partition between us, to feel the warmth of her touch. Minutes later a guard swings open my cell door. I look up to see Peter standing calmly in the entrance, dressed in his prison whites, a white sweater and white running shoes. I heave myself off the bed and rush to him, hugging him with my left arm.

He appears glad to be reunited, though he looks around the cell with less enthusiasm than I had. It seems he settled into a routine in Luman: they got four hours outside every day, he says, and he was enjoying speaking to Alaa. Alaa, I recall, is Alaa Abdel Fattah, the well-known blogger he had spoken fondly of when we met in the dungeon holding room beneath the State Security prosecution building. He tells me he believes Alaa is a true revolutionary, a fighter, and he is distraught over how Alaa's wife and his autistic son are faring. "I'd really like to help his son someday," he says fiercely.

I nod at the emotion in his voice. I will soon come to discover a deeply compassionate, humanitarian side to Peter that I had not had a chance to experience during our brief time together at the bureau.

It is the same compassion that takes many journalists, like my friend Steven Sotloff, to the most troubled corners of the world to help report on ordinary citizens caught in conflicts.

"What happened with the letter you smuggled out?" I ask now. "Did it get you in trouble?"

He shakes his head, explaining that although the warden was upset, he hadn't been punished. In it, he'd defended our journalism, dismissed any affiliation with the Brotherhood and advocated for press freedom.

He asks after Baher and I tell him he's been taken for questioning again, and how stressed out he's been about his wife, Jehan, on her own with two small children and pregnant with a third. "His kids think he's on a long business trip."

Baher arrives hours later, delighted to see both Peter and our more humane living conditions. He also brings news that, while his transfer was a glitch and he hadn't had to face another round of interrogation, he did connect with another prisoner—someone he knew—who had promised to find a way to pass my letter on to my family. There's a palpable sense of relief, a strength-in-numbers solidarity as we exchange prison stories, catch up on the past weeks.

Resourceful and energetic as always, Baher pushes my single bunk against the metal door and hops onto it to peer out the hatch. We take turns peering into the corridor, looking out to see a slice of the main- and second-level cells on either side. Baher calls out to our new prison mates and one by one they introduce themselves. Among them are Mohamed Badie, the supreme guide of the Muslim Brotherhood, who has headed the Egyptian branch of the international Muslim Brotherhood since 2010 and at times wielded more power than Morsi himself; Saad el-Katatni, former Speaker of Parliament and head of the Freedom and Justice Party; Hisham Kandil, former prime minister; and Bassem Ouda, Morsi's former minister of supplies. It's exhilarating to discover the identities of our new neighbours. All are top-ranking Brotherhood stalwarts—we would have considered an interview with any one of them a journalistic coup. For four years I have tried to get an interview with Badie, but he was well protected and gives only a couple a year. Now he's in the cell next to ours.

"*Ya* Baher," yells one of the inmates, his voice muffled from behind the door of his second-storey cell. "I carried you on my shoulder when you were a baby."

Others chime in with similar fond remembrances and ask after Baher's father. I discover that his father is not only a longtime Brotherhood supporter, but was manager of Misr 25 (Egypt 25), a privately owned TV channel funded by the Brotherhood and recently banned. I recall now a prisoner down the wing in Scorpion who had yelled "*Ya* Baher, I know your father." I'd dismissed the connection as insignificant at the time, but now I wonder if Baher's impressive ability to secure interviews with prominent Brotherhood representatives has anything to do with this. The reunion is unexpectedly touching. Then, as I translate the conversation for Peter, a worrying thought: his intimate Brotherhood connection might work against us during the trial ahead as we defend ourselves against the charge of acting on behalf of the Brotherhood against the state.

A moment later Baher surprises me again by informing our new prison mates that he wishes to start the Al Jazeera Talk Show in the coming days. I shake my head at his ease and audacity—and cannot wait to get started. The journalist in me is still awake, it seems.

As we settle into our cramped living space I engage in some gallows humour, playing the dictator with my colleagues. I stand stiffly in the middle of the cell, my voice commanding, my gestures exaggerated. "Peter, I appoint you minister of foreign affairs! Baher, you are minister of supplies in charge of food!" Their laughter feels like the best medicine on earth.

———

The next morning I awake to rays of sunlight filtering through the high, plastic-covered window. A guard brings us a box of salty white cheese, five loaves of flat round Egyptian *balady* bread, lettuce, tomatoes, onions, four eggs and an orange. A feast. Peter prepares breakfast, mixing the cheese and vegetables to create a surprisingly palatable meal—my Aussie cellmate is not only an accomplished journalist, he has a flair for food. Our first full day in Mulhaq Al Mazraa gets even better when the guard drops a copy of a local newspaper through our hatch.

"Fahmy," a voice yells moments later. "I sent you my newspaper with the guard until you arrange your subscription with the prison." It's Abou Elela Mady.

Minutes later, another prisoner sends us tea bags.

"Fahmy," the ever helpful Mady yells again, "you can order whatever you like from the supermarket outside, even ready-made meals. Someone will come to take your order. They charge twenty percent above market price, but it's worth it. Just make sure your family puts money in your prison account."

Peter fills three plastic cups with hot water from the tap in the bathroom and soon the three of us are sitting on the floor in a circle, eating breakfast and sipping lukewarm tea.

"Guys," Baher says happily in his lilting English, "this is such a beautiful morning. I like to have breakfast with you two. It's just beautiful."

I smile at Baher, but my mind is on other matters. "When any of us gets a family visit," I say, "we need to make sure we request lawyer visits so we can start planning our defense."

"That would be beautiful to see my wife and kids," Baher replies. "What a beautiful day that would be."

This time I look at Peter and smile. "Yes, Baher," I agree, "it's beautiful, beautiful." Peter and I laugh and it takes Baher a moment to realize we're teasing him. "Baher," I ask, grinning broadly now, "what's with this word 'beautiful' that you keep using?"

"I just love life today," Baher says. "Everything is beautiful."

"I'm going to call you Mr. Beautiful," I tell him and, indeed, as I spend more time with Baher, I come to realize what an apt moniker it is. In many ways his personal circumstances are far more difficult than Peter's or mine, yet he continually amazes me with his positive outlook and exuberance for life. He is an imprisoned man responsible for putting food on the table for his pregnant wife and two children and yet speaks enthusiastically about how he wants three more. Living with Baher would become a daily lesson in the art of the possible.

After breakfast, Baher and I make a list of supplies for our families to bring for us all during our next visit. Then afternoon arrives with a welcome announcement: we will be allowed outside together for an hour of exercise—Baher's and my first such privilege since our arrest more than a month earlier. We stand at our door barely able to contain our excitement as we wait for the guard to let us out. When he does, other prisoners call to us and we reach up to shake hands extended through hatches on our way out. Baher reminds them about the Al Jazeera show and issues invitations to all to participate.

"Welcome, *Beter*, welcome," Mohamed Badie, the Brotherhood's supreme guide, calls to Peter in stilted English. "Brotherhood good. No terrorist."

I enjoy watching Peter shaking hands with some of these leading figures and translate as much as I can.

"Brother Mohamed, tell Peter we are sorry for what happened to him," a man shouts from a second-storey cell. To my amazement he introduces himself as Hazem Abu Ismail, the popular Islamist politician who threw his hat in the ring as a candidate for president following the 2011 revolution, but was deemed ineligible by the government who claimed his deceased mother had held American citizenship. He vehemently denied it, insisting his mother had held only a green card, but the government would not be dissuaded.[70]

We emerge into the weak sunshine of an early February after-noon. I feel liberated as I walk beside Baher and Peter towards a sandy soccer pitch and I want to run, to jump, to throw my arms in the air. But such movement is not possible, so instead I stop and take in my surroundings: a small plot of garden, a weathered volleyball net, a set of soccer goal posts, the pale yellow sun, the glorious green foliage and sand-coloured houses beyond the prison walls. Wistfully, I pic-ture the home my parents still have in Maadi, a suburb just fifteen minutes away. I breathe in the fresh air and revel in the cool winter breeze on my face. I watch Peter and Baher bending, straightening and stretching their arms as they walk together. Nearby, guards tend a vegetable garden. I know that many of them live on farms outside the city in Cairo's rural outskirts and rely on prison work to supple-ment their meagre salaries. One guard assigned to watch us waters the greenery with a long hose. At one point Baher relieves the guard of the hose and waves it over the garden. I take another deep breath and watch Peter jog around the pitch, his gait loose and easy. I had been an athlete in my youth and feel the urge to sprint, to feel my legs propelling me over the long stretch of ground, but the pain in my broken shoulder stops me cold. Instead I begin walking briskly around the perimeter of the yard.

Baher is running laps around the field in Peter's footsteps. I smile as they pass me and look skyward to see an armed soldier watching us from a tower. Feeling a crazy sense of freedom, I wave to him and to my delight he waves back.

That evening after lockdown we begin what will fondly become known as the Al Jazeera Mulhaq Radio Show. Baher pushes my cot against the door and the three of us climb on top, crowding together near the small hatch.

"*Assalamu alaikum!* Peace be upon you," he bellows into the cor-ridor. "Welcome to the Al Jazeera Mulhaq Radio Show." Soon we see other faces at the hatches, hear the answering calls of prisoners in our wing: "*Wa'alaikum salam.* Peace be upon you, too."

Baher, at ease with our cohort, strikes the perfect tone. "Tonight, we would like to open with an ancient Brotherhood anthem and ask the Supreme Guide to sing for us."

I can hear the Brotherhood members murmur their approval. Mohamed Badie begins to sing, his voice deep and rich.

"Supreme Guide," Baher asks when he finishes, "can we talk about the January 25 revolution?" Again I marvel at my colleague, his instinct to get immediately to the core of things. As journalists, curiosity is our currency; the need to deeply understand the issues of the world, our passion.

"It is my pleasure," Badie answers. "I would like to correct the inaccurate information about the Brotherhood that's in the history books. But please," he adds thoughtfully, "translate for Peter."

Baher asks him why the Brotherhood did not support the youth in the brutal Mohamed Mahmoud riots in November 2011 when, nine months after Egypt's Arab Spring overthrew Mubarak, they had returned to the streets to voice opposition to the military's control of Adly's interim regime. But the Brotherhood—who had marched into Tahrir Square in such support—had remained passively on the sidelines as the violence escalated, and I had watched in horror as the street turned into a war zone in which dozens were killed, several thousand injured, and many lost their eyes in the targeted shootings by the dreaded police sharpshooter, "The Eye Hunter."

Badie admits that many saw their lack of support as a betrayal. "But the Brotherhood Guidance Bureau voted against it because we had set out to establish an unprecedented, fruitful relationship with the Supreme Council of the Armed Forces." He explains that they were also approaching the parliamentary elections and wanted to establish a stable political structure, not be seen to be fuelling more chaos on the streets.

That honeymoon phase between the military and the Brother-hood had soured as the power struggle between them escalated. Six months after the Brotherhood took power under Morsi, in December 2012, the military and the media united in their outcry against Badie when, during his weekly address as supreme guide, he openly called the military "corrupt." Badie defends himself, telling us his words were taken out of context.

I am not convinced. But it would hardly be wise to challenge him in front of his disciples.

I turn to Baher. "Ask him about the ongoing accusations that armed Brotherhood are terrorizing people, and that they used weap-ons against the police during the Rabaa dispersal."

"Don't believe these fabricated stories. The Brotherhood is a peace-ful group," Badie insists, saying that when he was on stage addressing thousands at Rabaa, he had shouted, "Our peace is more potent than bullets!" I had seen videos of a few people firing at the police during the dispersal, and the hate speech spewed on stage inciting protestors to violence was well documented. And I remember feeling sick to my stomach at the brutal scenes of the Rabaa massacre on TV, and at the sight of the charred and bloodied bodies in the mosque.

"Translate this for Peter," yells Bassem Ouda, Morsi's former minister of supplies. It quickly becomes apparent that it is impor-tant to the Brotherhood members—many facing dozens of charges ranging from inciting violence to terrorism and murder—that Peter, the Western journalist, understands their point of view.

"Yes, we took a defensive stand in Rabaa," Badie continues, "just as we did in Tahrir. In Rabaa we had to defend the legitimacy of our position as the elected government." He insists there was no systematic use of weapons, though he adds, "Of course we can't control isolated incidents by some of our youth, or fools who revert to violence."

I want to tell him I don't buy it, I've seen evidence to the con-trary, but I hold my tongue. I remember how the Morsi government responded when thousands of Egyptians protested outside the presidential palace against his constitutional decree granting himself absolute power. He allowed a group of armed Brotherhood supporters to disperse the protestors, sparking a bloody confrontation that left ten dead and more than a hundred injured.[71]

"What about the Marriott Cell?" someone yells and Baher takes it upon himself to explain our work as journalists. From his cell on the top floor, former prime minister Hisham Kandil requests details about our coverage of Iraq and the Arab Spring on a future radio show.

"We are sorry for your situation, Peter," Badie yells unexpectedly in his broken English, as if the Brotherhood is directly responsible for his incarceration.

Peter moves forward to call through the hatch and thank him: "All of you have been so kind since we've arrived," he says, telling them that he spent a month in Luman before coming here, has had many discussions and is beginning to understand the politics. I translate simultaneously as Peter tells them, "I'll share some of my experiences covering South Africa, the elections there and my work in South America in the coming shows."

"We want to hear about Australia, too," an inmate calls out. Baher wraps up our first radio show with the same tone of respect for the Brotherhood that he opened with, earnestly thanking them for participating before reciting a verse from the Quran to mark the end of the show.

As we lie on our bunks that night, the three of us are charged with enthusiasm. My mind is churning with questions for the next show, questions I would have had no chance of posing on the outside. "Let's plan to ask them about their opposing of the judiciary," I say, "or what they thought of Morsi granting himself absolute powers."

"Okay, Boss," Baher agrees happily as he readies himself for evening prayer. "It will be like the good old Marriott days again."

———

The following afternoon, during our coveted hour outside, the three of us are circling the perimeter when we hear a guard yell out, "*Ziyara!* Visit!" I look towards the building to see him beckoning us. The guard points at me. It is my visit! He nods at Peter, explaining that Australian embassy representatives will also visit him later in the day. I feel bad for Baher, but true to his positive outlook, he makes the best of the situation.

"Fahmy," he says, looking genuinely excited for me, "give Marwa the list of stuff we want and tell her to pass it on to Jehan, and ask Marwa to tell her to visit and to bring the kids."

I rush back to the cell. I duck my head under the tap in the sink, splash water on my face and run my hand through the one-inch bristle on my head. I carefully slip the small paper containing the list of needed supplies and several carefully composed tweets into the waistband of my prison bottoms. Minutes later, inmates cheer as I walk down the corridor.

"Fahmy, come here for a second," calls Abou Elela Mady and as I stop in front of his cell door, he quickly thrusts his hand through the bars of his high hatch and sprays me with cologne. "Enjoy your visit."

"Thank you," I say, touched by this encouragement from a man who has spent eight months behind bars with no trial date in sight.

The guard at the gate of the wing pats me down before escorting me to the visiting area. I see Marwa waving at me from a distance and quicken my pace. All of a sudden, she bolts from the visiting area and is in my arms before anyone can stop her. It's a breach of prison protocol, turning the heads of high-ranking officers observing us, but we don't care. I hold her for the first time since the arrest—a long, fierce embrace. When I finally let her go, the guard leads us to a table in a crowded visitation area where my parents sit waiting impatiently. I hug and kiss each of them in turn, overcome by emotion.

"You smell so good, *Habibi*," my mom says and I smile, grateful to Mady.

"It's prison chic," I say, feeling happier than I have in weeks.

"I brought you and the boys McDonald's." She hands me a brown paper bag. "There's also a tray of grilled fish, chocolate milk and Pepsi."

I thank her, feel Marwa's hand discretely find mine under the table, squeeze it tightly.

"*Habibi,* how is your arm?" my mother asks. "We are working on transferring you to a hospital, but the authorities are so resistant."

I can see the concern in her eyes and try to reassure her. "I have a bed, so that helps. Peter, Baher and I are together. Our cell is small but we have a shower, hot water and a toilet that flushes. I'm not sure how or why we were moved from that hellhole in Scorpion, but it's a miracle."

"I visited the head of the journalism syndicate, along with a group of foreign journalists, and he put pressure on the government to make it happen," Marwa says quietly and I stare at her in awe.

"*Hamdullah,* thank God," my mom says. "We see families of Scorpion prisoners on TV in tears since they've stopped the visits."

I grab my mom's hand and kiss it before turning to Marwa. "Baher asks—please call Jehan and tell her to visit Baher and to bring the kids. It's killing him not to see them."

"The court date has been set for February 20," my father announces. I take his news as a good sign, smile at him, but his expression is stony. "Your lawyer, Abou Bakr, is extremely worried about Baher's confession."

My mother frowns, whispers sharply to him, "Why now?"

"He has to know where he stands."

"What confession?" I ask.

It is Marwa who answers. "There have been leaks in the press. Apparently, he told the prosecutor that the managers in Doha had instructed him to film Tahrir Square during the protests against Morsi from an angle that would show it was empty of protesters. And he said the network changed his translation of Sisi's speech to

present Egypt in a state of civil war, and incite citizens to fight terrorism—meaning the Muslim Brotherhood."

I look at her and then at my father in disbelief.

"He also said the Al Jazeera English bureau was taking direct
orders from key Brotherhood figures during the coverage of the
Rabaa dispersal, including Gehad al-Haddad. He said you were
working illegally and hiding in the Marriott, and also something
about Peter smuggling in large amounts of undeclared cash through
the airport," my father adds.[72]

"What!" I say. "This is crazy. There must be a mistake. I can't
believe he'd say that. I wasn't even working with Al Jazeera during
Rabaa." I am grasping for reason. "What is Al Jazeera doing about
this? Have they refuted it? And what about my request that they pay
for an independent lawyer?"

I had rejected Al Jazeera's lawyers—my confidence undermined
by their evasive, disappointing actions in my early dealing with
them as bureau chief—and my family had hired Khaled Abou Bakr.

My father shakes his head. "We've paid fifty thousand dollars to
Abou Bakr. I had to sell my stocks. They have promised to reimburse
us, but we haven't see a penny yet."

Questions crowd my brain. "What is the press saying?"

"The whole world is behind you," Marwa replies. She tells me
CNN's Christiane Amanpour and other renowned journalists taped
their mouths shut in a video campaign that has gone viral, as has a
Twitter hashtag—#FreeAJStaff. Ordinary citizens and journalists
in newsrooms have staged global days of action, stands of solidarity,
vigils, and events in over thirty cities around the world, and the
online #FreeAJstaff campaign has garnered a quarter of a billion
Twitter impressions since February 1, dovetailing with the more
generic hashtag #JournalismIsNotACrime.[73]

I am very moved. "I thought I'd probably been forgotten already,"
I say. "Did you get my letter?"

Marwa nods.

"Great. Did you manage to publish it?"

For a moment no one answers. "No," Marwa says finally.

"What!" I explode, and direct my frustration at her. "I risked punishment writing that letter, Marwa, and Baher did, too, when he smuggled it out." To my horror I see tears well in her eyes and begin to roll down her face, and tell her I am so sorry, drying the tears around her eyes with my finger. "Forgive me."

"We stopped her from publishing it," my mom interjects. "Your journalist friend, Kareem Fahim from the *New York Times*, said it could hurt you."

"Son," my dad's voice is earnest, "you need to understand that your situation is different from Peter's. The government views us as Egyptians despite our Canadian passports. I don't want to alarm you, but our house is being watched and our phones are probably tapped. Even Baher's battle is different. His family is openly supportive of the Brotherhood on their social media platforms and he might be, too." This is a perspective I have not even considered from inside the bubble of Tora Prison. Though Parkinson's has gotten the best of his body, my father's mind is still sharp, and his perspective and experience invaluable.

"We are trying to garner both international and local support," he continues.

I have been relying on Al Jazeera to do the right thing, but I can see that he is right—it would be foolish to rely solely on the network. Or for that matter on my fellow journalists' good will and imaginative campaigns in my defense. It will all count together. Quickly, I rattle off the names of high-profile Egyptian politicians and diplomats who know me and I believe respect my work as a journalist. "Can you ask them for affidavits vouching for my professionalism and confirming that I have no affiliation with the Brotherhood?"

My parents fill me in on their conversations with the Canadian embassy—the consular staff will visit before the trial and they've placed Marwa's and my parents' names on a permission list granting extra visits.

"*Assalamu alaikum*, Brother Mohamed," a voice interrupts our conversation. Mohamed Badie, the supreme guide of the Brotherhood, enters the visiting room to meet his wife and daughter and I stand to greet him.

"Don't talk to this terrorist," my mom whispers fiercely. "The officers are watching closely." Of course: I have to be 100 percent circumspect in all my words and actions.

The guard tells us to us to wrap up and I feel a rush of panic. Have forty-five minutes elapsed already? It feels like I've just arrived.

"Check under the fish," Marwa whispers, her eyes holding mine.

"Be strong," I say, though I am already coming to understand that my fiancée is much stronger and more resourceful than I ever imagined.

"I'll try," Marwa promises. "I just don't want to lose my job."

I look at her tenderly, afraid of the toll my ordeal is having on her. From the corner of my eye, I see the guard approaching and slide the note from my waistband. "Give me your hand," I say to her in an urgent whisper, and her fingers find mine beneath the table. "Give this list of things we need to Jehan and post the tweets online."

"Let's go, Fahmy," the guard orders and I rise reluctantly from the chair.

"And don't forget to tell Jehan to come and bring the kids."

I hug her tightly and over her shoulder see my dad discretely slip the guard money. Reluctantly, I say goodbye to my parents. My mom has replaced her sunglasses to hide her tears and my dad, having provided such sage council, appears suddenly spent.

"I love you all," I say as I'm led away. I grasp the McDonald's bag, drinks, and extra clothing my family has brought, while the guard carries the tray of food. I look back one last time and see Marwa as I had first glimpsed her, beautiful, strong and stoic, waving vigorously to me from a distance.

When I return to our wing, Peter is outside the cell waiting to be taken to the warden's office for his embassy visit.

"We are going to court on the twentieth," I say.

"That is good news, Fahmy. Good news." Peter's blue eyes light up and he claps me hard on my shoulder.

"Man!" I yell, twisting away. "What's the matter with you!" Peter apologizes as the guard leads him away, and I enter our cell with my shoulder screaming again in pain.

I share news of the court date with Baher, but my thoughts are in turmoil: Why would he have said such things, I wonder? I recall his warm exchanges with the Brotherhood members. Have I misjudged Baher? Is he someone other than the engaging, conscientious journalist I've come to know and respect? I have no idea what to do with the information I've just learned—or how I will even begin to broach it. So I hand him the bag of McDonald's burgers and unwrap the tray my parents have brought. The food doesn't interest me; I want what it hides. I worm my finger along the foil-covered cardboard tray mounded with warm rice and topped with grilled fish, and find what Marwa hinted at—a neat square of pages, and a much-needed pen, wrapped in wax paper.

I unwrap it and lie on my bed to read and to escape the suffocating weight of Baher's confession. The first page is an international wire story from CNN on our arrest, with photos of each of us. The second is a copy of a petition signed by forty foreign journalists calling for our release. The last is a *New York Times* article decrying our incarceration. Moved, I pass the articles over to Baher. I study his face as he reads, weigh the angry words of accusation tumbling through my mind. As I am about to confront him, he jumps up.

"I almost forgot. Look what I made for you in the prison yard after you left for your visit," he points to two plastic water bottles filled with sand. "I thought you could use them as dumbbells to strengthen your shoulder."

"Thank you," I say, stifling my urge to question him. I take one of the bottles in my left hand and do a few curls before tucking them both under my bed along with my anger. Baher hasn't seen his wife or kids since his arrest, not wanting them to see him in prison, and is already suffering enough. I will wait for a better time. I tell him to pass on the papers to Peter, and that I am going to take a nap. I lie on my bed, turn my face to the wall. The news of his confession plays over and over through my mind. Finally, my thoughts settle on Marwa— her face, the feel of her body in my arms, her smile, her tears, her incredible strength—and I surrender to the sanctuary of sleep.

I awake to the clang of the cell door slamming shut and roll over to see Peter returning with gifts from the Australian embassy: a *Guardian* newspaper, a tin of chocolate biscuits and, incredibly, a package of new, brightly coloured underwear. He lifts a finger to his lips and I notice Baher, prostrate in the centre of the cell, praying. Peter places a foot on the metal frame at the head of my bed and climbs onto his top bunk to read the paper. His feet dangle inches from my face. Impatient, I wait for Baher to finish.

"The embassy convinced the warden to allow me to have monitored calls to my parents in Australia on a mobile phone they will bring during visits," Peter tells us. It's a good development—not just for Peter, but for all of us, potentially allowing us to convey and receive information critical to our defense. He relays that Al Jazeera's lawyer, Farag Fathi, will soon visit but, he says, there is some concern from the network that my hiring my own lawyer will confuse the defense.

I sit up. "I see Farag as a plumber dressed in a suit," I say bluntly. "I don't want him to represent me. Even Baher complained about him on my very first day of work." I ask Baher to show Peter the articles and recommend we use my contacts in Egypt and our combined contacts in the international media to exert influence in our case.

Peter reiterates that he thinks we should leave things to the Al Jazeera legal team; I tell him of the warning that Ragia—a human rights lawyer with her finger on everyone's pulse—gave me when she visited at the start. I am just not comfortable leaving our fate in the hands of Al Jazeera.

"Am I being naïve?" he asks earnestly.

"No," I say. "I just think it would be foolish to put all our eggs in their basket." My concerns, however, go deeper than the ability and reputation of our legal defense. My experiences with Al Jazeera from the moment I walked into the Marriott Hotel have shaken my trust in the organization's competence. When I express my concerns, the look on Peter's face suggests I am being disloyal, and, with Baher's own inexplicable behaviour in my mind, my frustration erupts.

"For me," I say passionately, "this is as personal as it is political. What's happening is an affront to everything I have fought for since the revolution." I explain that I participated in the Arab Spring as a citizen first, someone who had seen my father, my countrymen— shackled for thirty years under Mubarak—risk everything to achieve democratic freedom. I'd watched Egyptians, for the first time in their lives, peacefully assemble, protest, speak their minds, engage in a political process that Westerners take for granted. On January 25, I watched a young man die for his freedom. His future. All my anger boiling over, I can't stop myself. "The Muslim Brotherhood stole the revolution from the people simply because they were well organized and funded by governments like Qatar's. As a journalist, I've worked hard to decipher all that's happened in the last three years, to report it objectively. Then suddenly it's all a mirage, I'm under- mined by my own news agency, and I'm in prison. And it's not just about me," I say hotly. "Being labelled as Brotherhood puts my family at risk. Al Jazeera has dropped us into a hotbed of Egyptian politics, unprepared and unprotected. I'm worried, Peter. You know a lot about this part of the world, but you haven't *lived* it."

An awkward silence follows and I'm grateful when Baher breaks it. "Guys, how about we eat?" He holds up a brown paper bag. "We've got McDonald's." Peter and I readily accept, relieved to table the conversation. "Sorry I lost my temper," I say, and he waves off my apology. For the moment, all is forgotten as we enjoy the cold comfort of our hamburgers.

Despite our close quarters and tensions that simmer below the surface—and occasionally erupt—the three of us coexist peacefully. As with Baher's everything-is-beautiful attitude, I come to admire Peter's inner calm, self-discipline and spirituality. Though I don't know if he's a Buddhist, I come to think of him as one. He meditates every day, eyes closed, shirtless and cross-legged on his upper bunk, extending his practice weekly, and is equally regimented during our hour outside. The Australian embassy provides him with an exercise regime designed for Canadian airmen living in small quarters and he adheres to it religiously.

In small ways, in the weeks leading up to the trial, we make "the shoebox" home. Peter salvages the tinfoil wrapper from the cardboard food tray, fashions it into a circle, and affixes it to the wall beside his bed where it shimmers and catches the light, a precious talisman. Baher hangs a single photo of his children and I often catch him staring sadly at it. He and Peter collect empty plastic water bottles, peel their labels and ink the backsides of each with a large block letter. Over time we space them along the wall to create a long banner that reads: F-R-E-E-D-O-M N-O-W-! Peter writes long notes on rolls of toilet paper and I do the same on the backs of printed pages with the pen Marwa smuggled in. I also hoard paper bags for this purpose.

My arm has failed to improve much although the pain has sub-
sided somewhat. Though the prison will not release me to the hospital, I've begun receiving physical therapy sessions in the prison clinic
to improve the range of motion. I follow the supervising doctor's
advice and devise exercises in the cell using the sand-filled water bottles and a broom in hopes of restoring the function of my shoulder.

Still, at times we are lighthearted, as when Peter ribs me. "Fahmy,
are you going to spend all your prison time horizontally? Why don't
you give us a hand cleaning up here?" When I play my broken-shoulder
card, he doesn't buy it. "Yeah, yeah," he jokes and Baher chimes in.
"That is really a beautiful excuse, Fahmy."

At other times we debate passionately. Peter takes me to task for
my unequivocal criticism of the Brotherhood. He argues eloquently
that they, too, are entitled to due process, and in the end, I acquiesce.
We discover each other's pet peeves. For me, it's Peter's loud chew-
ing, for him, my insomnia and the restless movement of my legs as I
toss and turn. For us both, its Baher's haphazard ways. At night I lie
awake, try to make sense of Baher's confession and worry over the
trial ahead, going over every detail multiple times, until I finally fall
asleep around five o'clock. Peter awakes an hour or two later, so my
four-hour sleep, typically until nine, is always punctuated by the
sounds of quiet conversation and morning routines.

In my final family visit before the trial, I learn that an edited video
of our arrest at the Marriott has been leaked to Ahmed Moussa, a pro-
government anchor of Tahrir TV channel. The twenty-two-minute
segment portrays cinematic footage of the raid and our interrogation
interspersed with close-ups of our cameras and telecommunications
equipment set to a sinister score from the recent movie *Thor: The
Dark World*.[74]

"They're playing it all the time," Marwa tells me during a family
visit in February and I try to allay her concerns, saying people will
surely see through the propaganda. I focus instead on what my

lawyer, Abou Bakr, had informed her of: tomorrow he and the Al Jazeera lawyers will demand our release on conditional bail.

This is the hope I fervently hold on the eve of the trial as Peter, Baher and I prepare for the following day. Baher manages to borrow a mirror and an electric shaver from the former Speaker of Parliament Saad el-Katatni. After Baher trims my hair and shaves my beard, I look at my reflection in the mirror. It's the first time I've seen myself in almost two months. With a start, I see that my hair has grown in greyer and my face looks haggard. "But you do a better job than my local barber," I tell him.

A sense of anticipation, of lighthearted camaraderie, has taken hold of us as we sift through our prison whites seeking the most presentable for our first public court appearance. We counsel each other on our hair and clothes like boys preparing for a first date. Baher and I talk about being released on bail, while Peter cautions us against getting our hopes up. We brush off his reservations; fantasize about being with our families. When the three of us finally crawl into our beds that night I lie awake staring at the ceiling. It's not until the weak dawn light begins to glow through the high cell window that I finally fall asleep, my head filled with images of Marwa, my parents and our ride home together.

CHAPTER 12

THE CAGE

February 20–March 28, 2014

I have twice dreamt of the Cairo courtroom during my fifty-two days in this wretched place, but nothing prepared me for the first day of our trial.

Early in the morning we are reunited with the students, who are still incarcerated in Scorpion, in a small holding cell. Like us, they look haggard and nervous. Together we shuffle into a huge courtroom—also within Tora Prison—handcuffed together in twos; Sohaib and Shadi, followed by Peter and Khalid, and finally, Baher and me, all of us dressed in white prison garb. We are directed into a cage ten feet high, eight feet deep and half as long as a tennis court, running the entire left side of the massive, high-ceilinged room. I look out through the grey metal mesh onto rows of tiered wooden benches packed with hundreds of observers swivelling around now to look at us. Beyond them, at the front of the courtroom is the raised judges' bench, empty still. My nightmare has become reality.

I spot my mother and father and my brother Adel, who has flown in again from Kuwait for support, in the middle of the room. He stands and waves to me, and I feel as if he's reaching out to me with his strength. I catch my mother's eye, but my father doesn't turn, just sits stiffly facing forward. I wonder what it must feel like for him, a man who has fought for decades for justice and democracy in Egypt, to see his son caged and handcuffed like a common criminal. There, too, is my lawyer, Khaled Abou Bakr, looking reassuringly calm and confident in a black barrister gown. I search for Marwa, but there's no sign of her. I will discover later that Canadian representatives had neglected to include her name on the list when they requested permits for my family to attend.

Dozens of journalists fill the courtroom and several surge forward, their cameras trained on us, but they can't get close—white-uniformed officers, sitting two deep, occupy the bench seats nearest the cage, separating us from the public and the press. Beyond the buffer of military men are diplomats from the Canadian, Australian, British and Dutch embassies, as well as observers from human rights organizations like Amnesty International. I recognize local journalists, including several heavy-hitters from the international media: Alex Ortiz of CBS, Patrick Kingsley of the *Guardian*, David Kirkpatrick of the *New York Times*, Orla Guerin of BBC, Sharif Kouddous of *Democracy Now!*, my old friends Ian Lee of CNN and Sonia Dridi of France 24.

Minutes later, three judges enter through a large wood-panelled door at the front of the courtroom, followed by two state prosecutors, the bailiff and a bevy of clerks and security guards. The clerk asks the crowd to stand and I watch as the chief judge, Mohammed Nagi Shehata, lumbers up the stairs to the bench, and takes a seat in the centre of three stately chairs while the other judges settle on either side. Shehata is a portly man with heavy jowls and a thick black moustache that droops over his upper lip. Though the courtroom is far from bright, he wears dark sunglasses. The chief prosecutor, Mohamed Barakat, and state prosecutor, Rami el-Sayed—who I know well from my interrogations at state security—file in behind. Barakat, I later learn, has been handpicked for the trial by his father, Egypt's top judge, Prosecutor General Hisham Barakat, the man I often heard prisoners in Scorpion praying would be killed. As the crowd settles, I urge Baher, Peter and the students to raise their hands and bang their handcuffs on the cage. The racket of metal on metal reverberates through the room and I can see the cameramen turn their lenses on us, snap pictures that will make headlines across the globe.

"Honourable Judge," I shout, my voice echoing off the walls and high ceiling. "Can you remove these handcuffs?"

Shehata, recognizing the damaging optics, orders the guards to do so. Seconds later I see my father rise and say, "How can a respectable man be paraded in a cage like this?"

My lawyer rises to interject, saying my father is just upset to see his son in the cage.

"I will excuse you this time," the judge says. "Only because I understand your fatherly concern. Now, please sit down."

A guard enters the cage and removes our cuffs as the judge leans into the microphone in front of him to open the proceedings.

"This is not a fair trial," Sohaib calls out. "I've been physically tortured and haven't been allowed to see a lawyer."

The judge asks the court clerk to note Sohaib's objections and then motions to the chief prosecutor. Barakat stands and after reciting the opening verses of the Quran, reads out the names of twenty defendants on trial in the case. Mohamed Fawzy, our cameraman, is denoted "in absentia." He was arrested and interrogated at state security, where Baher saw him briefly, and then mysteriously released whereupon he immediately fled to Doha before his name appeared on both the charge sheet and on Egypt's no-fly list.

Thirteen defendants, including the three students with us in the cage, are individuals with whom I have no prior association at all. The final three are journalists, also being tried in absentia: our two British Al Jazeera correspondents, Sue Turton and Dominic Kane, who had returned to Doha shortly before our arrest; and a Dutch journalist, Johanna Ideniette, who I remember the prosecutor asked me about at my first interrogation. He lists the charges against all twenty defendants: fabricating false news broadcasts on Al Jazeera and the "world wide web" to harm Egypt's reputation and national security; stir strife with the intentional aim of portraying Egypt as a "failed state"; and spread terror among the general public. The accusations also include operating equipment without proper permits and supplying the Brotherhood with monies, supplies, equipment, machinery and information.

Prosecutor Barakat then singles me out for setting up the room in the Marriott as the base of the "media network." Additionally, Baher, the students and I are accused of being members of the Muslim Brotherhood, designated (though only just before our arrest) as a terrorist organization—a charge Peter and the other journalists are spared. Baher is also charged with possession of "ammunition"—the single bullet he had picked up as a memento during his time in Libya, which the police confiscated from his house during his arrest.

If convicted, these charges could result in a maximum penalty of fifteen years in prison.

A murmur ripples through the crowd and Peter asks what's going on. I move closer and begin translating as the lawyers for the defense make their statements. Farag Fathi, the lawyer hired by Al Jazeera to represent Baher and Peter, demands the court appoint an official interpreter for Peter; and then my lawyer, Khaled Abou Bakr, makes the plea we've been waiting for: that the court release us on bail. He highlights my medical injury, pressing the judge to act on compassionate grounds. He is eloquent and poised. Comfortable in front of the large crowd, he addresses the bench with conviction, dismissing all the charges and stating that Al Jazeera English is entirely independent of the Arabic international news channel and its banned local affiliate, Al Jazeera Mubasher Misr. By the time he wraps up and the judge adjourns for a brief recess to consider the request, some of the optimism I felt the night before has returned.

My family and an army of journalists cluster near the benches of guards in an attempt to get closer, in what quickly morphs into a mini-press conference.

"Tell us about prison," one yells.

"Our imprisonment is psychologically unbearable," I answer. "We are innocent men locked up twenty-three hours a day . . ." I grip the mesh as reporters snap photos, and take notes. "But we are strong."

Another reporter tells us that protests have been staged across the world calling for our release. A member of the Australian media addresses Peter directly, informing him that his parents are garnering a lot of support in Australia.

"I love my family, I am strong," Peter says, his voice too soft to be heard amid the clamour. I shout out his words and then translate the next ones. "We believe we'll be free, because we know we have done nothing wrong."

"The police raided my home and shot my dog," Baher yells. "Journalism is not a crime!"

We are still in the midst of our scrum, calling for more support, when the judges and prosecutors re-enter the courtroom and everyone returns to their seats. I grip the wire cage praying fervently that the judge grants our bail request.

"Adjourned until March 5," Shehata announces, and in the next breath, dashes any hopes of a homecoming. "Suspects to remain in detention."

———

During our two-week wait back in the concrete box that is our home, the daily Al Jazeera Mulhaq Radio Show becomes a form of sustenance, along with weekly family visits. Peter's brothers, Mike and Andrew, tag team, travelling from Australia to Cairo in turns to give Peter support. Once a week Mike drives to the prison to deliver clothes and books, which we have now been permitted access to, and our favourite treat: sushi. My family does the same, bringing local newspapers that contain op-eds about our case and photos of our trial. I begin to smuggle out tweets through Marwa hoping to bolster support in the international media and Canadian community.

The local media is largely unsympathetic, given their suspicion of the Brotherhood. But Marwa has managed to make impressive inroads. She has attained the affidavits that I'd requested (attesting I am not a Brotherhood member) from prominent friends of the government, and submitted them to the court. They are from figures like former secretary-general of the Arab League and minister of foreign affairs Amr Moussa, and Egyptian billionaire businessman Naguib Sawiris, with whom I'd established a close relationship as a reporter dating back to my time in Iraq. She has also convinced editors of several local papers to publish the statements—immediately after their publication, the prison allows me longer family visits. But my primary audience is not the guards, or even the public; it's Judge Shehata and the judiciary.

The judge wears the same dark sunglasses two weeks later and yells at Sohaib when he again complains of the torture he, Shadi and Khaled have endured, and of Scorpion's ongoing ban on family visits, which has prevented the students from seeing their families for forty days. My gaze settles on Marwa, so happy that she is there this time. The sight of her calms my nerves as prosecutors present box after box of conventional broadcast equipment seized during the raid as evidence of our terrorist activities. The offending items are nothing more than the tools of our trade—laptops, cameras, tripods, lights, memory sticks.

With a start, I see a familiar figure—the national state security officer who silently directed the man in the trench coat and the others the night of the raid on the Marriott Hotel. He rises from the front row behind the metal rail separating the judge's bench from the public gallery. Even without his brass-buttoned black uniform, I'd recognize him anywhere. He is a silent, frightening figure. I watch him walk to the open area in front of the judge to take the oath. Then, something unexpected: Shehata asks the media to stop filming, in fact forbids them to, during the officer's testimony.

The officer introduces himself as H, a senior officer in the Homeland Security Investigations Service, the security and intelligence apparatus of the Ministry of Interior. Listening to his twenty-minute testimony recounting the night of the raid and outlining the investigation against us, is painful, and his final summation of the facts downright erroneous.

"Through my investigations and the data collected," H says in a clear commanding voice, "I reached the conclusion that the suspect worked for Al Jazeera Mubasher [Misr], the channel banned by the administrative court because of its affiliation to the Muslim Brotherhood."

Furious, I yell, "I've been a journalist for more than fifteen years and I would never betray my country."

"Don't comment on the witness's testimony, or else . . ." the judge threatens, and Abou Bakr shoots me a warning look.

During cross-examination, Abou Bakr asks: "Who are your sources?" but H refuses to disclose them, calling them "secret sources."

He returns to his seat and another officer, one I do not recognize, takes the stand. On cross-examination of the second witness, Abou Bakr presses hard until he admits he doesn't know the difference between Al Jazeera's English channel and the banned Al Jazeera Mubasher Misr.

But any sense of victory is shortlived when the prosecutor cites Final Cut Pro—the video-editing software found on my laptop— as evidence of tools used for "fabrication."

Abou Bakr denounces him loudly. "Every journalist in this courtroom has this software on his laptop." I am grateful for his theatrical style. Farag Fathi appears mild by comparison, saying nothing to defend my colleagues, merely criticizing the court for failing once more to provide an interpreter for Peter. Baher and I take turns translating the proceedings and before the break I speak out again, asking the judge to grant me bail on a guarantee from the Canadian embassy that I will not leave the country.

Peter calls on Australian prime minister Tony Abbott to press his case. "We need him to speak out," he says, his quiet voice almost unheard amid the clamour, and I yell out his words to the press. "Everybody from the White House down has given his or her support to us, but we haven't heard from the prime minister." And it occurs to me that I have not heard from Canada's prime minister, Stephen Harper, either. Then the judge's words fall heavily on us as he again denies us bail and adjourns the court until March 24.

Back in the cell the three of us, discouraged, call the trial a farce. Peter bangs the wall in frustration vowing to punch the lead investigator if he ever sees him on the street. It's the first time I see this level of anger from my typically Zen colleague—an indication of the raw-edged emotions we are all experiencing. Our outlet is Mulhaq Radio: that night I stand on my cot relaying the unfair proceedings, railing at the trap we are caught in. Later, Peter reminds me that we are fortunate compared to many in our wing, like our neighbour, Wasat Party leader Abu Elela Mady, who has been jailed for close to eight months with no trial.

We are all strung out with emotion. Peter and I argue about the Brotherhood and Al Jazeera. "Peter, you don't know what's in their files," I say. "Many Brotherhood members may not have pulled the trigger, but they may have incited, funded, or fuelled the clashes that led to the deaths of people." With typical evenhandedness he concedes, but points out that even if he does not know if the Brotherhood inmates are innocent or not, he does know they are entitled to a trial.

But my most heated exchange is with Baher. Astonished that his damning confession has not yet been raised in court, and still fuming over what he has done, I finally confront him that afternoon, during our exercise hour, as he finishes jogging laps around the field.

"What the hell were you thinking?" I ask him. He replies that the prosecutor changed his words, possibly even added to them.

"That's impossible and you know it." My voice rises as I follow him back inside. "We're required to sign the bottom of each transcript page after interrogations and in the presence of our lawyers, so there's no way to change it. Don't lie to me, Baher," I say. "I need to understand why you did this."

I see Peter watching us from his perch on his upper bunk, a concerned look on his face as the two of us argue in Arabic, but am too angry to stop. "You told them that we were working *illegally* from the Marriott? Why would you say such a thing?"

Finally, his voice breaking, Baher says, "They threatened to arrest my wife. I had no choice. But I never mentioned you by name, I swear. I said that Dominic Kane was bureau chief."

I appreciate Baher's efforts to protect me, but his confession infuriates me. Doesn't he realize how incriminating it will sound when the prosecutor raises it in court? How damning it could be for us all?

Later, when I have calmed down, I tell Peter about Baher's confession and explain the nature of our argument. He urges me to be gentle with Baher, who has been silent and sullen ever since. I grab a few pieces of the notepaper I keep hidden beneath my mattress, and for the next hour craft a detailed letter to Salah Negm, Al Jazeera English's director of news, and Al Anstey, the managing director, demanding they provide evidence refuting Baher's confession in anticipation of the document being presented before the judges, which I'm certain must happen in the next hearing. I know footage exists proving Al Jazeera English (filmed before I joined) accurately portrayed the anti-Morsi protests, and did not film empty streets as Baher claimed—so all they have to do is simply present that footage. More importantly, I ask them to confirm that they did not alter Baher's translation of Sisi's speech to have him call for civil unrest. I also demand that Farag Fathi refute Baher's allegations when the confession document is presented in court and that the judge question Baher directly about it. I conclude with a warning: Baher's confession will negatively impact our case unless the network addresses the issue before the next court hearing.

Days after I manage to smuggle out the note, Al Jazeera English's head of deployment, Tamara Bralo—posing as Peter's distant relative—accompanies his brother Mike on a prison visit.

Al Jazeera does not share my sense of urgency. Tamara tells us that Al Jazeera English and the network believe Baher's allegations will just "disappear." The unlikelihood that the prosecution will choose not to present them, the sheer nonsense of that, infuriates me, hardens my anger into a sharp point. I find myself not just doubting the defense being provided by Al Jazeera's legal team, but seriously mistrusting my own network.

Then something hopeful. My father tells me during a family visit that the interim president, Adly Mansour, has replied to letters that my and Peter's parents have written asserting we have no ties to the Muslim Brotherhood and pleading for our release. Mansour's reply, which my father happily shares with me, guarantees I will receive proper medical attention and that all necessary steps will be taken to ensure a prompt and fair resolution to our case.

Two days before our third hearing, half a dozen heavily armed security forces wearing flak jackets, helmets and balaclavas collect me from my cell and drive me to a private hospital. Finally, my long hoped for wish is about to come true. As the prison transport truck pulls up at the hospital entrance, I peer through the small window and am thrilled to see Marwa, my mom, brother Adel, and a dozen journalists who I consider friends.

"Look at how they treat him," my mother sobs as several guards pull me from the back of the truck. "Why?"

I crack a joke to ease her pain, call my outing a "vacation" compared to the conditions in prison.

"Hey, Moody," NBC correspondent Ayman Mohyeldin matches my tone, "your NBA career is over. On the other hand," he adds, "if you write a book about this, maybe someone will actually read it this time." I laugh at his reference to *Baghdad Bound*, a book I'd written at twenty-nine and then self-published about my experiences as a stringer and interpreter for the *LA Times* during the US invasion of Iraq.

I am touched to see Ian Lee, my former CNN colleague, among the journalists again. "Hey, bro," he holds up a carton of Marlboro cigarettes he has brought for me. "I hear they use these like currency in prison." I clap him warmly on the shoulder as Sherine Tadros, a friend and Sky News correspondent jokes, "Maybe Salah Negm will promote you now." I smile, uplifted by their presence as they follow me through the hospital to the MRI screening area during what will be a brief visit before guards return me to prison later that day. Their solidarity is a welcome and powerful recognition that my battle is not just about our Al Jazeera trio; it's about press freedom for all journalists.

———

In court on March 24, a technical committee comprised of three members from Egypt's State TV, led by engineer Ahmed Abdul Hakim, who independently reviewed the evidence against us, submit their final report. It states the Al Jazeera English bureau has fabricated videos that spread false news "against the national security of the country." In his cross-examination, Abou Bakr is quick to point out that the three "independent" reviews from each of the technical committee members are near carbon copies of one another, containing the exact wording and summative comments. He demands the committee members present viable evidence to back the claims in their final report. The witnesses can provide none; only assert that they stand by their findings.

"Is broadcasting an opinion that opposes the government a crime?" my lawyer asks finally. "Or is it just journalism? This is the entire issue in this case."

I want to add that as journalists we are messengers, reporters of opinion, and regardless of or even despite our personal opinions, it is our job to report the voices of all factions on the street. Baher's confession does not come up. By the end of the hearing, I am optimistic that the defense has exposed our case as a sham, a show trial, and that the judges will have little choice but to acquit us.

What unfolds before the end of that same day reveals the brutality of the judicial system the three of us are up against. After a trial lasting a hundred minutes, a judge sentences 529 alleged Muslim Brotherhood supporters and members to death.[75] The sentence is for an attack on a police station in the southern city of Minya the previous August, the same day as the "dispersal" of the protestors at Rabaa Square that left so many dead. In disbelief, Peter, Baher and I listen to the verdict on a radio that Marwa has recently brought in for me. Among the sentenced are Mohamed Badie, the Muslim Brotherhood's supreme guide, and four others in our wing. As I await their return from court, I wonder what I can say to them, especially Badie, who occupies the cell beside us, while Peter pours out his emotions in the ever-lengthening letter he has been writing to his family on a roll of toilet paper.

Contrary to the sombre mood in prison, Badie returns in high spirits, proudly shouting that he is closer than ever to reaching paradise. The reactions from other Brotherhood prisoners during our talk show that night, however, are explosive, thunderous. I join their angry outbursts, our rage rattling the metal doors in our wing.

Early the next morning, in the wake of our outrage, the officer in charge of prison investigations calls me into his office with a warning. "End this talk show immediately. I don't need a headache," with the implicit threat: *neither do you.*

I tell Baher, "We've been taken off air. Again." He's on the verge of tears. During our months of incarceration, each of us has tried in his own way to maintain a sense of equilibrium. For Peter, meditation has become a solace, his daily practice stretching from minutes to hours. I realize that for Baher, his prayer and our Mulhaq Radio, with its solemn structure of opening with a Quranic verse, its questions carefully considered and delicately posed, and its nightly interviews with the Brotherhood's top minds, have been his anchor. Anger and determination, I realize, have been mine.

In the interminable waits between hearings, the unmarked elasticity of time, a new source of strength begins to emerge for me. It comes from reading books on personal and political struggle provided by our families and by embassy staff. Among my favourites are Nelson Mandela's *Long Walk to Freedom*, Barack Obama's *The Audacity of Hope*, and a book I come to again and again, Viktor Frankl's *Man's Search for Meaning*. Frankl was an Austrian neurologist and Holocaust survivor, and his reflections on his ordeal as a concentration camp prisoner in Auschwitz during World War II resonate deeply with me and also make my situation seem like a joyride by comparison. While I had only to accept the possibility of being in prison and potentially living with a permanent disability, Frankl had endured months of slave labour, faced the daily threat of dying in a gas chamber, and lost his wife, mother and brother in the camps. Yet he concluded that even in the face of extreme suffering, we may also find meaning in life. What matters, Frankl writes, "is to bear witness to the uniquely human potential at its best, which is to transform a personal tragedy into a triumph, to turn one's predicament into a human achievement. When we are no longer able to change a situation . . . we are challenged to change ourselves."[76]

Frankl's concept of Tragic Optimism—including turning suffering into achievement and drawing incentive from life's transitory nature to take responsible action—makes me reflect on my life as a journalist. I have never doubted that journalism is the true manifestation of who I am as a person. A drive to reveal the truth, to help the helpless, has been with me my whole life; yet I now realize that since my incarceration I've begun to see myself as the helpless one. Frankl's words embolden me. *Yes* becomes my new motto. *Yes* to being positive with myself, my cellmates and my family despite my frustrations. *Yes* to overcoming an injury that has robbed me of the full use of my right arm. *Yes* to fighting for justice with the one powerful tool I have—my instincts and skills as a journalist.

CHAPTER 13

ALLIANCE WITH THE DEVIL

March 29–June 15, 2014

Sending a clear message of defiance to our jailers, we decide to resume Mulhaq Radio, and talk of the recent mass sentencing of the Brotherhood members dominates the show in the ensuing days. Around the same time, the prison moves Sohaib, Shadi and Khaled into our wing, placing them together in a second-floor cell. Khaled, I discover, has staged a two-week hunger strike to protest his prison conditions and lack of family visits. I am shocked to see his transformation. When he arrived at Scorpion four months earlier he had been a well-built, clean-shaven, wisecracking young man. Now his prison whites hang loosely on a skeletal frame, he sports a long beard, and he's angry, potentially radicalized.

On March 31 I arrive in court to discover that my lawyer has not shown up, sending an associate in his place. I am not happy about it but a rare opportunity presents itself. In a highly unusual move, the judge calls the defendants out of the cage to address him directly.

As the cage doors opens, photographers stumble over each other to get shots of us, our faces no longer obscured by the metal lattice. Standing shoulder to shoulder in front of the judges, we each take turns speaking into a handheld microphone. I adamantly deny the charges of being a Brotherhood supporter and terrorist and defend our innocence. As if Frankl himself was directing me, I end my statement not with outrage, but levity. "I'm a liberal who has lived most of his life outside of Egypt. If you look at our Marriott bill, you'll see we ordered alcohol," I say, knowing Judge Shehata has a fondness for a drink. "Have you ever heard of a terrorist who drinks alcohol?" He chuckles and signals me to hand the microphone to Peter, who adds to our defense. "My knowledge of Arabic is effectively zero," he says through an interpreter. "The idea that I could have an association with the Muslim Brotherhood is frankly preposterous." Baher pleads his innocence, telling the judge his wife is pregnant and asking the judge to grant him bail so he can witness the birth of his third child. Which Shehata denies.

Over the next three months, the trial unfolds in an uneven, torturous rhythm. There is no certainty about how many more hearings we'll face or how long the trial will drag on. At one point, Khaled collapses in the cage. Judge Shehata, who continues to wear dark sunglasses, is impassive as, almost in tears, I help carry Khaled's body to the door.

The prosecution then begins to present its evidence—hours of bizarre video footage, audio clips and images culled from our seized laptops and cellphones are projected onto a large screen behind the bench. The hundreds of exhibits of visual evidence, at times bearing clear logos from other news networks, would be laughable if the stakes were not so high. There are stories from Peter dating back years, a documentary he made for the BBC on Somalia and the 2013 mall attack in Nairobi; farcical footage of trotting horses and revellers preparing for Christmas festivals, snippets of music videos, and even pictures of Peter and his parents on holiday.

The prosecution shows evidence from the hard drive of the network laptop I inherited when I became bureau chief. Prosecutor Rami el-Sayed smiles as video after video is presented featuring stories about the Brotherhood's anti-government protests, interviews with Brotherhood leaders, sheep farming and soccer. I cringe when a photo of me standing with a gun in each hand among gun-waving Libyan rebels flashes on the screen, remembering the day Sarmad snapped it on my cellphone while we were filming Gaddafi's seized assets for CNN's *BackStory*. Another CNN-related photo from my cellphone is of Mohamed al-Zawahiri from my 2011 interview and, with dismay, I watch the two prosecutors smile knowingly at one another, nodding their heads as if they've scored a decisive victory. I want to point out that most of these videos were shot before I even joined the network, or that sheep farming doesn't reveal much about the Brotherhood, but Abou Bakr signals me to remain silent.

However, the prosecution also reveals footage filmed in the Marriott under my management, including our report on the sorry story of "The Ruler Student," which later aired without our knowledge on the Al Jazeera Mubasher Misr channel, and Peter's report on the closure of hundreds of social and charitable organizations allegedly associated with the Brotherhood, and our coverage of a protest against this crackdown after the government had designated the Brotherhood a terrorist group.

April 27 is bittersweet: it's my fortieth birthday, day 119 behind bars. Although the MRI showed I would need an operation to correct the malunion of the bone in my shoulder and I had hoped to be in a hospital by now, nothing has come of it. Marwa, my mother and Nivine, a close cousin, arrive with two enormous birthday cakes, paper plates printed with colourful balloons and a present that touches me deeply: news that the Canadian Committee for World Press Freedom has awarded me their sixteenth Press Freedom Award and $2,000 in prize money.[77] I ask Marwa to give the money to the family of Mayada Ashraf, a young female journalist who was shot and killed a month earlier while covering clashes between police and Brotherhood supporters in Cairo. The cake, I hand out on the festive plates to the prisoners and guards in my wing. If anyone had asked me how I pictured spending my fortieth birthday, I'm pretty sure I would never have said eating birthday cake in prison with leaders of the Muslim Brotherhood.

In an ironic twist, the next of what will be our fifteen court hearings in total falls on May 3, which happens to be World Press Freedom Day. In the week since my birthday, I have crafted several tweets, which Marwa later sends out, thanking the tens of thousands of Canadians who have signed an Amnesty International petition calling for my release, and an acceptance speech to be read at an awards ceremony organized by the Canadian Committee for World Press Freedom in Ottawa the next night. In the speech smuggled out of prison by Marwa, I write that a key part of our defense has been to convince the judge of our professional integrity, to prove that we are journalists striving for the truth and not agents of terror. That day in court, I have an opportunity to deliver that message in person when the judge unexpectedly lets me out of the cage for the second time to address him directly.

I weigh my words as I walk towards the bench. I know that the foreign press is on our side, but I desperately need to win over the local press and the three men seated in front of me. I take a deep breath and present an emotional plea to the judges to recognize our innocence, expedite our trial and spare us the pain of prison. "Today is World Press Freedom Day," I say. "At least grant our request for bail. The world will be watching." I cannot see Judge Shehata's eyes behind his sunglasses. But a smile plays at the corner of his mouth and he dips his head forward.

"Happy World Press Freedom Day," he says, and orders me back to the cage.

On the streets of Cairo, another drama is unfolding, one we hotly debate on Mulhaq Radio. Egypt has begun the run up to its second presidential election slated for late May. General Abel Fattah el-Sisi, the man Morsi elevated to commander-in-chief of the army and who then ousted him a year later, has resigned his post in order to run for president. Sisi faces just one opponent, longtime liberal and political activist, Hamdeen Sabahi—a clear underdog who has already criticized Egypt's restrictive electoral environment, calling it "political theatre." The Muslim Brotherhood members in our wing agree with him. With most of their Freedom and Justice Party behind bars, and the Muslim Brotherhood banned as a terrorist organization, Sisi's victory is all but assured.

I have become convinced that the country needs a president with Sisi's strong background ties to the military—albeit a demo-cratically elected one—to counter the regional security crisis and unprecedented wave of Islamist terrorism that has gripped the country since Morsi's ouster. Many people think it a necessary step to stop religious fascists from erasing modernity and governing the country according to a strict version of Sharia law, to end escalating violence on the streets and avoid civil war. The country is polarized, crippled by conflict and unable to move forward. It is a stark choice. In the past year, Sisi has cracked down on Islamists, vowing to finish the Muslim Brotherhood. Sadly, he's done it by filling the prisons with many innocent men, caught up in the security sweep—Peter, Baher and I among them.

During our radio hour members of the Brotherhood express their outrage. "President Morsi's ouster was illegitimate," his former prime minister Hisham Kandil yells. "It was a military coup—and a conspiracy that began the moment he was elected!" Supreme Guide Mohamed Badie speaks, his voice broken with tears. "They killed my son Ammar, my first born, and not even the pretense of an investigation."

The prisoners are quiet. Many of them have lost sons, daughters and colleagues in the struggle. Baher ends the show immediately. Later, we can hear another prisoner sobbing in the post-prayer quiet, calling on God to grant him patience and vowing to avenge Badie's son's death.

Another night, Peter brings up Nelson Mandela's experience with the African National Congress, suggesting a similar path of reconciliation might serve Egypt. Badie is quick to dismiss Peter's suggestion, but Wasat Party president Abou Elela Mady and former Speaker of Parliament el-Katatni are onside. Together, they had crafted a reconciliation proposal to address the ongoing bloodshed between Brotherhood supporters and Egypt's security forces. They share their proposal with me when I return from my hour outside. It rejects Sisi's presidential nomination, as well as puts aside their previous demand to reinstate Morsi as president; it calls for new elections and for a new constitution, and demands accountability for the Brotherhood supporters killed in the Rabaa massacre. They decide to smuggle the draft out of prison and Mady later confides that it has been delivered to both the European Union and the US embassy in Cairo. Hearing this, I could only imagine how aggravated the military would be when they received word from the EU and US—two groups it had always accused of meddling in Egypt's internal affairs—that such a document had been delivered to them by imprisoned members of the Brotherhood.

Debate on Egypt's future also rages inside our own cell. During one of many heated exchanges, Peter voices his opposition to Sisi as Egypt's next president.

"Removing his uniform doesn't make him a civilian leader," he argues. "Just look at Gaddafi. Saddam Hussein. Sisi is just another dictator who will take Egypt down the same road."

And where are Libya and Iraq now?" I worry. "I want a democratically elected president, too, but one who understands the battle zone that North Sinai has become, who can protect our borders, someone with an inclusive strategy not an exclusivist like Morsi who is another Islamist with dreams of establishing an Islamic state, and who doesn't command respect from the police and military or even the Arab monarchs of the Arabian Gulf. Have you forgotten that Morsi was the first president to receive Hamas terrorists in the palace?"

Baher agrees with Peter. "The Brotherhood won fair and square," he says. "Yes, they made mistakes but they were democratically elected."

"What about the daily bloodshed on the streets, the breach of the US embassy, the lawlessness in Sinai?" I shout, pacing back and forth across the small cell. "Didn't you hear Hazem Abu Ismail, the Islamist imprisoned upstairs, who tried to run in the last election, say in the talk show that if he'd won he'd have cancelled the Camp David Accord with Israel?"

"Cracking down on dissent," Peter responds, "never solved anything. Egypt needs someone who can transition it to democracy like in South Africa and South America—countries like Brazil that went from a military dictatorship to a functioning democracy despite their poverty."

"But who, in this part of the world, could achieve that?" I ask. "And South America doesn't have thousands of Islamists willing to blow themselves up! Look, I saw the bodies laid out after Rabaa, I'm not condoning the human rights violations under Sisi, but what do you know about the Brotherhood, Peter? You sound like those foreign correspondents who parachute in for a two-week assignment and think they know it all!"

"You're right, Fahmy," Peter says. "I don't understand Egypt much, but I am here now and this has become my battle."

Chastened, I apologize, mortified by my frayed nerves, though still worried; we may disagree on politics but as journalists we share the same struggle, and I'm concerned for him that he doesn't see that in this battle for political power his own network is throwing him under the bus, and that whatever the Al Jazeera lawyers say to him about protecting his interests, they will be answering only to the network.

The three students are a bigger headache, wildcards who have been bundled with us in the case and who I am accused of supervising. One of the first requests our defense team filed was that Peter, Baher and I be tried separately from the students. The court, however, has denied this request despite confirmation from both sides that we do not know each other. What I do know from talking to the students is that police arrested them at a checkpoint in the early hours of January 2, 2014—days after they raided our offices at the Marriott. Khaled had been carrying a professional camera at the time; the cab headed to an apartment registered to Al Noor Media Production and owned by an Ahmed Abdo, another defendant we never met who is being tried in absentia. Officers had returned with the students to raid the media office the next day, confiscating computers, satellite broadcast equipment, satellite phones and cameras and Brotherhood flyers and posters.

In prison, I have learned they met a man named Alaa Adel during the Rabaa sit-in who offered them jobs at his newly established video production company. Alaa Adel provided the equipment and asked the students to film the protests and upload the footage to his accounts on Bambuser and Ustream. But I am still unable to figure out exactly why Khaled, Sohaib and Shadi are on trial with us.

The mystery is solved during our next hearing when the prosecutors present an audio recording of a conversation between the students and an unidentified man. The Al Jazeera lawyers for the defence, realizing the recording incriminates Al Jazeera as actively supporting the Muslim Brotherhood, protest it's inaudible. "I can hear it from my side," a judge says, overruling their objection.

I move to the front corner of the cage nearest the bench and press my ear against the cold metal, straining to hear. "My understanding is that it was for Al Jazeera," says an unidentified man and then I recognize Shadi's voice. "I tell you Dr. Amr Al Qazzas [listed as a high-profile member of the Muslim Brotherhood in the submission to the judge] gave me four cameras and three hundred dollars for each person filming. Some people from Al Jazeera were . . ." I lose Shadi's words before picking them up again "offering three to four thousand pounds . . . We covered many of the Friday protests for him until Al Jazeera started talking to our boys. It's all Al Jazeera Mubasher."

Unidentified man: "Who are you, I have a feeling I met you before?"

Shadi: "Shadi Ibrahim."

Unidentified man: "I don't understand what reports Sohaib sent to them . . . I sent to Al Quds and Aqsa TV channels supporting the . . . legitimacy. We produce . . . 60 to 70 percent of the work on Aljazeera.net. Some get two to three hundred dollars."

A new voice, perhaps another student: "We need money . . . we didn't have enough money to print flags when we entered Tahrir Square in the past days . . ."

Unidentified man: "Let me deal with Al Jazeera and we can possibly solve the problem. The guy in Al Jazeera wants to

help. He told me if anyone is facing security issues, tomorrow
he will get him a visa to Qatar."

It is numbingly clear that the prosecution is using the students' affiliation with the Brotherhood to cement its claims against us, although,
damning as its case against the students is, they have yet to produce
a shred of hard evidence connecting Peter, Baher and me to their
activities. During the recess, Sohaib, more brash than brains, makes
matters worse by telling an Australian reporter that he indeed provided video footage to Al Jazeera Arabic.

Baher's confession is often on my mind, even though, puzzlingly,
it has yet to be presented in court, but I do not mention it to him
again. What's done is done, I tell myself.

My faint hope that Al Jazeera is somehow working in our defense
behind the scenes is decimated during our next court hearing on May
15. That day Farag Fathi enters the courtroom and stops at the cage.
"The best thing you did, Fahmy," he says, "was hiring your own
lawyer. I am going to drop a bomb."

Puzzled, Baher and I look at one another and then translate his
unsettling words to Peter as Fathi approaches the bench to speak.

"Al Jazeera is offending Egypt," Fathi announces. "Against my
advice, they have launched an international lawsuit against Egypt
demanding a hundred and fifty million dollars compensation."
He shakes his fist in the air. "They have misquoted me and fabricated information about this trial on Al Jazeera's Mubasher [Misr]
channel."[78]

I'm unable to look at Peter or Baher as I watch Al Jazeera's lawyer—
Peter and Baher's lead defense—essentially melt down, criticizing
the very network that is paying him to defend them. I grip the bars
to keep my knees from failing as Farag continues angrily. "Al Jazeera
is using my clients. I have emails from the channel telling me they
don't care about the defendants, only about insulting Egypt."

In a move that stuns everyone present, Fathi then announces that he is quitting the case, and strides from the courtroom, leaving his clients high and dry. I watch as his black robe disappears through the courtroom door, reporters and cameramen dashing after him. When I look at Peter and Baher, their faces are white.[79]

Within days of Fathi's resignation, Al Jazeera releases a statement that would have once delighted me: "We now have the best legal representation working in harmony, focused on getting our journalists out of jail." Unfortunately, that representation is Yousri al-Sayed, a lawyer with little experience in criminal law. Peter and I still debate our differences of opinion about the network's loyalty or commitment to us, but our debates over Egypt's next leader end on June 3, after the presidential election when Abdel Fattah el-Sisi is confirmed as Egypt's next president with 97 percent of the vote (according to the government).

The rest of the month is an emotional rollercoaster ride. When we enter the cage on June 5 to hear the prosecution's closing arguments, the courtroom is shockingly empty. I look across the room to the opposite aisle where a crush of cameras is typically stationed, but there are none. My eyes sweep the centre benches looking for Marwa, my parents, local reporters and media stalwarts like the *Guardian's* Patrick Kingsley, who has not missed a court date. All are absent. I fear something sinister is afoot and look anxiously to Peter and Baher as Barakat, the chief prosecutor, takes the floor.

And now, finally, Baher's confession is brought forward. Barakat begins by reciting the questions posed in Baher's interrogation and his incriminating replies—that Al Jazeera allegedly asked him to alter his reports, including coverage of June 30 protests, when the network directed him to film Tahrir Square from an angle that showed it was empty; that the network changed Baher's English translation of Sisi's speech to imply Sisi had called for civil war; and that we worked illegally from the Marriott. "Hence," Barakat says sharply, "the defendant was aware of the channel's deception, and continued participating in transmitting lies, and working with the Brotherhood."

We later discover that the officer handling media access to the court had gotten into an argument with the journalists and refused to admit them but I am weak with relief that there is no press, local or international, present to record a single word of Baher's confession—it is damning.

Before the prosecutor begins making his case against the students, Judge Shehata calls the media into the courtroom. I fret as Barakat cites the students' confessions of participation in pro-Brotherhood protests; Sohaib outright admitting that he received cash for footage he sold to Al Jazeera, while Khalid doesn't deny his Brotherhood affiliations and media work for them. Barakat's voice grows louder as he builds, grandstanding, to his final remarks.

"The relationship between Al Jazeera and the Muslim Brotherhood was like an alliance with the devil, and their reports were intended to harm the state." He points a finger at me, calls me "a member of the terrorist Muslim Brotherhood organization responsible for establishing undercover media centres," accuses me of directly overseeing the work of the three students and the other defendants. His attack moves to Al Jazeera, whom he accuses of destroying Iraq, Syria, Libya and Yemen, and for exercising the same malicious intent toward Egypt. Barakat is almost shouting now, telling the court that "Al Jazeera journalists" did not obtain press passes or permits for their live transmission equipment, "a clear indication that they do not recognize the State, its laws and institutions."

Then the chief prosecutor makes his final plea to the bench: "We request that the court, without compassion or mercy, apply the maximum penalty for the abominable crimes they have committed. Mercy will bring the entire society close to darkness."[80]

———

On June 10 the defense lawyers begin their final arguments. Yousri al-Sayed, the new lawyer paid by Al Jazeera to represent Baher and Peter, stumbles on his way to the bench, forgets Baher's name, makes an ineffectual ten-minute statement that makes no attempt to contest Baher's confession and does little to rebut the serious allegations against his clients. Worse, he proclaims: "There are Al Jazeera spies in this courtroom." Yousef Al Jaber, Al Jazeera's head of cases and IP legal affairs is in the courtroom, but even so, the lawyer's actions are a mystery and an embarrassment. The students' lawyer, up next, rambles for an hour and a half until the judge cuts him off.

Then Abou Bakr takes the floor. He begins by establishing my credentials as a respected journalist with a long career working for reputable international networks. He proceeds to discredit the prosecution's flimsy case against us and its volumes of unsubstantiated, sometimes laughable evidence. He makes a strong case separating us as journalists from the network, and a clear distinction between Al Jazeera English and its pro-Brotherhood Arabic channels. Finally, he argues that although the Brotherhood was declared a terrorist organization on December 25, 2013, the government didn't enact this into law until April 8, 2014, so, technically, we could not be accused of being *terrorists* at the time of our arrest. His one-hour defense is so eloquent that the crowd applauds when he finishes. I'm glad that any good that may come of it will spill over onto Peter and Baher, despite the stupefying ineffectiveness of their lawyers.

In the final hearing five days later, I feel confident as the judge allows me out of the cage to address the court one last time. I bring the book I've been reading, George W. Bush's autobiography entitled *Decision Points*, and hold it up before him.

"In the prosecutor's case, it was mentioned that Al Jazeera ruined Iraq," I say. "It was George W. Bush who ruined it . . . when he entered Iraq. No TV channel can destroy a country or cause its demise.

It's an insult to journalists and media martyrs who lost their lives covering wars and revolutions." I wish I could read his expression behind the dark glasses. "You have had our computers, emails and cellphones for six months . . . I wish there was something to defend myself against, but there is not . . ." I say again that our arrest, and our treatment by a network that should have had its staff's best interests at heart, is politically driven. Ours is a political case.

I set the book before him. "I want you to know, too, that I have already received a sentence," I say. "Let me show you." I lift my left arm and circle it freely in a windmill motion. Then, painfully, I lift my right as far as I am able. It stops awkwardly below shoulder level. "That's as far as it goes—I now have a permanent disability . . . Please give us a verdict today."

A guard escorts me back to the cage, and then Shehata speaks, announcing the date that he and the stone-faced men on either side of him will decide our fate. "Judgment on June 23!"

CHAPTER 14

SENTENCED

June 24, 2013

Thank you Canada. I will be arriving soon for some love. No terrorism plans, I promise :)

The day before the verdict, I write out another tweet for Marwa to send out the next day. Since the final hearing, various high-powered Egyptian officials, including Amr Moussa, former secretary general of the Arab League, have told Marwa that there's a high probability we'll be acquitted. Despite the students' admissions and Baher's so-called confession, our lawyers are also cautiously optimistic the judges will rule in our favour. I am charged, buzzing with excitement at the thought that after fifteen trial hearings and 177 days behind bars, tomorrow we will be going home. I have spent the morning, before what I hope will be my last family visit, filling a piece of paper with tweets to friends and supporters—and a brief celebratory statement—which I plan to pass to Marwa to be published when the judge announces the verdict.

I fold the paper and carefully tuck it under the waistband of my pants. When I arrive in the visiting area, my parents and Marwa are beaming. I'm grateful to see my brother Adel again, who has flown in from Kuwait for the fifth time. Serendipitously, the new US secretary of state, John Kerry, has also arrived in Cairo that morning to meet with Egypt's newly elected president, Abdel Fattah el-Sisi—a visit I hope will play to our favour, though the revolving doors of politics strike me as amusing: not so long ago, during Morsi's brief tenure as president, Kerry had flown in to shake his hand, too, and assure him of the United States' cooperation and support.

Marwa has brought me a pint of Baskin Robbins chocolate ice cream, and I savour the melting but still delicious treat as we dream up plans for our future, anxious to make up for lost time. Two months earlier, we'd submitted a request to the Interior Ministry to get married while I was in prison, but had received no response. Now we discuss the idea of exchanging our marriage vows and hosting a freedom party on the same day. We talk about going dancing and hitting the beaches of Brazil, a country I'd visited and suggested as a potential honeymoon destination. Then we talk of Canada, making a home for ourselves in Vancouver, the beautiful west-coast city that I had fallen in love with when I'd moved there to attend college. Our imaginations race, and before we know it we are listing wedding guests—friends, family and journalists who have stood beside us throughout our fight for freedom. I lean into Marwa, find her hand under the table and slip her the folded paper. "Type the tweets and statement on your phone and send them to the press the moment I'm acquitted," I whisper.

My mom runs a hand through my hair, asking if Baher will be giving me another trim. I nod, tell her we've already picked out our outfits. "I'll be wearing white," I say, smiling.

Adel hands me a small Quran he has brought as a gift. Although we've had our political differences in the past, this ordeal has brought us closer. My dad says optimistically, "I think Al Shami's release is a good sign. The government doesn't want more bad press." Six days earlier, after 307 days behind bars, Abdullah Al Shami, a Cairo-based reporter accused of aiding the Brotherhood, was released from Tora on a health pardon after a 149-day hunger strike during which he lost close to forty pounds.

Back in the cell, our mood is upbeat. Rock music plays on Baher's radio as he trims Peter's hair. I tell them about my family's assurances, and that I think Kerry's visit will help.

"*Inshallah*, God willing, tomorrow at this time we will be with our families," Baher says. "I can't wait to hug my kids, Jehan and my parents."

"Guys," Peter interjects, standing to allow me a turn in Barber Baher's chair. "You need to curb your optimism a little."

I wave off his warning. "What's the first thing you're going to do when you're free, Peter?"

"Throw a good party," he says, relenting. "Then I'm going to take my family on a long sailing trip."

"I'm going to take my family on a vacation, maybe to a beach somewhere. Maybe to Disneyland," Baher enthuses. On the radio, the song "Wind of Change" by the Scorpions is playing. An omen. "Baher, turn it up," I say happily, and we belt out the lyrics.

That night at seven o'clock we tune into BBC to follow John Kerry's press conference on the heels of his visit with the recently inaugurated president. We huddle together, listening intently as we learn that the US has released $575 million in military aid, funding that the States had frozen after Morsi's overthrow, and that Kerry has recommitted to providing ten Apache helicopters. I know many of my media colleagues are at that press conference; will one of them ask the question that matters most to us in our cell? Then, finally: Has the secretary of state spoken to President Sisi about the journalists' court case and impending verdict tomorrow? We hear Kerry confirm that he discussed our case in his two-hour meeting with the president. "He gave me a very strong sense of his commitment to make certain that the process he has put in place, a re-evaluation of human-rights legislation, a re-evaluation of the judicial process, and other choices that are available are very much on his mind," Kerry says.[81] Vague as it was in political speak, we seize upon its promise.

In our final Mulhaq Radio Show that evening, I summarize the press conference to the Brotherhood inmates, only a handful of whom have access to radios. Former prime minister Hisham Kandil and former Speaker of Parliament, Saad el-Katatni, who have listened to the press conference, tell us that Kerry's visit is our ticket out of jail. I am secretly ecstatic but am careful to bridle my feelings, aware that Mohamed Badie and others have been sentenced to death while I am going home. In deference to them, we speak briefly of the death sentences and the lack of due process. In the case of Badie's verdict, the judge concluded his case after two hearings and without allowing the defense to present their full argument. As we close the nightly radio show that has kept me sane, I feel very lucky.

The next morning, dressed in a white, long-sleeved shirt and white training pants, I sit handcuffed to Baher in the back of the blue truck as it transports us across the prison complex to the courthouse. I glance at Peter, who is cuffed to Khaled, and wonder, not for the first time, what is going through his head. With little knowledge of the language, and in Egypt for only three weeks before being ensnared by its ruthless politics, Peter has impressed me with his tremendous poise and calm. I smile at Baher. His unfathomable confession notwithstanding, he, too, has impressed me by managing to remain cheerful over the past six months. The three of us have become a tight-knit unit in this long voyage, more brothers than colleagues, and I feel grateful for their friendship. I had, if not forgiven, at least tried to forget Baher's scathing confession. Any convulsions of anger toward him are dispelled when I see his children's tearful faces during prison visits. Instead, I direct my fury toward Al Jazeera for not challenging his confessions and hiring lawyers I consider unfit for such a case. I watch the three students reading their Qurans and quietly recite the few verses I have memorized since my incarceration calling on God to acquit me. Sohaib has written another prayer for me on a piece of paper, suggesting I read it before the verdict, and I tuck it into my pocket.

When we arrive at the courthouse, guards deposit us in a holding cell at the back of the building and remove our handcuffs. Baher and the young co-defendants pray while Peter and I anxiously await our final court appearance. After half an hour, the guards escort us to the cage. Walking into the courtroom feels like entering the ring for a championship boxing match. Spectators pack the benches and cameras are everywhere, their shutters clicking in rapid-fire succession. I am overwhelmed as I scan the room from the cage and see Marwa, my mom—my father, too frail and nervous to attend, watches from home—Adel, Peter's brothers, Mike and Andrew, in from Australia; for the first time, Canadian ambassador David Drake; the ambassadors from Australia, the UK and Holland, as well as international human rights observers and my friends in the media, all of whom have gathered to hear the verdict. I wave to the crowd with my good arm, but even it feels wooden, weighted.

Baher offers me a cigarette and I accept it to distract myself, puffing so hard that Sarah El Deeb, a friend and reporter from Associated Press shouts, "What's with the cigarette?" I put it out and shove my hands into my pockets. Feeling the note, I take it out and begin reading the Quranic verse Sohaib transcribed. Never in my life have I been as nervous as I am in this moment. My hands shake so badly that I have a hard time reading the words on the page. Marwa and my brother walk towards the cage to say hello, but the officers, stricter today than they previously have been, ask them to return to their seats. From the corner of my eye, I notice Peter wave, and I look up to see both of his brothers whistling and waving from across the courtroom—Mike gives us a thumbs up sign. I glance sideways at Baher. He looks as apprehensive as I feel. He had asked Jehan, now seven months pregnant, not to come to today's hearing. I wonder whether that makes it easier or more difficult for him.

Minutes later the bailiff walks in and loudly announces the arrival of the judges. We move to the front of the cage to get a better view of the bench and I pull Baher and Peter close to me, draping an arm around each of their shoulders. We huddle together, heads close, faces inches from the metal, as the judges take their seats. I can feel the intensity of Baher's emotion, see that he is barely holding himself together.

My own heart hammers wildly and I inhale in quick, shallow breaths. I focus my gaze on Judge Shehata's face, watch him finally remove his sunglasses to read the judgment before him. He begins without preamble: "Seven years of maximum-security incarceration for Mohamed Mahmoud Fadel Fahmy. Seven years of maximum-security incarceration for Peter Greste. Seven years to Baher Mohamed Hazim, and an additional three years for possessing ammunition."

I grab the metal cage to keep myself from collapsing. We clutch each other, Peter and Baher and I, all of us struggle to keep ourselves upright.

The judge sentences the students, Sohaib Saad, Khaled Abdel Raouf and Shadi Ibrahim, to seven years, and all those tried in absentia to ten. Only two defendants of the twenty bundled together in the case are acquitted—Shadi's brother and, surprisingly, the boy he was arrested with, Anas Beltagy, the son of the prominent Muslim Brotherhood leader jailed in Scorpion.

The courtroom erupts, but it feels like someone has muted the audio on the scene before me. I look into the crowd seeing, but not fully registering, images of journalists yelling, friends standing tearful and slack-jawed, our families crying. My gaze stops on the face of my mother, her usually smooth countenance collapsed, tears streaming down her cheeks. On Adel yelling furiously at the court. On Marwa's horrified expression, her hand raised to her mouth. Then, in a rush, the sound is back, chaotic. Deafening.

My anger returns with it. I want to express outrage but the students have started chanting loudly and I can't make myself heard. I scream, but it's like yelling into the face of a hurricane. I look at Peter and am surprised to see him waving his fists in the air, shaking them. Time moves in slow motion. I watch as several guards enter the cage, usher us all towards the rear door, but I am not ready. I will never be ready. Furiously, desperately, I grip the metal grille as several officers try to pry me off. Aggressively, I push the hand of one officer away, hanging on to the bar with every ounce of strength I possess with the other, screaming that they will pay for this. I can feel the mesh cutting into the underside of my fingers as officers wrench my arm, pull at my body, sending such spasms of pain through my shoulder that finally I surrender and let them push me towards the rear exit. I can see dozens of police standing by in full riot gear, and hear the students shouting a familiar chant: "*Down, down, military rule!*"

Outside, police surround us. Two yank my arms behind my back to handcuff me until a third orders them to stand down. The blue truck—the hated prison transport vehicle I'd hoped to never see again—rolls up and, pushed forward by the guards, we must climb into the back. Everyone takes a seat, but I refuse. Instead, I stand in the centre of the scorching, putrid box, delirious with rage, and yell my frustration to the world. When I finally collapse on the bench, Baher lays his head on my shoulder and breaks down. I loop my good arm around his head.

"Jehan is about to have a baby, Fahmy," he cries. "She can't handle this."

I have no words to console him. We are quiet on the ride back to prison, lost in our thoughts, only the steady hum of the engine and the sounds of Baher's occasional shuddering breaths to break the silence.

News of the verdict precedes our arrival: inmates solemnly murmur sympathies and even the guards are subdued as they lead us to our cell.

Peter climbs up to his bunk, and I lie on mine below him. I can hear his quiet sobs and I crane my head around to see him, his face to the wall. I open my mouth to speak, to comfort him, but Baher, lying on his own bed, shakes his head, whispers: "Leave him alone."

That night we forgo the talk show and remain in our bunks. I can hear the comments echoing along the corridor. Former prime minister Hisham Kandil, who possesses a radio, shouts: "Britain and the Netherlands have summoned the Egyptian ambassadors." This news heartens me: both countries have journalists tried and sentenced in absentia—Sue Turton and Dominic Kane, and an unknown Dutch woman, Johanna Indeniette.

"The Australians have released harsh condemnations," shouts former parliamentary speaker el-Katatni. "The international community is outraged. It will not end here."

I translate for Peter and turn on our radio hoping to catch news of Canada's reaction. Scrolling through the Arabic channels reveals near unanimous national support for the verdict and strong condemnation of the Marriott Cell and its journalists who conspired with the devil—the Brotherhood. Unable to tolerate the sound of prisoners reading Quranic verses, I turn up the volume as BBC's *Newshour* begins. The broadcast opens with an audio clip I have just lived: wrenching sounds of pandemonium in the courtroom marking the reaction to the judge's verdict. US secretary of state John Kerry calls the sentence "chilling, draconian."[82] British prime minister David Cameron condemns it as "completely appalling." Australian prime minister Tony Abbott has personally called Sisi to proclaim Peter's innocence and their foreign minister, Julie Bishop, states that the Australian government is "shocked," "deeply dismayed," and "appalled by the severity" of the sentence, and simply cannot understand how the court reached the verdict based on the evidence presented in the case. I listen intently for word from my own prime minister, Stephen Harper, or from John Baird, our minister of foreign affairs, but there is nothing. Canada's ambassador, David Drake, is quoted merely as saying, "We are very disappointed . . . we are digesting this. We have to put our faith in the judicial system." Lynne Yelich, John Baird's lieutenant responsible for consular affairs, has issued a news release saying she was very disappointed with the sentence, while Stephen Harper manages only a tweet asking for the Egyptian government's "co-operation" in returning me home.[83]

Feeling betrayed by Egypt and abandoned by my own prime minster, I want to shut myself off from the world. My family has told me how hard Canada's consular team in Egypt has been working, both on my case and to make my life in prison easier, but at this point I badly need swift, powerful intervention from the top. With the Canadian media also speaking out strongly, I'm beginning to understand how very hard it is to get a reluctant government to advocate forcefully for its citizens abroad when they are in desperate situations and facing grave human rights violations.

The next morning, after a sleepless night, I jump when the guard drops the daily newspaper *Al-Masry Al-Youm* through our hatch. I open it to a photo of Marwa in the arms of Leila Fadel, a friend and National Public Radio correspondent. Both women are crying. I've been able to hold it together until this moment, but seeing the look of devastation on Marwa's face undoes me. It's my turn to break down. I collapse on my bed, inconsolable, tears streaming down my cheeks. Peter approaches and lays a hand on my shoulder. At that

moment the reality of my future—the next seven years of my life
behind bars—begins to sink in.

Any lingering hope that this is all some terrible mistake disappears later that morning when a guard yells at us to pack our stuff.
We are moving to a new prison. We stuff clothes, food, bed sheets,
toiletries, the few plates and plastic utensils we own, our radio,
books, and our most coveted possession now that the heat of summer
is upon us—a box of bottled water—into plastic bags and cardboard
boxes and then pile our things in the corridor.

"Where are they taking us, Fahmy?" one of the students yells
from the top floor.

"I don't know," I say, "hopefully not Scorpion." Baher rushes to
speak to an investigation officer posted at the entrance to the wing
and returns minutes later with the answer. "They are taking us to
Mazraa Prison."

El Mazraa, or "The Farm," not to be confused with Mulhaq Al
Mazraa, is another building within the sprawling Tora Prison complex where former president Hosni Mubarak, his sons, and his government cronies are apparently detained.

News of our impending departure circulates quickly, causing a
commotion in our wing. Hisham Kandil and Bassem Ouda, returning from their hour outside, stop to say goodbye.

"Fahmy, be strong," Kandil says, shaking my hand. "You can get
out on appeal. Just distance yourself from the Qataris. Trust me, I know
from my time as prime minister how treacherous they are. Beware also
of Sisi's 'coup regime,'" he adds. "They are merciless. You were smart
to get pro-government figures like Naguib Sawiris, Amr Moussa and
Dr. Farouk El-Baz on your side, but don't forget Baher doesn't have
your connections or a foreign passport. He needs support to get out."

I thank him for his advice. The irony of being hugged at this
moment by Morsi's Muslim Brotherhood prime minister, as he says
goodbye, does not escape me.

We hustle from cell to cell, reaching up to the hatches to shake the extended hands. Many have pushed chairs or beds against their doors and I can see their faces pressed against the bars. A Brotherhood leader on death row who I do not know is tearful as he shakes my hand. Another prisoner, Sheikh Hazem Abu Ismail, the former presidential candidate, extends his arm through the bars, and touches my head. I look up to see that he, too, is crying.

"Allah protect you, Fahmy," he says, unabashed by the tears rolling down his face to dampen his long beard. "Take care of Baher." As I move to the next cell, I can hear the Sheikh call after me, "Keep your head up and don't bow down to anyone but Allah!"

I can barely contain my own emotion and glancing back, I see Baher wiping his eyes.

"We will miss the Al Jazeera talk show, but we'll keep it going," promises a former presidential aide who is also facing the death sentence. It is almost unbearable to shake his hand knowing I will probably never see him again; that he might be executed any day. Despite our differences, and an uncrossable political divide, I realize I have formed bonds with these men. Masks drop in prison. Politics become secondary to one's simple humanity. For the past six months, these men, some of them jihadists who call death and destruction down on the world for an inhumane ideology, have generously shared their food and meagre possessions. We have gotten to know their wives, sons and daughters, discussed their dreams, ideas and ambitions, and while I will never condone their ideology, I understand now the sentiment: "One's man terrorist is another's freedom fighter."

Among the many lessons learned during my time in prison is that the word "terrorist" has become a convenient political tool used by governments to label groups or individuals who oppose their interests— something that can be reversed overnight if those interests change. While there is no universal agreement on the definition of terrorism, the act is usually attributed to the threat or use of violence in pursuit of political, religious, or ideological aims by non-state actors.

The humanity I have discovered in these men does not alter the fact that during their rise to power and since their ouster, the entreaties by some Brotherhood leaders to their followers to take to the streets in protest has often ended in violence and bloodshed; that the Brotherhood's ultimate goal of establishing a religious state necessitates the end of a civic one. I have also come to understand the strategic and often duplicitous nature of the Brotherhood leaders, educated and patient men willing to play the long game and manoeuvre within established political norms to achieve their ultimate goal. The interim government's designation of the Muslim Brotherhood as a terrorist organization, right after Morsi's ouster, was undoubtedly a preemptive strike against a group that has, over decades, garnered significant grassroots support not solely as a political entity, but through its role as a social welfare organization providing health care, education and other services to thousands of impoverished Egyptians poorly served by the government.

Days before my arrest, I reported on the initiation of Article 86 in Egypt's penal code, which allows criminal courts to jail any member of a "terrorist" group, including the Muslim Brotherhood, for up to life in prison. At the time I understood the political expediency of this unprecedented move to brand the Brotherhood as terrorists, but I fretted that freedom of the press, human rights and the rule of law would also become casualties. Never in my wildest dreams, though, did I imagine that the crackdown on these "terrorists" would lead to me being convicted as one.

CHAPTER 15

WHAT WOULD I DO WITHOUT YOU?

June 2014

Inside Mazraa Prison, a security entourage searches us in a respectful, professional manner. At least a dozen high-ranking officers, investigation personnel and prison guards watch, curious about the infamous members of the Marriott Cell.

A tall, thin officer says, "The whole world is talking about you guys, even the White House." I later learn he's the warden of our wing.

"We're a very dangerous group," I say sarcastically. To my surprise, he smiles. We follow him down a corridor to our new home, a warehouse-sized cell with ten bunks, three bathrooms, a small kitchenette with a sink, a microwave, and an infestation of cockroaches. The cell houses four men, three of whom—Ibrahim, Hussein and Sayed—identify themselves as longtime, senior government employees in the Mubarak regime, imprisoned even before his overthrow. They've been in here for several years. They retreat to their bunks at the far end of the room as the fourth inmate, a large well-built man with a thick moustache, wearing tight cycling shorts and a dingy white tank top, rushes up to us. This remarkable figure introduces himself simply as Joe, tells us he's been in prison for close to ten years for using and selling counterfeit US money, announces "I'm your man here," then turns to the warden. "But I should be released in the next month or two, right sir?"

The warden has obviously heard this countless times. "We're still waiting for your release documents," he says dismissively, and pointing to the swarms of cockroaches, tells him to mop the floor. He jabs a thumb towards me. "That's Mohamed Fahmy. Coordinate with him."

I extend my hand and Joe shakes it. "Better you deal with Baher," I say quickly.

"A guard will bring you your blue uniforms," the warden tells us. "You can't leave your cell for the first week or so, and when you do, you'll wear the blue uniform at all times." The blue colour of the uniforms signifies to all that we are now convicted felons.

I protest that it's against regulations to confine us to our cells. "You're a convict now," he responds tersely, "and you'll get a visit once every two weeks, not once a week."

The blue prison garb turns out to be mismatched, ill-fitting rags, uncomfortably rough against the skin. They will be both our pyjamas and day clothes until we can arrange for our families to bring an acceptable alternative. I lay my belongings on an empty bunk and survey the living quarters of the four inmates we have joined. They occupy the last two bunks on opposite walls closest to the bathrooms and kitchenette. A modest cluster of furniture surrounds each bunk—a small fridge, TV, fan, table and chairs, even a portable closet—an attempt at comfort, but the sense of permanence is more depressing than the cockroaches.

Baher returns from his conversation with Joe—he has struck a deal. A guy named Shahat will mop the floor and make us coffee every morning. He will also bring us newspapers and clean the bathrooms. We just have to ask our families to deposit money in his prison account. The fee, roughly US$100 a month, is high, but that likely includes a cut for Joe.

I try to recapture some of the equilibrium and sense of purpose that Frankl's book once inspired in me. I carefully compose brief notes on an old paper bag I've brought with me from Mulhaq, 140-character missives to pass to Marwa, when she can next visit, to tweet out, entirely different in tone from the ones I had written two days earlier: *Qatar/Al Jazeera raised a $150 million suit against Egypt while I was hanging on a thread in a cage.* And: *We have become a bargaining chip between Qatar, Egypt and their coalitions.* I hide the notes, suspecting Joe is spying on us. When, later in the afternoon, a guard yells, "*Zeyara!* Mohamed Fahmy!" I am surprised. I rush to the bathroom, tear off the portion of the paper bag I've written on, fold it until it is small enough to hide undetected in my underwear, and then quickly flush the toilet before emerging.

I paste a smile on my face as I enter the visiting area where my parents, Marwa and Adel wait, conscious of my baggy, threadbare uniform and how much it must hurt them to see me here, a convict. "Hello, hello." My voice is a bright falsetto. "Welcome to my new home in the Farm." I hug them one by one. I am distressed by the shocked expression on my mother's face as she eyes my surroundings. "What do you think? Five-star treatment, Marriott style!" I attempt to be a good host, ordering sodas and bottled water from a modest kiosk in the visiting area for them, a coffee for myself. I tell them we are all in one big cell that looks like a small airplane hangar, along with former members of Mubarak's gang, and a petty criminal called Joe. "He has a poster of President Sisi on the wall above his bed," I say, and the laughter that follows is a relief.

"So you go from being with the Brotherhood to the pro-Sisi prisoners," my mom jokes. "Now you've seen it all."

My brother hands me a bucket of fried chicken, whispering that he stuffed some news articles under the chicken. I am ravenous but not for the food, desperate to know if there is any word from the Canadian government. My father is encouraging in his reply. "Listen, son, the world has erupted. The Canadian press is in an uproar over the government's lack of response to the verdict and the Canadian consular team are coming to see you tomorrow."

The view of John Baird, Canada's foreign minister, has changed little in the two months since he visited Cairo in April, when he used the same argument to justify Harper's failure to lobby for my case. Our conviction seems to have changed nothing. He has issued a statement saying "bullhorn diplomacy" will not win my release.[84]

"Lynne Yelich in Ottawa said Canada is very concerned," my mom says. "She—"

"*Concerned?*" I think of John Kerry's powerful recent statement, made even though there are no US citizens involved. I have not heard of Lynne Yelich before. David Drake, the Canadian ambassador, has not even met with the prosecutor. "They leave it to mid-level officials and send faxes to the foreign ministry instead of picking up the phone or going in person. It's not enough!"

"I spoke to CTV in Canada live right after the verdict," Marwa says, trying to cheer me up. "And to CNN for the first time. I am talking to everyone in the media now."

I take her hand, touched by her sacrifice that will surely jeopardize the job she loves. It could take months before we can launch an appeal and secure a retrial, so our best hope now is to get me transferred to a private hospital. Even though the MRI confirmed I need an operation, and despite the non-stop lobbying efforts of my family, the Ministry of Interior has repeatedly refused a hospital transfer. Still, I urge my family to keep pressing, hoping security at the hospital may be more lax and that I might be able to access my friends in the media, find a way to communicate with the lawyers, petition government officials.

We decide to focus on trying to make the transfer happen.

I realize, judging from the Canadian government's weak response to the verdict, that we are probably on our own for the next step. Abou Bakr does not specialize in appeals so he will be turning the application to appeal our case over to someone who does. Feeling both desperate and powerless to change things, we decide to all take separate action: Marwa is charged with physically knocking on the door of Egypt's interior minister and getting me that hospital transfer; my camera-shy mother agrees to appear on television to convince the local media that I am innocent; Adel will handle the foreign press; my father will get involved in pressuring Al Jazeera to hire a top appeal-court lawyer to try and secure a retrial—not idiots like Farag Fathi who either quit halfway through the case or who confirm the prosecution's accusations against us—and to continue to pummel Al Jazeera to honour their commitment to reimburse my legal fees for Abou Bakr, who I will want to rehire as my defense lawyer if our appeal should succeed.

At the end of our visit, Marwa hands me a bag with six blue T-shirts and trousers, underwear, socks, towels, batteries for the radio and a few books. How did she anticipate exactly what I would need? I am moved by her thoughtfulness. I ask her only for insecticide next time, and chlorine bleach to kill the cockroaches.

"I love you all," I say, overcome with gratitude. "What would I do without you?"

Back in the cell, I fish out the articles Adel has smuggled in. One of them is by British journalist Robert Fisk, a Middle East war correspondent since 1976, and author of several internationally acclaimed books on the region whose views I respect above all others. In journalism circles, Fisk is a giant—and to me personally, a hero. An Arabic speaker and equally respected by Westerners and Arabs, Fisk is one of the few journalists to have interviewed Osama bin Laden, which he did on three separate occasions. I'd heard his story of how, as he sat inside a tent surrounded by armed al-Qaeda fighters, bin Laden had tried to recruit him to Islam. Fisk's account of his reply, as he sought desperately for an answer that would not insult his terrifying host, is legendary: "'Sheikh Osama, I am not a Muslim. [. . .] I am a journalist. [. . .] And the job of a journalist is to tell the truth.' Bin Laden was watching me like a hawk. And he understood I was declining his offer. In front of his men, it was now bin Laden's turn to withdraw, to cover his retreat gracefully. 'If you tell the truth, that means you are a good Muslim.'"[85]

Fisk's article, entitled "The Jailing of Al-Jazeera Journalists: A Proxy in the War between Qatar and Saudi Arabia," and published in the *Independent* on the day of the verdict, adds important nuance to the story behind the conviction.

> Al Jazeera is a Qatari foreign policy project and Qatar supported the elected President, Mohamed Morsi, before Sisi rescued his beloved Egyptian people by chucking the bounder from power. And in one stroke, Egypt lost $10 billion in Qatari funding . . . The Saudis stepped in of course, as they have with the Sunni chaps now threatening Iraq, to underwrite all Egypt's debts (so long, of course, as Sisi leaves the Egyptian Salafists alone). And how to punish those pesky Qataris? Why, bang up their journos of course. For "aiding terrorists," for God's sake.[86]

Fisk's words remind me of a recent *Wall Street Journal* article that quoted Saudi prince Bandar bin Sultan, a former ambassador to Washington, saying that Qatar was "nothing but 300 people . . . and a TV channel." The "TV channel" being, of course, the pan-Arab Al Jazeera Network.[87]

I show Peter the articles and remind him that Al Jazeera was not upfront about the situation on the ground when they deployed him to Egypt—it reaffirms my belief that we must hire independent legal counsel for the next phase. But, to my dismay, Baher and Peter are still willing to accept a lawyer hired by the network for the appeal. I argue with them about this approach, trying to dissuade them, but they do not share my growing mistrust of our employer.

Living closely with the students now gives me the chance to delve more deeply into the shadowy connection. Shadi confirms what we heard in the audio recording, and that the Brotherhood took over the State TV broadcast truck sometime during the six-week Rabaa sit-in, and fed footage to the banned local Al Jazeera Mubasher Misr and Al Jazeera's international Arabic *and English* language channels. It's slippery, unethical conduct—and it forges a damning link between Al Jazeera English and the Brotherhood. That it occurred when I was a private citizen, weeks before I'd even accepted the job as English bureau chief, makes no difference of course.

Unlike Shadi, the budding cameramen Sohaib and Khaled were devoted to using their skills to support the Brotherhood—and had no knowledge of Al Jazeera's tenuous legal status. Nor, as young activists fighting the old regime, would they have cared even if they did. Sohaib, wild and self-confident as he was, had also hoped the money he earned as a freelancer would boost his chances of marriage to his girlfriend, Sarah—a dream the verdict has utterly destroyed.

Joe, our Sisi-loving cellmate, who chuckles at our passionate political debates, turns out to have been an eyewitness to one of the major events of the revolution. Joe escaped from Abu Zaabal Prison during the infamous mass prison breaks when armed gangs took advantage of the chaos on Cairo streets to free tens of thousands of prisoners—in their ranks were Brotherhood supporters and members, including Morsi himself—as well as known Islamist terrorists.

"It was like a war zone," Joe says. "Gunshots. Tear gas. Constant gunfire." Joe refused to leave his cell, fearing he would be shot like many escaping prisoners. "Then, out of the blue, an older, veiled woman walks into my cell calling for her son, a known drug dealer."

"Where was he?" I ask, riveted by Joe's account.

"I had no idea. He was detained in another wing and I told her that. But once I realized this old woman had just walked in, I ran out of the cell and sprinted for the gates." He pauses before going on to tell me that on his way out, he saw dozens of corpses of prisoners and some of guards he knew. He says: "There were several men wearing checkered black and white scarves, keffiyehs, running the prison break. I heard them speaking with Palestinian accents—they were Bedouin or Hamas, I'm not sure." I'd heard a rumour that masked, armed Bedouins mounted on bulldozers and driving pickup trucks had broken through the prison gates and that shadowy Palestinian gangs had orchestrated the simultaneous prison breaks. Rumours also abounded that the breakouts had been orchestrated by Mubarak's government to remind Egyptians that chaos and crime would be the offspring of their revolt, and to encourage protestors to clear the streets and return home to protect their families from escaped convicts.

Joe had spent months savouring his freedom until, realizing that his prison term was coming to an end, he had turned himself in. Unfortunately, he was an exception. Thousands of prisoners had apparently joined insurgencies in Sinai and across the Middle East. I recall the story of Ahmed Nofel, a prominent member of Hamas's al-Qassam military wing, who had escaped during the prison breaks, too, and was smuggled to Gaza days later through the tunnels in Sinai. He had returned to a hero's welcome in Gaza surrounded by hundreds of supporters. He told the crowd that he was ready to fight in the "next battle," and hoped to see the Muslim Brotherhood in power in Egypt and around the world. "They have spent thirty years being enslaved by the regime."[88]

Joe's story is a poignant and painful reminder to me that the Arab Spring, in which I had had such high hopes and which had arisen from pure and passionate popular dissent, also created unexpected and devastating consequences. We three journalists are living proof of it.

Days into our sentence, the prison authority grants us a daily outing from our cell. On some days it's an hour; on others, it's two. However, unlike Mulhaq Al Mazraa, they do not allow us outside the walls of the prison. Instead, we stroll up and down the corridors in our wing lined with cells similar in size to ours, each housing more than a dozen convicts. The men in our wing are not high-level political prisoners, but low-level military conscripts, all serving one- to two-year sentences, mostly for deserting mandatory military service. The authorities have instructed them not to speak to us so they gawk curiously as we pass. I try to enjoy the sunshine streaming through the barbed wire covering the open ceiling above. I enjoy watching Shadi teach Peter Arabic, and Peter return the favour, helping the student improve his English. We find ways to survive. To hope.

I discover a room in the wing that has been transformed into a quiet, lushly carpeted mosque, with rows of chairs at the back, two ceiling fans, and an audio system used by the sheikh for his Friday sermon. Although I'm not religious, the room is quiet, and feels like a sanctuary, a place where I can, at least briefly, put away the inner turmoil that threatens to consume me.

One afternoon a prison officer announces that the sheikh has arrived to test the prisoners' knowledge of the Quran. Those who pass the test will receive an extra family visit. I badly want this visit to scheme with my family, to smuggle out notes to the media and to advocate for my innocence. Baher, the students and I sit on the carpeted floor of the mosque surrounding the sheikh and await our turn to recite verses from the Quran. When mine comes, the students watch in amusement, barely keeping straight faces as I attempt to sweet-talk my way into my extra family visit. I inform the sheikh that I know only the first two verses of the Quran by heart. His jaw drops, but he nods for me to begin. I clumsily perform my short recital, stumbling over the words. A long silence follows my performance. Then the sheikh nods to the students and they and Baher take turns flawlessly reciting various verses of the holy book. It is no surprise that everyone passes except me. My only consolation is the entertainment my story provides to Peter when we relay the details of my bold but pitiful attempt.

CHAPTER 16

TWO STRONG WOMEN

July 5–August 30, 2014

I failed to memorize the Quran, but my prayers are answered. On July 5, a guard opens the door, yells the familiar refrain: "Pack your stuff!" This time, though, he also points a finger at me. "Fahmy, you're being transferred to hospital. You've got fifteen minutes."

I had hoped for it and badgered everyone for it. It had finally happened. But how? Joe has reminded me time and again that he can count on one hand the number of prisoners transferred out of Tora for medical care. I look at Peter and Baher dumbly then rocket into action, stuffing clothes, books and personal items into paper bags. I'm afraid they will change their minds. Peter and Baher come over and sit on my bed. I tell my friends I will use the time to meet the lawyers, speak to Al Jazeera, and lobby government officials. "I'll be back after the operation," I promise.

"Can I have your bed?" Sohaib asks and I smile.

"Sure, brother."

Joe shakes his head in amazement. Unexpectedly, he gives me a hug, vows to come and visit me when he's released. "Soon," he says.

This time there's no blue truck waiting for me, but a convoy of police cars, an ambulance and personal escort from the police general in charge of the police station in the district where the hospital is located. When we pull up at the entrance of the private As-Salam International Hospital on the Nile Corniche in south Cairo, I see Marwa standing outside, smiling. The glass doors slide open and we enter a pristine, air-conditioned foyer bustling with families, children, staff and the hubbub of hospital life. I am in such a state of euphoria that I scarcely notice the stares directed towards me, a blue-clad convict handcuffed to an officer and escorted by half a dozen police. Marwa quietly greets me and slips into the elevator behind us. We emerge on the seventh floor and the police hustle me down the hall and into a private room.

I am thrilled with my new home. It is bright and spacious, and the bed has clean white sheets.

"Handcuff him to the bed," the police general orders. He calls over a veiled nurse who stands nervously in the corner of the room. "This door is to remain locked at all times."

To my surprise Marwa, who has been standing quietly at the door, protests. "Sir, he is not a Brotherhood member. Handcuffing him to the bed could make his injury worse."

He ignores her, takes a last look around and, seemingly satisfied, steps outside with the officers. One returns shortly, introduces himself as Mohamed, second in command at the district police station, and handcuffs my left hand to the metal headboard. "I know your story inside out, Fahmy, and I know you're not Brotherhood." He winks before leaving the room.

Outside, I can hear Marwa pleading with the officers. The urgency in her voice tells me something is wrong.

"What's the problem?" I ask the nurse in the corner.

"I hear the prisoner in the next room wants you moved to another floor." She lowers her voice to a whisper. "It's the business tycoon Hisham Talaat Moustafa. He doesn't want to be next to a Brotherhood member."

Moustafa's story is well known across the Middle East. Courts sentenced the multimillionaire and former parliamentarian to fifteen years for ordering the brutal slaying of his girlfriend, famous Lebanese singer Suzanne Tamim. I have little time to dwell on the irony of a convicted murderer complaining about me—the officers return to tell me I'm moving, and the whole entourage escorts me to a room on the fourth floor. It is similarly spacious, with a flat screen TV and glass doors leading onto a balcony overlooking the Nile.

The police general enters, stating there are to be no visits without permission. Breaking this rule will result in an immediate transfer back to prison. Marwa follows him out, but turns to me and smiles before closing the door. I have no idea what's just happened, only that the handcuffs are gone.

Mohamed—the second in command—and two armed guards remain. "Fahmy," he says, "two guards will be inside the room with you at all times. They'll sleep here on the couches," he points at an L-shaped alcove inside and right of the door but beyond my line of sight. "Three police officers will be stationed in the room next door." Then he lowers his voice and confides almost conspiratorially, "You're here because the head of the country's prison authority himself ordered your transfer."

I nod as if in understanding, though I don't know why the man ultimately responsible for Egypt's prisons would do such a thing. I rather suspect Marwa has something to do with it.

"*Basha*, are the handcuffs staying off?"

"Don't worry," he replies, "Marwa spoke to me about this and we convinced the police general to keep the cuffs off. Just give it a day or two. All will be fine." And with another wink, Mohamed is gone, leaving me bemused but very happy.

The next morning I awake to the exquisite luxury of breakfast in bed. I relish the cup of Turkish coffee and glass of orange juice. There is no sign of the doctor but two new guards stand just outside my door, puffing on cigarettes and talking loudly. I turn the TV on to CNN and then I walk to the glass doors leading to the balcony. They are locked, but below me I can see cars moving along the corniche, and on the sidewalks ordinary people hurrying to their jobs, to school, to work. The morning sun glints brightly on the Nile, and palm trees dot the causeway that stretches along the river. An ordinary, beautiful summer day but I am cut off from it. I am still a convict and a traitor, confined to this room under armed guard; but compared to Peter and Baher, who remain inside Tora Prison, I am lucky.

I hear Ian Lee's voice on CNN and turn to see my former colleague onscreen. His report is on Egypt's hard economic times and the rise in prices on Cairo's streets. Seconds later, Ivan Watson is on air—the man who literally pulled me off Cairo's streets and into CNN as the Arab Spring was beginning. I am so glad to see my old friend's face, listen to his effortless delivery. He makes it look easy, but I know better. If people understood the amount of hard work a journalist puts into producing that final two-minute newsreel, they would be astonished. Journalists risk everything to build a career in this demanding field—personal safety, relationships, our lives. I recall escaping the first Gulf War with my family, fleeing Kuwait for the sanctuary of Canada. I was sixteen and had never tasted that kind of freedom. A little over a decade later, when I willingly entered Iraq on the first day of Operation Freedom as a rookie journalist, I didn't think much about safety. I wanted only to be on the frontline before anyone else. Despite the danger, I felt proud of every article or breaking news story we delivered. Waiting for days on the frontlines left me on edge, but also taught me patience. And taught me to respect the thin line between personal passions and journalism, and become adept at staying on the right side of it. Now it seems my colleagues and I have been caught up in Egypt's power struggle, and while the lucky streak that has seen me through four wars and the Arab Spring may have run out at the Marriott, I'll be damned if I let geopolitical score-settling and a Kafkaesque trial determine our destiny.

The view below me, the joy of a glass of orange juice and a good cup of coffee, Marwa's skill and commitment to getting me here, the support of my family, of colleagues and of ordinary citizens, have given me a surge of renewed energy. Such support is the difference between living and dying in a prison, I realize. I need to think of ways to keep our plight in the headlines—a reason to revisit the story and to seduce the press again, what we call a "peg" in the news world.

After work that day, Marwa appears at the door, beautiful in a floral dress. One of the guards rises to block her passage and tells her he can't let her in. She smiles disarmingly. "I am only bringing some food, books and the official case papers. You didn't get a call?"

"No visits. We have orders." He closes the door and as it swings shut, I can see the look of determination on Marwa's face. Minutes later she returns with a ranking officer.

"I have just had a talk with Marwa and it's clear you are not Brotherhood." He shakes my hand. "I can see you are both decent, liberal people. I only wish you'd never worked for Al Jazeera. You have half an hour. Enjoy."

I hug Marwa, overcome with gratitude and desire. I bury my face in her neck, pull her towards the cupboard away from the guards' sight. Nervously, she pushes me away, hands me a stack of bills.

"You have to pay off the guards every day," she says. I have no way to access my bank account and I know that she and my family are literally paying the price for my incarceration. She pulls out a take-away container from our favourite Cairo restaurant, asks if I want to eat with her, but I shake my head. Instead, I press her for information: What did she say to the officer just now? To the district police general yesterday? How is it that I'm even here? She recounts the conversations outside my hospital room, including a clever mention that my grandfather was a police general.

"I waited for five hours at Tora outside the door of the head of the prison authority at the Ministry of Interior. When I finally got to reception and told them I was the fiancée of the Marriott Cell guy, they freaked out at first, but then the head of the prison authority said he'd see me. Out of curiosity, I think. When he finally met me and saw I wasn't wearing a veil, he realized you are no Brotherhood member. He agreed to your transfer on the condition that the hospital gives us written approval first. But then the hospital wouldn't agree to admit you unless the prison authority approved it first."

"Shit. What did you do?"

"I had no choice." Marwa smiles mischievously. "I 'tipped' a hospital employee who wrote and signed the hospital approval. And then I tipped him to stamp it."

I stare at my fiancée in awe and disbelief. She has accomplished what no embassy or high-ranking diplomat has been able to.

"You've saved my life," is the little I can say, holding her to me. But she glances towards the guards, urges restraint, holds up the bag she is carrying. In it are the official case documents, interrogations, the verdict report and list of evidence against me, and the court transcripts that Abou Bakr has received from the prosecutor and given to Marwa for me to read. There are also boxes of cigarettes for "tips" to add to the stack of bills she's already handed me. Now I'm speechless.

A guard approaches us politely. "Mr. Fahmy, it's time."

"Slip them money," she whispers, and steps away into the bathroom.

I trail the guard to the door and discreetly palm each man a one-hundred-pound bill. "So you can buy food from the cafeteria or smokes," I say, nervously awaiting their reactions. Marwa was right. They beam. "You have an extra half hour, Mr. Fahmy," one offers.

"Thank you, guys." I hand both a pack of cigarettes and they step outside.

"It worked," I say happily, as Marwa reappears.

"Remember the second in command leading the transfer last night?"

"Mohamed," I say. "He kept winking at me."

"He asked me straight up for money—he called it a 'donation,' claiming it would be for renovations at the district police station. He wants me to meet him in Helwan tomorrow after work," she says, and my eyes widen. I had covered violent protests in Helwan, a rough neighbourhood in the suburbs near the prison. Not a place for an unaccompanied woman—at any time. I tell her it is too danger-ous, we cannot trust him. "What if it's a set-up or you're seen giving money to an official, or worse, assaulted."

"He's the one who appoints the guards at your door. I called him today when I got to the hospital and he talked to the officers in charge. He's the only reason they allowed me to see you."

She insists it is the only way. She will drive there in her car.

"Okay," I say finally, feeling sick that I was agreeing, "but don't get out of the car. Just throw him the envelope and keep driving." I say we must find a way to keep in touch.

She smiles slyly. "What do you think I was doing in the bathroom? I smuggled in your old BlackBerry and charger inside my under-wear. They only searched the food and my purse when I walked in. I wrapped them in toilet paper and put them in the garbage bin. Just keep the phone on your body at all times in case they search the room."

I look at her and grin. Fall in love all over again.

———

That night at ten o'clock, the guards lock me in the room and bed down on the couches just out of sight. My insomnia becomes my stealth advantage. I immediately turn off the lights, switch on the TV and take out my cellphone. By the time loud snores fill the room, I am surfing the Internet, scouring the Arabic and English international media coverage—trial hearings, opinion pieces, photos— paying special attention to Al Jazeera. Having next to no access to news while in prison was not only extremely frustrating for the three of us, it was a huge impediment to understanding the broader picture. The simple privilege of accessing the Internet dispells the terrible sense of isolation I'd felt in prison, and allows me to begin gathering essential information and strategizing about my next move. In the deep fold of night, I exchange messages with Marwa, urging her to be careful the next day, and with my brothers, Sherif and Adel, in Kuwait. I do not risk speaking on the phone, but stick to emailing and texting via WhatsApp, an encrypted instant messaging application. I log onto my Twitter account, @MFFahmy11, and tweet in the third person, to make it appear that someone else is tweeting on my behalf. This will become my routine and I will do this every night, all night, until finally around five in the morning, when I tuck my phone back into the pocket of the blue track pants that are my day and nighttime attire, and drift off to sleep.

At dawn, an officer knocks on the door without warning, and enters for an inspection. I can feel the hard edge of the phone in my pocket. He stands at the edge of the bed where I'm just drifting into sleep, and leaves. When I later ask the guards about this, they tell me that these inspections will happen daily at different times. I am now always alert for a sudden knock on the door or the turn of the handle.

That morning I begin sifting through the documents Marwa has brought, starting with the students' interrogation transcripts. While I know much of the information, some details are new. For example,

Khaled had initially worked for free until he realized his footage was being broadcast on Al Jazeera Mubasher Misr and on Anadol, a pro-Muslim Brotherhood Turkish news site. At that point he had demanded money from the point man, Alaa Adel, who had paid him a paltry 500 Egyptian pounds (US$58) per month for his services. Sohaib, on the other hand, had received a monthly salary of 1000 Egyptian pounds and been given a 600D Canon camera.

Baher's confession to the state prosecutor is not a surprise, though the impact of reading his actual words on the page is devastating. I read and reread the twenty-page document, underlining each and every word that incriminated us, stunned anew at his fabrications. One portion of Baher's interrogation transcript that still baffles me involves Peter and Dominic Kane:

> **Baher:** I learned that Dominic and Peter were able to bring in huge amounts of money in their suitcases when they entered through the airport. They used it for paying salaries and general expenses. Sometimes they were able to bring the money through their foreign bank accounts.
>
> **Prosecutor:** Why was Al Jazeera operating from the Marriott Hotel?
>
> **Baher:** Because a decision was issued ordering the channel to shut its offices. They set up a head office there and worked illegally from it.
>
> **Prosecutor:** Why did you continue working with the channel after these revelations?
>
> **Baher:** Because the pay was extremely good and I hoped they would not interfere with my work in the future.

I scan the bottom of each page to make sure Baher's signature is there, that the state prosecutor has not tampered with his confession, as Baher first suggested. I don't know what pressures they brought to bear on him, but I am distraught imagining the impact of his words on the judges. The wildness of his fabrications about Peter and Dominic floors me—and I almost laugh, remembering how hard I worked to convince head office to give him a $50 raise, if he was indeed making so good a salary. I elect to give him the benefit of the doubt. Perhaps he had seen the cash Peter carried for expenses and misconstrued what it was for. The big question still remains: Why didn't the Al Jazeera lawyers challenge this fabrication which became the pivotal evidence against us? Abou Bakr had expected the Al Jazeera lawyer to question the validity of how Baher's confession was obtained, as part of his defence of his client—that it was gathered under duress perhaps. In what must have been one of the briefest statements of defense I have ever heard covering these courts in my time as a journalist, the confession was not mentioned.

I am so lost in thought that I barely register the nurse who goes through my room to the balcony, unlocks the door and slides it open. Slack jawed, I watch her leave, and then I tentatively step out onto the balcony. I stretch, take in the fresh air, feel the warmth of the sun on my face, hear the sounds of street traffic below—all welcome delights though they cannot dispel my fear for Marwa, or the effect of Baher's troubling testimony.

I carry the pages containing the students' and Baher's confessions to the bathroom and quickly snap photos of the most damning. Then I attach them to an email addressed to Al Jazeera management demanding that they and their lawyers take swift action to deal with this before the appeal. Just as I hit the send button, a WhatsApp message pops up on my screen from Marwa: she has held off telling me—she is already close to Helwan where she is meeting the officer. Before I can say anything, I'm startled by a sharp knock on the bathroom door. I power off the phone, wrap it in toilet paper and hide it in the bottom of the garbage bin. Heart racing, I flush the toilet and open the door.

A doctor in a white lab coat stands outside. He introduces himself as Dr. Ahmed and asks me to remove my top for an examination. I am barely conscious of what he is doing. I am worrying incessantly about Marwa. I think of the poverty-encrusted streets of the Helwan district, the dangerous, loitering men who would see her immediately as fair game—an unveiled, beautiful woman.

The doctor is telling me he has seen my old X-rays and MRI. He will order a new MRI and a CT scan, says I will definitely need an operation. I hear him say it could have been avoided with proper care from the beginning. I'm required to do two daily physical therapy sessions in my room until the operation.

I need to focus. "What about my Hepatitis C, doctor?" I ask, I had not mentioned my dormant liver problem to the Scorpion medical officer knowing that it wouldn't make a difference, but I now hope this wild card will somehow extend my hospital stay. I tell him it was only detected last year, and I have no idea how I got it. Though it hadn't slowed me down, I raise it as a serious concern now, mentioning a medication called Sovaldi I'd learned about in prison that can frequently cure some types of the condition in three months. "Shouldn't we delay the operation until I'm better?"

He raises an eyebrow. "I'll request blood tests." He scribbles a note on my chart and is gone. I run back to the bathroom and pull out the phone to text Marwa when a WhatsApp message pops up again: *Mission accomplished. Financial transaction completed. Did they open the balcony door?*

Relief floods through me. I text back: *You did it! I love you! You are safe! And Yes! How did you do that?*

———

That afternoon, Marwa finishes laying two small carpets on the floor of the hospital room and arranging plants, before she will tell me what happened in Helwan. She also hands me a file stuffed with newspaper clippings of the trial.

"He was waiting for me in his car. I drove up and he rolled down the window. I was too scared to get out of my car, or to stop, so I threw the envelope out the window as I drove by."

I marvel at her courage and her strength. But she is already moving on. "We've requested a meeting with the minister of interior and contacted the President's Office, too. Now I think we need to try swaying Egyptian public opinion to your advantage using the local media."

I gawk at her in disbelief. She is besting me at my own game. We discuss preparing an electronic file—my bio, photos of my grandfather in his police uniform, copies of the official affidavits from prominent pro-government figures dismissing my affiliation with the Brotherhood—and emailing it to the local press. Explaining the real story.

"Who should I appeal to?"

I suggest she starts with Lamees El-Hadidi, the Oprah Winfrey of Egypt, then Wael Elebrashy, Amr Adeeb and Ibrahim Eissa— media icons who command an audience of tens of millions and not only shape public opinion, but are viewed by the government as the pulse of the street.

Days after Marwa's daring delivery, she floors me with another victory. She and Adel have indeed managed to meet with Mohamed Ibrahim, the Egyptian minister of the interior.

"I thanked him for transferring you to the hospital," Marwa tells me during her next visit. "I think he really likes Adel and me."

With Marwa using her government PR experience and working the media, I turn my focus to finding a lawyer to represent me in the appeal phase of my case. I asked my family to press Al Jazeera to hire someone we can trust, but one after the other Al Jazeera has rejected my suggestions, saying they do not "comply with the network's politics" or that Al Jazeera has "blacklisted" them. Incomprehensibly, they eventually hire a legal firm specializing in corporate law.

I am livid the day I receive this news. The deadline for submitting an appeal is August 23—a month away. I determine I must take action, even if I risk having my phone confiscated: I make a direct call to Mostefa Souag, Al Jazeera Media Network's director-general.

"Sir, your legal department can't sit in their air-conditioned office in Doha picking lawyers off the Internet," I say, using every ounce of restraint I possess to keep my voice in check so the guards will not hear me over the shower I'm running. "A terrorism trial of this magnitude needs a lawyer who has clout with the government outside the court and sympathy from the local media. You've caused enough damage with the lawyers you hired in the first place."

Souag admits, surprisingly, that they made a mistake, but have learned their lesson and this is a top-notch new team.

I tell him that I looked at their website, that they don't even list themselves as criminal lawyers. "We're not experimental rats," I fume.

Souag sharply advises me to support the network's choice. By the time the call is over my mind is made up: I will hire my own legal counsel for the appeal and hope Al Jazeera will pay the bill.

The next day a delegation from the Canadian embassy visits unexpectedly. I am sleeping when the guard announces their arrival, parts the curtains and opens the balcony door. I am startled and pleased to see Iman Sabry, who has been incredibly sympathetic and supportive to me throughout my ordeal. She introduces me to her consular colleagues Nicholas Bellerose and Marie Dextraze, as the guards pull up chairs for them. Iman hands me a small plastic bottle of Canadian maple syrup, a gift from Ambassador David Drake, whose term of office is soon to end.

I know from talking to Iman during my time in prison that the consular staff has worked hard, but must battle both lacklustre support from Ottawa and Egypt's bloated and slow-moving bureaucracy. Weeks earlier, my family and the Egyptian Journalism Syndicate had submitted an official request for a health pardon in the event I was sentenced, citing a procedural article that enables a convicted prisoner to be released if suffering a serious illness, especially if he has submitted an appeal likely to be accepted by the court. I ask the Canadian consular representatives if they could focus their energies on supporting this request. Can they press to meet personally with the interior minister and Sisi's presidential team? Can they urge Prime Minister Harper to pick up the phone?

Someone hands me information I had requested on Canada's Bill C-24, which Parliament had passed days after my sentence. I express concern about the controversial new bill, which allows the government to revoke Canadian citizenship from dual citizens convicted of terrorism, high treason or other serious offences. They reassure me, but I remain skeptical, worried that I am an ideal candidate. The law is a dangerous one that allows a minister to strip a person's citizenship with no judiciary oversight—a clear breach of due process. The staff notes my concern and leaves me with a cryptic, but potentially positive piece of news: a senior Canadian official is scheduled to visit Egypt soon.

With the August 23 appeal deadline fast approaching, I circle back to a well-respected human rights lawyer experienced in appeals that I had suggested to Al Jazeera, but who they'd rejected—Negad El Borei—asking if he would prepare and file the appeal documents before the deadline and represent me at the hearing when it finally happens. He agrees, offering his services at a reduced fee. Then fate steps in to deliver a gift of another magnitude.

After my sentence and unbeknownst to me, Dina Amer, my former CNN colleague now living in New York, had contacted a prominent human rights lawyer about my case. That lawyer's name is Amal Alamuddin. When my family tells me she has responded, indicating her willingness to represent Peter, Baher and me, I have no idea who she is. A quick Google search reveals that Amal Alamuddin is a respected barrister at London's Doughty Street Chambers, specializing in international law and human rights. Among her high-profile clients are WikiLeaks founder Julian Assange, and the former prime minister of Ukraine, Yulia Tymoshenko. She is British-Lebanese and she had recently been appointed advisor to former UN secretary general Kofi Annan in his role as the UN-League of Arab States joint special envoy tasked with helping find a resolution to the ongoing crisis in Syria. It takes a moment for me to realize that Amal has another high-profile connection—she was recently engaged to the renowned actor George Clooney.

Within days I am secretly communicating with Amal and her colleague, Mark Wassouf, on my cellphone via a WhatsApp group chat. She simultaneously begins discussions with Al Jazeera—though these talks break down in early August when Al Jazeera's management fail to commit to Doughty's financial requests. Left hanging with less than three weeks until our appeal deadline, I decide to call her directly. It is, for me, the start of an extraordinary professional relationship with a remarkable and courageous lawyer.

Marwa is my accomplice in reaching out to Amal. During her next visit, I convince the guards to allow us time alone in the hospital room. They smirk as they close the door. Straightaway, Marwa takes out her phone and we dial Amal in London. It is immediately evident that she is warm and direct; she is also cautious about protecting our lines of communication, suggesting Marwa download Telegram on her phone—a higher speed, more secure, encrypted instant messaging app that self-destructs messages—which I'm not able to do on my BlackBerry. To my delight, I learn that Amal is uniquely qualified when it comes to my case. She tells me that five months earlier she had co-authored a report on the independence of Egypt's judiciary for the International Bar Association's Human Right's Institute urging "the future Egyptian government to take action to promote the independence of the judiciary and prosecution services, in order to strengthen the rule of law in Egypt." In addition to her obvious knowledge of the battle we face, I'm impressed by her compassion, commitment to freedom of speech and her genuine belief in our innocence. I fill her in on my challenges with Al Jazeera, acknowledging that while Peter and Baher are willing to comply with the network's legal approach, I am not. Having had her own challenges with Al Jazeera, Amal quickly grasps that the only viable way to move forward is to represent me independently of the network. She asks if I can provide copies of the case files and I commit to have my brother send them that day.

Still, there is the issue of fees. The first trial has depleted my family's resources and I know that high-calibre international lawyers do not come cheap. I also fret that although I have some savings in the bank, none of my family members are authorized to access them.

"Amal" means hope in Arabic. This is what Amal gives me when she announces she'll waive her personal legal fees. She tells me that I have only to cover the firm's expenses and the costs of legal assistants who will work with her on the case.

I am overwhelmed with emotion.

Within twenty-four hours Adel has received the contract, and sends me images to review via WhatsApp. Before it's even signed, on August 18, Amal publishes a detailed, hard-hitting exposé on our case on the Huffington Post site that goes viral. Entitled "The Anatomy of an Unfair Trial," her article provides a scathing legal review of our case, calling it a "show trial" and a "travesty of justice." Shrewdly, the story contains a link to an Arabic translation.

Egypt has signed up to the International Covenant on Civil
and Political Rights, a human rights treaty that functions as a
"bill of rights" at the international level. Like Egypt's own constitution, this protects freedom of speech and guarantees the
right to a fair trial. Free speech means that reporting that
harms a country's image should not be criminal, especially
when—as in this case—there is no evidence that it is false, let
alone knowingly so. Under both international and Egyptian
law, a fair trial means independent judges, the need for evidence of guilt beyond a reasonable doubt, and due process. But
all of this was ignored in the journalists' case . . . This was a
battle for Egypt's identity, and Al Jazeera and Qatar would be
taught a lesson for supporting the Brotherhood in Egypt.[89]

It is an impressive media-savvy move less than ten days before
the appeal submission deadline. Then, days away from submitting
the appeal, Amal sends a hard-hitting nine-page expert opinion to
submit as an annex to the appeal. Her opinion notes that "Egypt has
ratified several international human rights treaties, including the
International Covenant on Civil and Political Rights ('ICCPR')
and the Convention against Torture and Other Cruel, Inhuman or
Degrading Treatment or Punishment ('CAT')" and that "the Constitution of Egypt provides that, once ratified, such treaties have
'the force of law' as an indivisible part of the national legal frame-
work . . . under both Egyptian law and international law."[90]

Amal further argues that the court's judgment in our case has
violated several of my rights, including my right to freedom of
expression, a fair trial, and arbitrary detention, and that the "evidence that is provided in the Judgment is either secret or irrelevant."
I'm impressed by the annex, though I worry about how the appeals
court will view her approach of using international human rights
covenants against Egypt's judiciary. Feigning the need for another

shower I duck into the bathroom with my phone and text Amal on WhatsApp: *You don't think the referral to international law as this excerpt from your appeal reads would aggravate the government? I don't want to be booted back to prison . . .*

Her reply is unequivocal: *No Mohamed. It stays in. My job is to get you out of prison and this is how we are going to do it.*

True to his word, my new appeal lawyer, Negad El Borei, quickly prepares and submits the appeal documents on my case, along with Amal's nine-page expert opinion, days before the deadline. But how will I pay my legal bills? Adel and I discuss this one night via WhatsApp and at some point land on the idea of a public fundraising campaign. Before dawn breaks, we have created a GoFundMe page calling for donations to support my legal fees, and published it online. Just seconds after the page goes live, a twenty-dollar donation pops up on my screen. In the days that follow, donations pour in from around the world. We will raise close to $45,000 over the next four months, thanks to the generosity of good people giving whatever they can afford. Some give beyond what they can afford, and many friends and fellow journalists, including Dominic Kane, Hoda Abdel-Hamid, Lyse Doucet and Bernard Smith, contribute. Journalists Martin Schibbye and Johan Persson—imprisoned in Africa for 438 days on terrorism charges and released in 2012—donate $10,000 through their Kality Foundation, established to provide emergency aid to journalists under threat. These and the small contributions ranging from $20 to $100 from complete strangers move me most. Often, these come with messages of solidarity—a "democratization force." I am overcome when I see a really significant sum from my old friend B, the man who competed with me for Marwa's affections at the 2011 Christmas party where I first met her.

To top things off, I receive an unexpected visit from Naguib Sawiris, who provided an affidavit for my original trial and released a statement on TV calling on the president to pardon me. One of the country's wealthiest businessmen and chairman of Osracom, an international telecommunications company, Sawiris had agreed to invest in a film I'd hoped to make about the Iraq War; it had fallen through, but we'd stayed in touch, reconnecting while I was with CNN. Sawiris, who Marwa has asked to come, is accompanied by Stephen Fuhr, his personal pilot, who is Canadian. Sawiris assures me he will do what he can to support me, as does Fuhr, who tells me he is considering running for the Liberal Party of Canada in next year's federal election.

Just as I am beginning to think everything is going my way, Mohamed, the officer who had taken the "donation" from Marwa, arrives with three others to tell me I am being transferred back to prison.

"Why, what's happened?" I ask, pulling the phone from my pocket beneath the bed sheets and furtively slipping it between the cheeks of my butt.

He reads out the written order he carries; he appears almost apologetic. "It says here you refused to do the operation. The nurses will help you pack."

I stifle the urge to mention the transaction. "I didn't," I say, stalling, but in truth I have been doing everything I can to delay the operation and buy time in hospital. "I only suggested the doctor check on my Hep C first."

Despite his sympathy, he is resolute. I rise from the bed and walk dejectedly to the bathroom squeezing the muscles of my buttocks together. I turn on the tap, slip the phone out and message Marwa on WhatsApp: *I am being transferred back to prison right now. The police commander is here. I'm taking the phone with me. They said I refused the operation.*

Her response is immediate: *What! I'm on my way to the hospital. Don't worry I have a meeting with the Interior Minister tonight. Don't get caught with the phone.*

I leave the charger in the garbage and walk out of the hospital handcuffed to a policeman and escorted by uniformed officers. My gait is slow, stilted, as I tightly clench my butt cheeks to keep the phone from slipping. Climbing into the blue transport truck without dropping it seems impossible, but somehow I manage it. Sitting, however, proves painful, so I lie back, feigning exhaustion. My relief is short-lived and panic flares as we pass through the prison gates. How in hell am I going to get through the metal detector?

I am sweating as the prison guards search my bags and put them through the baggage scanner machine. Then, without waiting for the guard to remove my handcuff, I pass through the metal detector, pulling him through with me. The alarm sounds and I shrug, holding up my cuffed wrist and looking at the guard with as much nonchalance as I can muster. My heart hammers in fear, but no one calls us back.

Returning to my former cell is bittersweet. I am demoralized at being back behind bars, but I am very glad to see Peter and Baher. I surmise Joe has been released, for Baher has taken over his bed and made the corner he once occupied into his own comfortable living quarters. After a warm reunion, I head to the bathroom and gratefully remove the phone. Somehow, it has been turned on during the transfer and I'm horrified to see the battery is hovering around 50 percent.

A message from Marwa reads: *We are on the way to meet the Interior Minister himself.*

How my fiancée has finagled another meeting with the minister in charge of the country's prisons is a mystery I have no time to ponder. I quickly text a response: *I am in prison with the boys. I have no charger and the battery is half-dead.* Then I wipe down the phone and emerge from the bathroom to see Baher smiling at me. Suddenly it occurs to me that because of Baher's father's strong Brotherhood connections, Baher has been unable to speak to or see his dad for the past nine months. I motion him over and confide that I have a mobile phone in my possession. His eyebrows rise in disbelief.

"Go call your dad, before the battery dies," I quietly urge, handing over my precious BlackBerry. "And don't forget to run the shower to cover the sound of your voice."

Baher grabs his towel, enters the bathroom, turns on the water. Remembering the documents I'd stuffed in my bag before leaving my hospital room, I pull them out and pass Peter a copy of Baher's testimony and the court verdict report. I have penned rough translations of passages in the margins of the Arabic document.

Peter scans them and is silent.

"I need you to understand the magnitude of what we're dealing with." We've had this discussion before, but I hope seeing the words in black and white will change his mind about their passive approach to their legal defense.

When Baher emerges from the bathroom a few minutes later, there are tears in his eyes. He furtively passes me the phone and then wraps his arms around my shoulders and hugs me.

The next morning, I smile grimly when a guard tells me to pack my stuff. I haven't even unpacked. Having no idea what's in store for me, I once again hide my phone between my butt cheeks before the guards escort me out of the prison. Twenty-four hours after I have vacated it, I'm back in the same hospital room, immensely relieved.

Marwa arrives shortly after to tell me she has had a second meeting with Mohamed Ibrahim, the Egyptian minister of the interior. I can only shake my head in wonder.

"He picked up his phone in front of me and yelled at his deputy saying, 'Why did you send Fahmy back to prison before the operation? I want him returned to the hospital immediately.'"

Most interestingly, he tells her he was opposed to referring our case to court. That he would prefer that Egypt punish Al Jazeera, rather than its employees. That he is convinced I am not Brotherhood, and that the three of us were used by the network. I marvel that she has been able to get such critical information from the minister, and think to myself that she'd make one hell of a reporter. It is the first sign we have had that the tide could turn. Ecstatic, I grab her and hold her tightly, thanking her again and again. I have a feeling that with Marwa and Amal in my corner, I am about to become Egypt's worst nightmare.

CHAPTER 17

THE NIGHT OF DISCOVERY

September 2–November 20, 2014

September 2 begins with one of the guards waking me with a warning that four officers from the prison authority are headed to my room—a reminder that although I am in a private hospital, I am also still very much a prisoner. That morning I had been too tired to hide my phone so had tucked it under my mattress with its charging cord plugged into the electrical socket. I bolt out of bed, yanking the charger out and drop it and the phone into the trash can seconds before the officers enter.

They tell me I am being taken to the government's forensic medicine office in central Cairo. They provide no explanation, but I have been undergoing a course of physiotherapy to strengthen my shoulder before surgery and while I am thrilled with the delay, I suspect the warden is not and that today's surprise outing is his way of ensuring that my prolonged hospital stay is legitimate.

Outside, three other prisoners are seated in the back of a caged pickup truck. I clamber in beside them and a guard handcuffs me to a long-bearded Islamist. I greedily drink in the hum and hustle of the streets as we drive through Cairo. The driver turns on the radio and amid the traffic noise I catch a snippet of a news bulletin announcing that ISIS has beheaded an American journalist in Syria. To my horror, a cheer goes up among the prisoners.

I turn to the man cuffed to me, suddenly cold: "Did you catch the name?" It is the second beheading in the past two weeks. On August 19, ISIS released a video showing an Islamic State fighter brutally beheading James Foley, an American journalist, in retaliation for the US bombing of ISIS positions in Iraq. That ghastly footage was accompanied by the threat to take the life of another American journalist in captivity if the US continued its bombing— and the kneeling figure was my friend Steven Sotloff.

The Islamist shakes his head, spits out a response. "He must be a spy. Why would an American put himself in such danger otherwise?"

I know why because I've been there. Risking one's life to get the story, to show the suffering, to try to make a difference, to stop the madness. I listen, aghast, to the conversation between the two young men handcuffed together in the back of the truck. "He's just one American. What about the thousands of innocent Iraqis killed by the US?" one asks.

"An eye for an eye," says the other.

I catch no more of the bulletin and am unnerved the whole time at the forensic medicine office. The minute the guards return me to my hospital room, I turn on CNN.

The image of Steven is a body blow. In the video footage, Steven, head and beard shaved, wears an orange jumpsuit and is kneeling on a desert plain while his killer waves a knife around his neck. His small glasses, the round curves of his warm face, and the kind smile

I remember from his visit to my apartment are nowhere to be seen. He keeps his expression inscrutable. He has the fortitude to hold himself upright.

For once I pray. I pray that his mind and heart were calm, that he felt proud of his work, of his unwavering and compassionate desire to bring the world's attention to those who needed it, that he died in the service of something important.

My friend's murder grieves me profoundly. He too held dual citizenship—Israeli and American. Yet neither of his passports protected him. I know his mother is the daughter of Holocaust survivors and I grieve for her as well as for Steven, who, I later learn, hid his Jewish identity from his kidnappers but managed to fast on the Day of Atonement, the holiest day in the Jewish calendar, claiming he felt ill that day. I think of the dangerous situations he has survived—street battles, wars, revolutions and conflict zones.

It enrages me that the hideous man who killed Steven and I are being labelled with the same name: *terrorist*. I am also disturbed by the increasingly sophisticated social media and public relations campaigns that groups like ISIS are using: dramatic videos like those of James's and Steven's beheadings, glorified footage of "freedom" fighters living on the fringes in lawless countries like Syria, brandishing machine guns or firing heavy artillery mounted on pickup trucks. While journalists—casualties of governments playing geopolitics—are being jailed as terrorists, the real terrorists roam freely, luring impoverished and disenfranchised young Muslims to their cause, those without hope for a better future, or a sense of identity.

The neutrality we uphold as journalists to report the story and to protect ourselves in the field does not seem to matter anymore. For as long as I can remember, journalists have been targeted, incarcerated and even killed for their fact-finding, truth-telling efforts, but I can recall nothing as sinister as what we are now experiencing, and what my colleagues across the Middle East are facing. We have become targets of both extremists and governments with scant neutral ground in which to operate safety. My loving friend, journalist Steven Sotloff, paid the price.

I am reeling that night, watching CNN, mourning Steven, when I learn of the sudden death of another friend, Sarmad Qaseera, the CNN cameraman whose laughter helped carry the two of us through Libya. When news of his fatal heart attack flashes on the screen, it is too much. I break down, sobbing uncontrollably. I had been chatting with Sarmad via WhatsApp nights earlier, bantering and planning a fun trip together after my release. The loss of two friends in a single day—journalists of true conviction—is almost unbearable.

It takes a glamorous event later that month to lift my melancholy mood. On September 27, my high-powered human rights lawyer, Amal Alamuddin, marries George Clooney in Venice. I follow news of their romantic wedding from my hospital room, cheering them on, unaware that Amal's rising celebrity status will soon become a PR crisis for the Egyptian government and a game-changer for me.

Amal and I—products of both Middle Eastern and Western cultures—had clicked immediately, and while the public and media fixate on her beauty, I quickly discover that her legal acumen, fierce determination and tireless work ethic are her greatest assets. During her honeymoon she communicates with me to discuss political developments involving our case and to collaborate on a statement to be published in concert with the release of a United Nations' review on Egypt's human rights record.

In the ensuing month, as I wait for the appeal decision, my operation, or any glimmer of reason why I am ensnared in this nightmarish situation, I stumble upon two investigative reports, both by Egyptians, that begin to open my eyes to the local politics at play in my case.

The first is by Nader Gohar, an experienced, highly-regarded local media service provider for Al Jazeera and dozens of foreign news organizations in Egypt over the past decade. I had met Nader on several occasions during my brief tenure with Al Jazeera English, renting equipment and hiring freelance cameramen from him when our Marriott team was overloaded. I find his article, entitled "Fahmy and Greste: How Al Jazeera Blundered Its Way to Journalists' Arrests in Egypt" on iMediaEthics, a non-partisan online website (formerly called Stinky Journalism) that investigates and publishes articles on journalistic ethics and ethical lapses.

"Al Jazeera English always tried to work separately from its sister Arabic channel [Al Jazeera Mubasher Misr] to avoid trouble with Egyptian authorities," Gohar writes. "This [approach] paid off, as the English channel resumed operation even when the Al Jazeera Arabic channel's offices in the same building were raided and shut down in July 2013."

Gohar's article reveals the reason for the raid on the English bureau on September 3:

> Al Jazeera English resumed operation until authorities discovered that the Al Jazeera Arabic was using Al Jazeera English to air footage filmed in Egypt. One of these stories was a report by Nicole Johnston, Al Jazeera English correspondent, on the social help Muslim Brothers were giving to Alhagana village near Cairo. This report was dubbed into Arabic and broadcasted at Al Jazeera Mubasher Misr, considered a pirate broadcasting channel in Egypt. Authorities raided the office of Al Jazeera English, and confiscated computers and a camera in September 2013.[91]

This transgression, I realize, had happened *before* I was hired as bureau chief. Which meant that the network management lied during my job interview when I had asked Salah Negm, Al Jazeera English's director of news, for assurances that Al Jazeera English would operate totally independently from the Arabic channels in order for me to take the job.

Shortly after I started as bureau chief, Nader Gohar had encouraged me to go the Cairo press centre, advise them of my new position with Al Jazeera English, and obtain press passes. At that time, I had already repeatedly asked the network for a proof of employment document that would allow me to do that, but it never arrived.

Following quickly on the heels of Gohar's report, I read another by the hard-hitting local journalist Mohanned Sabry, entitled "Did Al Jazeera Uphold Its Responsibility to Its Staff?" which traces the network's troubles in Egypt to early 2011 when it launched the local Arabic channel, Al Jazeera Mubasher Misr, following Hosni Mubarak's overthrow. Sabry notes that within three days of its inception, Gohar had terminated his work with the local Arabic channel. "The director of Mubasher Misr," Gohar told Sabry, "didn't hide his affiliation with the Muslim Brotherhood or his ideological background." Gohar learned that the director of the new channel had hired more than twenty-five staff with solid ties to the Muslim Brotherhood, the majority of who weren't journalists.[92]

On November 5, the day the United Nations' review on Egypt's human rights record is made public, Amal posts a forceful statement in both English and Arabic on her firm's website:

> The absurdity of the case has now been recognized both within and outside Egypt. Navi Pillay—the United Nations Secretary-General has condemned the verdicts. The UN High Commissioner for Human Rights concluded that the trial was "rife with procedural irregularities . . . in breach of international human rights law."

Pillay urges the Egyptian authorities to "promptly release all journalists . . . imprisoned for carrying out legitimate news reporting
activities, including Mohamed Fahmy."

Weeks earlier we had learned that a panel of judges in Egypt's
Court of Cassation—the highest judicial body in the country—will
hear our appeal on January 1, 2015. Amal's statement capitalizes on
this: "Egypt's highest court now has an opportunity to put things
right." She points a finger at Al Jazeera, saying it should "take positive steps to assist [Fahmy] in his bid for freedom and refrain from
taking any action that might undermine his cause."[93]

Amal's aggressive campaign has an effect. The Egyptian press
leads its coverage that day with her advice to Al Jazeera, while the
Western media picks up on her criticism of my unjust imprisonment.
Balancing the message for Eastern and Western media is no easy
task, but she manages to walk a thin line without losing her footing.
The international spotlight she shines on our case turns up the heat
on the government and precipitates a turn of events one week later.
On November 12, President Sisi issues a decree permitting the transfer of non-Egyptian convicts and suspects to their countries to be
tried or to have their punishment implemented there.[94]

I am elated. It is a face-saving move for the government and it
seems clear it will work in Peter's favour, which makes me very
happy. I recall Sisi's admission, during an interview four months
earlier with the country's newspaper editors, that the sentencing
of several journalists had created challenges for his government,
saying, "I wish they were deported after their arrest, instead of
being put on trial."[95] Amal and I wonder if the new decree will
apply to dual citizens, but still, she begins preparing for the possibility of my release, partnering with the Canadian criminal lawyer
Lorne Waldman, known as one of the most influential lawyers in
Canada, in the event my deportation results in imprisonment or a
trial in Canada.

In Cairo, the new decree becomes the talk of the town and together Marwa and I try to capitalize on the interest. Marwa, to my astonishment, manages to make two important and impressive personal connections. The first is with M.M., one of the secretaries to President Sisi. She has been trying for months to arrange a meeting with someone, anyone, in the President's Office and has finally done it, she announces during a hospital visit—she has an appointment at the presidential palace in a week's time. The other connection is with Lamees el-Hadidi, one of Egypt's top journalists and most-watched television talk show hosts.

Marwa saw Lamees and her friends in a coffee shop, she tells me. "It took me a long time to work up the courage to walk over and introduce myself, but finally, I thought: 'What do I have to lose?'"

Lamees will become one of my staunchest advocates, and the friendships Marwa forges with other local journalists will ensure the press releases and media advisories that she writes up and personally delivers are published and aired. Soon Egyptian journalists and TV anchors who once called me a terrorist and barely knew my name begin defending me.

Marwa's meeting with M.M. seems less definitive. She reports back that it was very brief and that he made no promises. Still, it is closer to the ear of the president than anyone else has come.

The Canadian media is already doing an impeccable job covering my story, and many journalists have picked up on our critique of Prime Minister Harper's mild stance—a sentiment readily embraced and supported by the NDP, the official opposition at the time, and the Liberal Party.

Then an unexpected gift is delivered to my bedside when Tamar Weinstein, a CBC senior producer for *The Fifth Estate*, the country's top investigative news program, arrives in Cairo. I had been answering her queries on WhatsApp, but am very impressed when she shows up in my hospital room posing as the wife of an Egyptian uncle living abroad, convincing the guards she has approval to visit. With our mutual passion for investigative journalism, Tamar and I bond immediately. I provide her with documents and official court transcripts that support our assertions of negligence and misrepresentation by Al Jazeera, hoping her documentary will unveil the truth about my situation, and keep our story at the forefront.

I continue to scan the local news on television and in every newspaper I can get my hands on, as well as by surfing the Internet on my BlackBerry during my many trips to the bathroom and through my wakeful nights. On the afternoon of November 20 I am surprised to see footage of Sisi meeting an envoy of the emir of Qatar—the first sign of detente between the two nations since Sisi took office five months ago. The chief of the Saudi royal court also attends the meeting, apparently brokered by the Saudi government, and advocates for turning a "new page" in Egyptian–Qatari relations.

Later that same evening, when my friend and fellow reporter Sonia Dridi of France 24 news channel and her colleague Marc Perelman interview President Sisi in the wake of this dramatic dénouement and days before his first European visit, I'm hoping they won't forget me and my colleagues. Flanked by my guards, with whom I am developing a comfortable camaraderie, I watch the interview on TV, marvelling at Sonia's skill and eloquence as she presses Sisi about Iraq, Libya, Syria, ISIS, and the human rights abuses in Egypt. Then, nearing the end of the interview: a question about the possibility of a presidential pardon for the Al Jazeera journalists. I feel like cheering as Sisi replies, "Let me just say this issue is currently under discussion so that we may find a solution."

The guards grin. Two nurses rush into my room and congratulate me, and an officer from the room next door barges in yelling, "You are going home!" I'm cautiously optimistic: I know that Sisi is prone to conciliatory rhetoric when it serves his political goals. But

I also wonder: Why is Egypt's president so responsive all of a sudden?

Marc Perelman notes later in his coverage that there is "clearly something going on right now behind the scenes between Egypt and Qatar . . . [Sisi's] body language seemed to indicate that . . . part of the negotiations . . . between Egypt and Qatar . . . involve these three journalists, but it also involves diplomatic concerns."[96]

I have long sensed that there are larger politics at play, but had no opportunity to investigate while at Tora Prison. That night, searching the Internet, I stumble upon an underreported private accord called the Riyadh Agreement. Eight months earlier, while imprisoned in Mulhaq with Peter and Baher, I saw a brief mention of the agreement in a state-owned Egyptian newspaper. Signed in Riyadh, Saudi Arabia, on November 23, 2013, between Qatar's thirty-four-year-old emir and the king of Saudi Arabia and in the presence of key members of the Gulf Cooperation Council—a political and economic union involving Saudi Arabia, Bahrain, Kuwait, Oman, the UAE and Qatar—the accord had committed the young emir to implement changes to Qatar's foreign and domestic policies, including preventing Brotherhood and radical Islamists from appearing on Al Jazeera and preaching from Qatari mosques, ending Qatar's financial support and aid to the Brotherhood and Islamist groups in the region, restricting the network's criticism of Egypt and member Gulf nations, and expelling Brotherhood fugitives, including Brotherhood secretary-general Mahmoud Hussein.

The Riyadh Agreement was signed one month before our arrest. Al Jazeera's chairman, Hamad bin Thamer Al Thani, a cousin of Qatar's emir, must have known about the terms of the agreement, and Qatar's promise to stop promoting the Muslim Brotherhood and criticizing Egypt's government on its Al Jazeera channels. Yet it seems the man ultimately responsible for Al Jazeera ignored these terms. In the month that followed the signing of the Riyadh

Agreement the network continued to criticize Egypt and to promote the Brotherhood on its Arabic channels, including translating and airing our English-language reports on the banned Al Jazeera Mubasher Misr channel still broadcasting from Doha.

Above all, Al Jazeera had breached the agreement covertly by asking us to cover the almost daily anti-government protests by Brotherhood members and supporters. I remember the network's request for me to report on Sisi's strange and potentially damaging dream. That request had occurred at the very time that Qatar had agreed that its network would refrain from hypercritical anti-government broadcasts.

I can't believe that no one in the media has connected the dots, but then again, other journalists aren't staying up all night trying to make sense of why they're incarcerated for being a terrorist.

The media *had* reported the growing tensions between the Gulf neighbours, and word had also leaked out that diplomats who attended the series of meetings around the Riyadh Agreement had witnessed the severity of the rift when the ailing Saudi King had harshly rebuked the emir of Qatar for his questionable motives in the region. Tensions came to a head eight months ago when Saudi Arabia, Bahrain and the UAE recalled their ambassadors from Qatar and threatened to expel it from the Gulf Cooperation Council (GCC). Egypt recalled its ambassador to Qatar days later. I discover a BBC article dated March 5, 2014—three months after the signing of the Riyadh Agreement—citing "interference" and "security and stability" as the reasons for the diplomatic rift:

> [T]he three countries had made "major efforts to convince Qatar" to implement a November 2013 agreement not to back "anyone threatening the security and stability of the GCC whether as groups or individuals—via direct security work or through political influence, and not to support hostile media."[97]

Digging deeper, I discover that President Obama had discussed regional tensions during a visit to Saudi Arabia shortly after the recall, perhaps due to the unique and strategic relationship the US has with both Qatar and Saudi Arabia. More recently, Qatar had succumbed to regional and possibly US diplomatic pressure, expelling seven Muslim Brotherhood fugitives wanted in Egypt. Included were the Brotherhood secretary-general, Mahmoud Hussein, Morsi's former minister of planning and international cooperation, Amr Darrag, and the radical Islamic cleric Wagdi Ghoneim—a man previously investigated for terrorism in the US and recently implicated in transferring funds to Jabhat al-Nusra, an al-Qaeda affiliate in Syria. Qatar also agreed to bar Muslim Brotherhood leaders from appearing as guests on Al Jazeera TV, including Sheikh Yusuf al-Qaradawi—at one time an admired scholar but, more recently, one of the most hardline clerics of the Brotherhood, calling for fatwas against Israel, sanctioning violence, promoting suicide bombings and stoking religious hatred through his sermons. And Qatar promised to review the network's hypercritical stance on Egypt and neighbouring Gulf nations.

Finally, I unearth news that four days ago, on November 16, during a meeting in Saudi Arabia, Qatar had formally recommitted to abide by the Riyadh Agreement. In response, Saudi Arabia, the UAE and Bahrain promised to return their respective ambassadors to Qatar. In the bathroom I watch a news clip of the Saudi king acknowledging the "great role" of Egypt in backing the Riyadh Agreement. It is a historic moment: King Abdullah said he was "sure that the leaders of thought and opinion and the media in our countries will seek to achieve . . . convergence from which we aim to end all odds, whatever their causes might be."[98]

Over the past few days, I had been astonished by the dramatic shift in Al Jazeera Mubasher Misr's rhetoric. Anchors who had previously described Sisi as the "leader of the military coup" are now referring to him as the "elected president after the coup," and for the first time Al Jazeera news bulletins describe Mohamed Morsi as Egypt's "ousted" president.[99] No wonder Sisi had been so conciliatory during his interview with France 24 earlier that night.

I contact the person I know will understand the wider implications of my discovery: Amal. Over a series of long WhatsApp messages, I explain to her that it is not simply our actions on the ground, but the shadowy geopolitics between the Middle East's major players that has landed me, Peter and Baher in prison.

In one of the first bloody confrontations of Egypt's Arab Spring, police violently fire water cannons and tear gas at us as we peacefully head to Tahrir Square, pushing us back across the Kasr el-Nile Bridge on "The Friday of Rage," January 28, 2011.

Tahrir Square in central Cairo on February 9, 2011, the sixteenth consecutive day of protests demanding "democratic change" and the end of the thirty-year-long presidency of Hosni Mubarak. Two days later, Mubarak relinquishes authority to Egypt's Supreme Council of the Armed Forces.

(left to right) In a photo taken November 8, 2001, Osama bin Laden, then-leader of al-Qaeda, sits with his successor, Ayman al-Zawahiri, who is now listed by the US government as "The Most Wanted Man in the World" with a US$25 million bounty on his head. Ayman is the older brother of the Salafi jihadist Mohamed al-Zawahiri (far right), who I interviewed for CNN on July 29, 2012. We met again as inmates in Scorpion Prison.

A photo taken July 29, 2013, of a poster in downtown Cairo praising Army Chief General Abdel Fattah el-Sisi alongside an image of US president Barack Obama, bearded and depicted as a supporter of the Muslim Brotherhood.

Current Supreme Guide of the Muslim Brotherhood, Mohamed Badie, attends a press conference in Cairo. Badie, arrested in the weeks after Morsi's fall, was detained in the cell adjacent to ours; Baher Mohamed, Peter Greste and I "interviewed" him in prison for our mock Al Jazeera Live Radio Show.

The revolving door of Middle Eastern politics: US secretary of state John Kerry meets with former president Mohamed Morsi (left) in Cairo on March 3, 2013; and then with President Sisi on March 13, 2015. Sisi was instrumental in the ouster of Morsi on July 3, 2013.

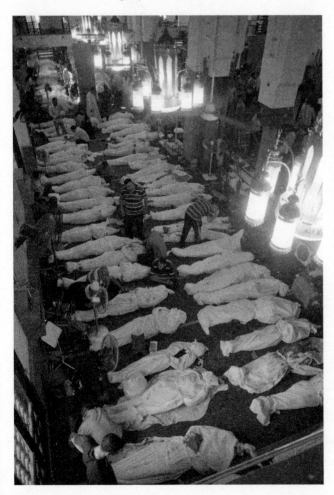

In the aftermath of the Rabaa massacre of August 14, 2013, I went to Al Eman Mosque in Cairo to interview the families of the dead trying to identify their loved ones. Fans and ice blocks were being used to keep the bodies cool. While Muslim Brotherhood leaders had used anti-military rhetoric to incite violence, Human Rights Watch reported that nearly 1,000 demonstrators were killed when state security forces opened fire on the pro-Morsi crowd.

Security forces stand guard outside an entrance to the sprawling Tora Prison complex, which contains Scorpion, the maximum-security wing reserved for terrorists and political leaders.

We appear in court in Tora Prison, March 5, 2014. Locked inside the court-room cages (left to right): me (with my arm in a sling), Baher Mohamed, Peter Greste, and three students—the so-called Marriot Cell.

In a rare occurrence, Baher Mohamed, Peter Greste and I are allowed out of the cage to address Judge Nagi Shehata (top centre) on March 31, 2014.

I am allowed out of the cage once again to address Judge Shehata, ironically on World Press Freedom Day, May 3, 2014, telling him, "Journalists have to speak to all sides to do their job."

(left) Amnesty International promotes the #FreeAJStaff campaign featuring journalists with tape over their mouths—it garnered the support of millions worldwide. (right) One of many memes shared widely on social media.

Out on bail before the retrial verdict, and joined on stage by lawyers (left to right) Dr. Mohamed Hamouda, and Joanna Gislason and Gary Caroline, who flew in from Canada, we announce our multi-million-dollar lawsuit against Al Jazeera on May 11, 2015.

Two strong women: (left) My fearless wife, Marwa Omara, appears on Canadian television on August 31, 2015, after the court sentencing, appealing to Stephen Harper and his government to take action, which he had signally failed to do. (right) Distinguished human rights lawyer Amal Clooney arrived in Cairo on August 28, 2015, for the retrial defense.

Press scrum in the courtroom, as we await the verdict, flanked by Marwa (left), Amal Clooney (centre), Canadian ambassador Troy Lulashnyk (right) and Dutch ambassador Gerard Steeghs (far right).

With Marwa and Amal Clooney on either side, and Baher Mohamed leaning forward to grasp my hand in the court room, before the judge announces the retrial verdict.

Marwa (left), with Amal Clooney, breaks down in court as the judge in the retrial hands down a sentence of three years, August 29, 2015.

September 23, 2015: the moment of release. Turfed out unexpectedly from the prison van onto the street, Baher and I, still in our prison uniforms, celebrate with our wives in exhausted relief.

"If you ever doubt that campaigns and advocacy make a difference . . . I am living proof that they do." On arrival home in Canada, the first move was to advocate for other imprisoned Canadians though the Fahmy Foundation and to present, in Ottawa, a Protection Charter laying out how the government might best proceed when Canadian citizens are detained overseas.

CHAPTER 18

BETRAYAL

November 24, 2014–February 12, 2015

Amal, as always, is quick to capitalize on developments. She has
been lobbying the UN, US and the UAE—Egypt's close political
and economic allies—hoping they will press Sisi's government for
a pardon. As the news of reconciliation emerges, she applies for my
deportation, begins engaging with the Egyptian government, and
releases a pointed yet diplomatic statement aimed at the three governments with the power to influence my release: Egypt, Qatar
and Canada.

  She calls on Al Jazeera to "respect the spirit of the Riyadh Agreement, which requires that parties should not foment hatred between
groups but rather work openly and cooperatively with each other
in a spirit of reconciliation." She calls on Egypt's top judge to grant
me a temporary release on health grounds pending my appeal, and
welcomes Sisi's new law allowing Egyptian authorities to transfer
foreign nationals for trial or incarceration in their home countries.

"Mr. Fahmy should benefit from this law and be returned to Canada as soon as practicable," she urges, and highlights a recent comment by Sisi that he's considering granting me a presidential pardon. "A pardon by the President," she writes, "would be in line with the spirit of the recent Riyadh Agreement approved by the states forming the Gulf Cooperation Council, including Qatar, and supported by Egypt."[100]

When it comes to Canada, Amal is direct, referencing the Avaaz petition initiated by my brother Sherif: "Almost 50,000 Canadians have signed an online petition calling on the Canadian government to take 'urgent public action to fight for [Mr. Fahmy's] release.' Yet so far senior officials have been shamefully quiet about the travesty of justice that has led to the illegal detention of their citizen. We have spoken with Canadian officials . . . and it is hoped that they will now take active steps to support Mr. Fahmy's release and transfer him to Canada forthwith."

I secretly reach out to the venerable Middle East correspondent Robert Fisk to give him my thoughts on the connection between the Riyadh Agreement, Al Jazeera, Egypt and our imprisonment. In true unflinching Fisk fashion, his story appears on December 5 in the *Independent*:

> Mohamed Fahmy is an angry man. And so he should be. He says that he and his two colleagues from the Qatari-based al-Jazeera channel—Peter Greste and Baher Mohamed—were imprisoned by the Egyptians to "teach Qatar a lesson" because the emirate supported the banned Muslim Brotherhood.[101]

Fisk goes on to list my grievances against Al Jazeera, namely that "through its own negligence, [the network] unwittingly endangered him and his colleagues in the days before and after their arrest." His article quickly becomes a hot topic on Egyptian talk shows and later, on December 22, I feel a huge sense of satisfaction when Al Jazeera

Mubasher Misr, banned in Egypt before our arrest yet still broadcasting ilegally into Egypt from Doha, closes for good—which it should have done by law from the moment it was banned eighteen months ago.

Fortified by Fisk's article and the more sympathetic narrative our case is starting to garner from the local media, I prepare for a different challenge: surgery. After the intensive physiotherapy the operation is finally scheduled to take place in the early weeks of December. On the morning of the operation, I hide the phone and charger in the inside pocket of a bag under my bed. Marwa, her mother, and my brother Adel have arrived and they follow me and the guards as the nurses wheel the gurney down the hall. There's a moment of levity when we reach the doors to the operating room and the staff stop the guards from entering with me. I wave jauntily, and see the guards smiling as the door swings closed behind me.

My guards and I have developed an unlikely bond, forged by my substantial "tips" and sharing food, sleeping quarters, and a bathroom. At one point I entered the bathroom to discover one of the guards had left his gun there and I gently ribbed him for his carelessness when I handed it back. I have come to empathize with their struggles to support their families, and their inability to sustain dignified lives despite crushing hours of work. And they have become a lifeline for me, warning me of surprise inspections by prison officials, allowing in visitors not approved by the prosecutor's office, and taking me on nighttime walks around the hospital. The genuine concern beneath their smiles, and the reassuring looks on the faces of my family, are the images I hold in my mind as I feel the prick of the anesthetist's needle.

I awake hours later in a state of delirium, a deep throbbing in my shoulder. The guards tease me, telling me that I yelled out: "We have to protect Sinai from the terrorists! We have to protect Egypt!"

though I have no recollection of it. The doctor arrives to tell me that he has screwed a seven-inch metal plate into my humerus. My shoulder is again immobilized in a sling. The good news is that I will need at least eight weeks of recovery and physical therapy before the hospital will release me to the prison.

Christmas Day arrives with an unexpected bedside visit that will have a devastating impact. Three men appear at my door, ordering the guards out. Each wears a tailored suit and sunglasses, carries an air of sophistication. These are not police or military, they look like high-level civil service bureaucrats. What happens next is like something out of a B-rated spy movie.

A tall man with greying hair is first to speak. He asks how my shoulder is, nods solicitously.

"Your family is a respectable one," a second man says, removing his sunglasses. "And we know your grandfather served on our country's police force."

I thank them and ask for their names.

"Our names are not important, Fahmy. We have been asked to facilitate the renouncement of your Egyptian citizenship."

"My Egyptian citizenship?" Caught off guard, I sit up straighter in my bed. "Why would I want to renounce it?"

"We know you're not a Brotherhood member, and neither is Peter Greste. But your dual nationality prevents the president from implementing his decree in your case. This could be your ticket out of prison. This request comes from the top. We only want to help you," he says smoothly, taking a seat on the side of my bed.

"But why do I need to renounce my citizenship?" I protest again. I tell them that my lawyer, Amal Clooney, already applied for deportation after the president issued his decree. I explain that I have been a Canadian citizen since 1995 and my Egyptian passport should not be an obstacle.

Unexpectedly, he changes tack, asking if Al Jazeera is paying Amal Clooney's fees. It is an odd question. I explain that I am doing so myself. That I have raised and borrowed money to do so and that it is ridiculous to think my world-renowned lawyer has anything to do with Al Jazeera.

He changes tack again—"Do you get visitors here?"—and my mind races to decipher the reason. Do they know I receive unauthorized visitors in addition to family, lawyers and embassy staff who have permits from the prosecutor? I reply carefully. For the sake of the guards as much as myself I do not mention the visits of Naguib Sawiris and Stephen Fuhr or the CBC's Tamar Weinstein, who have managed to slip by them. Unnerved, I demand confirmation as to who they are and on what authority they are here.

The officer on the bed reaches into his suit pocket, pulls out his cellphone, punches in a number. "Yes, sir, I am with Fahmy in the hospital," he says into the receiver before handing me the phone.

"Mohamed, I hope your arm is getting better. This is S. I am a deputy to the minister of the interior. We know you're innocent. We are trying to extract you and your Australian colleague."

My mind spins to hear that "they" know I am innocent. "Then why don't you just let us go?"

S says it is not his decision and urges me gently, "Just renounce it." He tells me he watched me in court, that he knows I am patriotic and that Al Jazeera lied to me about their legal status in Egypt. "Nationality is in the heart, not on a piece of paper. It's the only way out. You can always return as a tourist and reapply for your citizenship. Be smart."

He ends the call and I feel the sweat on my forehead. I am being given an impossible choice: my freedom or my Egyptian citizenship. My phone sits under the bed sheets, and I wish to hell I could call my lawyers, but it's impossible. The men who surround my bed stare at me intently. I want to tell them: *No!* Though I have Canadian citizenship, and a deep kinship with Canada where I lived and studied as a young man, my Egyptian citizenship is also important to me: it is part of my heritage. A part of my history. I want to say that I came back to help create a better future for the country—a cause that my father and my grandfather worked hard for. I am a Westerner, but I am an Easterner too. I see the world, walk through it, with two identities, two perspectives. But they are assuring me that the Egyptian government needs a face-saving way to deport me, and renouncing my citizenship right now will give it to them. They make clear that this opportunity will not come again. I say that if they guarantee it, and it is the only way, and I can get my citizenship back again, then I will do it to free myself from this nightmare. They insist it is the only way, and it will be managed confidentially.

One of them hands me a pen and paper, asks me to copy the words he dictates. My hand shakes as I write: *I renounce my Egyptian citizenship of my own will and with no coercion exerted on me.* I scribble my signature beneath the statement as the officer pulls out an inkpad and asks me to press my thumb into it. I stamp the paper with my thumbprint. When I share news of what has transpired with my loved ones and with Amal they try to encourage me, saying I am one step closer to gaining my freedom. But all I feel is a deep loss. Officially, I am not an Egyptian anymore.

On January 1, one year after our arrest, Egypt's Court of Cassation hears our appeal. Although Peter, Baher and I are not permitted to attend, Juris and Lois Greste, Peter's parents, have flown in from Australia; Adel from Kuwait. They are with Marwa and my mother in the courtroom—my dad being too sick to attend. All the reporters who showed up to cover the hearing are banned from the courtroom, so gather outside to await the decision. The court can uphold the sentence or overturn it and issue a retrial. As I wait in hospital, I cross my fingers that we will be released on bail pending retrial. I wonder what Peter and Baher are feeling during this nerve-wracking morning. I watch the Twitter feeds of trusted friends, following the hashtag #FreeAJStaff. Finally, word comes from the *Guardian*'s Patrick Kingsley, the only reporter to have covered every hearing, that the judge has overturned the lower court's ruling. In its reasoning for the decision, the Court of Cassation said the "criminal court's verdict lacked evidence to support its ruling" and "was hasty in pronouncing the verdict." It also said the prosecution had failed to prove how we had joined the Brotherhood or that an act of "terrorism" had actually occurred. And it noted: "The judgment was based on an invalid procedure, and thus is, itself, invalid. Thus, it follows that the appealed judgment should be annulled to allow for the retrial of the applicants."[102]

I'm escstatic that the judge ruled in our favour and that our case has been remanded for retrial, but also deflated that our request for bail is denied. In a moment of reckless defiance, I snap a photo of myself from my hospital bed flashing a victory sign and tweet the photo, attaching a message that reads: *A retrial is a milestone toward victory in our free press battle. Our spirits are bulletproof!* The photo is immediately posted on many news sites including the Al Jazeera website, and for the remainder of the day I wait anxiously for the police to come and confiscate my phone.

Two weeks later, a piece of good news: Canada's Foreign Minister, John Baird, is slated to arrive in Cairo shortly for a series of meetings with the Egyptian government on bilateral trade, ISIS and, I hope, my deportation. After renouncing my citizenship, Amal had resubmitted the deportation paperwork with the support of Canada's new ambassador to Egypt, Troy Lulashnyk, who had replaced David Drake in September. The timing of Baird's visit could not be better, even though he had refused a request to meet with Amal and our Canadian lawyer Lorne Waldman prior to his departure to discuss the deportation decree. The law is uncharted water for all governments involved—Australian, Canadian and Egyptian—and it remains to be seen whether the Egyptians will deport me if there is no guarantee I will stand trial in Canada or serve my time in a Canadian prison. But that is a requirement of deportation—whatever one's country might subsequently decide at the other end.

Baird addresses my case at a press conference at Cairo's Fairmont Hotel amid a crowd of media shortly after he arrives. Answering a question about what would happen to me if deported, I hold my breath as Baird responds: "In Canada we would have no basis to put Mr. Fahmy on trial. That would not be an option which would be acceptable to the government of Canada."[103]

I feel like I've been sucker punched. My foreign minister has just made it more difficult for the Egyptian government to justify my deportation without losing face, and potentially slammed the door on my legal exit. I head for the bathroom to write a brief statement on my cellphone and send it to Amal: *I understand that the ability of the Canadian government to help me is limited by the rules of diplomacy. But I do believe that Prime Minister Harper could do more to obtain my release if he were to directly intervene in our case. My situation and the ongoing legal limbo that I am enduring affects all Canadians who are in the Middle East, because it shows that anyone, regardless of how innocent, can become a victim of the political turbulence here.* Minutes later she posts it on Doughty Street Chambers' website in English and Arabic where it is quickly picked up by the Canadian press.[104] Later, I lie in my hospital bed listening to my words read out on CBC TV, hoping that Prime Minister Harper is listening. After all, I've wagered my Egyptian citizenship on it.

A week later, King Abdullah of Saudi Arabia dies, leaving the reconciliation he brokered up in the air. I worry that his death will affect the fragile Egyptian-Qatari relationship as I follow CNN's extensive coverage of his funeral. And with good reason. The Riyadh Agreement is buried with the king and Al Jazeera returns to its anti-government programming on Egypt, including a condescending description of President Sisi during coverage of the fourth anniversary of the January 25 revolution. That day, Al Jazeera Arabic broadcasts a speech from Qatar by the one-time scholar and godfather of the Muslim Brotherhood, Sheikh al-Qaradawi, during which he urges all Egyptians to join the protests against the current government as their religious duty.

Seeing me bereft, the guards allow Marwa to stay late at the hospital one evening. We are sitting together in my room, Marwa scanning the Arabic Twitter timelines on her cellphone when suddenly her face turns pale. Tears fill her eyes and she drops the phone on the bed and runs outside to the balcony. I grab her phone and read the tweet on the screen: *A presidential decree had been issued to deport Peter Greste to continue his punishment period in Australia.*

Peter will be leaving Egypt on an afternoon flight the next day. I recall the look of fear and incomprehension on his face that night of our arrest as he was swept up in a political battle that is not his, and I think of how he has suffered, harshly imprisoned in a foreign country in which he is unable to understand the language or the culture. That he has survived the ordeal so well is a testament to his internal strength. I am happy that tomorrow will mark the end of my friend's traumatic ordeal.

I scan for any mention of my name but there is none. On the balcony, Marwa's back is turned to me, her hands gripping the rail as they did the night I was arrested. I get up from the bed and walk out to her, turning over what I will say to comfort her: the wonderful news of Peter's release is a breakthrough in our fight for freedom. Then I will myself to believe that it is.

———

The next morning I watch the sun rise over Cairo, infusing the dawn sky with a hazy orange light. The media response is building over the news of Peter's deportation. The rumour is that he has secretly left Tora Prison, and is booked on a flight out that afternoon. There is speculation about my and Baher's fates. BBC's Orla Guerin interviews Marwa and lifts her spirits, telling her that she is optimistic that I'll be next. Canada's ambassador, who I quickly come to call Ambassador Troy, has secured an appointment today with Egypt's prosecutor general, Hisham Barakat. It's the first time a Canadian ambassador will meet face-to-face with Egypt's top judge on my case, despite numerous previous requests. Although dedicated and supportive, Canada's consular staff has until now been given access only to middle-ranking government representatives or ministers with no real influence on the president. Barakat, however, has the power to give them what they want.

In late afternoon, a Foreign Ministry official finally confirms on Twitter that Peter's plane has taken off, bound for Cyprus, en route to Australia. My friend and colleague is free, and for a blessed moment my happiness in that overrides all else.

Ambassador Troy reports in. Despite Peter's release, Prosecutor General Barakat will not offer assurances on my deportation, claiming he did not receive my deportation paperwork in time. Amal texts to warn me that this could be another political play since she submitted the deportation request around the same time Peter's lawyer had done so. Egyptian talk shows air conflicting opinions, some supporting his deportation citing a clause in Sisi's decree allowing the president to release a prisoner "whenever the higher interest of the state dictates it."[105] Our case is a political hot potato, and considering the international pressure on Egypt, it seems that it might indeed be in the "higher interest of the state" to get an imprisoned foreign national out of the country. Other local media protest Peter's release, citing discrimination against Egyptians like Baher who are left behind. The debate becomes more volatile when the Australian foreign minister Julie Bishop announces that Peter, now safely on his way home, will not be tried or imprisoned when he returns to Australia.

My hope that renouncing my Egyptian citizenship would remain a secret as my three impeccably attired visitors had promised is shattered the next day when the Interior Ministry releases a statement that I relinquished my Egyptian citizenship five weeks earlier. Quickly, it is picked up on local media as a "betrayal," which is devastating.[106] On the other hand, could it be that the Egyptian government is setting the stage for my deportation? Or Canada? John Baird had said that helping me was "somewhat more complicated" because I held both Egyptian and Canadian citizenship, and indeed just hours later he announces that my release is "imminent." Ecstatic, I let out a whoop. The guards lounging outside my door rush inside and I fill them in on the news. Then I head to the bathroom and call in a favour from a man who I feel owes me one—Salah Negm, director of news at Al Jazeera. I had communicated with him only once since my transfer to the hospital when I requested Al Jazeera hire better lawyers for the appeal and urged the network again to contest Baher's confession. Now I text him to ask if he can ensure news of my possible deportation receives intensive coverage on Al Jazeera English's channel in hopes this will increase the chances of success. He agrees and I wonder, dispassionately, if our unjust incarceration and the vast international media our case is attracting has made us poster boys for Al Jazeera English.

From the balcony I gaze happily at the blue sweep of the Nile; admire the green cuff of trees that line its banks. Cairo seems suddenly magnificent again, the sprawl of this city of twenty-two million people a marvel. As the networks report my impending freedom, I catch a brief item featuring Peter's family back in Australia holding a huge poster with his picture and the words "Thank You." Their appreciation plays well in the Egyptian media.

As I ready myself for deportation, a WhatsApp message from Salah Negm pops up on my phone telling me that Al Arabiya, a prominent Saudi-owned TV channel based in Dubai, is reporting that I have been released. I immediately text Amal. This time it's her mother, Baria Alamuddin, a charismatic former journalist and influential PR expert with powerful connections in the Arab media, who intervenes. Baria calls Al Arabiya, demanding a correction, and a short time later Amal messages me that the channel has removed the story from its news ticker. By then, however, word of my release is out.

Within hours, scores of journalists are outside the hospital, many finding their way to the fourth floor hoping to snap photos of me leaving and overwhelming the guards who turn them away. Somehow, Wael Hussein, a BBC producer I know, makes it past them and into my room. I admire his tenacity and am very pleased to see him, but as much as I would like to speak, I tell him he needs to leave—my deportation is not official and I need to protect myself. For all my guards' covert leniency, visits are still officially banned, and punishable by a return to prison.

February 3 brings unexpected news: John Baird announces his resignation. Although he'd done little to advance my case, a change in minister could upend negotiations. I make a secret call to the Canadian ambassador. He assures me that despite Baird dropping out of the picture, I *will* be leaving. "It is only a question of when."

Marwa and I spend the next evening together plotting our exit. We have dreamt of this moment. Fought for it. She and our families have paid a heavy price over the last year, and worked tirelessly. And, as she feared, her increasingly high-profile lobbying efforts have affected her work at Vodafone and made relations between her and her colleagues uncomfortable. What's worse, the company has demoted her from a senior PR position to an administrative job in the security department. That night as we sit together on my bed, I help her draft a resignation letter.

"How honest do you want me to be," I tease her.

"Just say that I will be getting married and moving to Canada," she replies, smiling.

It's true. As soon as I'm released, we plan to marry, to fly to Canada, where we will put all this behind us. Begin anew. We scan Air Canada flights out of Cairo. The next day, Adel brings me several bags filled with winter clothes and I enjoy another phone conversation with Amal. She agrees to reserve a conference room at the Four Seasons Hotel in Toronto and to meet me there upon my arrival for a joint press conference. She cautions me to say little until I've boarded the flight. Our bags are packed.

Then, on February 8, Hisham Barakat, the prosecutor general, announces that Baher and I will return to court within the week to face retrial.

I think of the Egyptian security officers who persuaded me to renounce my citizenship, saying it was "the only way out"; of the assurances from Canada's former Foreign Minister that my release was imminent. Sitting in my hospital room it is difficult not to feel betrayed and abandoned by Stephen Harper and his government. On his visit to Cairo a year earlier, Baird had said Canada was "tremendously concerned" about the Muslim Brotherhood.[107] They know full well that I am not Muslim Brotherhood, so why isn't my prime minister calling Sisi as the Australian prime minister has done for Peter? Is it perhaps that I'm an immigrant, an Arab who fits all too easily into the "terrorist" stereotype? I wonder if I am not Canadian enough in the eyes of my government, if my skin is a shade too dark, or my name a tad too ethnic sounding. I note that some comments on social media call me a "Canadian of convenience." The sentiment baffles me. The Canada I know was built and defined by immigrants, is strong and unique because of their hard work and culturally diverse contributions. More than twenty percent of Canada's population is foreign born and all but its First Nations were immigrants at some point over the last few hundred years. My family, like millions of others, had come to Canada fleeing oppression and violence, drawn by Canadian values of democracy and freedom. Ironically, it was my desire to fight for these same values that drew me back to Egypt during the Arab Spring four years ago.

My faith in diplomatic channels at a low ebb, and having exhausted all other options to press for my deportation, I turn to social media. I ask Adel and Marwa to contact a Canadian who I hope will help publicize my plight and encourage the Canadian public to put pressure on the Harper government. They contact Tarek Loubani, an emergency physician and humanitarian who—along with filmmaker John Greyson—was arrested in Cairo in October 2013 and imprisoned for fifty-three days. Loubani calls John's sister, Cecilia, and she immediately puts the skills and contacts she has gained in the campaign to free her brother and Tarek into action, devising a #HarperCallEgypt Twitter campaign that she launches on February 9. The hashtag quickly trends on Twitter, and the Canadian and international press pick up the story.

In the Egyptian media the backlash has continued to grow since Peter's release, over the injustice of foreign nationals going free while citizens like Baher are left behind. The hashtag #To_be_an_Egyptian_is_not_a_crime trends equally strongly on Twitter as Middle Eastern analysts weigh in expressing solidarity with Baher.

News that I've renounced my Egyptian citizenship is proving personally disastrous. To the wildly patriotic public I am now the man who shunned his country and sold out his nationality to get out of prison. I am now branded "Mohamed Fahmy the traitor" by the media. When Abou Bakr gets permission to visit me in the hospital, since he will be acting for me again in the retrial, I plead with him to find a way to allow me to address the court to explain my actions. Renouncing my citizenship was an act of desperation—it cut me deeply to sign the document in the hospital that day, and had I known then that it would not stop the government from returning me to prison, I never would have done it. Now, in the court of public opinion, I have been tried and convicted. Worse, in three days I will face a judge again, one who will not be immune to this. I lie awake fretting how to redeem my tattered reputation.

CHAPTER 19

BEDOON

February 12–24, 2015

On the morning of Thursday, February 12, I am jittery as I dress for the first hearing of our retrial. I put on my blue bomber jacket—returned to me on my transfer to the hospital. My hands shake as I adjust the white straps of my sling around my neck and waist. I had asked Adel to bring me a large Egyptian flag, and I fold the red, white and black fabric into a small, neat square and then tuck it inside the front of my pants. I follow the guards downstairs to the waiting ambulance. The driver addresses me as the "man who renounced his citizenship." I drop my head, humiliated.

Re-entering the courtroom where our four-month-long trial occurred evokes a dark sense of déjà vu. It was here that Judge Shehata sentenced Peter and me to seven years in prison, and Baher to seven plus an extra three for possessing his single bullet from Libya. A thick soundproof layer of glass has been added around the cage, presumably to keep us from speaking out in court this time or talking to the media. The only joy is being reunited with Baher—and even the students. I learn Khalid has been accused in another case called the "Helwan Brigades," and surely has an even longer road ahead than we do.[106] We stand together, staring out through the thick glass, humbled by the sight of the hundreds of supporters and journalists. We wave to Marwa and to Baher's wife, Jehan, standing together near the front of the courtroom, Marwa wearing a tailored black suit, Jehan in a modest smock, her head covered by an azure blue scarf. I congratulate Baher on the birth of his third child, Haroon, five months earlier. Though he could not be present for the birth, both my mother and Peter's parents had been there to support Jehan and her family. Al Jazeera had announced the birth on TV.

The crowd's attention turns to the front of the courtroom as three judges, the bailiff, prosecutor and a series of guards enter through the stately wooden door and climb the short staircase to the bench. Hassan Farid, the new chief judge, is bull-chested with a round, fleshy face and bushy grey arch of moustache. I am relieved to see that, unlike his predecessor, he wears no sunglasses. Through speakers inside the cage, we hear him call the court to order. Then Judge Farid throws a curveball. He adds a new charge to our case: that we were broadcasting without a licence in deliberate defiance of the law. Inside the cage, Baher and I look at one another. Was this the reason the network did not respond to my repeated requests to move us out of the Marriott back to our office, or give me the documentation I needed to obtain press passes for the team? If the charge is true, it is not just a matter of the network shoddily failing to provide us with press passes, but of operating illegally. Yet they are not providing any evidence.

In another troubling twist, the judge repeatedly calls Peter's name, including him in the list of defendants in our retrial, which Baher and I find comical, as President Sisi has personally signed Peter's deportation order.

My lawyer through the first trial, Khaled Abou Bakr, back in court to defend me once again, delivers an impassioned speech focusing on the Court of Cassation's decision to annul the court's prior judgment based on lack of evidence, "insufficient and contradictory motivation," and procedural violations in issuing the warrant for our arrest. He also points out that the Court of Cassation determined there were insufficient elements under Article 86 of the Penal Code to uphold the conviction that we'd committed acts of terrorism, or were guilty of joining a group that uses terrorism to achieve its objectives. When Abou Bakr finishes, he asks the judge that I be let out of the cage and I exhale in relief when he agrees. Abou Bakr, a consummate showman, introduces me to the court as "Mohamed Fahmy, the Egyptian." I walk to the front of the court and clutching the microphone in a damp palm, I begin: "Your Honour, renouncing my Egyptian citizenship was a very difficult decision. I didn't ask to give up my Egyptian citizenship. I was asked to do so." I tell the court how senior government officials had pushed me into giving up my citizenship so they could deport Peter Greste and me and because this case has become a nightmare for Egypt.

I hear murmurs from the crowd behind. Knowing Peter will forgive me, I invoke his example. "How is it that a defendant who was with us in this case, convicted of the same charges, is now sitting on a beach in Australia? As defendants in this case, we request that all of us be treated equally by the honourable Egyptian judiciary, and take this opportunity to clarify that, as the Court of Cassation stated, there is no evidence linking us to the Muslim Brotherhood." I reiterate the findings of the Cassation Court that the evidence against us had not been serious enough to warrant arrest and that we had committed no violent act worthy of a terrorism trial.

I end my speech, reach beneath my waistband with my left hand, pull out the Egyptian flag and hold it high above my head before the judges. I turn to face the press gallery. I cannot raise my right arm

past my shoulder, but clutch the other side and lift the flag so reporters can see it. The audience applauds as the guards escort me back
to the cage, and the judge calls a recess. I wait, cut off from the press
and public.

Fifteen minutes later the judges and their entourage shuffle back
into the courtroom and to my utter surprise, Judge Farid announces
I will be granted bail. I look at Baher and the students, an awkward
silence hanging between us. When he confirms that the defendants,
with the exception of Kahlid, will be released, I embrace Baher.
Though I cannot hear anything, I can see the courtroom erupt,
people clutching each other, applauding. I see Marwa jumping in
the air, clapping and crying, and among the members of the press, I
spy my former CNN colleague and friend Ian Lee, grinning broadly.
Baher, Peter and I had been refused bail so many times during our
previous trial that I had given up on the idea that it would ever
happen. Today's announcement feels unimaginably sweet. The
judge's voice drifts in through the speakers. He declares that as I am
no longer an Egyptian citizen, I am required to pay CDN$41,000,
while Baher and the students will be released without bail. He bans
any travel and orders us all to report to the police station every day
as a condition of our parole. Then he sets February 23 as our next
hearing date.

Today being the last day of the workweek, I'm required to post
bail at the prosecutor's office by noon or remain under guard at the
hospital over the weekend. I had asked the Al Jazeera lawyer representing Baher to request financial support from the network in the
event I was released on bail at some point. However, I had little faith
the network would follow through, and they have not. But knowing
I would need money if deported, my parents have withdrawn funds
and have it in safekeeping at their home. Adel bolts from the courtroom. I later learn that he raced home to retrieve the money while
my lawyer Abou Bakr pulled strings to keep the cashier waiting at

the prosecutor's office. The two then hurried to meet the cashier and post bail.

News of my release precedes me to the hospital. The officers and guards and nurses with whom I've formed close bonds over the past months converge on my hospital room and we exchange emotional goodbyes before the police drive me to the station in the south Cairo neighbourhood of Maadi—close to my parents' home—where they drop me off. As the car passes through a perimeter of heavily fortified cement barricades, I glimpse the families of detainees waiting outside laden with plastic bags. I know that the bags are filled with food and clothing, and that these families are hoping to negotiate visits with their loved ones. I feel a surge of empathy for them and for the men behind bars.

As a journalist in Egypt, I had often heard recently released prisoners use the term "on asphalt" and I understand why now—I feel as if I've been born again as my feet strike the street's asphalt. I lean against a lamp post and take in the powdery blue light of dusk, my body infused with an indescribable sense of lightness.

When Marwa pulls up, I jump into her car, pull her into my arms and hold her as we laugh and cry at once. "Let's get out of here," I say, turning up the music. Marwa stomps on the gas and we head for my parents' home, a ten-minute drive away. My mother answers the door wearing her nightgown, and her face is filled with joy as she hugs me. Over her shoulder I see my father, dressed in a robe. He looks both more frail than the last time we met, and happier than I can ever recall.

The next morning Marwa and I drive to the Maadi Police Station to check in. I'm led to the well-appointed office of a youthful major. With a start, I realize I know him—he was in charge of our wing in the Mulhaq Al Mazraa Prison. He greets me warmly and over sweet mint tea confides that he is convinced Peter, Baher and I

are innocent pawns in a larger political game, before sliding a piece
of paper across the desk. The document, from the Ministry of Interior,
states that I must relinquish my Egyptian national identity card,
driver's licence and Egyptian passport.

"The Egyptian police confiscated them all when I renounced
my citizenship," I explain.

He pauses then nods in understanding. "Very well, show me
your Canadian passport, please, so I can confirm your identity and
open a file on you."

I shake my head. "The police took my Canadian passport during
the raid. The embassy asked for it many times while I was in prison,
but the police say they've lost it."

He laughs. "You are a Bedoon."

I smile weakly at his reference to a little known minority num-
bering tens of thousands—living largely in Kuwait, Iraq and some of
the Arabian Gulf states and not to be confused with Bedouins—who
are "without nationality." These "illegal residents" cannot obtain
birth or marriage certificates, have difficulty receiving state benefits,
and often face severe discrimination. He is flummoxed, and does
not know what to do, telling me he has never seen a case like it. He
finally tells me to bring a notepad back the next day with my photo
stapled to it, and he will sign the page every day when I come. And
because as a result, they have no official record of me, I must always
report to this same station.

Back in the car I suggest to Marwa that we head to the city centre,
anxious to put prisons and police encounters behind me. I gaze at
my fiancée as she confidently manoeuvres through Cairo traffic
towards the upscale Zamalek district. I feel carefree. Aimless. As
we pass the Marriott Hotel, I ask her to pull into the parking lot.
She looks at me strangely, but does as I ask. All I really want at this
moment is to sit in the lush green surroundings of the hotel's famous
garden promenade and enjoy a cold beer in the sunshine—it will be

my first drink in 411 days. I also want to talk about our future, starting with marriage. We had applied to be married several times while
I was in prison, but our requests had been denied. Now that I'm out
on bail, I want to change that.

As we wait for our drinks, we are shocked to see the waiter who
knocked on our door the night of the raid, allowing the police in to
search the room and arrest me. I wave him over.

"Please don't be angry," he says, apologetically. "The police
forced me to knock on your door that night."

"It's all water under the bridge," I say, full of equanimity, and
visibly relieved, he rushes away.

I remove my phone from my pocket, revelling in not having to
look over my shoulder or scurry to the bathroom to use it, and snap
a selfie of Marwa and me flashing victory signs. I upload the photo
to my Twitter account and post my first tweet since my release: *Free
sunshine @CairoMarriott where it all started with my better half Marwa
Omara. Till death do us part. #Thankyou.*

Over the next half hour several Canadian journalists who had
flown into Cairo to cover the retrial make their way to the gardens
of the Marriott. I am thrilled to put faces to the names of these foot
soldiers who have kept my story alive: the CBC's Derek Stoffel and
Saša Petricic, and Radio Canada's Marie-Eve Bédard and Sylvain
Castonguay. Cairo-born Daniele Hamamdjian, who had closely
covered and sympathetically reported on my situation for CTV, asks,
"Are you ready for an on-camera interview?"

I shake my head. I feel unable to face cameras at this moment,
although in a couple of days, I will gladly talk to Gillian Findlay who
is working with Tamar Weinstein—the producer who had visited
me in hospital—on the CBC TV's *Fifth Estate* documentary about
my case. Still, the camaraderie of my fellow Canadians and colleagues is joyful, and I happily share my feelings about being free,
my intention to continue to push for deportation. Marwa has been

busy on the phone—still tirelessly working the press on my behalf. Now she places her cell against my ear. I give her a questioning look and then hear a man's lilting British accent. It's Robert Fisk on the line. I have said I am not giving interviews, but for this venerable correspondent who has lived in and reported on the Middle East for as long as I've been alive, of course I make an exception.

"Mohamed," he says teasingly, "since this is your first interview, feel free to speak your mind on the angle of your preference."

Fisk's article, "Freed Al-Jazeera Journalist: Why Can't Canada Get Me Home?" is published the next day and conveys my frustration at the Harper government's "failure" to secure my deportation: "Now I'm out, I want to leave. My name is on a no-fly list at the airport. I need the Canadians to get me off that list, to get the signature of the prosecutor to get me out and to apply the same laws and procedures they applied to Peter." I went on, "The hardest thing is to be an innocent man behind bars. And with people not realising that you are just an innocent journalist. Yes, it's an infringement to imprison journalists. But this case must also be seen at a geopolitical level. It is geopolitical score-settling and we were the pawns."[108]

Within a week of my release, Diaa Rashwan, the head of the Egyptian Journalists Syndicate, arranges a meeting with Egypt's Prime Minister Ibrahim Mahlab and we visit his office. I am hoping he can provide an explanation about why, though I had renounced my Egyptian citizenship, I had not been deported. The prime minister has no answer, but is sympathetic to my plight, calling me "son" and discussing my grievances against Al Jazeera.

With no official passport or identity documents, my mother worries about me travelling the streets of Cairo and the repercussions if I should be stopped at a police checkpoint. But now that I'm out on bail, nothing is going to stop me from embarking on the most important investigative journalism assignment of my career: researching the role Al Jazeera played in my arrest and conviction as a terrorist and figuring out why, despite a sympathetic ruling from Egypt's highest court, and the overtures on deportation from the governments of Egypt and Canada, I am still facing a retrial.

Hoping for answers, I visit Nader Gohar, Al Jazeera's longtime media service provider whose scathing article against the network I'd read while in hospital the previous October. I find him at his studio overlooking the Nile in central Cairo's Agouza district. A trim, fine-featured man with a grey halo of soft curls, Gohar knows well the distinction between the English and Arabic channels. He became concerned early on by the bias and distortions of news on Mubasher Misr, and proceeded to sever ties with it after discovering that it had not met the licensing conditions from day one. He explains that, unlike CNN or other non-local channels that are licensed in Egypt as foreign media offices, the Al Jazeera Media Network was granted a licence from the investment minister under different conditions: that it establish itself as a registered company rather than a foreign media office, set up the channel's local office in Cairo's Free Trade Zone, and broadcast only from a studio at Cairo's Media Production City via a rented channel on Egypt's NileSat satellite. Al Jazeera didn't meet some of these conditions, opening a broadcast studio in central Cairo and operating mobile broadcasting units across the country, all without the required permits. But they got away with it, Gohar says, because of their strong ties with the Brotherhood. Gohar's assertions make me even more uneasy about the new charge against us that Al Jazeera English had been operating without a broadcast licence.

Since I had visited him to ask his counsel when I started as bureau chief, I now fill him in on my frustrations and repeated efforts to convince Al Jazeera management in Doha to provide the official documentation I needed, which would have given me the credentials to present myself as the new bureau chief at the press centre in Cairo's

State Television Office and apply for press passes for me and my team as he had advised. But without the documentation, I couldn't do so.

Gohar believes that had Al Jazeera applied for accreditation for me and my staff, the government would have granted it, since it had no issue with Al Jazeera English (which is why the Egyptian authorities allowed the English channel to continue operating after police raided and shut down Mubasher Misr's office—located in the same building as Gohar's —in July 2013).

I also speak to Farag Fathi, the former Al Jazeera lawyer. I hadn't spoken to Fathi since he walked out on Peter and Baher during our trial, and want to find out why he dropped the case so unceremoniously. He is surprisingly candid now when we meet, sharing with me an email exchange with the network just weeks before he did so. On April 7, 2014, he had written to Al Jazeera's senior council, Yousef Al Jaber, to complain that Al Jazeera Arabic had misquoted him in its coverage of the trial. Ignoring his complaint, Al Jaber asked Fathi to take on a new client, a man the network had recently hired. Fathi says furiously that the client was Gamal Nassar, a well-known senior member of the Brotherhood who had been accused in a high-profile terrorism case and who I later discover works at the Al Jazeera Center for Studies in Doha, a think tank and research arm of the network providing in-depth analysis of current affairs, geopolitics, and strategic developments in the region.[109]

As Peter, Baher and I and our families fought to distance ourselves from Al Jazeera and the Muslim Brotherhood in the eyes of the courts and a distrustful public, Al Jazeera was not only hiring Brotherhood members but asking the lawyer defending us against charges of Brotherhood ties to simultaneously defend a prominent Brotherhood member.

Amid my investigations, another worry weighs on my mind: marriage. With no way of knowing whether I will be freed or sentenced during my retrial, and concerned for Marwa's status and protection should I be sent back to prison, I am anxious to make our union official. However, our plans are stymied yet again: foreigners who wish to get married in Egypt must present a passport to the Justice Ministry. What's worse, I soon discover that the Canadian embassy requires approval from the Egyptian judge in my retrial before they can issue me a replacement Canadian passport.

While there is no further mention of the new charge against us, the near-farcical issue of my passport arises during our second retrial hearing on February 23. Before the judge adjourns, Abou Bakr asks the court that my Canadian passport be returned.

"Who took your passport?" the judge asks.

"The security forces during the arrest, Your Honour," I say.

"The Canadian ambassador is here in the courtroom," Abou Bakr interjects, pointing at Ambassador Troy Lulashnyk who is sitting in the courtroom with members of his consular team. "If you tell him to issue a new one, he will."

To my relief, the judge agrees that Canada can issue me a new passport once I file a report at the police station declaring my previous passport lost.

That same night I hunker down in front of the TV to watch a BBC 4 exposé entitled, "Al Jazeera in Egypt: The Inside Story," the first television documentary to try to unravel the situation for a mainstream audience. Channel 4's Jonathan Miller opens with his account of interviewing more than a dozen current and former Al Jazeera English correspondents who have worked in Egypt in the past four years. All speak of the network's cavalier approach to the safety of their journalists. One unnamed reporter describes Al Jazeera English as a "Kafkaesque world in which decisions on the ground were undermined by directions from Qatar." Only the former Al Jazeera English Middle East correspondent Anita McNaught agreed to appear on camera. "There has never been any acknowledgement

by Al Jazeera management in public that they got sucked into the
Muslim Brotherhood game that was being played out in the Middle
East," she says. "Everyone working at Al Jazeera English came to
recognize that Al Jazeera's pro–Muslim Brotherhood bias in some of
its reporting [. . .] put its staff in greater and unnecessary danger."[109]

My pulse quickens when I see the gaunt face of Salah Negm,
director of news for Al Jazeera English and the man who assured me
everything was fine when he hired me. He and Miller stand in Al
Jazeera's well-appointed Doha newsroom as Miller reveals that days
before Peter Greste's arrival in Cairo, Al Jazeera's own head of security had advised against deploying further teams to Egypt, saying
it was too dangerous. I lean forward on the couch, scarcely breathing
as I wait for Salah's response.

"There is no concrete evidence that someone told us: 'Don't
work in Egypt.' Never happened."

Miller tries another tack. "I understand that there was a diplomatic warning that there was a prospect of your bureau being closed
down at one point?"

"Can I interrupt you for a moment," Salah interjects, "because
that line of questioning is really dangerous. I don't want to continue
this line. Al Jazeera is not under trial now."

Miller presses on. "The allegation about you, sir, in particular,
is that you knowingly put some of your staff, over several years, in
harm's way?"

"I'm sorry. Excuse me." Salah cuts him off, raising a hand. "I am
not going to take [these] allegations."

By the time Miller wraps his story and the Channel 4 anchor
relays Al Jazeera's official statement denying all allegations, I am as
certain of Salah Negm's and Al Jazeera's guilt as I am of my own
innocence. The network withheld the information, which they had
in hand, as to the status of the English bureau when they hired me
in Doha; continued lying about the dangerous situation on the

ground in Egypt, despite numerous enquiries from me and other staff; and additionally continued to put us all at grave risk by rebroadcasting (and distorting on occasion) our footage on banned Arabic channels. While I am happy the international media is starting to put Al Jazeera's actions under the microscope, I have the sinking feeling that I am in for a lengthy retrial.

Dutifully, as I have done each day, I report to Maadi Police Station first thing the next morning to sign in and to file a police report on my lost passport that I immediately submit to the Canadian consular team. Days later the embassy calls me in and Marwa drives me to their office to pick up my new passport. Instead, Ambassador Troy presents me with a letter he has received from Citizen and Immigration Canada. The letter references Section 9 of the Canadian Passport Order, which states that the minister may refuse to issue a passport to an applicant who "is subject to a term of imprisonment outside Canada or is forbidden to leave a foreign state or the territorial jurisdiction of a foreign court."

I read the closing sentence of the letter in disbelief: "The passport program will provide you a travel document as soon as the court signals definitively that one is required and the court travel restrictions are lifted."

I am incredulous, as is the embassy's Iman Sabry, who handles immigration and visa files and has been working on my case throughout. She shakes her head—she has never seen a case like this. The issue of my Canadian passport makes headlines in Canada and Egypt. Ambassador Troy personally visits Egypt's Justice Ministry to try and remove the roadblock to Marwa's and my marriage. However, the Ministry stands firm: they require my Canadian passport before they will permit us to exchange wedding vows. In the meantime, I am effectively stateless and though out on bail, still a very long way from being a free man.

CHAPTER 20

RETRIAL

March 5–August 25, 2015

The retrial is another frustrating ordeal. I return to court on March 5 for a mere ten minutes: two key witnesses for the prosecution fail to appear and Judge Farid adjourns until March 8. Outside the courthouse, I take advantage of the impromptu press gathering to announce the launch of the Fahmy Foundation, a non-profit organization based in Vancouver to provide financial support to journalists and prisoners of conscience and to advocate on their behalf. During my incarceration I vowed to use the publicity I was receiving to highlight the plight of and provide protection for other journalists behind bars for simply doing their jobs. I mention Shawkan, a liberal Egyptian photographer arrested on August 14, 2013, during the Rabaa dispersal and wrongly accused of being a member of the Muslim Brotherhood, and who is still imprisoned as of September 2016.[111]

When I return to court three days later, the key witnesses for the prosecution unbelievably fail to appear for a second time so the judge adjourns our retrial once more, until March 19. Abou Bakr manages to at least press him again on the issue of my passport (without a passport one can be stopped at any time by the police and detained for lack of identification, as I had recently been). Outside the courthouse, my anger bubbles over: "We come here and we respect the court, but it's very unusual that witnesses don't appear twice in a row [. . .]. It's a legal limbo and we're caught in it."[112]

With the retrial stalled, and unsettled by the recent charge that the English bureau was operating without a broadcast licence, I decide to press ahead with the lawsuit against Al Jazeera and communicate my plans to my Vancouver lawyers, Gary Caroline and Joanna Gislason, who agree to help research the question that plays in my mind: How widespread is the network's breach of journalistic ethics—and to what end? The Canadian legal team turns up the name of Aktham Suliman, a former Al Jazeera Arabic bureau chief in Berlin who claimed, in Germany's *Der Spiegel,* to have resigned over the network's unethical practices, asserting that during his time with the network, Al Jazeera Arabic became the "palace broadcaster for Morsi," and ordered that Morsi's decrees be portrayed "as pearls of wisdom." "Such a dictatorial approach would have been unthinkable before," Suliman told *Der Spiegel.* "Al Jazeera [now] takes a clear position in every country from which it reports—not based on journalistic priorities, but rather on the interests of the Foreign Ministry of Qatar . . . To maintain my integrity as a reporter, I had to quit."[113] He sends an email stating that the network also asked him to travel to Egypt during the 2011 revolution without equipment, and to avoid identifying himself as a journalist upon entry at the Alexandria airport—the same operating advice it gave Peter when they assigned him to Egypt. What is most shocking about Suliman's account is how the management in Doha responded when he asked how he would work in Alexandria with no cameras or crew: it informed him that Brotherhood supporters would escort him and facilitate his assignments on the ground.

I track down another former Al Jazeera Arabic reporter named Ali Hashem who, along with two other staff members, recently resigned from the Beirut bureau, protesting the network's bias and whitewashing of events unfolding in Syria. Hashem tells me that in May 2011, during the early stages of the conflict in Syria, he filmed dozens of armed gunmen engaging with targets inside Syrian territory, and his crew witnessed armed groups entering Syria three weeks earlier in April, some with Kalashnikovs and rocket-propelled grenades. According to Hashem, Al Jazeera headquarters refused to air the footage and told him to "forget that there are armed men," revealing a media agenda that could only be interpreted as deliberate support of Qatar's anti-Assad stance and its narrative of a civil uprising. Hashem claimed on the Russian government's TV channel, RT, that Al Jazeera paid US$50,000 to smuggle satellite phones across the border to Syrian rebels "to ensure they would get an inside picture."[114]

The idea that a major network is *shaping* rather than objectively reporting on the story—and in this case, one that has considerable effect on events in the Middle East, and is potentially contributing to the intractable situation in Syria—is, of course, troubling.

During one night of research, I come across a disparaging video commentary on the network by Adel Iskandar, a media scholar and communications professor at Simon Fraser University who had in 2006 co-authored a book praising the network: *Al Jazeera: The Story of the Network That Is Rattling Governments and Redefining Modern Journalism.* More recently, he was quoted as saying to Mohamed Elshinnawi on Voice of America News: "Al Jazeera used to have a firewall between its governmental funding and its broadcast content, but when the Qatari government decided to support Islamist groups in Egypt, Syria, Libya and Tunisia, viewers began to see a transformation in Al Jazeera from [a] professional investigative approach to [being] an outpost of the Qatari government propaganda machine."[115]

What changed your mind? I ask Iskandar, when I reach him by phone in Vancouver. His short answer: the Arab Spring. He tells me that between 2009 and 2012, during the public unrest in the Middle East, revolutionary politics became an important tool for Al Jazeera, boosting its popularity as protests escalated across the region. But juggling competing grassroots and government aspirations and an increasingly complicated political landscape, the network found itself spread too thin. At that point, Iskandar says, it decided to align itself with particular political Islamist organizations across the region, including the Brotherhood, courting Islamist actors and parties in every country in the region. "By doing so, the network could create a more extensive reach, sphere of influence and presence on the ground."

"And the Qatari government [the network's owner]?" I ask. He explains that the collusion of the network's programming with political Islamist actors worked seamlessly with Qatar's foreign policy, one that hinges its regional influence on similar groups of Islamist parties in Egypt, Syria, Libya, Yemen and elsewhere. And with a strong and growing alliance with Prime Minister Erdogan's AKP Party in Turkey—the Justice and Development Party, a political organization led by Erdogan and inspired by the Muslim Brotherhood—both the Qatari government and, by extension, Al Jazeera demonstrated a clear preference for the Muslim Brotherhood's particular brand of political and societal progress in the region.

"When they [the Brotherhood] were the opposition, they were deemed revolutionary—such as in Libya, Syria and Yemen. When they formed governments—as in Egypt during Morsi's term, and Turkey—they lost their revolutionary credentials. This complicated the picture for Al Jazeera and the Qatari government." Having put all their eggs in the basket of political Islam, when the first tremors of popular dissent and the youthful cry for "freedom" were heard from Tunisia to Tahrir Square and beyond in Turkey, Libya and Yemen, the network was taken by surprise. In a last-ditch effort to salvage its political connections in Egypt, and to continue supporting them around the region, it attempted to access areas where it no longer had an active presence by employing citizens to collect coverage of Islamist movements. Even in Syria, in late 2011, with the Syrian revolution turning to civil war, Iskandar believes Al Jazeera began broadcasting footage collected by opposition protestors and armed militias directly on its news programs. With little evidence and few attempts at corroboration, the percentage of such unreliable or deliberately biased content going to air from Syria, Libya and, later, Yemen and Egypt (particularly after Morsi's fall), was significant by the standards of any major news organization with a journalistic commitment to accuracy.

"Al Jazeera picked a side in the conflict and ran with it," Iskandar tells me, "and when the station was unable to deliver coverage from the ground, they relied on footage and reports produced by Islamist opposition groups and armed militia factions. This technique became their modus operandi in Syria where the stakes and the costs are extremely high—particularly to journalists."

After taking the job as bureau chief I had watched Al Jazeera's grainy coverage from Syria, wondering where the hell they were getting it. Iskandar believes there is truth to the claim—like that of former Al Jazeera Arabic reporter Ali Hashem—that the Qatari government provided communication facilities and equipment to tip the conflict against the Assad regime, including satellite uplinks for distribution of footage. This gave Al Jazeera an advantage over its competitors: the network was essentially recruiting protestors and fighters to become citizen journalists and information gatherers for its news programming. "Since the Syrian opposition to Assad, particularly those aligned with the Muslim Brotherhood and similar groups, were ideologically harmonized with the Qatari policy in the country," Iskandar says, "the coverage often went straight to air without verification, clarification, or corroboration."[116]

Gary Caroline and Joanna Gislason connect me with Stephen Howard, a Vancouver-based communications strategist who uncovers a classified WikiLeaks cable published in the *Guardian* confirming that the US has long known what Iskandar told me. Sent to Washington by the former US ambassador to Qatar Joseph LeBaron in 2009, the cable reads:

> Over the next 36 months, Qatar will continue to [. . .] pursue its classic vulnerable small-state policies aimed either at pleasing as many players as possible or—where competing demands make this impossible—at containing and counter-balancing irritation caused by these policies. We expect Qatar therefore to persist in supporting problematic players such as Hamas, Hezbollah and Syria, even as it attempts to strengthen its relationship with the United States and its GCC [Gulf Cooperation Council] neighbors. We expect the trend in favor of using Al Jazeera as an informal tool of [Qatari] foreign policy to continue undiminished.[117]

The geopolitical influences the network is bringing to bear take a further swerve when we return to court on March 19. Judge Farid asks the head of the technical committee, Mohamed Abdel Hakim, to take the stand. Bald and barrel-shaped, Abdel Hakim's testimony at our first trial stated that our footage that he and his team reviewed was fabricated and a threat to Egypt's national security—an accusation that weighed heavily in our conviction.

"Tell the court about the footage you reviewed," the judge orders.

Abdel Hakim hesitates, head slightly bowed, before answering quietly, "I did not see the footage and I did not write a report on it."

My jaw goes slack.

"Then why did you say that you saw it in the first place?" the judge yells. Dumbfounded, we strain to hear Abdel Hakim's response, but he gives none. Judge Farid, his expression grim, confers with his colleagues for several minutes, then orders a new technical committee be struck to view the footage, cracks his gavel forcefully against his block, and booms, "Court adjourned!"[118]

I throw an arm around Baher's shoulder and pull him in, and catch Marwa's eye as she files out of the courtroom looking ecstatic. As she nears the door, I see Abdel Hakim approach her. Outside the courtroom, I rush to her side. "What did he say to you?"

Marwa grins happily. "'Fahmy is innocent.'"

Another country is being drawn in to the swirling politics. My inability to get my Canadian passport back, which had been seized when I was arrested, continues to distress me, and Amal, in her usual indomitable style, releases a pointed statement that appeals to Prime Minister Harper from the Canadian public to pick up the phone and personally intervene have "so far fallen on deaf ears"; that the Canadian government had assured me I would be deported and when I was not, their only response had been a short statement from a junior minister calling for my release. "Such sheepish whimpers are woefully inadequate when it comes to enforcing an agreement reached with a sovereign state regarding a citizen's release from detention."[119]

Ever supportive and sympathetic, Caroline visits Ottawa to lobby for a replacement passport on the grounds that there is nothing in Canadian law that should prevent me from getting a new one. "The only impediment is Canada," he tells the Canadian Press.[120] The issue hits the floor of the House of Commons where the Opposition New Democratic Party's Paul Dewar, who has long championed my cause, takes Canada's new foreign affairs minister, Rob Nicholson, to task. "We know the Passport Order gives the government the authority to grant a passport in this case," Dewar states. "Why haven't you granted him one? [. . .] Is that the standard of service you're giving to Canadians abroad? If so [. . .] it is a matter of incompetence, and it's disgraceful."[121] I manage to arrange a phone call with the Liberal Party leader, Justin Trudeau, and soon his tweet pops up on my Twitter feed: *Spoke w/ @MFFahmy11. Egyptian govt needs his passport for ID purposes. Our govt refuses to re-issue it. @pmharper: Why refuse? #NotMyCanada.* He, too, raises my case during question period, pressuring the prime minister to act.[122]

I reach out to my friend Ayman Mohyeldin, a former Al Jazeera English bureau chief in Cairo during the revolution, and now anchoring *Road Map*, his own show on MSNBC in New York. Ayman immediately grasps the nuances of the issue and on April 15 he hosts MP Paul Dewar and me live from Ottawa and Cairo. "It's egregious," Dewar tells Ayman. "There is no real rationale for denying him a passport. Either it's deep, deep ignorance of their own powers, or [the Canadian government] is being dismissive of Mohamed's rights."[123]

Finally, a resolution to my passport woes comes a week later when I arrive at the courthourse on April 22 for the next retrial hearing. As I approach the gate, my cellphone rings. It's Iman Sabry asking me to meet her and the Canadian ambassador in the parking lot. I look around, spy the embassy driver waving to me, and change direction, moving towards the embassy's white SUV. Ambassador Troy Lulashnyk sits in the front passenger seat holding up a manila envelope. I look at him questioningly as he hands it over. Inside is a small white booklet. I pull it out and stare at the gold embossed coat of arms, and then the words: CANADA TEMPORARY PASSPORT. For a moment I am speechless. I do not ask how or why, I am only deeply grateful. Iman assures me that I will receive the blue permanent passport in a week.

"Thank you," I say to the ambassador and Iman.

I rush into the courtroom and return to the cage feeling buoyant and for once looking forward to the day's proceedings. The outspoken Christian billionaire businessman, Naguib Sawiris—who had visited me in the hospital—has agreed to testify on my behalf as a character witness. At sixty, Sawiris is still youthful, with dark, heavily lidded eyes crowned by a broad forehead. When the judge calls him to testify, I watch heads turn excitedly as he strides to the front of the courtoom.

"I've known Fahmy a long time," he tells the judges. "We are friends who meet in public places. Mohamed Fahmy has no relation to the Muslim Brotherhood organization and he is not a Muslim Brother."

If anyone has the ability to sway public opinion, it's Sawiris. Wielding his television channel, ONTV, he strongly opposed the Muslim Brotherhood during their rise to power and time in government. Nor is he a friend to Qatar or Al Jazeera. Typically critical, today, in his hour-long testimony, he praises the English channel, distinguishing it from its Arabic counterparts, which he calls "unprofessional and biased." As the head of a live, pan-Arab television channel, Sawiris also tells the court that a distinction must be made between journalists and the network that employs them. "The organization, not the correspondent, is responsible for what is broadcast," Sawiris says forcefully.[124]

I celebrate my forty-first birthday five days later at Cairo's Riverside, a nightclub overlooking the Nile owned by Sawiris. The lounge is electric that night, bathed in blue light and throbbing to the pulse of music. It's a far cry from my last birthday spent eating cake in a cockroach-infested prison with members of the Brotherhood. Marwa and I laugh, drink and dance the night away with friends, the weight of the trial momentarily lifted.

Armed with my new passport, and in an attempt to normalize my life, I move out of my parents' home and rent a furnished flat in central Cairo, even though it means a longer drive to check in at the Maadi Police Station each day. My apartment becomes a one-man investigative newsroom. During the day I welcome reporters; late into the night, I scour the Internet and tap my media and personal contacts to help defend myself in court and carefully build the case against Al Jazeera. My Canadian lawyers and I have chosen May 11 to announce my lawsuit against Al Jazeera. They arrange to fly to Cairo, and I book a conference room at the Four Seasons Hotel overlooking the Nile. But there's an impediment: as a former Al Jazeera journalist convicted of being a Muslim Brotherhood terrorist and undermining national security, there is zero chance that Egypt's press centre will grant me permission for a live broadcast.

One night Marwa and I are having dinner at the Five Bells, an outdoor restaurant near my apartment, when she sees the respected Egyptian lawyer Dr. Mohamed Hamouda seated nearby. Swarthy and square-jawed with a head of thick, coal-black hair, Hamouda's high-profile clients have included the sons of former president Hosni Mubarak and many Cairo businessmen. Having met him on a couple of previous occasions, Marwa says, "Let's ask if he'll help us." She rises from the table before I can stop her. Hamouda is gracious and invites us to sit. I tell him about my lawsuit against Al Jazeera, and to my surprise he agrees to help us for a contingency fee.

I feel his influence immediately. I'm in Hamouda's office when he unleashes his charm on the director in charge of the press centre via speakerphone. "You are asking me why we are renting the conference room, Mr. Director," Hamouda says with mock effrontery. "Well, we are planning to have an orgy!"

The director is contrite. "I trust you, of course, and your client has spoken bravely against Al Jazeera."

"Don't worry," Hamouda assures him, "what we are announcing

will ignite the interest of the country. Just warn your people and the management at the hotel that there will be at least a hundred journalists from all over the world attending."

It turns out to be no exaggeration. Marwa and I have invited a long list of local and foreign media, arranged simultaneous translators, and even created an enormous wooden backdrop, a midnight-blue billboard with bold yellow letters that reads: JOURNALISM IS NOT POLITICAL ACTIVISM. Adding to our firepower, Sawiris confirms that he will air the announcement live on ONTV.

One day before the press conference, Robert Fisk and his Afghan-Canadian wife fly into Cairo to meet with us. Fisk is en route to Syria for yet another stint in one of the world's most dangerous conflict zones, but makes time for lunch at the Marriott. I feel a rush of warmth when I see him. Almost seventy, Fisk has a ruddy complexion, a thatch of slightly dishevelled grey hair, and behind rimless glasses, keen blue eyes. We have not seen one another since the days of the Arab Spring, but his passion, intellect and vigour are undiminished. Unable to attend the coming conference, Fisk offers to write a "teaser" article. Titled "Al Jazeera Plays a Dangerous Game in Egypt," it appears the morning of our announcement:

> In a few hours' time, in Cairo, Mohamed Fahmy will hold a press conference, which every reporter will want to observe. The Al Jazeera journalist, who spent 411 days in Egypt's gruesome Tora prison on trumped-up state charges of "terrorism," refused, even after a long Cairo lunch [. . .] to tell me exactly what he's going to say. But I have a dark suspicion that by the time he finishes speaking, his employers at the Qatari television network will rue the day he was ever sent to trial.[125]

That afternoon I am perspiring as I enter the conference room packed with journalists and lined with dozens of cameras, and take my seat

at the podium table. Flanked by my Canadian lawyers on my right
and Dr. Hamouda on my left, I ask those present to stand for a
minute of silence honouring journalists killed globally—a number
the UN lists at seven hundred in the past decade.

Then I pick up my speech from the table with a trembling hand.
Training my eyes on Ian Lee in the front row, I nervously begin:

> We journalists are not meant to be the friends of any govern-
> ment. We exist to ask the why, to dig for and to report the truth,
> and to pose difficult questions to politicians . . . That is what
> the fourth estate is about. In my modest fifteen-year-old career,
> I don't remember the world being so cruel to us journalists with
> more than two hundred journalists around the world jailed
> and sixty killed in 2014. The abuse of this so-called war on
> terror has to stop being used as an excuse to limit free speech
> in what seems to have become a partial global war on journal-
> ists. Egypt put three journalists on trial instead of punishing
> the network . . . I am here to announce that I will set the record
> straight and put Al Jazeera on trial in Canada's top court.

A murmur ripples through the room. Camera flashes explode.
I press on, feeling more confident as I accuse the network of deceiv-
ing us as employees, breaching our contract, acting negligently,
and using us as political pawns. "The reality is that Al Jazeera is not
only biased towards the Muslim Brotherhood, they are sponsors.
My intent in launching the lawsuit," I conclude, "is to draw the line
between journalists who have no malicious intent and a network
that has breached the code of ethics of journalism and imperiled lives
on the ground."

Joanna Gislason announces the details of the suit against the
network: $100 million in punitive and remedial damages for negli-
gence, breach of contract, and misrepresentation.[126]

"Why are you suing in Canada?" one journalist asks during the brief question period that follows. It is Dr. Hamouda who responds with a blunt and painful reminder: "Since surrendering his Egyptian citizenship, Fahmy is seen as a traitor in Egypt."

After the announcement, I become a lightning rod for several high-profile Qataris living in exile keen to relate what they know. One is Khalid Al-Hail, a reform-minded businessman calling for a constitutional monarchy in which power resides with an elected Parliament, not the emir. Speaking via Skype from London, Al-Hail confides that he was jailed, electrocuted and beaten by Qatar's state security agency in 2010 and 2014 before fleeing to the UK to seek political asylum.[127] "The royal family spends millions on public relations companies to promote Al Jazeera and to clean up their dirt," he says.[128] Another is the former Qatari official spokesman in the early '90s, Fawaz al-Attiya, a British national who fled to London after accusing then–prime minister Hamad bin Jassim Al Thani of siphoning millions of dollars of state funds into his own bank accounts. He tells me in an interview that Al Jazeera has been compromised from its very beginning. His book questioning the dealings and intentions of many prominent Qataris, including the ruling Al Thani family, landed him in a Qatari prison for nearly fifteen months for "divulging state secrets"—a charge he fiercely denies.

He recounts his personal involvement in Al Jazeera's 1996 inception after Qatar's emir at the time, Hamad bin Khalifa Al Thani, became troubled that the citizens of the Middle East had to rely on CNN for coverage of the first Gulf War in Iraq in 1991. He proposed launching a local channel that could also compete with the Saudi-owned Middle East Broadcasting channel. "He wanted to match the media influence of the Saudis." On April 21, he came across a newspaper article stating that BBC's Arabic Television, which was owned by Saudi king Fahd's cousin, had been pulled off the air after criticizing the Saudi government. Quickly, al-Attiya convinced the prime minister and members of the Qatari cabinet to fly to the UK to meet the recently disbanded BBC Arabic team. He describes how they "gathered the journalists in the house of the Qatari ambassador in London, and in a matter of three days they were set up at the prime minister's residential compound in Doha." Months later, on November 1, 1996, a network was born.[129]

According to al-Attiya, in the three years following its launch, the network's budget came directly from the Qatari Foreign Ministry. Working in the presidential palace, he regularly communicated requests from Prime Minister Hamad bin Jassim al Thani to his cousin who was head of Al Jazeera. "I instructed him to spin the coverage in a way that suited our views in the Qatari Foreign Ministry," al-Attiya admits. "That way, Al Jazeera would criticize other countries, but not Qatar." He blames the former prime minister for orchestrating the unethical and highly politicized coverage of Syria, Libya, Egypt and Iraq during the popular uprisings.

Digging into his assertions, I unearth a *Guardian* article dated December 6, 2010—a month before the start of Egypt's Arab Spring—that underscored the extent to which Qatar wielded its media network as a foreign policy tool. According to US embassy cables leaked by WikiLeaks,

> "[Qatari prime minister] HBJ [Hamad bin Jassim] had told Mubarak 'we would stop al-Jazeera for a year' if he agreed in that span of time to deliver a lasting settlement for the Palestinians," according to a confidential cable from the US embassy in Doha in February. "Mubarak said nothing in response, according to HBJ."[130]

On May 30 I awake to a flood of calls from the media. Mohamed Soltan, a young Egyptian-American serving a life sentence for participating in pro–Muslim Brotherhood protests against the government, has been deported after relinquishing his Egyptian citizenship. Two days earlier, former US secretary of defense and CIA chief Leon Panetta had met with President Sisi in Cairo. In no mood to talk to the press about my own prime minister's shortcomings, I focus on my next hearing. On June 1, state prosecutor Hassan Fathi presents his closing arguments.

"Standing before us today are those who would divide our people; those who have lied to us and accused us of lying." He speaks of the students and submits a transcript of their audio testimony to the judge, and reiterates parts of Baher's confession: that Al Jazeera had asked him to alter his reports—including coverage of anti-Morsi protests on June 30, 2013—to "film Tahrir Square from an angle that shows it empty" and that Baher had translated a speech by General Sisi in a way that incited civil war. In the cage, I seethe, recalling my entreaties to Al Jazeera to contest these allegations, and their belief that Baher's testimony would "disappear." Now nearing the end of our retrial, they haunt us.

The prosecutor then addresses the charge that Judge Farid added against us at the first retrial hearing—the curveball that has been worrying me through the six weeks of delays. He pulls out a document, waving it dramatically. "We have just received evidence that *all* Al Jazeera channels were banned." He points out triumphantly that this includes Al Jazeera English at the time we were employed there. If the evidence is valid, it is confirmation that the network lied to us from day one. It also means the judgment in the retrial may not go in our favour.

I ask Dr. Hamouda if he can help confirm the veracity of the document. He moves swiftly. He locates and obtains an affidavit from Mohamed Sulaiman, Al Jazeera's senior accountant in Cairo from June 1, 2013—three months prior to my arrival—to October 3, 2014. "As part of my work for AJ, I was required to visit the Egyptian Media Production City complex . . . to obtain AJ

statements of account. I learned . . . that AJ did not have the necessary [broadcast] licences . . . and when I reviewed AJ's commercial
register, I found that they had expired." His affidavit also confirms
that the network's practice of paying Brotherhood supporters to
film demonstrations was well-established:

> AJ broadcast these recordings on its banned channels and
> through the Internet. Management provided Brotherhood sup-
> porters with small cameras in order not to be discovered. Al
> Jazeera in Doha paid the Brotherhood supporters by deposit-
> ing funds directly into their personal bank accounts in Egypt.

Two days after the hearing, our defense lawyers finally obtain
and share a copy of the prosecutor's evidence. It's a document from
NileSat, the company that grants Egypt's broadcast licences:

> Subject: Decision issued to ban all Al Jazeera channels from
> broadcasting out of Egypt . . . A decision was issued by the
> executive board of the Media Production City dated March 7,
> 2013, granting preliminary permission to set up a project
> called "Al Jazeera Media Production and Satellite Broadcast-
> ing." A contractual agreement was not signed [by Al Jazeera]
> with the NileSat company therefore a decision was issued by
> the Production City on September 8, 2013, to cancel the previ-
> ous approval.

There it is, in this impersonal document. But what really floors
me is the timing: Al Jazeera's licence was cancelled two days after
they appointed me bureau chief on September 6. Which means,
quite simply, that for more than three months the Doha management
concealed that fact from its employees—a detail that could land us
in prison for a long time.

Three days later our defense begins its closing arguments. Abou Bakr systematically refutes each accusation in the long list of charges against me, including that there was no evidence that national security had been compromised by our video footage, that the discredited technical report vindicates us, and that if there were any issues with licences, it is Al Jazeera who should be accountable. I had talked to Abou Bakr about directly contesting Baher's testimony, but he advised me that this is the domain of Baher's Al Jazeera lawyer Mohamed Wahba who will address it in the final hearing for the defense. Still, three weeks later, the day the defense is to conclude its arguments, I enter the cage with a sense of foreboding.

After almost eighteen months since Baher made his "confession," we will finally see it defended in court. Wahba challenges the prosecution's allegations, saying that "[Baher] did not prepare any report showing the Egyptian state in a bad light" and "did not follow any directions from the channel in this regard." The "report" in question is a video report aired on Al Jazeera English on July 25, 2013 (six weeks before I joined the network), that "quoted" then-general Sisi calling for Egyptian citizens to take to the streets in a mass rally against "terrorism"—a presumed reference to supporters of recently ousted Muslim Brotherhood President Mohamed Morsi.[131] This report was seen as an incitement to civil war and has been a major factor in the charges against us. Baher's lawyer asserts that Baher's "role was limited to translating the said speech without having any role in preparing the report." Wahba further defends Baher by stating that the translation had been doctored subsequent to his initial translation of it, that Al Jazeera took his words "out of context," and that Baher refused network directives to "fabricate" news and portray Egypt in a negative light.

When Baher's lawyer finishes, I study the impassive face of Judge Farid. Is the defence too little too late?

I prepare a brief speech before we arrive in court for the final hearing on June 29. I run the words over and over in my mind as I wait my turn to speak.

When the judge finally calls me to the floor, I am prepared to make the most convincing speech of my life. I stand before the bench, dressed in a dark suit and tie, and begin earnestly: "If I had known almost two years ago when I accepted the job that Al Jazeera was operating illegally, I never would have taken it."

The judge nods, and I press on, paraphrasing Sawiris. "The responsibilities of a network are different from the responsibilities of its journalists—"

A policeman approaches the judge as I speak, and whispers in his ear. I am in mid-sentence when the judge bellows, "Enough! Enough!" Without warning he adjourns the hearing, announcing the court will deliver its verdict in a month.

I stand bewildered as the judges hurry from the courtroom. But the reason is quickly apparent: a car bomb has blown up the convoy of Prosecutor General Hisham Barakat, Egypt's top judge. The man with whom Marwa and my mom had a five-minute audience and who had sent thousands of Islamists, secularists and journalists to prison, is dead. The Egyptian affiliate of ISIS, Sinai-based Ansar Bait al-Maqdis, had recently called for attacks on the judiciary. And I recall the nights in Scorpion, when I lay listening to the men in their cells praying to God to take the life of Barakat. The retrial is again adjourned when the judge calls in sick. Then, more distressing news: Sohaib, one of the students, has "disappeared," rumoured to have been picked up by police. Two weeks later the twenty-two-year-old appears from an undisclosed location on an eleven-minute video released by the Ministry of Defense. In it he confesses to charges in relation to a large terrorist cell that the military says has threatened national security and targeted police officers in collaboration with Muslim Brotherhood cells in Turkey and Syria. Watching the subdued demeanor and wooden performance of the once brash student, I worry his confession was forced.

I show up at the courthouse on August 2, downcast to discover the verdict is again postponed—this time to August 29. Amal Clooney, who is closely following developments from London, releases a statement on her firm's website, noting, "It has not escaped observers that [August 29] comfortably postdates the visit of US Secretary of State John Kerry as well as the planned celebrations of the new Suez Canal waterway scheduled for August 6, with various world leaders in attendance. The verdict may be coming later; but the world will still be watching."[132]

Amal urges President Sisi to pardon me if sentenced, and submits another deportation request in an effort to extricate me from the possibility of returning to prison if the conviction goes against us for a second time. She decides she must come in person. While thrilled, I am also concerned for her. After she co-authored an International Bar Association report critical of Egypt's government and judiciary, experts advised her to launch the report in London since she risked arrest if she did so in Cairo. When I broach my concern, she dismisses it, sending a letter to the prime minister's office saying she is coming to Egypt for my sentencing.

Unsure of my fate, Marwa and I rush to get married before the verdict. If I must return to prison, she will at least have the protection of being a married woman. On August 17, armed with my new Canadian passport and required documents, we head to the Ministry of Justice.

I offer a bit of gallows humour as we approach the entrance of the bustling ministry in downtown Cairo. "Maybe they will allow conjugal visits in prison."

The official at the "foreign marriage desk" doesn't recognize me and I hand him the papers, hoping he will expedite the process so

we can get on our way. I had gotten permission from the major at
the Maadi Police Station to check in by phone rather than in person
over the next week and have booked a flight that evening to the
picturesque seaside resort of Sharm el-Sheikh on the Red Sea where
we will spend our honeymoon. He looks over our papers and frowns.

"Mr. Fahmy, the letter from the Canadian embassy has the
proper stamp, but is not signed by the ambassador."

"Sir," I say, my voice rising, "the letter would not be stamped
without the approval of the ambassador. Why does he have to sign
it personally?"

Those are the rules, he says, looking at his watch, and tells us to
come back another day with the signature. For him, this issue is
simply an annoyance at the end of his workday. For me, it is the last
straw.

"This is not acceptable," I snap. "I'm going to call the prime
minister." I pull out my cellphone as the officer watches skeptically.
I have not spoken to Prime Minister Ibrahim Mahlab since I visited
him shortly after being released on bail, and am not sure he will
accept my call. To my surprise, he picks up the phone.

"Mr. Ibrahim. I hope you are not too busy," I say in a rush. "I am
calling you from the Ministry of Justice. I have all my documents,
and they still won't let me get married. Can you please help me?"

"Get married! Who is this?"

"Mohamed Fahmy."

"Oh, Fahmy, you caught me off guard. I was wondering who
was calling me about getting married. Where are you now?"

"I am at the Ministry of Justice," I explain, "and I have all the
documents required, but—"

"Okay," he interrupts. "Let me make some calls."

The marriage official has risen to his feet and is gawking at me.
"I'm sorry, I didn't realize you are the Al Jazeera journalist from the
Marriott Cell."

Marwa and I smile at one another as the man rushes off to get us coffee. Minutes later, another official enters announcing he works in the justice minister's office, and he takes us up to the top floor.

Months earlier, Marwa and I had bought gold wedding bands and had them engraved with our names. I pull the rings from my pocket. It's finally happening. Marwa and I sit facing one another behind the desk as the official signs our paperwork, rambling on about Egypt's political scene. I hear nothing, see only the lovely face of the woman who is about to become my wife.

"Witnesses?" the official asks, and I stare at him blankly. "You need two witnesses to sign your wedding certificate." We had not thought to invite family or friends to bear witness.

"Don't worry," he says, stepping into the hall and returning with two janitors. Smiling, mops in hand, they sign our wedding certificate. I grab Marwa's left hand, slip the band onto her ring finger, and she does the same for me. "This is a good Egyptian woman who has stood beside you like a champion," the official says. "Take care of her."

"I can't believe that I agreed to marry a terrorist," Marwa jokes later as we board the plane to Sharm el-Sheikh. That evening we check into the Marriott Hotel overlooking the water and try to relax. We walk the beaches, eat in open-air restaurants, and revel in one another's company, but the shadow of the verdict hangs over us. When Amal calls to strategize about her visit, I joke that we are even: we have each spoken to the other during our honeymoons.

On our return to Cairo, I receive a startling, unexpected invitation from D.T., Sisi's top presidential aide—a man who is never far from the president's side and always appears next to him on TV footage in Egypt and abroad—who asks me to the Al-Ittihadiya Palace in Heliopolis for a private meeting. Such an invitation is unheard of for an ordinary citizen, let alone a journalist on trial for crimes against the state in Egypt. I am nervous and bewildered as I arrive at the grand building clutching the only ID I own and that I've been asked to bring: my Canadian passport. At least two dozen presidential guards stand inside the gate. They are expecting me. One confiscates my cellphone, and walks me through two metal detectors before another official greets me inside the palace and leads me upstairs to an opulent waiting room. Someone brings coffee and I sip cup after cup as I wait, clueless as to why I have been summoned, and thinking about the many presidents who have occupied this palace in Egypt's recent history. One was assassinated, two remain in prison, and history has yet to decide President Sisi's fate.

Finally, the door to an inner office opens and I stand and greet President Sisi's impeccably dressed aide. Behind him is another man who introduces himself as M.M., the president's secretary; I recognize his name as the contact with whom Marwa has established a connection within the President's Office.

"Mohamed, it's a pleasure to meet you," D.T. says, shaking my hand and inviting me to sit. "I called you here just because I wanted to meet you in person. As you know this case has become a real disturbance."

I nod, unsure how to respond. In a nearby chair, the presidential secretary takes notes but does not speak.

"You can tell your elegant lawyer, Amal Clooney, that she is welcome to visit us in the presence of the Canadian ambassador."

Of course, I seize the opportunity to assert my innocence, that I spent only three months with the English channel and never supported the Arabic platforms.

D.T. scrutinizes me. "I've seen you speak on TV and watched your press conference against Al Jazeera. How is your lawsuit going?"

It occurs to me that with the launch of my lawsuit against Al Jazeera, the government and I are in the same trench, fighting the same enemy. "It's been filed in Canada by my Canadian legal team, with the assistance of Dr. Mohamed Hamouda, my Egyptian lawyer," I answer carefully. "The evidence that the network operated in bad faith and deceived us is incontrovertible."

"You know, you have a very persistent wife," he says, catching me completely off guard and exchanging a look with the presidential secretary. "I have followed her lobbying efforts with government officials and the Egyptian media. You are a fortunate man."

"Yes, sir. We just got married, thanks to the prime minister's help."

He smiles. "When is your court date?"

"August 29," I say, and venture a question. "What do you think will happen?"

"I don't know. We have no contact with the judges. But don't worry, Fahmy," he says, "if you go to prison, we will take care of you."

I leave the presidential palace feeling unsure of the reason behind our meeting and uneasy. I can only hold fast to the slim hope that my lawsuit against Al Jazeera and the efforts of my new wife and Amal mean my case is being viewed sympathetically at the very highest levels of the Egyptian government. I immediately call Amal to brief her, as the presidential aide's final words play over in my mind. *If you go to prison, we will take care of you.* It's an outcome I cannot bear to think about. Hopefully, with the inroads Marwa has made and Amal on her way to Egypt, I won't have to.

CHAPTER 21

VERDICT

August 28–October 6, 2015

On August 28, the day before the verdict is to be read, Marwa and I check into the Four Seasons Hotel in the heart of Cairo to await Amal's arrival. She is flying in from London and will check in under a different name. Tonight we will meet and tomorrow morning travel to court together to face the judge.

Our room overlooks the Nile and to the north I can see the Kasr el-Nile Bridge. It seems like yesterday that I was one of the determined, optimistic mass of Egyptians streaming into Tahrir Square demanding freedom and justice. Almost four years after the revolution, the country has not achieved either.

Marwa entreats me to relax, but I cannot. Family and friends call with encouraging words, and the media bombard us with requests: everyone wants an interview with Amal—her presence here is attracting widespread attention. Finally, a WhatsApp message pops up on my phone. Amal has cleared customs and is leaving the airport

with the Canadian ambassador. She calls soon after she arrives, and
Marwa and I ride the elevator to her floor. Over the last year Amal
and I have planned, lobbied and strategized, carrying out much of
our interaction on a contraband phone from my hospital room. We
have exchanged dozens of messages and shared emotionally charged
moments, and yet we have never met.

She opens the door and without hesitation warmly embraces each
of us in turn. She is down to earth and taller than I had imagined.

"How was your trip?" I ask.

"Shorter than your long march to freedom," she says, smiling.

I feel like we are meeting an old, trusted friend, and her calm
presence momentarily chases our stress into the shadows. As we
settle down, Amal mentions that George has been following every
twist and turn of the case, and is as outraged as she is. In the seconds
it takes to register that George is, of course, George Clooney, her
husband, she is down to business. Reassuringly, she says we have
every reason to hope for an acquittal, but must prepare for the possibility of a conviction. A presidential pardon, she tells us, is her first
priority and preferred option. She pulls deportation and pardon
requests from her briefcase, and walks me through them, saying she
will submit these to the Egyptian authorities in the event of a conviction. I sign the papers reluctantly, feeling as if I am signing my
own death warrant.

Amal is not permitted to speak or defend me in an Egyptian
court, but we strategize about how she can leverage her reputation
to put pressure on the government to pardon or deport me. Though
it makes me slightly nauseous, we discuss a list of government officials she and the Canadian ambassador should try to meet with if
the worst-case scenario should come to pass and I am sent back to
prison. She has already secured a meeting with the justice minister
Ahmed Al-Zind, scheduled to take place after the verdict, should
it be necessary, and—following up on my impromptu meeting with

D.T., Sisi's presidential aide, and his invitation to Amal to visit—she and Ambassador Troy have requested a meeting with the president himself, and are awaiting confirmation. Sisi, Amal reminds us, has consistently said that he wished our case had never happened, that it has been damaging to Egypt's reputation and that he would seek to intervene if I am convicted. Seeing the concerned look on Marwa's face and mine, she adds that both, of course, will be unnecessary if I am acquitted. On the other hand, although she rarely uses media except as a last resort, she promises us that if I am re-sentenced tomorrow, she will speak to the media, and reach out again to the highest-level political channels she can. Then we talk hopefully about meeting again in Canada.

The next morning, I dress in my best dark suit. I run my statements over and over in my head.

Amal is waiting for us in the lobby. In her hand she holds a white folder bearing the large imprint of a red maple leaf—a subtle nod to Canada. Minutes later, Ambassador Troy arrives and escorts us to his embassy car. Sitting in the back seat of this armoured vehicle, flanked by Amal and Marwa, my two-woman-strong army, I am the one who feels bulletproof. I am incredibly proud to have them as my champions, proud of the fight they have both put up. Marwa has morphed from a shy, media-averse woman to a courageous expert at negotiating the byzantine police and prison systems, and a savvy, strategic spokesperson. She has gained access to, and respect from, the highest levels of government, including from M.M. Amal has been fearless, a brilliant tactician, and peerless at delivering the clear, consistent messages to the world and the government that anything but an acquittal will be a terrible miscarriage of justice. I reach for Marwa's hand, holding it tightly all the way to the courthouse.

I hang back as Amal, Marwa and Ambassador Troy enter the courtroom and are engulfed by a mob of reporters, photographers and cameramen. They disappear under a thicket of swaying boom mics, and I watch white–uniformed police clamber on top of benches to get a glimpse of Amal.

The words of the presidential aide have run like a looping news-feed through my head for the last few days: *If you go to jail, we will take care of you.* I shoulder my way through the media scrum. The room is so crowded I have to shuffle down a row of benches to reach Amal and Marwa. I squeeze in between them and see Baher, dressed in a cheerfully coloured shirt as if he expects to be sitting on a beach this afternoon like Peter. He reaches his hand out to say hello and I grab it tightly, raise our arms in a gesture of solidarity. The report-ers throw questions at us. Amal acknowledges them with gracious smiles, but does not answer. The impact she has in saying nothing, by holding her counsel, is very effective.

I am uplifted to see all the journalists—Canadian, Middle Eastern and international—who have kept our story alive and not allowed us to "disappear." So many feel like loyal friends, here again for the final chapter of the story. I watch Marwa in awe as members of the local media greet her warmly, and wish us luck. With all the camera shut-ters clicking and reporters jostling for a sound bite, the atmosphere is electric. A grab bag of correspondents from *Entertainment Tonight* and Rotana, a Middle Eastern celebrity network, clamour around Amal. An island of calm amid the commotion, she leans her head in close to mine and whispers, "Are there always this many reporters in the courtroom?"

I admit that today there are more than usual.

Moments later the bailiff bellows out the names of the defendants. Peter is named again as being tried in absentia, as are my British col-leagues, Sue Turton and Dominic Kane, and veteran Egyptian cam-eraman, Mohamed Fawzy. The defendant named Johanna Indeniette is also listed in absentia. I recently discovered Johanna Indeniette is the name the investigators mistakenly gave to Rena Netjas—the Dutch freelance reporter I met with at the Marriott. Quick-thinking

Dutch embassy officials picked up on the error and spirited Netjas out of the country. A fictional woman has all this time stood trial in her place.

I turn to Marwa, pull her close and hug her. Then I stand back to look at her. I can see her bottom lip trembling. Amal rises, extends her hand, and firmly shakes mine.

"Please look after Marwa if this all goes bad," I say.

Furtively, I slide my trusty BlackBerry into the waistband of my trousers and let it slip down into my underwear. I stride quickly towards the cage and when I reach it, wish I hadn't been in such a hurry. Behind me, I hear someone yell, "Take care, Champ. We're with you!"

Just as I'm about to enter the cage I look up and spot H., the distinguished brass-buttoned national state security officer who orchestrated the raid on the Marriott. He stands in uniform, flanked by police officers, near the door to the judge's chambers. He sees me, and then looks away quickly.

Baher, Shadi and I are locked into the cage, where we find Khalid and Sohaib who have been trucked in from prison. I haven't seen Sohaib since he was abducted in early July, his whereabouts unknown until his disturbing video confession from Tora Prison appeared on TV weeks later. The students embrace Baher and me like brothers.

I quietly ask Sohaib if he was tortured to confess. The young student has not been broken, but I see an angrier man—one who has morphed from the hotheaded twenty-year-old I met behind bars in Scorpion to a jaded convict. He speaks firmly and looks me straight in the eye as he describes how he was stripped naked, beaten, electrocuted on his genitals, and hung from his arms until he confessed to a crime he didn't commit. His words break my heart and I don't dare ask about Sarah, the woman he wanted to marry using the money he saved from selling protest footage to Al Jazeera. He is to face a military tribunal for allegedly staging attacks against the army.

"I am not scared of death," he tells me, knowing that his fate could be the death sentence.

The judges and the prosecution team enter the courtroom. Sealed in the soundproof cage, I hear nothing from the outside and press my body close to the grille, straining to decipher the expression on Judge Farid's face. He appears jowly and stern as he settles himself on the bench behind a bank of microphones.

I watch as if in slow motion he depresses the button on his mic. His voice suddenly booms into the cage, and one by one he intones the names of those being tried in our case. And then: "In the name of the Egyptian people . . ." I watch his mouth open and the courtroom seems to warp in front of me as his words float though the speaker. "The court finds the defendants guilty." Through the roaring in my ears I hear Baher's, Shadi's and my names and then the sentence: three years.

Baher grabs me and we hold on to each other, our bodies leaden with the effort of staying upright. Chaos erupts in the courtroom. I see Marwa burst into tears and Amal's stony expression as she reaches to comfort her. I lose sight of them as a swarm of reporters closes in, cameras firing. Police officers and guards shove and yell, trying to control the pandemonium.

Inside the cage there are no goodbyes. The guards immediately hustle Baher, the students and me through the rear door and down a hallway to the holding cell. Before closing the door on us, one of the guards says derisively to me, "Why did you even come to court today? Who walks to hell on his own two feet?"

In the cell, I slump on the hard bench. Baher and the students look shell-shocked. As soon as I hear the deadbolt turn, I reach into my pants, pull out my phone and frantically begin sending contacts to Marwa: the presidential aide, reporters, officials. I cannot remember what strategies we discussed with Amal the night before, only that we had, in the end, all talked hopefully about a meeting in Canada, and Marwa and I about freely walking the streets of Vancouver.

I check Twitter and see that the verdict is starting to trend in Canada, London and Australia, the rising outrage scrolling in real time. I want to jump onto Twitter and express my rage, I want to fight and lash out, but I cannot reveal that I have a phone. My BlackBerry starts to vibrate and I recognize the number of the national state security officer, H, who I had glimpsed in court. I do not know why he would be calling, only that if I answer, he will know I have a phone. It's a chance I can't afford to take.

I see that Amal has wasted no time unleashing her fury to the press, and is sounding the alarm about the wider implications of the verdict: "It sends a message that journalists can be locked up for simply doing their job, for telling the truth and reporting the news. And it sends a dangerous message that there are judges in Egypt who will allow their courts to become instruments of political repression and propaganda."[133]

I fire Amal a WhatsApp message thanking her for speaking out so courageously. No Egyptian lawyer would dare criticize the Egyptian government as she is doing today.

She texts back: *Don't thank me now. You can thank me when I get you out.*

The familiar sound of keys jangling and a deadbolt turning alerts us to the arrival of the guards who will transfer us to Tora. I shove the phone down the back of my pants, wedging it again between the muscles of my buttocks just as the door swings open. The guards lock Baher, Shadi and me together using two sets of handcuffs, and escort us out, while Sohaib and Khalid are hauled out together and pushed into another prison transport truck, likely bound for a different prison. The cuffs are wrenched so tightly around my wrists that my hands turn blue. I ask him to loosen the cuffs, but he scoffs.

"It's a short drive to Mazraa Prison. Toughen up," he says.

———

Mazraa Prison. A different section of Tora from Mulhaq Al Mazraa, where Peter, Baher and I had been detained before. I recline awkwardly on the metal bench in the filthy, airless and sweltering truck, resting on one hip to avoid the discomfort of sitting on my phone. The temperature outside is over 40 degrees Celsius; inside, it's a furnace. Still dressed in the suit I had carefully chosen for court, I am bathed in sweat. Chained together, Baher, Shadi and I try not to retch from the stench.

The walk from the truck into the prison is the constant nightmare that wakes me from sleep. Inside, the cuffs come off and the guards ask us to empty our pockets. I fumble in my pockets and toss my wallet onto the table along with my only piece of ID, my hardwon Canadian passport. The guard, who is skinny and at least a decade younger than me, gestures toward my wedding ring.

I refuse, telling him that my fingers are too swollen, but really I can't bear to give it up.

He regards me impassively. "Take it off." My throat tight, I surrender my wedding ring.

He is watching closely as I remove my pants in slow motion, one leg at a time, clenching my buttock muscles to keep the phone in place. Thankfully the guards let me keep my boxers on. One tosses the blue prison uniform at me. I yank the blue pants over the Italian leather dress shoes I had chosen for court.

"Through the metal detector," barks a guard.

Baher throws a worried look in my direction, but there's no avoiding it. Sure enough, as I pass through, the metal detector rings. I pause, try to look surprised, as four officers and another guard move in, demanding I remove my clothing.

"It's from the operation he had in the hospital," says Baher. "He's got a metal plate in his arm."

I could hug him. Instead I pull the collar of the prison shirt off my shoulder to reveal the long, ugly scar.

"Okay," the officer in charge says, "let him pass."

Guards escort us to a cavernous cell with rows of low, rusty metal bedframes covered in thin, dirty mattresses. There appear to be four prisoners currently living here. I feel apathetic, unable even to choose a bed. Before I can slip into the washroom to remove my phone, the guard announces that the warden and several high-ranking generals are on their way for a visit.

Minutes later, at least half a dozen uniformed and plainclothes officers enter our cell. One introduces himself as the head warden of the entire Tora complex. He extends his hand. Surprised, I take it.

"It's pandemonium out there, Fahmy. Your wife and your brother are making a lot of noise. And tell me, why is Amal Clooney, the movie star's wife, in the picture?"

I am affronted on my lawyer's behalf. "She is my international lawyer. She just happens to also be George Clooney's wife."

His eyebrows go up. "And why is the Egyptian government summoning the British ambassador if you are not even British?"

"Because two British journalists in the case were sentenced in absentia and the ambassador publicly protested the verdict."

"You, Baher and the student will live here alone. I am ordering the other prisoners out. Tomorrow, someone will paint the cell while you three are out enjoying some exercise in the sun." He looks at the resident prisoners. "You four, pack up. You're moving." Wordlessly, they begin packing their belongings. I know too well how they feel.

He tells me that my wife has special permission to visit tomorrow—she does not have to wait the customary thirty days. And my family has been given permission to deliver a bag with clothes and food tonight—outside the usual hours. "We've granted you a rare exception," he smirks, "so you can tell your famous Hollywood friends you are being treated well."

Baher is as surprised as I am. "It must be the press," he speculates. "They're worried someone will complain if they don't treat us well." But I wonder if this is what the presidential aide meant when he said, *We will take care of you.* It seems to me that while many members of the government may think I am innocent and feel uneasy about what has happened to me and Baher, that has not saved us from the judiciary's verdict and from being sent back to prison.

When the warden and his entourage leave, I rush to the bathroom to remove my phone, crestfallen to see that it has switched itself on between leaving the holding cell and now, and the battery is almost dead. Under other circumstances I'd find this something to laugh about, my absurdly powerful buttocks, but in the moment I don't find it funny at all.

I message Marwa to ask what's happening. She replies immediately. She has called the prime minister's office manager and secured a meeting. The justice minister, however, has cancelled on Amal, possibly because of her scathing comments after the verdict, calling the judiciary a "tool of state repression."[134] And they have yet to hear from President Sisi's office. She adds that Amal has arranged interviews with the CBC's Middle East correspondent Derek Stoffel, the BBC's chief correspondent Lyse Doucet and the country's popular Lamees el-Hadidi at the hotel that evening. I silently cheer Marwa, Amal, and every journalist I know. I tell my wife I love her and make one request: *Please bring a phone charger.* I know she'll find a way to get it past security. I ask her to thank Amal.

When I emerge from the bathroom, Baher and Shadi are kneeling on the floor, praying. I look across their bent backs to the peeling cement walls, the grimy floor. I am despondent. Past believing that the judiciary or the government will deliver justice.

A couple of hours later guards arrive with a huge bag filled with supplies. Such after-hours deliveries are unheard of. Baher, Shadi and I sift through the contents, dividing clean pairs of underwear, socks, towels, bed sheets, pillowcases, snacks and bottled water. Marwa has not forgotten a thing: hairbrush, toothpaste, batteries, a radio, books, and—most essential—more pens and another notepad. She has even included an iPod loaded with my favourite music along with ear-buds. The next morning, half a dozen prisoners arrive and start daubing fresh white paint on the pocked walls. Another arrives to fix one of the ceiling fans. The guards open the cell door and Baher takes a stroll down the corridor to meet the other prisoners. The authorities are bending over backwards to show we are not being mistreated, but these acts of favouritism do not move me. Shadi lies on his mattress, depressed, mumbles about this "theatrical play" orchestrated by the superpowers, and about George Orwell, Big Brother and the Ministry of Truth.

Later that day we get news of visitors and the guards lead us to the communal visiting area. Jehan and Baher's children are there, and so are Marwa and Adel. Marwa recounts the details of her, the ambassador's, and Amal's visit to the prime minister's office. When pressed on the urgency of a deportation or pardon, he'd replied, "It's not in my power." Only the president could authorize my release.

"Before we even left his office it was all over the press."

"And the meeting with President Sisi?" I ask.

Her face is sombre. "His office told us he is on a visit to Russia and then travelling directly to China. There is no way Amal can meet with him before she leaves."

But Amal has made a direct plea to President Sisi in an interview with Lyse Doucet: "President Sisi, you have previously promised that you would intervene to pardon the Al Jazeera journalists when the judicial process is over. Please do so now. And if for any reason you're not willing or able to do that now, then please send my client home to Canada just as you sent his colleague back to Australia."[135]

Trying to cheer me, Marwa reaches into her waistband, leans close to whisper in my ear, "I got the charger and a new phone card for you."

I shake my head. "Don't give them to me."

A look of incomprehension, then disappointment, comes over her face. She knows that means we will only be able to communicate during official prison visits. But I am also, for the first time, afraid of what would happen, what further charges could be laid if I'm caught with it.

Seeing my depression, she tells me that Amal will be continuing to act from London. That Caroline and Gislason, and Peter Klein, the Emmy Award–winning journalist, documentary filmmaker and director of the University of British Columbia's Graduate School of Journalism, are gathering signatures from hundreds of Canadians to pressure Stephen Harper to call President Sisi on my behalf. And that she and my brother are meeting with M.M. and Ambassador Troy separately right after the visit. "The wheels are in motion," she says reassuringly.

Before they leave, Adel says he feels he has to let me know that our father, struggling with colon cancer and Parkinson's, has taken a turn for the worse following the news of my three-year sentence. I feel gutted by what I have put him through. Put all of them through.

The next morning I stay in my bed while Baher and Shadi are released for our one-hour outing. I try to listen to the music Marwa's compiled on the iPod—a mix of rock, jazz, reggae—but it does little to boost my morale. In an effort to rouse me, Baher approaches me after lockdown and shows me the *Alwatan* newspaper: Marwa is on the front page in an interview entitled "Wife of Al Jazeera Journalist Appeals to President for Pardon." Shadi proclaims loudly that the tide is turning: to see the wife of a convicted Al Jazeera journalist on the front page of a pro-government newspaper is a first.

A few days later, Marwa visits again and tells me that George Clooney has spoken out about my case at the Toronto International Film Festival, and, like Amal, called on the Canadian government to do everything it can to secure my freedom. The generosity of taking the time to do so on behalf of his wife's intractable case touches me. Then she leans in and whispers that Naguib Sawiris has called her. "He told me he got confirmation that you will soon be released."

I am not convinced. If our passionate and powerful billionaire friend was not able to sway the authorities during the trial, I am not sure he can do so now. Marwa grabs my hand and squeezes. At that moment, she notices that I no longer have my wedding ring. Our eyes meet and we both fall silent. At the table beside us, Baher plays a game with his kids, reaching to tickle them, then pulling his hand back. They shriek with delight.

"What about Baher?" I ask "Did you ask Sawiris about him?"

She looks hurt. "I have to focus on you. Baher has Al Jazeera on his side working for him, promoting him regularly on their social media and TV."

She tells me Justin Trudeau has written to Prime Minister Harper again, urging him to personally intervene; and NDP leader, Thomas Mulcair, has called the Egyptian ambassador in Ottawa. She pulls out a folded paper and discreetly hands it to me. I read the paper quickly, an open letter by three hundred notable Canadians and addressed to Stephen Harper demanding he call President Sisi and seek my release. I am humbled by the names I see: former Canadian prime minister Paul Martin, former supreme court justice and UN commissioner for human rights Louise Arbour, internationally acclaimed author Naomi Klein, and a number of recognized academics, doctors, writers, journalists and members of Parliament.

"Thank you," I say, but I'm speaking to all Canadians, and to every journalist and member of the public who has written, tweeted or spoken out on my behalf.

As the days pass, I struggle to create a daily routine, to channel the advice of Viktor Frankl to find meaning in suffering. I sketch out ideas to better protect and improve consular services to Canadians imprisoned abroad and to protect journalistic freedoms. During Marwa's next visit, I tell her about the charter I have begun drafting.

She stares at me blankly, and then bursts into tears. "I tried everything," she says in a stuttering breath. "I even managed to reach the number-two man in the palace. I told him about your medical situation, the patriotism of your family, your pride in your Egyptian nationality and your pain over the loss of your citizenship." Marwa's voice breaks. "He stopped me and said it was hopeless. He told me that a series of pardons would be announced soon, but your name would not be on the list."

For the first time in the twenty months since my ordeal began, I wonder if I have the energy to keep fighting. Days later, on the small television in our cell, Baher, Shadi and I watch news announcing that in late September 2015, President Sisi will attend the seventieth session of the United Nations General Assembly in New York City. Prior to the visit, around the time of the national Muslim holiday of Eid al-Adha, Sisi is expected to announce numerous pardons in a public relations attempt to move ahead Egypt's bid to get re-elected to a seat on the UN Security Council.

"Don't get too excited. Our names won't be on the list," I say, flatly.

Baher and Shadi look at me strangely, rising to get ready for their afternoon prayers. I roll over on the bed grabbing my pen and notebook, the only form of devotion I have.

On September 23 my younger brother, Sherif, pays me a visit from Kuwait. Between his job at a bank and his newborn baby, he has had few chances to get away. Now, with Adel having exhausted his vacation leave, it's Sherif's turn and I am delighted to see him.

Moments after he arrives, Marwa joins us in the visitor area, electric with energy. Pulling a chair close, she steals a glance over her shoulder to the other side of the room where Baher is visiting with Jehan and his children. She leans in and whispers in my ear, "Your name has been included on the pardon list."

I stare at her, uncertain. She whispers that she has been in touch with M.M., the president's secretary, who has assured her, but I must tell no one.

I lean my head on her shoulder and hold her close.

Baher calls out, "What's going on, Fahmy?"

"Nothing." I let go of Marwa. I hold up the bag of sweets she has brought. "My favourite," I say, offering some to Baher's children.

When the visiting hour ends, Marwa hugs me and I wave good-bye to her and Sherif. I return to the cell and sit very still. The door opens a short time later and a guard calls me. "The warden of Mazraa wants to speak to you, Fahmy. You. Alone."

Baher stares at me curiously.

I follow the guard down a long corridor to the warden's office. A blast of cold air from the air conditioner hits me as I enter. He sits behind a large desk, a smug grin on his face, and in two chairs next to it are Marwa and Sherif.

"Congratulations, Fahmy, you've been pardoned!" The warden rises and reaches out his hand to me, saying something about having just received a call from national security, as my tearful younger brother jumps out of his chair and gathers me in a bear hug. He tells me he and Marwa were on their way out when they called them back to the office. When he lets me go, I pull Marwa into my arms. I wipe the tears from her cheeks. I say a silent thank you to Amal, to all those who have continued to pursue legal and diplomatic avenues for my release since the conviction, and to the many journalists and citizens who have helped put pressure on the Egyptian government to make this happen.

I turn to the warden and ask him about Baher but he says he does not know—he has only been told about me. He claps me on the back and tells the guard to return me to my cell. As soon as I am back I walk to the television and turn it to the local news. Baher, sitting on his bed, stares at me suspiciously. I can't look at him, don't know how to begin to tell him I have been pardoned and he hasn't. All I can think about are his wife and children.

On the small set, the news anchor begins announcing the pardons. One hundred prisoners pardoned. And then, as if in a dream, I hear our names: Canadian Mohamed Fahmy, Egyptian Baher Mohamed. Shadi's name is on the list, too.

Baher whoops with joy. We grab each other and begin jumping and dancing just as the door opens and a guard yells: *Pack your stuff!*

I have never been so happy to hear the familiar words. Within minutes, guards return our belongings, including my invaluable passport and wedding ring, and whisk the three of us from our cell and out of the prison, load us into a white minivan. An officer drives us a short distance, and stops in front of my old high school, the Cairo American College. They tell us to get out and we tumble onto the street. Baher, Shadi and I stand blinking in the bright sunshine as if we have just been spit out of a dark tunnel. We are haggard, still wearing our blue prison garb, clutching our belongings in plastic bags, with no money or mobile phones and staring at each other in joyous disbelief.

A cab comes flying down the street towards us, stops and Marwa jumps out. She races towards me, flies into my arms. We hug and kiss and laugh at once. Baher's wife, Jehan, arrives minutes later. I am still hugging Marwa when the journalists arrive. Amal calls soon after. She sounds as euphoric as I feel, and then tells me to wait a moment. "George wants to talk to you."

Clooney's voice resonates in a rich, familiar way. "Fahmy, you've kept me up late too many nights in LA following this case." He talks about politics and international human rights issues, about corruption and about his own experience doing humanitarian work.

"People," he suggests, "will want to hear about this, not just about freedom of the press but what this whole case reveals about the geo-politics of it all."

His words bolster my commitment to fight for press freedoms and the safety of journalists, and ignite my determination to share my understanding of the political ambitions that are bloodying the region today—and which so deliberately and carelessly knock insig-nificant pawns out of the way. I will, at least, try to do that.

Two weeks later Ambassador Troy informs me that my name has been removed from the no-fly list. I promptly book tickets for Marwa and me to fly out of Cairo to Canada with a stopover in London to see Amal. On October 6, the ambassador and Iman Sabry accompany us to the airport to make sure all goes smoothly. Marwa and I are practically shaking with excitement as we hand our passports to the security officer. He scans them, punches a few com-puter keys. Suddenly he frowns, gets up and walks away with our passports. He returns a few moments later accompanied by an armed police officer.

"What do you do for a living?" the officer asks.

I tell him I am unemployed.

He narrows his eyes, looks Marwa and me up and down. "Unem-ployed? You don't work for Al Jazeera?"

My heart skips a beat. "I used to."

"You are the leader of the Marriott Cell," he says with an unmis-takable tone of satisfaction. "You are banned from travelling. Your name is on the no-fly list."

I turn to Iman in shock as she translates the conversation to Ambassador Troy. "Sir," she says to the passport official, "we were told by national security that Mr. Fahmy's name has been removed."

"I've been pardoned. *Pardoned!*" I fight to keep my voice under control.

"What should we do?" Marwa begs the passport official. "We'll miss our flight."

He taps the counter officiously with my passport, shrugs, then strides away, leaving the police officer watching over us.

Fifteen minutes tick past as Iman makes frantic calls, to no effect. Over the airport PA we hear a boarding call for our flight.

"Call M.M. at the president's office," I whisper to Marwa in desperation. She steps away to make the call and less than a minute later turns, her eyes bright with hope. "He said he would call airport security and hung up right away."

We hear the final boarding call for our Air Canada flight.

Suddenly the passport officer reappears, hustles over, stamps both our passports with a flourish and hands them back. "Run," he says.

Ambassador Troy takes off in the lead. I have never seen a middle-aged man in a suit move so fast. Marwa runs behind him, her long hair flying. I sprint alongside her, clutching our carry-on. When we arrive at the gate, the staff beckons us impatiently. I hand my mobile phone to Marwa and grab a smiling Ambassador Troy. We pose for a photo under the gate's yellow billboard. The tweet I post with the photo minutes before our plane takes off says: *A glorious end to our battle for freedom!*

CHAPTER 22

FREEDOM IS ONLY HALF THE TRUTH

October 6, 2015–September 30, 2016

My flight home to Canada is a slow unwinding, as we arc across Europe to the UK for a reunion with Amal. On October 7 we meet under happier, celebratory circumstances at London's Frontline Club, a renowned media venue dedicated to conflict reporting and championing independent journalism. My arrival, with Marwa and Amal at my side, feels like a homecoming for us all. As I move through the crowded room, my former Al Jazeera English colleague, Dominic Kane—still sentenced to ten years in absentia along with Sue Turton and Mohamed Fawzy—wraps me in an emotional bear hug, calls me "Boss." The title makes me cringe, bringing back the stress of the months working together in the Marriott Hotel, which changed everything.

"You're in London," he says in near disbelief, clasping a hand on my shoulder.

"Yes," I say, though I can't quite believe it either.

The weightless feeling of being free pervades me as I settle on stage in front of dozens of my colleagues. I am grateful to them all. Amal is to my left and my longtime friend Lyse Doucet, who will interview us, is on my right. My eyes settle on Marwa, sitting elegantly in the front row beside Amal's renowned mother, Baria Alamuddin.

"Thanks to all the journalists of the world and the unity that was put behind this cause," I say. "It really, really made a difference." Even when in solitary confinement without sunlight, I explain, "the advocacy that was happening outside was slipping through the concrete walls."[136]

Amal is relaxed and forthcoming, recounting something of the high-level diplomatic pressure brought to bear on Sisi after our second conviction. She notes the timing of the two key events we believe led to Baher's and my eventual pardon: the start of the Muslim holiday of Eid al-Adha on September 23—a traditional time of reconciliation, including announcing prisoner pardons— and President Sisi's scheduled address to the United Nations in New York the very next day, surmising that he did not want our case to overshadow his UN visit. In a candid moment, she also reveals that we secretly communicated via WhatsApp using my contraband phone. The champagne we sip after the presser feels like our official declaration of victory.

Four days later, Marwa and I board the flight to Toronto, surprised when half a dozen passengers and two Air Canada cabin crew ask to pose with us for photos. One woman confides that her daughter decided to be a journalist after reading my story. "Thank you for your stand against Stephen Harper," a woman in the seat behind me whispers. "He has to go in the election next week. Please don't stop."

In *Man's Search for Meaning*, Victor Frankl says, "Freedom is not the last word. Freedom is only part of the story and half of the truth." Freedom, Frankl says, degenerates into arbitrariness unless it is exercised with a sense of responsibility.[137] I know that if I do not use my new-found freedom and fame to promote individual, journalistic and political freedoms then my entire prison ordeal will have been meaningless.

The mention of the upcoming federal election underscores for me the absolute importance of our most treasured individual freedom: the right to vote. Prime Minister Harper's mild stand on my incarceration in Egypt cut me deeply, making me feel that as a Canadian citizen I was not worthy of my government's protection. I felt both threatened and demeaned by Bill C-24, recent legislation allowing the government to unilaterally revoke passports of dual or foreign-born Canadians convicted of terrorism and other serious offences abroad, even when those convictions may be unjust or expedient. Harper's election talk of "old-stock" Canadians, banning the niqab in the public service, and starting a telephone tipline to report "barbaric cultural practices" was utterly at odds with Canada's values of inclusiveness and pluralism; on the contrary, these sentiments were thinly veiled anti-Muslim tactics designed to incite fear, divisiveness and racism.[138]

Arriving at Toronto's Pearson International Airport reinforces my resolve to protect the Canada I cherish, one that has managed to maintain positive public sentiment towards multiculturalism, and foster social integration of immigrants in Canada despite a growing international climate of fear and protectionism. In contrast to my exit from Egypt, Canadian airport officials hustle Marwa and me through customs, requesting photos along the way.

We check into our hotel and then wander the streets of Toronto beneath a bright autumn sun. It's Canadian Thanksgiving and I am overcome with emotion as we move freely without threat of arrest or violence, a scenario I have imagined countless times in prison. I spy a Canadian flag amid the towering Toronto skyline, and snap a photo of Marwa and me with it in the background, and then post the photo on Twitter with the message: *Happy Thanksgiving Canada! Walking the streets of Toronto with my wife is a truly liberating feeling! We feel safe, free & at home! #Love.*

Seeing Canada through Marwa's eyes is uplifting. I had tried many times to explain what life in Canada felt like, the reality of living in a country where one is rarely judged on one's gender, race, religion or political affiliation. Now, I revel in her excitement over the diversity and sense of freedom that surrounds us: gays, Jews wearing kippas, Jamaicans with Rastafarian dreadlocks, veiled Muslim women, Sikhs with colourful turbans, all co-existing peacefully. I am reminded of why I came to Canada as an immigrant teenager escaping conflict and repression in the Middle East. The values enshrined in the Canadian Charter of Rights and Freedoms form the beliefs I carried with me as a journalist when I returned to the Middle East to report on the Iraq War and, later, the Arab Spring. They are the values I championed as a private citizen during the Egyptian revolution, and held up as a justifiable end as men and women put their lives on the line to achieve freedom. Canadians, most of whom have never been without individual freedoms, sometimes take them for granted. Having mine stolen from me makes me appreciate what we have in Canada and want to safeguard it.

My first opportunity arises the next day when Marwa and I, along with Gary Caroline and Joanna Gislason, join Tom Henheffer of Canadian Journalists for Free Expression (CJFE) to speak to the media at Toronto's Ryerson University. "While you, here, citizens in Canada and around the world, clearly understood the urgency of the situation we faced in prison in Egypt, the Harper government did not," I say. "Sitting in that prison cell, it was difficult not to feel betrayed and abandoned by Prime Minister Harper."[139]

Meeting the government opposition leaders, Justin Trudeau and Tom Mulcair, over the next two days is edifying. Trudeau welcomes Marwa and me at his hotel suite with cold beers and youthful zest.

He forgoes handshakes for hugs, his photographer quick to snap a photo of us for Trudeau's Twitter feed. Behind his PR savvy, however, Trudeau is genuine and open, thoughtfully discussing the importance of journalistic freedom in present times. Our meeting with Tom Mulcair a day later is a more extravagant affair that includes a media scrum at his hotel. Flanked by our spouses and standing in front of a row of Canadian flags, I formally thank the principled and hard-working NDP leader for taking the prime minister to task in the House of Commons.

"Who are you voting for?" a reporter asks. "Are you planning to sue Harper?" I tell him I have no intention of being punitive, only to ensure loopholes in consular protection are revisited to prevent issues for other Canadians. "You do know who I'm *not* voting for, that's for sure," I say, and the room erupts with laughter.[140]

Walking casually with my friend Samantha Monckton to vote in Vancouver five days later means the world to me. In recent years, I have stood outside polling stations in Egypt, Iraq and Libya covering elections and talking to citizens who dream of real democracy. Often I feared that voters could be in danger, and sometimes they were, armed men attacking the stations with Molotov cocktails, gunfire, and even bombs. Still, every election the people returned, hoping always for a better outcome, a better future.

As we watch the election coverage that night, Marwa and I hug and dance when Justin Trudeau is declared the winner. Our euphoria reminds us of the dance we did in my apartment in Egypt the day the Brotherhood was ousted. Such moments of hope are what we hold dear.

Inspired by the possibility I see anew in Canada, I revisit the notes I took in prison. In partnership with Alex Neve—secretary general of Amnesty International Canada who tirelessly spearheaded the Canadian campaign for my release—and with the help of Gary

Caroline, we craft a twelve-point Protection Charter, which I had first begun scribbling in jail. Its aim is to reform Canada's consular laws, policies and practices for dealing with Canadians imprisoned or detained abroad. During my incarceration, I discovered that consular assistance to Canadians, even those facing human rights violations abroad, is discretionary. The first point in our proposal tackles this issue, saying: It is time to enshrine the right to receive consular assistance and the obligation to provide it in Canadian law.

The proposal also calls for greater transparency and consistency on the questions that tormented me while incarcerated: When will a minister take up a case? When and how will family members be informed of key developments? When and in what manner will government work with lawyers and civil society groups? When, and to what extent, will the government speak out publicly about a case? How best can we ensure individuals in prison receive medical treatment and legal representation?

Not all cases of Canadians detained abroad involve naturalized citizens—frequently those experiencing human rights violations are permanent residents or spouses or family members of Canadians. Such is the case with my fellow inmate at Scorpion, Khaled al-Qazzaz, the University of Toronto engineering graduate—a Canadian permanent resident—who, after almost two debilitating years in prison, was finally released and allowed to return home with his Canadian wife, Sarah, and their four young children in August 2016.[141]

Our charter is endorsed by Gar Pardy, former director of consular affairs, who later releases an invaluable report entitled *Canadians Abroad*, echoing the concern that by maintaining "Crown prerogative," the government retains the right to act as it deems appropriate on matters not governed by statutes, including consular affairs. Pardy shares a list of twenty-eight countries that have embedded consular protection in their national laws, or through judicial decisions. The disparity is stark between Canada and countries like the United

States, where the government's "clear and universal duty" to protect Americans in foreign countries is enshrined in law, or Germany,
where there is a "constitutional duty" to provide protection to
German nationals in relation to foreign states.[142] Like Pardy, I feel
strongly that Canadians—more than 1,400 of whom are detained
abroad—deserve the protection of their government, whether
hyphenated citizens or not. He revealed that the Conservative government refused to abide by international norms, citing its 2007
decision to stop requesting clemency for Canadians on death row.
He and others also point to decision-making based on political interests rather than objective measures of just and humane treatment.

On January 26, Alex Neve, Gary Caroline and I travel to Ottawa to
unveil the Protection Charter. When Marwa and I, chaperoned by
Stephen Fuhr—recently elected a member of Parliament, who had
visited me in hospital back in Egypt—enter the viewing gallery
overlooking the floor of the House of Commons, we are both surprised and overwhelmed to receive a standing ovation. The welcome
reminds us again how different and remarkable this country is.

    I am further encouraged when Minister of Foreign Affairs
Stéphane Dion announces that Canada will return to a policy of
consistently seeking clemency on behalf of all Canadians facing the
death penalty abroad—one of the twelve points in our Protection
Charter. In May 2016, Dion supports a second point in our proposal,
announcing Canada will take initial steps towards signing the UN
Convention against Torture.[143]

Coming through my ordeal a free and able man while many of my
colleagues have lost their lives in the field leaves me feeling humble
and very fortunate. It's with this sense of privilege that I settle into
my new appointment as adjunct professor at the University of
British Columbia and the first journalist-in-residence at the Global

Reporting Centre. The centre was established by Peter Klein, one of our unflagging supporters while we were on trial, himself the son of immigrants who fled the Hungarian revolution in 1956. Our faculty residence, situated in a lush forest overlooking the Pacific Ocean and North Shore Mountains, is utopian. At times, as I stare out the window at the verdant university landscape surrounded by towering trees, the majestic mountains beyond, I realize that the escapism I indulged in while in prison to maintain hope is now my reality.

I am keen to share my experiences with the students, many of whom have followed my case. In our lectures, I tell them that getting one's hands dirty in the field, talking to real people, and bearing witness to their stories makes a difference. The students are quick to raise concerns about protecting oneself in the field, and even have me questioning my own hubris. I concede there are no guarantees that journalists operating in conflict zones will emerge unscathed, regardless of hostile-environment training or other precautions. Citing my own experience, we review the ugly side of journalism: the risks to reporters when networks use journalism as a form of political activism, exposing their employees to serious repercussions— Al Jazeera and its Qatari owner being the most extreme example of what happens when the media use their platforms as weapons to spread propaganda and frame political agendas.

When I began this journey I believed that if my team and I held fast to good, honest journalism, everything would be all right. And that's where I was wrong. Capital and politics are increasingly controlling the corporate media, often fed by sensational, headline-grabbing stories that keep ratings high and result in biased journalism. So what's the answer? How to direct young aspiring journalists? Or the public who rely on us to report the truth? What I have learned is to question everything and not believe that any single source is above bias. I have come to trust specific journalists, ones I follow closely, and attempt to be vigilant, educated and active. We no longer live in a world where we can afford to be passive recipients of news, whether from a major network or from social media.

In the case of the Middle East, the most dangerous and volatile conflict zone today, many respected journalists tiptoe through the political minefield that exists between reporting government propaganda and upholding journalistic ethics. In Egypt, for example, some journalists have become blatant agents of the regime (like the journalist who leaked the video of our arrest after adding dramatic music to it), while others continue to critique government misman agement and strive to highlight the increasing domestic problems such as poverty, the poor quality of education, the clampdown on NGOs, corruption, inadequate health care, high unemployment, the devaluation of the Egyptian pound, and the drop in tourism due to terrorism.

Journalists' hard work can also put them in danger—especially those reporting from conflict-torn places where they might become political targets—as was the tragic case for my courageous friend Steven Sotloff. More than 70 journalists were killed worldwide in 2015—some of them personal friends and acquaintances—and 199 remain behind bars. In summer 2016 I travelled to Geneva and had the opportunity to lobby the UN to take immediate action by appointing a special representative to the UN secretary-general for the Safety of Journalists, echoing and supporting similar demands by Reporters Without Borders and other reputable press-freedom orga nizations. This special envoy will bear responsibility for monitoring compliance by UN member states in keeping with their obligations under international law—a requirement fundamental to ensuring we hold governments accountable.

Even in a Western democracy, vigilance is necessary. Reporters Without Borders listed Canada in eighteenth place in their 2016 World Press Freedom Index and Reporters Without Borders describes the tenure of former Canadian prime minister Stephen Harper as a "dark age" for journalism in Canada—a period during which the federal government's focus on secrecy and control systematically undermined the Canadian public's right to know.[144] "The right to know" and "responsible journalism" are deeply intertwined.

In the United States and elsewhere, the anti-Islamic rhetoric of people such as Donald Trump and Marine Le Pen are constantly reiterated by the media, inflaming and exploiting fear while adding credence to the Islamist claims that the West is waging war against Islam, and feeding directly into the narrative that the Islamic extremists then use to recruit young, disenfranchised Muslims.

What is most dangerous about this anti-Islamic rhetoric is that it fails to acknowledge the vast majority of the world's 1.6 billion Muslims, who are largely peaceful. The Islamist extremists who I encountered in prison operate more like gangs than religious adherents, and have little or no connection to the world's mainstream Muslims.

Dangerous rhetoric from Islamist leaders further fans the flames of recruitment. One example is a recent video entitled "We Are All Osama," released by Osama bin Laden's son Hamza, who entreats al-Qaeda supporters to seek revenge for the death of his father, killed by US Navy SEALs along with his brother Khaled in the 2011 raid on their compound in Pakistan. Now in his early twenties and purportedly being groomed before his father's death as his heir apparent, Hamza also vowed to continue the global jihad against the United States and its allies. In a recent interview, Hamza's sister-in-law Zaina (the wife of Omar, the fourth eldest of bin Laden's nineteen children now living in Qatar), told me Hamza, who has been underground for several years, had been detained in Iran until 2010 before travelling to Pakistan with his mother, Khirah.

I asked Zaina if she thought Hamza's audio message would resonate globally and inspire his father's disciples to avenge his death.

"Yes, I do," she told me, "but Hamza is making a grave mistake. I think he's being manipulated by Ayman al-Zawahiri."[145]

Less than two months after my release, I had an opportunity to speak at the World Democracy Forum in Paris and meet with members of the European Union to advocate for imprisoned journalists. My visit coincided with the gruesome series of coordinated terrorist attacks that left 130 people in that city dead. Some of the Paris attackers were young men born and raised in France and Brussels before becoming radicalized and travelling to Syria to join ISIS.

As Marwa and I walked through the tearful crowds to pay our respects at a memorial across the street from the Bataclan theatre, I had a flashback to my time in Scorpion and my visit to the "dungeon of radicals," where I witnessed Islamist leaders' efforts to radicalize the young men incarcerated with them. Many of those young men—secular as well as Muslim, boys like Shadi and Sohaib and Khaled—had lost hope after the revolution disintegrated. Some, like me, were innocent; others merely zealous college students arrested for participating in pro-Brotherhood protests. Whatever the reason, those youths did not arrive in Scorpion as murderers. I now stood face-to-face with the chilling result—prisons across the Middle East have become breeding grounds for terrorists, not rehabilitation centres. I'd followed the journeys of some: the lucky ones received pardons, others were freed on bail for lack of evidence after sometimes spending years behind bars. Still others served out their sentences. On release, many of them slipped through Egypt's porous security net to neighbouring Turkey, or on to Syria. Others remain on the path of what they call a "revolution" against Egypt's current regime.

I was recently encouraged by reports in the Egyptian media that an Islamic scholar and advisor to President Sisi visited some of the Brotherhood and ISIS youth in Scorpion and two other prisons to investigate the potential for a de-radicalization program. The news gave me hope for the imprisoned youth in Egypt. So I called one young prisoner, a college sophomore I'd befriended in prison, who I knew had smuggled in a phone. A staunch sympathizer of the Brotherhood, the young man confided that he'd been among dozens of youth assembled in a prison yard to listen to Sisi's envoy urging the prisoners to renounce their violent views and embrace the government's "road map" for a peaceful and democratic Egypt. At the end of the lecture, the young prisoner told me, an officer who had accompanied the scholar and who identified himself as representing the military's Moral Department polled the gathered youths.

"He asked us to raise our hands if we would still join anti-government protests if we were released the next day. Each and every one of us raised our hands."

"Why?" I asked.

"Because we have nothing left to lose."

It took prison time for me to understand that the oft-used phrase "al-Qaeda-inspired extremists"—a phrase I, too, have used in my reporting from the Middle East—has a complex flip side to it: it's also the heavy hand of repressive governments that inspires extremists to join al-Qaeda and ISIS.

In contrast to the Egyptian youth radicalized in prison, many extremist Muslims in France and Brussels, for example, were not well integrated socially or culturally into the mainstream. It appears they were likely discriminated against as visible and or religious minorities, and treated as second-class citizens. In fact, recent reports suggest that Western countries in which anti-Muslim sentiment, and barriers to immigration and integration are high, produce more ISIS recruits and are more likely to come under attack by Islamic terrorists.[146]

These findings underscore why the Canadian model, which supports social integration of immigrants through jobs, language instruction, welfare and housing, might make Canada one of the safest countries on earth for refugees. While the Conservative government detoured from this traditional approach, Canadian citizens didn't, electing the party with the most immigrant-friendly platform. And since his election, Trudeau's historical welcome of thousands of Syrian refugees may have in short order reversed years of damage created by Conservative anti-Islamic messages of fear and distrust.

The dangerous marriage of politics and news is more important today in our media-driven world than ever before in history. Al Jazeera forsook its once-admired slogan, "The Opinion and the Other Opinion," thanks to Qatar's political ambitions and its agenda-setting attempts across the Middle East. But the world has been taking note: in addition to the pressure brought to bear on Qatar in the Riyadh agreement to back off its pro-Brotherhood editorial line, Al Jazeera's offices have been shut down in Egypt, Kuwait, Saudi Arabia, Iraq, Syria, Bahrain, Jordan, Israel, Algeria, Morocco and the Palestinian Authority in the West Bank—as well as further afield in China and India. Al Jazeera will not regain its stature without balanced reporting—including a critical appraisal of Qatar's shortcomings—and that's unlikely to happen under the autocratic rule of its owner, the Al Thani family.

Qataris living in exile, who oppose the current regime, like Mona Al Sulaiti, daughter of Qatar's current minister of communication and transportation, want the network to ask the tough political questions Qataris want answered. For example, why has Qatar allowed the Taliban, one of the world's most ruthless terrorist groups, to establish a diplomatic office in Doha, and why has the emir turned a blind eye to prominent Qataris and members of his own family funding Islamic extremists in Syria, Libya and Iraq? Such political questions are always intertwined with human rights—of which freedom of expression is one: When will the courts gain a measure of independence? When will alternative media voices be heard? Why do they target intellectuals like the poet Mohammed al-Ajami, sentenced to life imprisonment for insulting the emir in a poem—a case that received worldwide attention but was scarcely covered by Al Jazeera during the four years he spent in prison before his recent pardon?

And because of the actions of networks such as Al Jazeera, the reputation of citizen journalism, once believed to be the authentic and trustworthy voice of the independent citizen at the heart of emerging events, broadcast directly through social media, is becoming increasingly tarnished. The network's deliberate pro-Islamist recruitment of impoverished, politically disenfranchised young people has warped the meaning of "citizen journalism"—that once open, grassroots avenue for individuals to submit information to established networks.

Language is a weapon in itself. In leaked emails in 2016 highlighting Al Jazeera's biased coverage supporting militant groups like Jabhat al-Nusra in Syria, Kelly Jarrett, executive producer of news at Al Jazeera English, allegedly instructed her reporters to stop referring to al-Nusra as "al-Qaeda affiliated" and to describe its members as "rebels."[147] Al Jazeera also ordered its reporters to refrain from using words like "jihadists," "terrorists" or "extremists" when referring to al-Nusra fighters, editorializing that deceives viewers.[148]

There are brave people who stand up to powerful interests all over the world—often at great peril. The actions of Al Jazeera, for example, have endangered the lives of its staff, or put them at risk of lengthy jail sentences—as in our case, or that of the Egyptian cameraman and our former colleague Mohamed Fawzy, sentenced in absentia to ten years in prison. Assigned by Al Jazeera to the Washington bureau, he was left in legal limbo by the network who had not secured proper documentation for his US visa. Fawzy, unable to return home to his family without being arrested and in limbo in the US as a designated "terrorist," was left with no choice but to launch a multi-million-dollar lawsuit against Al Jazeera in

Washington. Shannon High-Bassalik, a former senior vice president
of programming and documentaries at Al Jazeera America (which
shut down in April 2016 after its $500 billion investment in the new
channel garnered only 30,000 viewers),[149] filed a lawsuit against the
network in New York for "unlawful" treatment of employees and
biased coverage, alleging that: "As ratings failed to live up to the
expectation of management, Al Jazeera openly decided to abandon all
pretense of neutrality in favour of putting the Arabic viewpoint front
and centre, openly demanding that programs be aired to criticize
countries such as America, Israel, and Egypt." Article 4 of her counsel's
claim states: "Dedicated journalists like High-Bassalik were told that
if this abandonment of journalistic integrity led people to deem them
'terrorists' that was an acceptable risk for the Company to take."[150]

My imprisonment has left me more skeptical than ever about the
web of international coalitions and governments—especially our
Western governments—who can't seem to agree on who the actual
terrorists are, including the Muslim Brotherhood. Perhaps Christiane
Amanpour's September 2014 CNN interview with Sheikh Tamim
Al Thani, the emir of Qatar—one I watched from my hospital
bed—best captured Qatar's obscure foreign policy on this important
and complex issue. "Qatar has been blamed and criticized [. . .] over
the years for funding these movements," Amanpour carefully stated
in reference to Qatar's unwavering support for Islamist groups designated as terrorists.[151]

    "There are differences [among] some countries about who are
the terrorists and who are the Islamist groups," the emir replied,
"but we don't consider them as terrorists." By "them" the emir was
likely referring to groups like the Muslim Brotherhood, Hamas and
Jabhet al-Nusra, an al-Qaeda affiliate in Syria that later broke ties
with the group on July 30, 2016, and changed its name to Jabhat
Fatah al-Sham, or Syria Conquest Front.[152]

Countries such as Qatar, ambitious for potential control in Syria are, to some extent, supporting al-Nusra, whose Islamist militants are fighting both ISIS and Assad's regime, which is indiscriminately killing its own citizens with barrel bombs and chemical weapons.

And what of the Muslim Brotherhood, the group that the government of Egypt labelled as "terrorist" but whose stature is less clear in other parts of the world? In February 2016, the US's House Judiciary Committee passed the Muslim Brotherhood Terrorist Designation Act of 2015—a Republican bill calling on the Department of State to assess the status of the Muslim Brotherhood as a terrorist organization. In a statement introducing the bill, Republican Mario Díaz-Balart noted, "The Muslim Brotherhood continues to pose a global threat."[153] Dr. Eric Trager, a fellow at the Washington Institute and an expert on the politics of Egypt and the Muslim Brotherhood, later told me in an interview, "That bill is basically the work of a very small sliver of the far right of the Republican Party, and centrist Republicans—particularly in the Senate—aren't inclined to do anything about it." He goes on to say, "This is partly political: centrist Republicans appear wary of supporting a measure that would bolster that small faction within the party that sees a 'Sharia' conspiracy everywhere. But it is also a matter of policy: while the Muslim Brotherhood is strongly disliked across the American political spectrum, there are certain countries in which communicating with Brotherhood groups is necessary, such as Tunisia." He concludes by stating: "Designating the Brotherhood would therefore constrain US policy, and Congress is typically hesitant to go that far."[154]

Similar sentiment exists towards the Muslim Brotherhood in the United Kingdom. A December 2015 government report titled "The Muslim Brotherhood Review," co-authored by the former British ambassador to Saudi Arabia John Jenkins, states that the Brotherhood "promotes and sometimes takes a role in violence;

seeks world domination of Sharia, or Islamic, law; and views other religions as illegitimate."

"The movement is deliberately opaque and habitually secretive," former prime minster David Cameron told the press after the release of the report, which highlighted the Brotherhood's clandestine operations, centralized hierarchical structure, and secretive support for Palestine's Hamas.[155]

The emergence of this anti-Brotherhood rhetoric from the West was a huge political win for President Sisi and his coalition of Arabian Gulf states. Still, critics question why the UK stopped short of designating the Brotherhood a terrorist organization. I believe the UK's and the US's caution is to avoid alienating its allies Turkey and Qatar, which are major Brotherhood supporters. It also avoids provoking Brotherhood sympathizers in other parts of the world. And if the US government was to designate the Brotherhood a terrorist organization, the potential Islamist backlash against it is something to fear.

Defeating the epidemic of extremism won't be achieved until governments cooperate with civil liberties organizations to provide better futures for youth and minorities as a bulwark against radicalization and terrorism. It also won't come without journalists having the freedom to truthfully tell the stories of the oppressed and disenfranchised, both within conflict zones and in authoritarian regimes. For that to happen, leaders like Egypt's President Sisi and Turkey's President Erdogan need to stop branding journalists as terrorists through vague terrorism laws, and realize that journalists are working to expose the terrorists they strive to defeat.

When groups like the Muslim Brotherhood, contrary to its proclamations of being democratic, benevolent and mainstream, seek to march countries like Egypt along the dangerous road of Islamic fundamentalism, its actions must be challenged by both those in political power and by journalists. The result when they fail to do so is the terrible tide of violence sweeping across the Middle East and North Africa with every regime change and comes at a huge cost: a lawless power vacuum.

As a journalist covering Egypt's uprising, seeing streets stained red with blood of civilians from both camps, one thing is clear: the revolution and the end to Murbarak's iron grip created space for and emboldened Islamic factions. Nor is it surprising that, without robust democratic institutions, the long-established and well-organized Muslim Brotherhood were able to seize power under his successor, Mohamed Morsi. It would only have been a matter of time, however, before Salafi jihadists like Mohamed al-Zawahiri, and many younger militant Islamists who follow his violent form of Islam, would have vied for power with the Brotherhood. If that had happened, the barely contained and underreported conflict between the military and Islamists in Sinai would have exploded into a full-fledged civil war that would likely have spilled into neighbouring Israel. Such conflicts are often a harbinger of state disintegration.

In times of terrorism the balance between security and civil liberties necessarily tilts towards the former. For now, Egypt has avoided the fate of its neighbours like Iraq, Syria, Yemen and Libya. For that, President Sisi deserves credit. Egypt, a country of ninety million people, the most populous and politically pivotal in North Africa and the Arab world, is still standing. But at what a cost. Sadly, the crackdown on dissent by his government has branded the country as a "big prison" and a "nation of fear" in the eyes of the world. Although Sisi may have subdued the violence, he has yet to provide the much-needed bread for Egypt's masses, mitigate their poverty and nourish the growth of freedom and social justice that many gave their lives for during the revolution.

What is not in question is that the eighteen days that shook Egypt in January 2011—and indeed the unprecedented uprisings right across the region that we have come to know as the Arab Spring—were a popular and powerful awakening by a youthful generation that still burns with the dream that, in time, it can enjoy economic opportunities and a secure future.

I long to see the many innocent journalists and youth still in Scorpion set free—students like Khalid, tried in the Marriott Cell case with us, currently on a hunger strike and recently photographed in a wheelchair. Or Sohaib, sentenced to life in prison. And I wonder about the freedom given to Mohamed al-Zawahiri, recently released from Scorpion on a questionable health pardon—a move many experts believe was to appease his militant followers in Sinai.

Just after being pardoned, I appeared on BBC's *HARDTALK* program with Stephen Sackur, a veteran Middle East reporter. After peppering me with questions about torture in Egyptian prisons, and the travesty of our case, he took me to task.

"It's fascinating to me that you have been deprived of your Egyptian passport and yet you still say, 'I want to be Egyptian. I want my passport back,'" since respected international human rights and civil liberties organizations like Freedom House deem Egypt's current human rights situation to be worse than at any time under Hosni Mubarak's thirty-year rule. "Why?"

"It's a matter of principle," I told him, but that was only half the truth.[156] What I didn't say is that Egypt is not Hosni Mubarak—just as Iraq is not Saddam Hussein and Syria is not Bashar al-Assad. Egypt is not Mohamed Morsi or Abdel Fattah el-Sisi or the next president who will take over. It is a country with a seven-thousand-year legacy rich in cultural traditions and shaped by a strong sense of national identity. It is an identity embodied in its history, culture and political passions. The beliefs I hold about Egypt come not from the stories I've covered as a journalist, or the ordeal I have endured as an accused terrorist, but from my father and my grandfather, men who believed in justice, discipline and the civil liberties that make countries like Canada great.

My Canadian identity is a proud one, too, one that is rooted in the realization that my adopted country embodies the values that my Egyptian forefathers dreamt of attaining and that current citizens of Egypt, and of countries across the Middle East, still fight for and one day hope to achieve.

NOTES AND SOURCES

I am grateful to those acknowledged below who have enriched my understanding; and the responsibility for any inadvertent errors or omissions is mine alone.—Mohamed Fahmy

CHAPTER ONE

1. Mohamed Fadel Fahmy, "Al Qaeda Leader's Brother Says Terror Group Far from Defeated," CNN, last updated August 3, 2012, http://security.blogs.cnn.com/2012/08/01/zawahiris-brother-says-al-qaeda-far-from-defeated/.

2. Human Rights Watch, *Black Hole: The Fate of Islamists Rendered to Egypt* (New York: Human Rights Watch, 2005), 5, 25–6, www.hrw.org/reports/2005/egypt0505/egypt0505.pdf.

3. "Egypt: Rab'a Killings Likely Crimes against Humanity," Human Rights Watch, August 12, 2014, www.hrw.org/news/2014/08/12/egypt-raba-killings-likely-crimes-against-humanity.

4. Elsharq TV, "حصريا: أحمد المغير الهيثم لهيثم خليل:أبوخليل هذا ما منعنا من استخدام السلاح في #رابعة . .!" [Exclusive: "Ahmed Al Mogheir to Haitham Khalil: This is what stopped the protesters from using weapons in Rabaa"], YouTube video, uploaded August 15, 2016, www.youtube.com/watch?v=HLZ3U2J9isg&feature=youtu.be&app=desktop.

5. Nic Robertson, "Al Qaeda Leader's Brother Offers Peace Plan," CNN, September 10, 2012, last updated September 11, 2012, www.cnn.com/2012/09/10/world/meast/zawahiri-peace-plan/.

CHAPTER THREE

6. "CNN: Anderson Cooper: 'I've Been Hit Like 10 Times in Egypt Protests,'" YouTube video, uploaded February 2, 2011, accessed September 9, 2016, www.youtube.com/watch?v=0K-lfUuEBLM.

7. Ashley Fantz, "Why Are Reporters Being Attacked?" CNN, February 4, 2011, www.cnn.com/2011/WORLD/meast/02/04/egypt.journalist.attacks/.

8. "Mubarak Intensifies Press Attacks with Assaults, Detentions," Committee to Protect Journalists, February 3, 2011, https://cpj.org/2011/02/mubarak-intensifies-press-attacks-with-assaults-de.php.

9. Christiane Amanpour, "Omar Suleiman on the Crisis," ABC News, February 6, 2011, http://abcnews.go.com/ThisWeek/video/omar-suleiman-crisis-12852023.

10. David Blair, "The Fixer in the Shadows Who May Emerge as Egypt's Leader," *The Telegraph*, February 24, 2009, www.telegraph.co.uk/comment/personal-view/4800970/The-fixer-in-the-shadows-who-may-emerge-as-Egypts-leader.html.

11. Stephen Soldz, "The Torture Career of Egypt's New Vice President: Omar Suleiman and the Rendition to Torture Program," Information Clearing House, January 31, 2011, www.informationclearinghouse.info/article27384.htm.

12. Matthew Cole, Sarah O. Wali, "New Egyptian VP Ran Mubarak's Security Team, Oversaw Torture," ABC News, February 1, 2011, http://abcnews.go.com/Blotter/egypt-crisis-omar-suleiman-cia-rendition/story?id=12812445.

13. See Chris McGreal and Jack Shenker, "Hosni Mubarak Resigns—and Egypt Celebrates a New Dawn," *The Guardian*, February 11, 2011, www.theguardian.com/world/2011/feb/11/hosni-mubarak-resigns-egypt-cairo; "Egypt Crisis: President Hosni Mubarak Resigns as Leader," BBC, February 12, 2011, www.bbc.com/news/world-middle-east-12433045.

CHAPTER FOUR

14. Mohannad Sabry, "The Students: The Untold Details of the Al-Jazeera Trial," Atlantic Council, December 19, 2014, www.atlanticcouncil. org/blogs/menasource/the-students-the-untold-details-of-the-al-jazeera-trial.

CHAPTER FIVE

15. Ben Wedeman, "CNN: Voices from a Benghazi Rally," YouTube video, uploaded February 24, 2011, www.youtube.com/watch? v=Qyb1uXUbJWY.

16. Reza Sayah, "Pro-Democracy Activists Allege Torture by Egyptian Soldiers," CNN, March 18, 2011, www.cnn.com/2011/WORLD/ meast/03/17/egypt.activists/.

17. Ivan Watson and Mohamed Fadel Fahmy, "Thousands Demonstrate in Tahrir Square," CNN, last updated April 1, 2011, http://edition.cnn. com/2011/WORLD/meast/04/01/egypt.protests/.

18. "Constitution of Egypt, Article 2: Islam as State Religion and Source of Law," Berkley Center for Religion, Peace, and World Affairs, https:// berkleycenter.georgetown.edu/quotes/constitution-of-egypt-article-2-islam-as-state-religion-and-source-of-law.

19. Mohamed Fadel Fahmy, "Egypt's Muslim Brotherhood to Run Candidates for Half of Parliament," CNN, last updated April 30, 2011, http://edition.cnn.com/2011/WORLD/africa/04/30/egypt.muslim. brotherhood.candidates/.

20. Mohamed Fadel Fahmy, "Filmmaker Warned Bin Laden about Attacking Civilians," CNN, last updated May 8, 2011, http://edition. cnn.com/2011/WORLD/africa/05/06/egypt.filmmaker.bin.laden/ index.html.

21. Fareed Zakaria, "Why They Hate Us," CNN, updated June 20, 2016, www.cnn.com/2016/04/08/opinions/why-they-hate-us-zakaria/.

22. Ivan Watson and Mohamed Fadel Fahmy, "Sadat's Unrepentant Killer Aims for Political Future," CNN, last updated April 14, 2011, http:// edition.cnn.com/2011/WORLD/meast/04/14/egypt.sadat.killer/.

23. Diana Magnay and Mohamed Fadel Fahmy, "Smuggling Along a Tense Border a Lifeblood of Bedouin," CNN, last updated June 14, 2011,

http://edition.cnn.com/2011/WORLD/meast/06/13/egypt.bedouin.
smuggling/.

24. Mohamed Fadel Fahmy, "Islamist Militant Group Resurgent in Egypt,"
    CNN, August 10, 2011, www.cnn.com/2011/WORLD/africa/08/09/
    egypt.islamists/.

25. Isabel Kershner and David D. Kirkpatrick, "Attacks Near Israeli Resort
    Heighten Tensions with Egypt and Gaza," *The New York Times*, August
    18, 2011, www.nytimes.com/2011/08/19/world/middleeast/19israel.
    html?_r=1.

26. Associated Press, "Egyptian Protesters Break into Israeli Embassy in
    Cairo," *The Guardian*, September 10, 2011, www.theguardian.com/
    world/2011/sep/10/egyptian-protesters-israeli-embassy-cairo.

27. "Israeli Embassy Ransacked in Cairo," YouTube video, uploaded
    September 9, 2011, accessed September 9, 2016, www.youtube.com/
    watch?v=iXravWgNOKA.

28. Ivan Watson, "Angry Crowd Turns on Journalists Reporting Embassy
    Attack in Egypt," CNN, last updated September 11, 2011, http://edition.
    cnn.com/2011/WORLD/meast/09/10/egypt.journalists.targeted/.

29. Margaret Myers, "Margaret Warner Recalls How Mohamed Fahmy
    Helped Newshour Crew Escape an Attack," PBS NewsHour, June 23,
    2014, www.pbs.org/newshour/updates/margaret-warner-recalls-
    mohamed-fahmy-helped-newshour-crew-escape-attack/.

30. "CNN Journalist Injured in Attack Near Sirte," CNN, September 19,
    2011, http://edition.cnn.com/2011/WORLD/africa/09/17/libya.war.
    journalists/.

31. David Blair and Richard Spencer, "How Qatar is Funding the Rise of
    Islamist Extremists," *The Telegraph*, September 20, 2014, www.telegraph.
    co.uk/news/worldnews/middleeast/qatar/11110931/How-Qatar-is-
    funding-the-rise-of-Islamist-extremists.html.

32. Mohamed Fadel Fahmy, "Egyptian Officer Suspected of Being 'The
    Eye Hunter,' Shooting Protesters," CNN, last updated November 26,
    2011, http://edition.cnn.com/2011/11/25/world/africa/egypt-eye-
    hunter/; "Egyptian 'Eye-Sniper' Police Officer Sentenced to Three
    Years," Ahram Online, March 5, 2013, http://english.ahram.org.eg/
    NewsContent/1/0/66147/Egypt/0/Egyptian-eyesniper-police-officer-
    sentenced-to-thr.aspx.

CHAPTER SIX

33. Kristen Chick, "Egyptian Graffiti Artist Ganzeer Arrested Amid Surge in Political Expression," *Christian Science Monitor*, May 26, 2011, www.csmonitor.com/World/Middle-East/2011/0526/Egyptian-graffiti-artist-Ganzeer-arrested-amid-surge-in-political-expression.

34. David D. Kirkpatrick, "Egyptian Soccer Riot Kills More Than 70," *The New York Times*, February 1, 2012, www.nytimes.com/2012/02/02/world/middleeast/scores-killed-in-egyptian-soccer-mayhem.html?_r=0.

CHAPTER SEVEN

35. "Muslim Brotherhood's Mohammed Morsi Wins Egypt's Presidential Race," *The Guardian*, last updated June 24, 2012, www.theguardian.com/world/middle-east-live/2012/jun/24/egypt-election-results-live#block-36.

36. The FBI's "Most Wanted Terrorist" Poster for Ayman al-Zawahiri: www.fbi.gov/wanted/wanted_terrorists/ayman-al-zawahiri/download.pdf.

37. "US Flag Burned as Protesters Storm Cairo Embassy," *The Telegraph*, September 12, 2012, www.telegraph.co.uk/news/worldnews/africaandindianocean/egypt/9537517/US-flag-burned-as-protesters-storm-Cairo-embassy.html.

38. David Ariosto, "Protesters Attack U.S. Diplomatic Compounds in Egypt, Libya," CNN, September 12, 2012, www.cnn.com/2012/09/12/world/meast/egpyt-us-embassy-protests/.

39. Bassem Mroue, "Prominent al-Qaida Figure Killed in US Drone Strike in Syria," Associated Press, April 8, 2016, http://bigstory.ap.org/article/2b6f19281b4d4a50949ad9d44872105d/prominent-al-qaida-figure-killed-us-drone-strike-syria.

40. Brian Whitaker and Tom McCarthy, "US Ambassador Chris Stevens Killed in Libya—As It Happened," *The Guardian*, September 13, 2012, www.theguardian.com/world/middle-east-live/2012/sep/12/libya-egypt-attacks-muhammad-film-live.

41. "16 Egyptian Soldiers Killed at Israel Border," Ahram Online, August 5, 2012, http://english.ahram.org.eg/NewsContent/1/64/49660/Egypt/Politics-/UPDATE---Egyptian-soldiers-killed-at-the-Israel-bo.aspx.

42. "The Most Important Man in the Middle East," *TIME*, December 10, 2012, http://content.time.com/time/covers/0,16641,20121210,00.html.

43. Wolf Blitzer, "Exclusive: Wolf Blitzer Interviews Egyptian President Morsy," CNN, January 7, 2013, http://situationroom.blogs.cnn.com/2013/01/07/exclusive-wolf-blitzer-interviews-egyptian-president-morsy/. See also "Interview with Egypt President Mohamed Morsi" (transcript), CNN, January 12, 2013, www.cnn.com/TRANSCRIPTS/1301/12/sitroom.01.html.

44. "Egypt's President Morsi Calls Jews 'Apes, Pigs,'" The Christian Broadcasting Network, January 6, 2013, www.cbn.com/cbnnews/insideisrael/2013/january/egypts-president-calls-jews-apes-pigs/?mobile=false.

45. Fady Salah, "Islamists Escalate Media City Sit-In," *Daily News Egypt*, December 11, 2012, www.dailynewsegypt.com/2012/12/11/islamists-escalate-media-city-sit-in/.

46. David D. Kirkpatrick, "Leaks Gain Credibility and Potential to Embarrass Egypt's Leaders," *The New York Times*, May 12, 2015, www.nytimes.com/2015/05/13/world/middleeast/leaks-gain-credibility-and-potential-to-embarrass-egypts-leaders.html?_r=0.

47. See Hussein Amin, "The Nature of the Channel's Global Audience," in *Al Jazeera English: Global News in a Changing World*, ed. Philip Seib (New York: Palgrave Macmillan, 2012), 34–35.

48. Associated Press, "Court Orders Closure of Al-Jazeera Egypt, Brotherhood TV," New Delhi Television, September 3, 2013, www.ndtv.com/world-news/court-orders-closure-of-al-jazeera-egypt-brotherhood-tv-533478.

49. "'We Aired Lies': Al Jazeera Staff Quit Over 'Misleading' Egypt Coverage." July 8, 2013, Al Arabiya, http://english.alarabiya.net/en/media/2013/07/09/Al-Jazeera-employees-in-Egypt-quit-over-editorial-line-.html.

50. "Video Shows Egypt Generals Plotting Media Gag," Al Jazeera, October 3, 2013, www.aljazeera.com/news/middleeast/2013/10/video-shows-egypt-generals-debating-media-gag-201310365144226112.html.

51. Amy Austin Holmes, "Sisi's US Army War College Thesis: 10 Years Later," March 15, 2016, Mada Masr, www.madamasr.com/opinion/politics/sisis-us-army-war-college-thesis-10-years-later; Gen. Abdel

Fattah el-Sisi, "Democracy in the Middle East" (dissertation), US Army War College, 2006, https://assets.documentcloud.org/documents/1173610/sisi.pdf.

52. "Egyptian Forces Arrest Qataris at Al Jazeera Office in Cairo: Report," Reuters, December 11, 2013, www.reuters.com/article/us-egypt-qatar-raid-idUSBRE9BA1CE20131211.

53. Rezaa Kasu, "Egypt: A Campus Revolution?" Al Jazeera, December 14, 2013, www.aljazeera.com/programmes/insidestory/2013/12/egypt-campus-revolution-2013121474643100889.html.

54. Richard Spencer, "General Sisi 'Dreamed He Would Rule Egypt,'" *The Telegraph*, December 12, 2013, www.telegraph.co.uk/news/worldnews/africaandindianocean/egypt/10514821/General-Sisi-dreamed-he-would-rule-Egypt.html.

55. Patrick Kingsley, "Egypt: Frenchman Dies in Police Custody Amid Rising Tide of Xenophobia," *The Guardian*, September 18, 2013, www.theguardian.com/world/2013/sep/18/egypt-frenchman-dies-syria-morsi.

CHAPTER EIGHT

56. "Those Who Harm Egyptians Will 'Vanish from the Face of the Earth': El-Sisi," Ahram Online, December 26, 2013, http://english.ahram.org.eg/NewsContent/1/64/90106/Egypt/Politics-/Those-who-harm-Egyptians-will-vanish-from-the-face.aspx.

CHAPTER NINE

57. Lawrence Wright, *The Looming Tower* (New York: Knopf, 2006), 39.

58. Eric Trager, "Where Did They Go Wrong?" Washington Institute, August 12, 2016, www.washingtoninstitute.org/policy-analysis/view/where-did-they-go-wrong.

59. Richard Barrett, The Islamic State (Washington, DC: Soufan Group, 2014), http://soufangroup.com/wp-content/uploads/2014/10/TSG-The-Islamic-State-Nov14.pdf.

60. Anthony Shadid, "In Iraq, Chaos Feared as U.S. Closes Prison," *Washington Post*, March 22, 2009, www.washingtonpost.com/wp-dyn/content/article/2009/03/21/AR2009032102255.html.

61. "How Many People Fight with ISIS and How Much Territory Does it Control?" *The Times of India*, December 24, 2015, timesofindia. indiatimes.com/deep/islamic-state/questions-and-answers/How-many-people-fight-with-ISIS-and-how-much-territory-does-it-control/ articleshow/50312965.cms.

62. "Nusra Leader: Our Mission is to Defeat Syrian Regime," Al Jazeera, May 28, 2015, www.aljazeera.com/news/2015/05/nusra-front-golani-assad-syria-hezbollah-isil-150528044857528.html; "[FULL] Interview Al Jazeera with Syaikh Abu Muhammad al Jaulani (27 Mei 2015)," YouTube video, uploaded May 27, 2015, www.youtube.com/ watch?v=1EVaBgSAJ3o.

63. Thomas Joscelyn, "US Counterterrorism Efforts in Syria: A Winning Strategy?" The Long War Journal, September 29, 2015, www. longwarjournal.org/archives/2015/09/us-counterterrorism-efforts-in-syria-a-winning-strategy.php.

64. "Egyptian Salafist Muhammad Al-Zawahiri, Brother of Al-Qaeda Leader: We Don't Recognize Elections or President Morsi; Calls for Jihad against the Jews," MEMRITV, Clip No. 3611 (transcript), October 4, 2012, www.memritv.org/clip_transcript/en/3611.htm.

65. "Cairo rocked by deadly bomb attacks," Al Jazeera, January 24, 2014, www.aljazeera.com/news/middleeast/2014/01/cairo-rocked-deadly-bomb-attacks-2014124103138914258.html.

CHAPTER TEN

66. Samuel Westrop, "UK Funds Terror Connections: Islamic Relief Worldwide," Gatestone Institute, July 3, 2013, www.gatestoneinstitute. org/3792/islamic-relief-worldwide-terrorism.

67. "'Destroy the Idols,' Egyptian Jihadist Calls for Removal of Sphinx, Pyramids," Al Arabiya, November 12, 2012, https://english.alarabiya. net/articles/2012/11/12/249092.html.

68. "Egyptian Cleric: Boston Bombings 'Message to America,'" The Clarion Project, April 18, 2013, www.clarionproject.org/news/egyptian-cleric-boston-bombings-message-america#.

CHAPTER ELEVEN

69. "Morsi, Mady Shall Be Investigated Over Claims of Intelligence's Thugs: Dina A. Fattah," Amwal Al Ghad, March 27, 2013, www. amwalalghad.com/en/news/egypt-news/15738-morsi-mady-shall-be-investigated-over-claims-of-intelligences-thugs-dina-afattah.html.

70. Jacey Fortin, "Egypt Presidential Candidate Abu Ismail Says Mother Not American Citizen, Blames Opponents," *International Business Times*, April 5, 2012, www.ibtimes.com/egypt-presidential-candidate-abu-ismail-says-mother-not-american-citizen-blames-opponents-434216.

71. "Egypt: Investigate Brotherhood's Abuse of Protesters," Human Rights Watch, December 12, 2012, www.hrw.org/news/2012/12/12/egypt-investigate-brotherhoods-abuse-protesters.

72. Mohannad Sabry, "Did Producer Lead Al Jazeera Coworkers Straight to Jail?," Al-Monitor, October 23, 2014, accessed August 30, 2016, www.al-monitor.com/pulse/originals/2014/10/jazeera-journalists-egyptian-prison.html.

73. The #FreeAJStaff Tumblr page: http://freeajstaff.tumblr.com/.

74. "Video of Al Jazeera Journalists' Arrest Causes Uproar," Mada Masr, February 3, 2014, www.madamasr.com/news/video-al-jazeera-journalists%E2%80%99-arrest-causes-uproar.

CHAPTER TWELVE

75. Asma Alsharif, "Egyptian Court Sentences 529 Brotherhood Members to Death," Reuters, March 24, 2014, www.reuters.com/article/us-egypt-brotherhood-courts-idUSBREA2N0BT20140324.

76. Viktor E. Frankl, *Man's Search for Meaning* (Boston: Beacon Books, 1959), 135.

CHAPTER THIRTEEN

77. "Jailed Al Jazeera English Journalist Mohamed Fahmy Wins World Press Freedom Award," Canadian Journalists for Free Expression, May 1, 2014, www.cjfe.org/jailed_al_jazeera_english_journalist_mohamed_fahmy_wins_world_press_freedom_award.

78. John Beck, "Defense Lawyers Abruptly Quit in Egypt's Adjourned Al Jazeera Trial," VICE, May 15, 2014, https://news.vice.com/article/defense-lawyers-abruptly-quit-in-egypts-adjourned-al-jazeera-trial.

79. Helen Davidson, "Peter Greste's Lawyers Quit in Court, Accusing Al-Jazeera of 'Vendetta,'" *The Guardian*, May 16, 2014, www.theguardian.com/media/2014/may/16/peter-grestes-lawyers-quit-in-court-accusing-al-jazeera-of-vendetta.

80. Alexandra Zakreski, "#FreeAJStaff: In Disturbing Turn of Events, Prosecutors Request Maximum Jail Term," Canadian Journalists for Free Expression, June 5, 2014, www.cjfe.org/_freeajstaff_in_disturbing_turn_of_events_prosecutors_request_maximum_jail_term.

CHAPTER FOURTEEN

81. Jay Solomon, "John Kerry Voices Strong Support for Egyptian President Sisi," *The Wall Street Journal*, June 22, 2014, www.wsj.com/articles/john-kerry-arrives-in-egypt-on-unannounced-visit-1403426551.

82. "Kerry Condemns Al Jazeera Journalists' Sentences as 'Chilling and Draconian,'" Middle East Eye, June 23, 2014, last updated February 12, 2015, www.middleeasteye.net/news/kerry-condemns-al-jazeera-journalists-sentences-chilling-and-draconian-590718538.

83. "Jailed Egyptian-Canadian journalist Mohamed Fahmy sentenced to seven years in maximum security prison," *Ottawa Citizen*, June 23, 2014, http://ottawacitizen.com/storyline/jailed-egyptian-canadian-journalist-mohamed-fahmy-sentenced-to-seven-years-in-maximum-security-prison; Robert Sibley, "Canada Demands Release of Fahmy," *Montreal Gazette*, August 31, 2015.

CHAPTER FIFTEEN

84. The Canadian Press, "Baird Says 'Bullhorn' Diplomacy Won't Free Mohamed Fahmy," *Maclean's*, June 24, 2014, www.macleans.ca/news/canada/bullhorn-diplomacy-wont-free-canadian-journalist-in-egypt-says-baird/.

85. Robert Fisk, "My Deadliest Moment with the World's Most Dangerous Men," *The Independent*, May 2, 2011 (originally published March 22, 1997), www.independent.co.uk/voices/commentators/fisk/robert-fisk-my-deadliest-moment-with-the-worlds-most-dangerous-men-2278036.html.

86. Robert Fisk, "Robert Fisk on the Jailing of Al-Jazeera Journalists: A Proxy in the War between Qatar and Saudi Arabia," *The Independent*, June 23, 2014, www.independent.co.uk/voices/comment/robert-fisk-a-proxy-in-the-war-between-qatar-and-saudi-arabia-9558306.html.

87. Amam Entous, Nour Malas, and Margaret Coker, "A Veteran Saudi Power Player Works to Build Support to Topple Assad," *The Wall Street Journal*, August 25, 2013, www.wsj.com/articles/SB1000142412788732 3423804579024452583045962.

88. Harriet Sherwood, "Egyptian Uprising Enables Jailed Hamas Militant to Escape," *The Guardian*, February 21, 2011, www.theguardian.com/world/2011/feb/07/egypt-protest-hamas-militant-escapes.

CHAPTER SIXTEEN

89. Amal Clooney, "The Anatomy of an Unfair Trial," The Huffington Post, August 18, 2014, last updated October 18, 2014, www.huffington-post.com/Amal-Alamuddin/egypt-unfair-trial_b_5688388.html.

90. Mohamed Fadel Fahmy, "How Al Jazeera, My Employer, Failed Me in Egyptian Court," *The Globe and Mail*, March 5, 2015, last updated March 6, 2015, www.theglobeandmail.com/opinion/fahmy-how-al-jazeera-my-employer-failed-me-in-egyptian-court/article23322748/.

CHAPTER SEVENTEEN

91. Nader Gohar, "Fahmy and Greste: How Al Jazeera Blundered Its Way to Journalists' Arrests in Egypt," iMediaEthics, October 8, 2014, www.imediaethics.org/fahmy-and-greste-how-al-jazeera-blundered-its-way-to-journalists-arrests-in-egypt-commentary/.

92. See Mohannad Sabry, "Did Al Jazeera Uphold Its Responsibility to its Staff?" The Tahrir Institute for Middle East Policy, November 15, 2014, http://timep.org/commentary/al-jazeera-responsibility/.

93. Press Statement by Amal Clooney and Mark Wassouf, November 5, 2014, www.doughtystreet.co.uk/documents/uploaded-documents/ 2014_11_05_-_Press_Statement_English.pdf.

94. "Egypt's Sisi Decrees Law on Repatriating Foreign Prisoners," Reuters, November 12, 2014, www.reuters.com/article/us-egypt-jazeera- idUSKCN0IW2ET20141112.

95. Ali Abdelaty, "Egypt's Sisi Says He Wishes Al Jazeera Journalists Were Not Tried," Reuters, July 7, 2014, www.reuters.com/article/us- egypt-sisi-aljazeera-idUSKBN0FC00T20140707.

96. "Egypt's Sisi Considering Pardon for Al Jazeera Journalists," France 24, last updated November 20, 2014, www.france24.com/en/20141120- egypt-general-sissi-exclusive-france-24-libya-jazeera-journalists

97. "Gulf Ambassadors Pulled from Qatar Over 'Interference,'" BBC, March 5, 2014, www.bbc.com/news/world-middle-east-26447914.

98. "Saudi King Invites Egypt to Join Reconciliation with Qatar," *Daily News Egypt*, November 19, 2014, www.dailynewsegypt.com/2014/11/ 19/saudi-king-invites-egypt-to-join-reconciliation-with-qatar/.

99. Ian Black and Patrick Kingsley, "Qatar Shuts Down Pro-Islamist TV Channel in Thaw with Egypt," *The Guard*ian, December 23, 2014, www.theguardian.com/world/2014/dec/23/qatar-shuts-down- islamist-channel-egypt-directlk.

CHAPTER EIGHTEEN

100. Press Statement by Amal Clooney and Mark Wassouf, November 24, 2014, www.doughtystreet.co.uk/documents/uploaded-docu- ments/20141124_-_PRESS_STATEMENT_English.pdf.

101. Robert Fisk, "Al-Jazeera Journalists Imprisoned by Egypt to 'Teach Qatar a Lesson' for Supporting the Muslim Brotherhood," *Belfast Telegraph*, December 5, 2014, www.belfasttelegraph.co.uk/opinion/ columnists/robert-fisk/aljazeera-journalists-imprisoned-by-egypt- to-teach-qatar-a-lesson-for-supporting-the-muslim-brotherhood- 30800779.html.

102. "Egypt Court: Lack of Evidence Led to AJ Staff Retrial," Al Jazeera, February 9, 2015, www.aljazeera.com/news/middleeast/2015/02/ egypt-court-lack-evidence-led-aj-staff-retrial-150209193838826.html.

103. "Mohamed Fahmy Disappointed John Baird Couldn't Resolve His Case," CBC, January 15, 2015, www.cbc.ca/news/politics/mohamed-fahmy-disappointed-john-baird-couldn-t-resolve-his-case-1.2901476.

104. Ishmael N. Daro, "Mohamed Fahmy: 'PM Harper Could Do More to Obtain My Release,'" Canada.com, January 15, 2015, http://o.canada.com/news/mohamed-fahmy-578318.

105. Jessica Hume, "Fahmy deportation negotiations in 'critical phase,' Baird says," *Toronto Sun*, January 6, 2015, last updated January 6, 2015, www.torontosun.com/2015/01/06/fahmy-deportation-negotiations-in-critical-phase-baird-says.

106. Rami Galal, Pascale el-Khoury (translator), "Egyptian Prisoner Renounces his Nationality to Escape Sentence," Al-Monitor, June 8, 2015, www.al-monitor.com/pulse/originals/2015/06/egypt-prisoner-renounce-nationality-jail-sentence.html#ixzz4Jm8ojbcZ.

107. "Canada 'concerned' about Muslim Brotherhood," Al Jazeera, April 17, 2014, www.aljazeera.com/news/middleeast/2014/04/canada-concerned-about-muslim-brotherhood-2014417194344335577.html.

CHAPTER NINETEEN

108. Robert Fisk, "Freed Al-Jazeera Journalist: Why Can't Canada Get Me Home?" *The Independent*, February 13, 2015, www.independent.co.uk/news/world/middle-east/freed-al-jazeera-journalist-why-can-t-canada-get-me-home-10045889.html.

109. Rhonda Roland Shearer, "Exclusive: Al Jazeera Accused of Money Laundering by Fmr [*sic*] Lawyer for Greste, Fahmy, Imprisoned Journalists in Egypt," iMediaEthics, October 8, 2014, www.imediaethics.org/exclusive-al-jazeera-accused-of-money-laundering-by-fmr-lawyer-for-greste-fahmy-imprisoned-journalists-in-egypt/?new.

110. Jonathan Miller, "Al Jazeera in Egypt: The Inside Story," Channel 4 News, February 23, 2015, www.channel4.com/news/al-jazeera-greste-peter-fahmy-baher-muslim-brotherhood.

CHAPTER TWENTY

111. Nick Logan, "Mohamed Fahmy starts foundation to help imprisoned journalists," Global News, March 5, 2015, globalnews.ca/news/1866735/mohamed-fahmy-starts-foundation-to-help-imprisoned-journalists/.

112. Jared Malsin and Kim Mackrael, "Mohamed Fahmy in 'Unprecedented Legal Limbo' as Retrial Postponed Again," *The Globe and Mail*, March 8, 2015, www.theglobeandmail.com/news/world/fahmy-in-unprecedented-legal-limbo-as-retrial-postponed-again/article23351234/.

113. Alexander Kühn, Christoph Reuter and Gregor Peter Schmitz, "After the Arab Spring: Al-Jazeera Losing Battle for Independence," *Der Spiegel*, February 15, 2013, www.spiegel.de/international/world/al-jazeera-criticized-for-lack-of-independence-after-arab-spring-a-883343.html.

114. "Ex-employee: Al Jazeera provided Syrian rebels with satphones," RT, April 4, 2012, last updated April 5, 2012, https://www.rt.com/news/al-jazeera-rebels-phones-lebanon-281/.

115. Mohamed Elshinnawi, "Qatar's Activism Sparks a Backlash," VOA, January 17, 2014, www.voanews.com/a/qatars-activism-sparks-a-backlash/1832277.html.

116. Adel Iskandar, in discussion with Mohamed Fadel Fahmy, June 21, 2016.

117. Robert Booth, "WikiLeaks Cables Claim Al-Jazeera Changed Coverage to Suit Qatari Foreign Policy," *The Guardian*, December 6, 2010, www.theguardian.com/world/2010/dec/05/wikileaks-cables-al-jazeera-qatari-foreign-policy.

118. Shadi Bushra, "Egyptian Court Adjourns Al Jazeera Trial after Witnesses Admit Lapses," Reuters, March 19, 2015, www.reuters.com/article/us-egypt-jazeera-idUSKBN0MF18520150319.

119. Diana Mehta, "Fahmy Family's Lawyer Amal Clooney Lashes Out at Harper Government Over 'Woefully Inadequate' Response," *National Post*, February 28, 2015, news.nationalpost.com/news/canada/amal-clooney-mohamed-fahmy-egypt-detention-harper-gov-response.

120. Diana Mehta, "Mohamed Fahmy's Lawyer: Canadian Government 'Only Impediment' to Getting Passport," *The Huffington Post*, April 7, 2015, www.huffingtonpost.ca/2015/04/07/canadian-government-only_n_7019774.html.

121. Kady O'Malley, "Mohamed Fahmy: NDP Demands Government Invoke Passport Power," CBC, April 2, 2015, www.cbc.ca/news/politics/mohamed-fahmy-ndp-demands-government-invoke-passport-power-1.3019611.

122. "Trudeau appeals to Harper on behalf of Mohamed Fahmy," Global News, February 18, 2015, globalnews.ca/video/1837330/trudeau-appeals-to-harper-on-behalf-of-mohamed-fahmy.

123. Ayman Mohyeldin, "Canada Refuses to Issue New Passport to Al Jazeera Journalist Mohamed Fahmy," MSNBC, April 15, 2015, www.msnbc.com/msnbc/watch/canada-denies-its-own-citizen-a-passport-428604995775.

124. Sharif Abdel Kouddous, "Mohamed Fahmy Defended in Court by Egyptian Media Tycoon," *Toronto Star*, April 22, 2015, www.thestar.com/news/world/2015/04/22/mohamed-fahmy-defended-in-court-by-egyptian-media-tycoon.html.

125. Robert Fisk, "Al Jazeera Plays a Dangerous Game in Egypt," *The Independent*, May 10, 2015, www.independent.co.uk/voices/comment/al-jazeera-plays-a-dangerous-game-in-egypt-10240116.html.

126. Agence France-Presse, "Al-Jazeera Reporter Sues Network for $100M Over Egypt Detention," *The Guardian*, May 11, 2015, www.theguardian.com/media/2015/may/11/al-jazeera-reporter-egypt-detention.

127. I spoke with Dr. Najeeb Al Nuami, former justice minister of Qatar and lawyer of Khaled Al Hail. Dr. Al Nuami corroborated Al Hail's story and verified Al Attia's claims and later became an invaluable resource in my research on Al Jazeera and Qatar.

128. Khalid Al-Hail, in discussion with Mohamed Fadel Fahmy, May 20, 2015.

129. Farwaz al-Attiya, in discussion with Mohamed Fadel Fahmy, June 28, 2016.

130. "Qatar Uses Al Jazeera as Bargaining Chip: WikiLeaks," ABS-CBN News, December 6, 2010, http://news.abs-cbn.com/global-filipino/world/12/06/10/qatar-uses-al-jazeera-bargaining-chip-wikileaks.

131. "Egypt Rallies Defy Army Chief's Call," Al Jazeera, July 25, 2013, www.aljazeera.com/news/middleeast/2013/07/2013724101110977227.html.

132. Amal Clooney, "Courtroom Nightmare Continues for Canadian Mohamed Fahmy in Egypt—It Is Time for Sisi to Set the Al-Jazeera Journalist Free," February 8, 2015, www.doughtystreet.co.uk/news/

article/press-statement-courtroom-nightmare-continues-for-canadian-mohamed-fahmy-in.

CHAPTER TWENTY-ONE

133. Ahmed Aboulenein and Michael Georgy, "Amal Clooney Warns of 'Dangerous Message' as Al-Jazeera Journalists Are Sentenced to Prison," *The Daily Mirror*, August 29, 2015, www.mirror.co.uk/3am/celebrity-news/amal-clooney-warns-dangerous-message-6343200.
134. Amal Clooney, "The Anatomy of an Unfair Trial," ibid.
135. Lyse Doucet, "Amal Clooney's Dilemma Over Al-Jazeera Trial," BBC, August 31, 2015, www.bbc.com/news/world-middle-east-34105301.

CHAPTER TWENTY-TWO

136. Jeremy Singer, "Mohamed Fahmy and Amal Clooney Speak in London," *ET Canada*, October 7, 2015, http://etcanada.com/news/32070/live-mohamed-fahmy-and-amal-clooney-speak-in-london/.
137. Frankl, *Man's Search for Meaning*, 155–156.
138. Edward Keenan, "When Stephen Harper Refers to 'Barbaric Culture,' He Means Islam—an Anti-Muslim Alarm That's Ugly and Effective Because It Gets Votes," *Toronto Star*, October 5, 2015, www.thestar.com/news/canada/2015/10/05/when-stephen-harper-refers-to-barbaric-culture-he-means-islam-an-anti-muslim-alarm-thats-ugly-and-effective-because-it-gets-votes-edward-keenan.html.
139. Ilina Ghosh, "Freed Canadian journalist Mohamed Fahmy sets sights on change," Ryerson Journalism Research Centre, October 15, 2015, http://ryersonjournalism.ca/2015/10/15/fahmy-says-canada-needs-better-protections-for-citizens-in-trouble-abroad/.
140. "Mohamed Fahmy Thanks Tom Mulcair for Support During Egypt Detention," CBC, October 13, 2015, www.cbc.ca/news/canada/toronto/mohamed-fahmy-addresses-media-at-ryerson-university-1.3268195.
141. The Canadian Press, "Khaled Al-Qazzaz back in Toronto after release from Egypt," *Toronto Star*, September 2, 2016, www.thestar.com/news/canada/2016/09/02/khaled-al-qazzaz-back-in-toronto-after-release-from-egypt.html.

142. Gar Pardy, *Canadians Abroad: A Policy and Legislative Agenda* (Ottawa: Canadian Centre for Policy Alternatives, 2016), 6, 17, 45, 67.

143. Lee Berthiaume, "Canada to Fight for Lives of Citizens Sentenced to Death in All Countries, Including the U.S.," *National Post*, February 15, 2016, news.nationalpost.com/news/canada/canada-to-fight-for-lives-of-citizens-sentenced-to-death-in-all-countries-including-the-u-s.

144. "Canadian Press Freedom Suffered Through 'Dark Age' During Harper Era: RSF," *The Huffington Post*, April 20, 2016, http://www.huffingtonpost.ca/2016/04/20/press-freedom-reporters-without-borders_n_9737012.html.

145. Zaina bin Laden, in discussion with Mohamed Fadel Fahmy, September 4, 2016.

146. Daniel Hiebert, "What's So Special About Canada? Understanding the Resilience of Immigration and Multiculturalism" (Washington, DC: Migration Policy Institute, 2016), 16–18.

147. "Al Jazeera instructs staff to refrain from calling al-Nusra Front 'al-Qaeda,'" Middle East Eye, September 22, 2015, www.middleeasteye.net/news/al-jazeera-instructs-staff-refrain-calling-al-nusra-front-al-qaeda-1671552331.

148. Cheryl K. Chumley, "Al Jazeera English bans words: 'Terrorist,' 'Islamist,' 'jihad' off-limits to news employees," *The Washington Times*, January 28, 2015, www.washingtontimes.com/news/2015/jan/28/al-jazeera-english-bans-words-terrorist-islamist-j/.

149. John Koblin, "Al Jazeera America to Shut Down by April," *The New York Times*, January 13, 2016, www.nytimes.com/2016/01/14/business/media/al-jazeera-america-to-shut-down-in-april.html?_r=1.

150. Michael Calderone, "Former Executive Charges Al Jazeera America with Discrimination, Biased Coverage in Lawsuit," *The Huffington Post*, June 11, 2015, www.huffingtonpost.com/2015/06/11/al-jazeera-america-lawsuit_n_7563944.html.

151. Mick Krever, "Qatar's Emir: We don't fund terrorists," CNN, last updated September 25, 2014, http://edition.cnn.com/2014/09/25/world/meast/qatar-emir/index.html.

152. "Syria War: Who Are Jabhat Fateh al-Sham?" BBC, August 1, 2016, www.bbc.com/news/world-middle-east-36924000.

153. "Editorial: The Muslim Brotherhood and the US," *Al-Ahram Weekly*, March 3, 2016, http://weekly.ahram.org.eg/News/15648/21/Editorial--The-Muslim-Brotherhood-and-the-US.aspx.

154. Dr. Eric Trager, in discussion with Mohamed Fadel Fahmy, June 3, 2016.

155. Rowan Scarborough, "Britain's Report on Muslim Brotherhood Contradicts U.S. Views on Group," *The Washington Times*, December 28, 2015, www.washingtontimes.com/news/2015/dec/28/muslim-brotherhood-report-by-britain-contradicts-u/.

156. "BBC HARDtalk—Mohamed Fahmy—Journalist and Author (1/10/15)," YouTube video, uploaded October 2, 2015, www.youtube.com/watch?v=ELCMz_-eLk8.

PHOTO CREDITS

MOHAMED FAHMY, a dual Canadian-Egyptian award-winning journalist, war correspondent, and author, entered Iraq on the first day of the war in 2003 with the *Los Angeles Times*. He has reported extensively on the Middle East and North Africa. In 2012 he was among the CNN team honoured with a Peabody Award for the network's coverage of the Arab Spring. He won the Tom Renner Investigative Reporting Award in 2012 for producing the CNN Freedom Project documentary series *Death in the Desert*, which exposed the trafficking of Sub-Sahara Africans to Israel through Sinai-Egypt. He was appointed Al Jazeera English Egypt bureau chief in September 2013. He is the recipient of the Canadian Committee for World Press Freedom Award from UNESCO. He and his wife, Marwa Omara, founded the Fahmy Foundation non-profit in 2015 to provide financial assistance and advocate on behalf of imprisoned journalists and prisoners of conscience worldwide. Upon returning to Canada he joined the University of British Columbia as an adjunct professor.

www.fahmyfoundation.org

CAROL SHABEN is author of *Into the Abyss,* an award-winning national bestseller *The Washington Post* described as "deeply satisfying . . . gripping and emotionally affecting." She won two National Magazine Awards, a Gold for Investigative Reporting and Silver for Politics and Public Interest. Like the "two strong women" in *The Marriott Cell*, Carol is of Arab heritage. She is a former international trade consultant and CBC writer/broadcaster, and at twenty-two worked as a journalist in Jerusalem.